The Musical Comedy Films of Grigorii Aleksandrov

The Musical Comedy Films of Grigorii Aleksandrov
Laughing Matters

Rimgaila Salys

intellect Bristol, UK / Chicago, USA

First published in the UK in 2009 by Intellect,
The Mill, Parnall Road, Fishponds, Bristol, BS16 3JG, UK

First published in the USA in 2009 by Intellect, The University of Chicago Press,
1427 E. 60th Street, Chicago, IL 60637, USA

A catalogue record for this book is available from
the British Library.

Cover design: Holly Rose
Copy-editor: Jennifer Alluisi
Typesetting: John Teehan

ISBN 9781841502823

Contents

Introduction

When the audience wants to laugh, it's no longer a laughing matter for us!

– Nikolai Erdman[1]

The title of this book is, of course, multivalent. Erdman's "no longer a laughing matter" quip expressed his wry reaction to Grigorii Aleksandrov's invitation to write the script for the first Russian musical comedy film, *Veselye rebiata* (*Happy Guys*), which was part of a governmental cinema initiative and consequently an invitation one was obliged to take very seriously. "Laughing *matters*" bears upon the reasons for the popularity of Aleksandrov's musical films. "*Laughing* matters" refers to the sources and technologies of his comedic practice. These meanings of "laughing" and "matters" comprise the central issues of the following chapters.

This book is concerned with four Aleksandrov films: *Happy Guys* (1934), *Tsirk* (*Circus*, 1936), *Volga-Volga* (1938) and *Svetlyi put'* (*The Radiant Path*, 1940).[2] I have devoted one chapter, presenting both history and interpretation, to each film. In the sections on production history I chronicle the untold story of the making of these films: their genesis, the circumstances surrounding their creation, and the evolution and significance of successive scripts. I argue that the content and form of the musical comedy films can best be understood via the deformations caused by the competing discourses that created them. My account is based on both archival research and published sources.

I have examined all surviving scripts; some versions have not survived, but are described at least partially in studio documents or newspaper articles. The designations of the various types of scripts differ from contemporary western terminology because the script development process in Russia did not parallel American practice, nor were the component parts of each category consistent. Soviet directors did not always produce detailed written scripts, nor did studios always require uniformity. For example, after the success of *Happy Guys*, Aleksandrov was permitted to begin filming *Circus* without even a completed script. Three types of script are discussed in the following chapters. The literary script (*literaturnyi stsenarii*) was presented to the studio in order to obtain a contract. It is more or less equivalent to the modern scenario, defined as a prose version of the planned plot, sequence of events, and roles, sometimes including partial dialogues. The director's script (*rezhisserskii stsenarii*) was, in theory, authored by the director and is generally equivalent to the modern screenplay, defined as a series of master scenes, providing all dialogue, essential actions, character movements, and sometimes shot and mise-en-scène directions. In Aleksandrov's case, the author(s) of the literary script collaborated extensively on plot development and dialogues. The montage script (*montazhnyi stsenarii*) was the final version of the script, which included dialogue, directions for movement, scene length, shot specifics, and music directions. Several increasingly elaborated versions of each category of script were produced as dialogues and subplots were added or changed.

Each of these three categories of scripts required approval by the studio and—to varying degrees at various times—by cinema's central administrative organization, GUKF, the Chief Administration of the Film and Photo Industry (simplified to GUK in 1937 and replaced by the Cinematography Committee in 1938). As a result, at different stages, scripts underwent revisions for both artistic and ideological reasons. A case in point is the development process for *Volga-Volga*, which was particularly difficult. Multiple versions of the script were required because of Aleksandrov and Nil'sen's inadequate initial literary script, because of studio objections to the director's script, and—after a change of leadership both at Mosfil'm and GUK during the purges—further revisions to the rough cut of the film.

The analytical section of each chapter deals with topicality and cultural context, narrative development, genre paradigms, comedy, formal filmic devices, the interplay of music and lyrics with narrative, and the encoding of socialist values through myth, fairy tale and folklore, and gender. By emphasizing ideological values in its striving to create a unified culture, Socialist Realism suppressed issues of genre in the arts. Furthermore, national cinemas, with their encoded genre traditions, have never been purely homegrown products, even when closely linked to figurations of nation-state. Scholars have written about the functioning of ideology and myth in the Aleksandrov films, but have largely ignored their roots in the American musical and comedy traditions. Aleksandrov's sojourn in Hollywood, his friendship with Chaplin and visit to Disney Studios are simply mentioned, as is, less frequently, the notebook in which he recorded plots and gags borrowed from American films.[3] I argue that Aleksandrov's films preserve the genre paradigms of the originating model of the American musical, including its associated comedic tradition, using both creatively to inscribe the foundation myths of the Stalin era in the national consciousness.[4]

According to Rick Altman, the syntax or deep structure of the American musical consists of a dual-focus narrative strategy of alternation, confrontation, and parallelism between the male and female leads, which is more important than chronological progress. Hero and heroine may appear in parallel or alternating scenes, in duets or parallel solos; they may confront each other repeatedly in various situations. Male and female are further identified with opposing cultural values, which the musical seeks to reconcile. The formation of male and female into a couple invariably parallels the success of a venture or task in the narrative. A secondary couple or a love triangle, consisting of the primary couple and a male or female rival, typically fulfills a comic function.[5] Beginning in the early thirties, American musicals regularly use direct address and include diegetic audiences as a means of both integrating the external audience into filmic space and influencing its perceptions through applause. Although Aleksandrov also employs these filmic operations, Trudy Anderson points out that the Aleksandrov musicals additionally seek to create community through aperture, by extending cinematic space out into the real world.[6] Narrative realism is combined with the formal patterning of music and dance, and the traditional cinematic hierarchy of image over sound is reversed at climactic moments. Altman divides the corpus into three semi-permeable thematic categories—the fairy tale, show, and folk musicals.[7] The latter two, which are concerned with putting on an artistic performance and doing the work of the nation or community respectively, bear on the Aleksandrov films.

Except for World War II musicals, which take place in the present, the American folk musical typically constructs a nostalgic, mythicized version of the national past, as in *Oklahoma!* and *Meet Me in St. Louis.*[8] *Circus* and *Volga-Volga*, which are hybrids of the show and folk musical, also celebrate national myths, but are instead set in a utopian and mythicized present, while the core events of *The Radiant Path*, in spite of its proleptic finale, take place in a recent, happier past. Many American show musicals are organized so as to justify a final revue with multiple production numbers[9]; this is also the case in *Happy Guys*, *Circus*, and *Volga-Volga.*

The Aleksandrov musicals all follow a standard narrative paradigm of the musical film—the transformation of a talented, spunky underdog into a professional, personal, or civic success. While Valentina Serova, Tamara Makarova, Marina Ladynina, and Zoia Fedorova created the image of the wholesome, energetic, impulsive, determined, straightforward and slightly naïve heroine of the thirties and forties, Liubov' Orlova made her contribution toward the creation of the type, with a more sophisticated coloration.[10] Both the "before" and "after" versions of her heroines are attractive, sympathetic, positive types. But in Aleksandrov's films, cinematic illusion merges with the reality of Orlova's stardom: the underdog country girl is typically transformed into a version of the actress herself, either in the guise of a stage performer or offstage, as an elegant, cultured, modern urban woman. In *Circus*, however, where the quietly elegant offstage persona of Marion Dixon already corresponds to Orlova's refined tastes, her heroine, who must become fully Soviet, dons the parade dress of a *fizkul'turnitsa* (female athlete) in the final scenes of the film.

As a non-hermetic genre, the musical film often incorporates different types of comedy into its corpus. In my discussion of Aleksandrov's use of both physical and verbal humor in the individual musicals, I rely on Noël Carroll and Tom Gunning's work on the categories of gags and Kristine Karnick and Henry Jenkins on comedian and clown comedy.[12] Because Socialist Realism stipulates absolutes, such as the positive hero and the vision of a perfect society, and operates with black and white binaries, the Soviet arts always struggled with humor as a potentially destabilizing and subversive modality. Through his early work with Eisenstein, and later with Erdman, who embodied the 1920s satiric tradition in his plays, Aleksandrov was no stranger to destabilizing humor. Although he experimented with all types of comedy, from slapstick to irony, his comic sensibility was forced into retreat by the end of the 1930s. According to Iurii Saakov, Aleksandrov's favorite writer was Gogol'.[13] Not surprisingly then, the early comedy *Happy Guys* is populated with grotesque bourgeois figures and colored with graveyard humor. In *Circus*, the elements of melodrama are abrogated by ironic cinematic devices that tell the audience, "Don't take this seriously." In *Volga-Volga*, scriptwriter Erdman was responsible for the satirical treatment of the bureaucrat Byvalov and ironic remarks hidden in plain view regarding the peripeties of authorship. *The Radiant Path*, the last pre-war film, reprises the satirical treatment of the bourgeoisie from *Happy Guys* in the depiction of servant Tania's mistress, and retains the slapstick Taldykin line, but as a marker of aesthetic judgment in the Stalin era, irony is here replaced by its polar opposite—the grandeur of spectacle.[14]

Katerina Clark's work on the Socialist Realist novel and Stalinist culture has produced a number of concepts that are particularly important for Aleksandrov's musicals. High Stalinism's reorientation from the horizontal social relations of the 1920s to a vertical hierarchy included the organic and legitimizing metaphor of the Great Family, consisting of political leaders as "fathers" with Stalin as the patriarch, positive heroes as model "sons," and the nation as "family-tribe." In Soviet society, the positive hero had a dual goal: to complete a task in the public sphere and to resolve the inner tension between natural "spontaneity" and socialist "consciousness," attaining the latter with the help of a Party mentor. A description of the extraordinary hero demanded extraordinary—and simultaneously legitimizing—forms borrowed from folklore and fairy tale. In a philosophical reorientation, Socialist Realism abandoned revolutionary positivism for a type of idealism emphasizing transcendence and mysticism. At the highest level then, the positive hero achieved consciousness and higher knowledge through a transformative encounter with one of the father-leaders in the Kremlin. This idealistic inclination also led to millennial thinking in which a glorious future invested the present with its significance, typically blurring the chronological line between the two.[15] Potekhin, the hero of the first musical film, *Happy Guys*, is imbued with the transgressive persona of jazz performer Leonid Utesov; the cardboard figures of the later male heroes (Martynov, Trubyshkin, Lebedev) all exude classic unimpaired, patriarchal soviet masculinity, as attenuated by comedic context.

Complementary to Clark's insights is Hans Günther's work on the Stalinist encoding of Jungian archetypes. In Foucauldian terms, the practice of Soviet society can be seen as the creation of a mythology based on the actualization of four ancient archetypes: the hero, the enemy, the wise father, and the mother.[16] The hero-son and wise father archetypes essentially correspond to Clark's descriptions. Although the truly sinister enemy is not a pivotal figure in the utopian world of the musical, Altman notes that a villain is most common in the folk musical as the melodramatic threat to the well-being of the romantic couple and their world.[17] In Stalinist Russia, the term *vrag naroda* (enemy of the *people*) points to its archetypal signification. Aleksandrov ultimately defangs his villains in *Circus* and *Volga-Volga* through irony, and the kulak-arsonist in *The Radiant Path* is easily unmasked by Tania early in the film. Both Kneishitz's arrest and the capture of Samokhin serve to unify the audience in *Circus* and the factory workers in *The Radiant Path* in righteous indignation. The folkloric, rather than Christian, aspect of the ancient Slavic "mother" archetype comes to the fore in Stalinist culture as a familiar and therefore legitimizing trope. In the musical films, the maternal archetype, a revival of the cult of "mat' syra-zemlia" ("mother damp-earth"), is present in fertility imagery and is spatially encoded as "Rodina" ("homeland" or "motherland"), always with maternal signification. It is worth noting that Aleksandrov was successful for as long as the archetypes and myths of the Stalin era were operative, but ultimately he remained a prisoner of the time. After *Vstrecha na El'be* (*Meeting on the Elbe*, 1948), a mediocre Cold War spy flick with archetypal enemies, he never made another successful film.

Why were Aleksandrov's musical comedies the most popular films of their time? There are various reasons: the specifics of traditional Russian culture, the national interest in Soviet contemporaneity, and the syntax of the western musical film genre in its imbrications with audience values and the dominant ideology. Aleksandrov recognized that Russia was a singing country with a rich tradition of folk and urban melodies. The population would eagerly accept musical films with songs that would live outside the movie theatre as a popular genre, the *massovaia pesnia* (mass song), replacing the solemn revolutionary hymns of the twenties.

Unlike most Soviet directors, Aleksandrov was uniquely equipped to make musical comedy films. Eisenstein's early dramatic productions, in which Aleksandrov acted, were not lacking in humor and, according to Kushnirov, an atmosphere of mischief and trickery reigned in Eisenstein's film group, the "Iron Five." He and his assistants delighted in playful pranks, such as pushing a naked Tisse out into the hallway on a hot day or hiding a dummy made up as a decaying corpse in Maksim Shtraukh's bed.[18] From his stay in Hollywood, Aleksandrov was familiar with the syntax of the American musical, and he would later use western-style spectacle to showcase Soviet achievement, while demonstrating the moral superiority of the USSR in *Circus* and its technological ascendancy in *Volga-Volga*. He was blessed with natural comic vision: "No matter what was happening around me, I would invariably see the humorous in the terrible commotion and muddle, and store it in the piggy bank of directorial memory."[19] While Aleksandrov was well acquainted with the work of the great cinema comedians—Chaplin, Lloyd, Keaton, and the Marx Brothers—it was Disney cartoons that initially inspired his use of rhythmical motion to music, his lively tempo and precise timing, the musical staging of chaotic group scenes in *Happy Guys* and *Volga-Volga*, and the exploitation of classical music favorites in comedy chase scenes.[20]

Aleksandrov was obsessed with capturing Soviet modernity on film; when the new red stars were put up on the Kremlin towers, he was the first to show them to Soviet citizens in *Circus*. He had the gift of identifying and integrating into his films the most innovative and impressive achievements and emblematic events of the culture: the Moscow metro, May Day parades on Red Square, the Volga-Moscow canal and the new Moscow port terminal, the latest Soviet steamships, and the monumental All-Union Agricultural Exhibition, which opened in 1939. Thanks to his American experience and gifted collaborators, such as cinematographer Vladimir Nil'sen, Aleksandrov produced the most technically advanced Soviet films of thirties and forties, packed with innovative special effects. He further endeared himself to Russian audiences by stubbornly pursuing slapstick and satirical comedy at a time when its undignified and potentially subversive aspects were viewed with suspicion by the cinema authorities. At the same time, his sense of timing and tempo was far superior to that of many contemporary comedy directors, such as Semen Timoshenko in *Tri tovarishcha* (*Three Comrades*, 1935), Antonina Kudriavtseva in *Lenochka i vinograd* (*Lenochka and the Grapes*, 1936) or Igor' Il'inskii in *Odnazhdy letom* (*Once in Summer*, 1936).

Finally, Aleksandrov put an end to the 1920s cult of ugliness in Soviet cinema, which was driven by the figuration of the exploited peasant-proletarian body, such as Marfa Lapkina in Eisenstein's *The Old and the New* and the anti-classical norms of the avant-garde—the angular *jolie-laide* Aleksandra Khokhlova, the Countess in Kuleshov's *Mr. West in the Land of the Bolsheviks*. At a 1939 filmmakers' conference, Aleksandrov made his case in the politically correct context of "affirmative" comedy:

> It was fashionable here to consider beauty an unnecessary element in Soviet art. This was especially the case in the time of Futurism and Cubism. Any kind of beauty was perceived as petty-bourgeois, as Mossel'prom, as lemonade ideology and the like, and to this day many comrades are afraid of beauty. But I think that Soviet comedy can't exist without beauty. If bourgeois comedy focuses only on discrediting a number of things, on struggling with the environment, we will not only struggle with elements of the old mentality, not only eradicate elements of the old consciousness, we will simultaneously affirm the new. But how can you affirm the new without beauty?[21]

In *Circus*, Aleksandrov reintroduced classic aesthetic norms to Soviet cinema in their contemporary western figuration, primarily through the influence of Art Deco.

Both in the West and in Soviet Russia, the successful musical film simultaneously accommodated the values of the audience and the ideological concerns of the producer, whether the Hollywood studio system or the Soviet government. While the American musical integrated free enterprise capitalism and nationalism into its narrative, the Soviet musical incorporated Stalinist ideology and nationalism. While the western musical attempted to hide the profit motive, the Stalinist musical strove to mask the power motive. Aleksandrov's films both reproduced the dominant ideology and gave people what they wanted—entertainment, escape from the travails of the everyday, and hope for a better life. Yet sitting squarely among the events of everyday life were the arrests of 1937–38. And here a memoirist recalls the palliative illusion of Orlova's performance in *Circus*: "Her smile shone in the dark of the endless year of 1937, her voice warmed our hearts and inspired hope, her heels tapped out a melody of unrealizable happiness..."[22] The classic scene of Marion Dixon's dance on the cannon, with the accompanying jazz song in English and broken Russian, has been reproduced in revisionist glasnost' films on the Stalin years as emblematic of the paradoxes of the era. In *Koma* (1989), a rousing party performance of "Mary's Song" by the wife of a Gulag officer is intercut with sharply contrasting scenes of camp life. Tsymbal's 1988 film *Zashchitnik Sedov* (*Defense Attorney Sedov*) uses the dance on the cannon episode in a more nuanced way. In 1937, Moscow lawyer Sedov arrives in a provincial town where, as attorney for the defense, he stubbornly demands interviews with three imprisoned agronomists accused of wrecking. This everyman good citizen, who insists on observing Soviet law, thereby exposing himself to arrest, spends an evening at the local movie theatre, laughing and enjoying Orlova's performance on the cannon. The narrative provides him only this one moment of respite as he becomes an unwitting pawn in the political games of higher powers.

In its genre conventions, the musical film functioned easily within the paradigm of Socialist Realism. Whether apprehended as escapism or wish-fulfillment, the central thrust of film entertainment is utopian: "Entertainment offers the image of 'something better' to escape into, or something we want deeply that our day-to-day lives don't provide. Alternatives, hopes, wishes—these are the stuff of utopia, the sense that things could be better, that something other than what is can be imagined and maybe realized."[23] Given the strongly utopian tendencies of Socialist Realism, defined by Zhdanov as "reality in its revolutionary development," and permeated with the drive to transpose the radiant future into the present, the musical provided a site at which the ideological motive coincided with the desires of the audience. Aleksandrov's films achieved this mediating goal representationally through comedy, spectacle, and direct ideological statement, as well as through embedded myth, fairy tale, and folkloric codes. The folk genres rehearsed in the musicals were familiar to formerly peasant urban audiences, thus legitimating Soviet power as being of the people. Fairy tales with happy endings, such as Cinderella and Vasilisa the Fair, complemented the life-affirming qualities of the musical film. The nonrepresentational features of Aleksandrov's musicals (music and song, rhythm) served the same convergent function, melding personal and ideological utopias.

The narrator in Milan Kundera's *The Unbearable Lightness of Being* comments on the Communist usurpation of existential optimism: "The May Day ceremony drew its inspiration from the deep well of the categorical agreement with being. The unwritten, unsung motto of the parade was not 'Long live Communism!' but 'Long live life!' The power and cunning of Communist politics lay in the fact that it appropriated this slogan. For it was this idiotic tautology ('Long live life!') which attracted people indifferent to the theses of Communism to the Communist parade."[24] The historical optimism of Socialist Realism, grounded in a Marxist understanding of history, thus engendered a celebration culture, which was consonant with the happy-ending world of the musical—all of which attracted otherwise apolitical citizens to Aleksandrov's films.

The superficial character development in the musical parallels the schematicism of Socialist Realism, which outlined and concentrated the cultural dominants of the era without psychologizing. The integration essential to the musical film, which reconciles opposing communities and values, symbolically establishes the unified culture so important to Socialist Realism.[25] In both the fairy tale, which Aleksandrov employs in his films, and the musical, tasks are completed with relative ease and the improbable is presented as ordinary, thus dovetailing with Socialist Realism's normalization of the fantastic. In *The Radiant Path*, after setting her first record, Stakhanovite Tania Morozova tells her fellow workers: "What did I do that was so special? Everyone can do this."

Aleksandrov's shrewd choice of Isaak Dunaevskii for his composer assured the success of his musical films. Their collaboration lasted until the ever-political Aleksandrov, under the pressure of Stalin's anti-Semitic campaign, broke with Dunaevskii by recruiting a reluctant Shostakovich to write the music for *Meeting on the Elbe*. The two men never spoke again and *Vesna* (*Spring*, 1947), Aleksandrov's final film with Dunaevskii was also his last real success. Dunaevskii came to the cinema from years of experience at the Kharkiv Drama Theatre, the Moscow Satire Theatre, and the Leningrad Music-Hall. He later recalled that the theatre experience had helped him develop "a concrete musical vocabulary, the ability to think theatrically in music, i.e., to perceive a musical image realistically."[26] Dunaevskii termed himself "the singer of Soviet success" ("pevets sovetskogo preuspevaniia")[27], and his compositions were indeed the musical accompaniment to the celebration culture of high Stalinism. Aleksandrov himself was an amateur musician who understood the necessary primacy of good music and song driving the narrative in a musical film. In composing for Aleksandrov's films, Dunaevskii moved from the largely accompanying music of *Happy Guys* toward the integration of music into the film as its dramaturgical engine, culminating in the symphonization of film in *The Radiant Path*. His expressed aim was to compose songs intended both to function organically in the cinematic narrative and then to acquire a second life outside the movie theatre, as mass songs for the general population.

Dunaevskii was a loyal supporter of the Soviet project and even an admirer of Stalin until the beginning of the anti-Semitic campaign of 1948. A 1930 letter characterizes his self-imposed movement toward conformism:

> The religion of the Soviet land is industrialization, socialism, class warfare. Right here, right now. They demand that we become servants of this cult. *They* are right in this...I'm a loyal person, but I don't glitter with any hyper-revolutionary convictions. But I'm a living person...You can't ignore what is happening now—the most colossal break, the most colossal revolution...I can't stand the sanctimoniousness and hypocrisy of certain prominent figures who stand over art and control it, but I can't not agree with them when they demand art for themselves, and not for us. They don't deny beauty, they can't deny it, but they see it in other things. And we must look with their eyes and create their beauty, until it becomes ours too, until we begin to believe in it too with our whole being."[28]

Ultimately Dunaevskii was less concerned with politics than with the simple joy of living, which inspired all of his music. For Dunaevskii, living was composing: "I don't think about work. In general, I don't think about needing to work. I walk around, read, busy myself with something, and seemingly pay no attention. But meanwhile inside, a serious process is underway and then, after harnessing all these components, the work appears."[29] His innate love of life translated into a talent for expressing happiness, lyrical emotion, youthful energy, and a festive holiday atmosphere corresponding perfectly to the historical optimism of a society that in 1934 was experiencing a relatively improved standard of living, a more plentiful supply of food and manufactured goods, and industrial expansion. To the end of his days, Dunaevskii repeated that the addressee of his songs was the young people of the country: "You are a representative of youth, the youth to whom I have dedicated and continue to dedicate all my creative work."[30] Like the inveterate optimist Aleksandrov, Dunaevskii chose to celebrate the normal, positive aspects of life that continued during the abnormal purge years, and it is only during the war years that he was less prolific, admitting to a friend, "Apparently my muse—is a muse of a peaceful time."[31]

Dunaevskii's preferred collaborator was satirist Vasilii Lebedev-Kumach, a master of the *pesnia-plakat* (song-poster) or aphoristic mass song, the lyrics of which provided a semantic shield for any perceived ideological deficiencies in Aleksandrov's musicals. Dunaevskii himself was less concerned with the words to his melodies and once gave a candid description of his work with Lebedev-Kumach:

> Kaganovich, the transportation commissar, calls us in and says: It's shameful that the railroad kingdom doesn't have a song so, please, make us one by June when the wives of our senior officials gather. Lebedev and I walked out, looked at each other and began to think what we would write. After agreeing about the idea of the work, I don't care at all what words he writes. It's important to start from one and the same national

> idea. My task is to transfer it to music and his task is to embody it in words. When I tell him that this sort of line doesn't work for me, sometimes he tells me that he has nothing to put into the bar. We meet each other half way. Sometimes the couplet is his, but the refrain is mine."[32]

German and Khait's "Aviamarsh" ("Aviators' March," 1920) enjoyed its greatest popularity during the early thirties, becoming a source of motifs for the mass songs of the 1930s–40s, particularly those of Lebedev-Kumach.[33] While Dunaevskii often grounded his melodies in folk and urban songs, Lebedev-Kumach exploited in his lyrics the traditional motifs of the folksong—daring, rapid motion and energy, longing for spatial expanses. His mass songs did not, however, tell a story, but were primarily declamatory and his lyrics for the Aleksandrov films parsed the vocabulary of Stalinist myth: Motherland, broad expanses, Moscow as sacred center, geographical periphery, freedom, happiness and laughter, youth, dynamism, the heart, hero, enemy, vigilance, defense.[34]

Music is an essential component of public ritual, so that the mass songs were sung and repeated during ceremonies, parades, and holiday celebrations, fostering a sense of transcendental unity in the population.[35] Mass songs also played on ubiquitous radio loudspeakers, becoming part of the rhythm of everyday life. As a result, Lebedev-Kumach's lyrics, embedded in Dunaevskii's engaging and memorable melodies, were validated as truth through constant repetition. Dunaevskii summed up their task:

> The song—especially in light of its enormous importance in our country—is a crystal-clear musical genre, reflecting our entire great present day, our beautiful yesterday and marvelous tomorrow. The large in the small! This means that a song is first of all an artistic work where, in the space of a few bars, the author must give a cluster of feelings, images, and moods. A song is a work in which the will and sense of purpose of the author's creative aspirations must and cannot weaken for its entire duration—from the first to the last musical and verbal signs. Finally, a song must be permeated with an enormous, winning creative sincerity. From one heart—to millions of hearts (and not just to millions of ears)—that is the watchword of my songs.[36]

As a creative personality, Aleksandrov remains something of a mystery. Director Mikhail Romm characterized him as both a Khlestakov, the foppish imposter-hero of Gogol's *The Inspector General* and "fortune's darling" (*vezunchik*), from whose jacket Mosfil'm and even Lenfil'm directors came to tear off buttons for good luck as they went into production on a new film.[37] Critic Maia Turovskaia, a member of the editorial board at Mosfil'm for many years, lays out the conundrum in its most extreme terms:

> We considered him to be the most stupid person at Mosfil'm. He was handsome and absolutely stupid. But when I began to work on him—he was long dead, it was no longer possible to ask anyone anything—I began to think: first of all, would Eisenstein have taken as the co-director of his films...a person of such classic stupidity, as he seemed to be? All of his relations with the Soviet authorities turned out very strangely: he could permit himself things that no one else could. To depict Soviet life as absolutely stupid, as he did [in *Volga-Volga*], *that* no one but he could permit himself.[38]

When I began this project in 2002, Neia Aleksandrovna Massal'skaia, one of Aleksandrov's few surviving co-workers, an assistant director on *Happy Guys* and *Circus*, communicated the following opinions. Massal'skaia saw Aleksandrov primarily as a shrewd organizer who had a nose for choosing good actors and talented associates, such as cameramen Vladimir Nil'sen and Boris Petrov, and secondly as a skilled film editor. In relation to her own duties in casting actors and arranging shooting schedules, she characterized Aleksandrov as a "*barin*" (gentleman-squire), who preferred not to be involved in any of the details of production. In contrast, Massal'skaia viewed Orlova as the consummate professional who scrupulously prepared her roles, working out every movement and line of dialogue. There were no temper tantrums during shooting: on the set Orlova was simple, modest, and unassuming with the film crew, although often unwell, even in the early years. Massal'skaia remembers her sitting with a hot water bottle for a liver ailment in the intervals between shooting for *Happy Guys*; nevertheless she was never one to complain.[39]

Three factors problematize the task of writing the history of Aleksandrov's musicals: the director's own testimony, the dispersal of his archive, and the "de-Stalinization" of the films. In his published memoirs, *Gody poiskov i truda* (1975) and *Epokha i kino* (1976), Aleksandrov is an unreliable narrator who, not surprisingly given the time, suppresses information but also distorts and exaggerates facts for greater effect. While Aleksandrov was fond of telling tall tales about his past, Orlova, the most popular film star of the Stalin years, carefully guarded her privacy. As a result, the lives and deeds of the couple have become the stuff of legend and sensation during the perestroika and post-Soviet years, thus complicating the task of documenting the history of their films. The Aleksandrov-Orlova estate was inherited by the director's grandson, Grigorii, who immigrated to France, apparently taking the archive (or what remained of it) with him. According to Naum Kleiman, the grandson had first promised to give the archive to Muzei kino, but then changed his mind.[40] Nonna Golikova, the granddaughter of Orlova's sister, states that the director's son and his wife Galina threw out Orlova's archive, fragments of which Vnukovo neighbors retrieved and gave to the Golikovs.[41] During past years, stories have also circulated about archival materials found in the Vnukovo dump (the Aleksandrov-

Orlova dacha was rented for many years to foreigners) and of other materials sold to private collectors. The most reliable and intelligent biographical source on Aleksandrov and Orlova is Mark Kushnirov's *Svetlyi put', ili Charli i Spenser* (1998), based on the author's conversations with the director and with Orlova's concert accompanist, Lev Mironov.

The versions of Aleksandrov's musical comedies available to us today may be likened to the contemporary appearance of the older Moscow metro stations, which no longer display statues and mosaics of the Leader. During the Khrushchev years, the names of purged cinematographer Vladimir Nil'sen and exiled scriptwriter Nikolai Erdman were restored to the titles of the films on which they worked, but the films were also cleansed of references to Stalin, and these censored images were mostly not reinserted when the films were restored during the 1970s. Wherever I have found authoritative references to such omitted footage, I have included descriptions of them. The recent DVD version of *The Radiant Path* (Master-Teip, 2006) does restore the Stalinist footage: Tania Morozova's speech to the factory workers with a Stalin portrait on the left wall; Tania driving through the Pavilion of Mechanization and past Merkurov's Stalin sculpture at the Agricultural Exhibition (Fig. 1); her speech at the textile pavilion with a Stalin statue at the far right of the frame (Fig. 51); her conversation with a foreign ambassador by yet another Stalin sculpture.

Because of the large number of archival references in this text, I use documentation endnote style in which the first note referring to a source provides the publication information found in a bibliographic entry. Except for the conventional spelling of certain Russian names, such as Eisenstein and Gorky, the Library of Congress system has been used to transliterate Cyrillic names and titles. In the text, I have tried to provide the original spellings of non-Russian surnames and city names, but I have used Library of Congress transliteration in the endnotes to facilitate bibliographic searching. Where dialogues or lyrics are reproduced in Russian transliteration for reasons of analysis, I provide translations, either immediately following or in endnotes after the first occurrence. Because of varying citation practices for archival clippings, in a few instances, such as references to the periodicals *Kino* and *Za bol'shevistskii fil'm*, either the issue number and year or the full date (day, month, year) may be cited. Where rare newspaper clippings are cited, the page number may be missing because of incomplete archival information.

My research on this project has been funded by the National Council for Eurasian and East European Studies, the International Research and Exchanges Board, and the University of Colorado at Boulder. For their assistance and advice I am indebted to R. Dunaevskaia, E. Al'pers, M. Lebedev-Kumach Deeva, M. Turovskaia, E. Stishova, Tim Riggs, P. Rogers, my two reviewers, and the staff of the Russian State Archive of Literature and the Arts, Gosfil'mofond, the NII Kinoiskusstva Library, the Russian State Library at Khimki, and the Union of Cinematographers Library.

Figure 1.

Endnotes

1. Grigorii Aleksandrov, "Komediia nikomu ne nuzhna, krome...zritelia," *Sovetskii ekran*, 23 (1974): 18.

2. I have not included *Vesna* (*Spring*, 1947), which can be considered a musical in the broad sense because it contains music and song that emanate from the diegesis rather than inserted as theme song or separate accompaniment on a non-diegetic soundtrack. However, unlike the earlier Aleksandrov films, *Spring* does not consistently privilege sound and rhythmic movement over image at its climactic moments, nor does it transform diegetic music into the transcendence of supra-diegetic music (diegetic singing transitions to singing with a sourceless, non-diegetic orchestra). I follow here Rick Altman's definitions in *The American Film Musical* (Bloomington, IN: Indiana University Press, 1989) 63–71. Except for its ending, in which diegetic speech leads to singing and non-diegetic orchestration, the song and dance numbers of *Spring* are mostly motivated realistically as stage performances or a party sing-along. In contrast, Kostia Potekhin of *Happy Guys* disrupts the illusion of diegetic reality by performing "Spasibo serdtse" ("Thank you, heart") sitting outside on a tree branch, but with full orchestral accompaniment. In *The Radiant Path*, Tania's marching among her rows of weaving machines forms the rhythmic bridge to her singing of "Marsh entuziastov" ("The Enthusiasts' March"), complete with supra-diegetic orchestration, as she works to set a Stakhanovite record. The classical image over sound hierarchy is reversed: Tania's movements are now an accompaniment to the music track— her singing and the triumphant orchestral music.

3. Kushnirov, *Svetlyi put', ili Charli i Spenser* (Moscow: Terra-Knizhnyi klub, 1998) 80. After viewing Aleksandrov's mediocre *Odna sem'ia* (*One Family*, 1943), Eisenstein remarked sarcastically that the "Hollywood notebook was used up." (Iu. Saakov, *Liubov' Orlova i Grigorii Aleksandrov* [Moscow: Algoritm, 2005] 184). V.A. Razumnyi, who knew Aleksandrov in the mid-1970s, recalls seeing the *kartoteka smekha* (laughter file), the director's collection of gags, comic situations, jokes and witticisms. (http://razumny.ru/alexandrov2.htm. Accessed Apr. 26, 2009).

   Trudy Anderson and especially Richard Taylor were the first scholars to foreground non-representational aspects of the Soviet musical. See Richard Taylor, "But Eastward, Look, the Land is Brighter: towards a Topography of Utopia in the Stalinist Musical," in *100 years of European Cinema. Entertainment or Ideology?*, eds. Diana Holmes and Alison Smith (Manchester: Manchester University Press, 2000) 11–26; Trudy Anderson, "Why Stalinist Musicals?" *Discourse*, 17.3 (Spring 1995): 38–48.

4. Aleksandrov's films did not employ a characteristic device of certain, but not all, American musicals, perfected by Fred Astaire: the emergence of song and dance directly from the rhythms of the surrounding diegetic world. See Natasha Drubek-Maier, "Zvuki muzyki. (Anti-)medium v sovetskikh muzykal'nykh komediiakh," *Sovetskaia vlast' i media*, eds. Hans Günther and Sabina Hängsen (St. Petersburg: Akademicheskii proekt, 2006) 578-92.

5. Altman, 19–20, 24–28, 31–33.

6. Anderson, 44–45.

7. Altman, 71, 110, 122–28.

8. Altman, 272.

9. Altman, 202.

10. See Oksana Bulgakova, "Sovetskie krasavitsy v stalinskom kino," *Sovetskoe bogatstvo. Stat'i o kul'ture, literature i kino*, eds. M. Balina et al. (St. Petersburg: Akademicheskii proekt, 2002) 391–411.

12. Noël Carroll, "Notes on the Sight Gag," *Comedy/Cinema/Theory*, ed. Andrew Horton (Berkeley: University of California Press, 1991) 25–42; Tom Gunning, "Crazy Machines in the Garden of Forking Path: Mischief Gags and the Origins of American Film Comedy," *Classical Hollywood Comedy*, eds. Kristine Brunovska Karnick and Henry Jenkins (New York: Routledge, 1995) 87–105; Henry Jenkins and Kristine Brunovska Karnick, "Introduction: Acting Funny," *Classical Hollywood Comedy*, 149–67.

13. Saakov, *Liubov' Orlova i Grigorii Aleksandrov*, 13.

14. See Leonid Heller, "A World of Prettiness. Socialist Realism and Its Aesthetic Categories," *Socialist Realism without Shores*, eds. Thomas Lahusen and Evgeny Dobrenko (Durham, NC: Duke University Press, 1997) 64.

15. Katerina Clark, *The Soviet Novel. History as Ritual*, 3rd ed. (Bloomington and Indianapolis: Indiana University Press, 2000) 114, 136, 147–51, 162, 175.

16. Khans Giunter, "Arkhetipy sovetskoi kul'tury," *Sotsrealisticheskii kanon*, eds. Kh. Giunter and E. Dobrenko (St. Petersburg: Akademicheskii proekt, 2000) 743–84.

17. Altman, 289.

18. Kushnirov, 71.

19. Kushnirov, 71.

20. Disney's rhythmical "Skeleton Dance" was a favorite (Kushnirov, 78). In "Whoopee Party," the musical chaos must be broken up by the police.

21. G. Aleksandrov, "Tvorcheskoe soveshchanie, sozvannoe Komitetom po delam kinematografii v Dome kino po voprosu o razvitii sovetskoi kinokomedii 16-17 noiabria 1939 goda," *Zhivye golosa kino*, ed. L. A. Parfenov (Moscow: Belyi bereg, 1999) 145. For comments on Aleksandrov's rejection of avant-garde aesthetics in his films, see Sabine Hängsen, "Film als Erbe anderer Medien. Das Lied in den Filmkomödien Grigorij Aleksandrovs," *Die Musen der Macht*, eds. Jurij Murašov et al. (München: Wilhelm Fink Verlag, 2003) 187-209.

22. S. Nikolaevich, qtd. in Kushnirov, 9.

23. Richard Dyer, "Entertainment and Utopia," *The Cultural Studies Reader*, ed. Simon During, 2nd ed. (London: Routledge, 1999) 373. (First published in *Movie* 24 (1977): 2–13.)

24. Milan Kundera, *The Unbearable Lightness of Being* (NY: Harper and Row, 1987) 249.

25. On unified culture see, for example, Margarita Tupitsyn, "From Factography to Mythography: The Final Phase of the Soviet Photographic Avant-Garde," *Kultur im Stalinismus*, ed. G. Gorzka (Bremen: Edition Temmen, 1994) 206–224.

26. I. Dunaevskii, qtd. in I. V. Nest'ev, *I. Dunaevskii* (Moscow, 1967) 10–13.

27. I. Dunaevskii, qtd. in M. Iankovskii, "Stranitsy druzhby," *I. O. Dunaevskii. Vystupleniia. Stat'i. Pis'ma. Vospominaniia*, ed. E. A. Grosheva (Moscow: Sovetskii kompozitor, 1961) 324.

28. I. Dunaevskii, Jan. 14, 1930 letter to K. Ia. Goleizovskii, *Kas'ian Goleizovskii. Zhizn' i tvorchestvo* (Moscow: Vserossiiskoe teatral'noe obshchestvo, 1984) 193–94. For a sympathetic but clear-eyed explanation of Dunaevskii's politics, see Naum Shafer's introduction to *Pochtovyi roman. Perepiska I. O. Dunaevskogo i L. S. Rainl'*, ed. N. Shafer (Moscow: Kompozitor, 2001) 4. Shafer is the most

erudite contemporary Dunaevskii scholar in Russia. The most recent book on Dunaevskii published in the West is Matthias Stadelmann's well-researched *Isaak Dunaevskij – Sänger des Volkes* (Köln: Böhlau Verlag, 2003). Dmitrii Minchenok's *Isaak Dunaevskii* (Moscow: Olimp, 1998), a biography partially based on taped interviews with Dunaevskii's elder son, Evgenii, contains many factual errors and cannot be considered a fully reliable source.

29. "Stenogramma, doklad Dunaevskogo v Muzykal'nom nauchno-issledovatel'skom institute o muzyke v kino," (May 7, 1937), RGALI (Russian State Archive of Literature and the Arts), f. 2062/1/332.

30. I. Dunaevskii, Feb. 21, 1952 letter to L. G. Vytchikova, I. O. Dunaevskii, *Izbrannye pis'ma*, eds. I. Person and M. Iankovskii (Leningrad: Muzyka, 1971) 145.

31. I. Dunaevskii, qtd. in M. Iankovskii, "Stranitsy druzhby" 324.

32. "Stenogramma, doklad Dunaevskogo v Muzykal'nom nauchno-issledovatel'skom institute," (May 7, 1937).

33. Iurii Mineralov, "Kontury stilia epokhi. Eshche raz o massovoi pesne 30-kh godov," *Voprosy literatury*, 7 (1991): 17–19.

34. For a recent analysis of the themes of the mass song, see Karsten Brüggemann, *Von Krieg zu Krieg, von Sieg zu Sieg* (Hamburg: Verlag Dr. Kovač, 2002).

35. See E. Petrushanskaia, "O 'misticheskoi' prirode sovetskikh massovykh pesen," *Russian Literature*, 45 (1999): 87–102. Petrushanskaia points to Bulgakov's framing of the phenomenon as diabolical in *The Master and Margarita*, when office workers, conducted by trickster-demon Korov'ev, are unable to stop singing "Slavnoe more sviashchennyi Baikal" until cured in Stravinskii's clinic.

36. I. Dunaevskii, "O tvorcheskoi strastnosti," *Sovetskoe iskusstvo*, Nov. 28, 1938, qtd. in *Isaak Dunaevskii. Pesni. Ocherk o zhizni i tvorchestve*, introd. G. Golub (Moscow: Muzyka, 1983) 10.

37. Iu. Saakov, *Liubov' Orlova i Grigorii Aleksandrov*, 12.

38. "Veselye rebiata," Radio Svoboda program, http://www.svoboda.org/programs/cicles/cinema/russian/HappyGuys.shtml. Accessed May 10, 2007.

39. Interview with Rimgaila Salys, Feb. 16, 2002, Moscow.

40. "Litsa. Na dache Orlovoi zhivut inostrantsy," *Argumenty i fakty*, Jan. 29, 2003.

41. Golikova, Nonna. *Aktrisa i rezhisser* (Moscow: Vagrius, 2005) 250.

Chapter 1

Veselye Rebiata

Happy Guys

"We want to laugh and we have the right to laugh with the laughter of victors."

– Boris Shumiatskii, 1935

"Your work is useless. It is not yet time for the Soviet people to laugh. They have very many serious matters to attend to."

– RAPP critics[1]

I. THE BATTLE FOR COMEDY

In May 1932, when Grigorii Aleksandrov returned to Russia after an absence of three years, he found himself in the right place at the right time, for it was precisely the centralization of cultural policy during 1931–32 that made possible the appearance of the first Soviet musical comedy film.[2] The March 1928 Party Conference on Cinema had been the watershed moment for the still relatively diverse and fragmented film industry. The Conference resolution prescribed clear ideological purpose: "Fiction film must actually become a medium of Communist enlightenment and agitation, an instrument of the Party in educating and organizing the masses around the basic tasks of the period of socialist construction.... The main criterion for evaluating the formal and artistic qualities of films is the requirement that cinema furnish a 'form that is intelligible to the millions.'" The resolution specifically mentioned the need to "pay special attention to the creation of Soviet comedy."[3]

The December 1931 Plenum of the VTsIK Council of Cultural Construction criticized the lack of a unified plan for cultural policy, and in January, A.S. Bubnov, the People's Commissar for Enlightenment, called for a five-year plan in the arts.[4] At the time of Aleksandrov's departure abroad, the Russian Association of Proletarian Writers (RAPP), which stridently championed a proletarian culture opposed to modernist experimentation, was in the ascendant, though it never gained official Party sponsorship. On April 23, 1932 a Central Committee decree dissolved RAPP and established a single Union of Soviet Writers, thereby bringing writers of different persuasions into a single organization and at the same time taking control of cultural policy. The April decree served as a weathermaker for all the arts and led to analogous organizational changes in architecture, art, and music.[5] In recalling the musical climate of the early thirties, Isaak Dunaevskii credited above all the liquidation of the Russian Association of Proletarian Musicians (RAPM) and its dogmatic views as opening the door to the jazz music of *Happy Guys*.[6] And it was the State, in the person of its functionaries, that for reasons of cultural policy commissioned Aleksandrov to make a comedy film and later defended him against all critics. The cinema industry had a new leader, Boris Shumiatskii, who had been appointed after Sovkino was replaced by the more centralized Soiuzkino in 1930.[7] Shumiatskii was to play a pivotal role in the making of *Happy Guys*.

Yet in spite of the attention to and official encouragement of cinema, during the early 1930s it became progressively more difficult to make a film for two reasons: a proliferation of controlling bureaucratic entities in the government, the Party, and in film studios, which had veto rights over scripts, and Stalin's direct involvement in the approval of completed films for release to the nation. In June 1932, the cultural propaganda section of the Komsomol Central Committee met with film organization leaders, directors, and scriptwriters to push its agenda of greater Komsomol involvement in filmmaking.[8] In February 1933, the State further expanded its direct supervision of the film industry: Soiuzkino was replaced by the Chief Administration of the Film and Photo Industry (GUKF), which reported directly to the Sovnarkom (Council of People's Commissars).[9] As a result of such moves, in 1933 the largest Soviet film studio, Soiuzfil'm, paid advances for 129 scripts, of which only 13 were approved for production.[10] Film comedy had fared no better, in spite of the 1928 Party Conference's encouragement of comedy. Writing in 1934, a *Komsomol'skaia pravda* critic pointed out that of the eighty Russian films released the previous year, only three were comedies. To meet audience demand, enterprising theatre administrators were screening worn-out copies of 1920s Russian and American comedies. "'An Evening of Laughter,' 'Four of the Merriest Comedies in One Show,' 'I. Il'inskii in His Best Comedy'—these advertisements achieve their aim almost automatically: the tickets sell out long before the beginning of a performance."[11] The same critic also noted that it had been several years since any new foreign films had been shown in the Soviet Union, a clear indicator of the xenophobia that would fuel the debate over *Happy Guys* during 1933–34.[12]

At its June 7, 1933 meeting, the Organizing Bureau of the Central Committee established a film commission (Kinokomissiia), to be chaired by Party functionary Aleksei Stetskii, with Bubnov, commissar for Enlightenment, and Shumiatskii among the members. The Kinokomissiia's mandate was to: 1) examine GUKF annual lists of film topics and make recommendations for action to the Organizing Bureau, 2) screen and approve completed films before their release, and 3) organize a contingent of script reviewers composed of writers in the Party and highly qualified propaganda and Party workers. In addition, film topics could not go into development without the approval of the Central Committee.[13] At the next level, Stalin became the chief curator of the arts in Russia. Film was his special favorite, which explains both why relatively few filmmakers suffered during the purges and also the decline in production as compared to the second half of the 1920s.[14] From mid-1933 onward, Stalin and members of the Politbiuro viewed and vetted all Soviet films before their release, and his taste and reactions determined their ultimate fate.

Nevertheless, the two years preceding the assassination of Kirov in December 1934 are seen as a period of relative thaw— within the context of the Stalinist system.[15] There had been a relatively good harvest in fall 1933, and the 17th Party Congress in early 1934 called itself the "Congress of Victors." The tempo of forced industrialization, which had driven the Soviet economy into crisis, was slowed during the second five-year plan. The ethos of asceticism and self-sacrifice propagated during the first five-year plan gave way to the ideal of a "cultured and prosperous life" that included the development of leisure time activities, which had been under strict ideological control since the time of the Great Break. It is only within the context of this measured relaxation of cultural control, which also permitted the dissemination of western popular culture such as jazz music, the foxtrot, and tango, that the making of *Happy Guys* became possible.

A closely managed press told the population that, with the success of the first five-year plan, a new socialist order of economic power and plenty had arrived. Reportage now stressed a joyous celebration of Soviet accomplishments that continued throughout the Soviet era but reached its performative apex during the 1930s. Even before Stalin's 1935 "Life has become happier" declaration and precisely during 1933–34, when *Happy Guys* was being made, the press implanted happiness with a musical accompaniment in the consciousness of their readers: under the caption "Nynche zhit' veselo!" ("Life is Happy Now!"), a 1933 issue of *Komsomol'skaia pravda* printed a large photo of a smiling young Komsomol boy playing his accordion. In early 1934, the headline for an initiative to manufacture better musical instruments read: "Industriia vesel'ia vykhodit v pokhod. Bol'she garmoshek, gitar, balalaek!" ("The Merriment Industry Begins a Campaign. More Accordions, Guitars, Balalaikas!").[16] It is not surprising then that the authorities turned their attention to musical comedy film as an appropriate correlate to the newly created image of Soviet success.

The production history of *Happy Guys* is a fascinating case study, brimming with passionate ideological controversy and political machinations during a transitional period of the Stalin era when a public discourse still existed in the Russian cultural community. In May 1932, the government had refused Eisenstein and Aleksandrov's request to purchase their *Da zdravstvuet Meksika*! (*Que viva México!*) footage from Upton Sinclair; their most recent collaborative project thus came to nothing.[17] On July 8, Shumiatskii met with the two men to discuss the Eisenstein group's future plans, of which the most immediate was to make a Soviet comedy. Eisenstein announced plans to film, jointly with Aleksandrov, *Samoe zabavnoe...* (*The Most Amusing Thing...*), a comedy based on a script by Boris Shklovskii with dialogue by Nikolai Erdman.[18] But nothing came of the project. In late summer 1932, Shumiatskii took Aleksandrov, who had just returned from the United States, on an informational visit to Gorky, warning him that Stalin might also be present at the writer's dacha. According to Aleksandrov, the conversation with the General Secretary initially concerned *The Five-Year Plan*, a documentary film the director had put together from the holdings of Amkino, the Soviet film distribution office in New York City, and had shown during his lectures on the Soviet Union that summer. Stalin then began speaking of the successful completion of the first plan: "Our people, the Bolshevik Party has every reason to look to the future with optimism. Art, unfortunately, cannot keep up with the tempo of economic construction.... Everyone knows the people like joyous, buoyant art, but you don't want to take this into account. What's more," Stalin continued with undisguised irony, "people who suppress everything funny haven't disappeared in art. Aleksei Maksimovich," he addressed Gorky, "if you aren't against gaiety and humor, help stir up the talented literary people, the masters of laughter in art."[19] Mark Kushnirov gives a parallel, more down to earth, account of the visit, which highlights the role of Aleksandrov's personality in his being chosen as director for *Happy Guys*:

> Apparently interested, [Stalin] listened to the account of foreign countries, asked questions from time to time, nodded approvingly and laughed. Gorky asked Aleksandrov to sing some Mexican songs. He tuned a guitar that luckily happened to be in the house, sang "Adelita," "Sandunga," and something else. He sang like a professional, thereby eliciting the approval of his exalted listeners. Before saying good-bye, Stalin said, "As far as I can tell, you are a very witty and cheerful man. Our art very much needs such people. Especially now. Unfortunately, for some reason our art is ashamed to be cheerful and funny. It lags behind life. This is not proper."[20]

The idea for a film-operetta had come out of Shumiatskii's conversations with Lev Kamenev, one of the formerly powerful old Bolsheviks with whom he maintained friendly relations.[21] Once assured that Aleksandrov had made a good impression, Shumiatskii then offered him the chance to make a musical comedy film based on Leonid Utesov's Tea-dzhaz (theatrical jazz) and his current stage show *Muzykal'nyi magazin* (*The Music Store*).[22] Shumiatskii even provided the first name for the film, *The Jazz Comedy* (perhaps by analogy to *The Music Store's* subtitle "Dzhaz-klounada") and arranged for Aleksandrov to travel to Leningrad to see Utesov's show. *Happy Guys* carried various names in the process of its evolution. *Jazz Comedy* was initially used in the press, but the first script was called *The Shepherd* (*Pastukh*). By July 1934 Shumiatskii refers to the film as *Happy Guys*. The GUKF chief had originally proposed the musical comedy project to Eisenstein, who wouldn't bite. Aleksandrov accepted without consulting his former teacher and colleague, which Eisenstein understood as a defection from his camp.[23]

Stalin's comedy "initiative" became operative in fall 1932 when the Central Committee called a meeting of directors and scriptwriters under the slogan, "Smekh—rodnoi brat sily" ("Laughter is the brother of strength"), intended to push the film industry toward producing sound comedies to replace the cinematic farces and bourgeois urban songs of the 1920s.[24] The best directors, such as Protazanov, Kozintsev and Trauberg, Dovzhenko, Room, and Eisenstein responded enthusiastically, although few were able to complete their projects. In August 1932, Eisenstein (without Aleksandrov) began working on *MMM*, a comedy about the adventures of a modern man in medieval Russia. In his memoirs, Aleksandrov cites his dislike of the idea as the reason for his break with Eisenstein, but it is more likely that Shumiatskii's offer of an independent project was more influential at this stage in Aleksandrov's career.[25] In a late interview, Aleksandrov also admitted, "I consciously tried to choose another genre for myself than the one he had chosen. I wanted to, if one can express it this way, 'choose the opposite.'"[26]

Happy Guys was not in any way the product of amateurs. The scriptwriters Nikolai Erdman, whose 1925 play *The Mandate* had been a sensation in Meierkhol'd's theatre, and Vladimir Mass were the best stage satirists of their time. Aleksandrov had apprenticed and collaborated with Eisenstein for ten years. His cameraman, Vladimir Nil'sen, had been trained by Tisse during their years with Eisenstein. A trained dancer and singer, Orlova was already an operetta star in Nemirovich-Danchenko's musical theatre, and had acted in two films, Iurtsev's *Alyona's Love* and Roshal''s *Petersburg Night*, both 1934. Dunaevskii had been composing and conducting successfully for the theatre in Kharkiv, Moscow and Leningrad since 1919. Musician and singer Leonid Utesov was a music-hall star, conductor of the most popular Soviet jazz orchestra, and had acted in three films, *The Firm of "Antanta and Co."* (1923), *The Career of Spir'ka Shpandyr'* (1926), and *The Strangers* (1928).[27]

In 1932, Utesov was a much more significant public figure than Grigorii Aleksandrov. During a 1927 trip to Paris, Utesov had been bitten by the jazz bug and soon formed his own orchestra, which made its debut in Leningrad with the 1929 Tea-dzhaz program. Utesov had heard both the Jack Hilton and Ted Lewis orchestras abroad; Tea-dzhaz and Utesov's later shows, including *The Music Store*, were influenced by Lewis's informal and synthetic performance style. Utesov and his crew not only played in a highly professional manner, but each orchestra member also acted, danced, or sang as part of the theatrical-musical presentation. The orchestra was tremendously popular with Soviet audiences starved for good, non-ideological entertainment, and Utesov with his musicians were mobbed by crowds of admiring fans both in Leningrad and on tour in the provinces. However, in the music world and official circles, where RAPM, with its emphasis on heroic socialist construction and proletarian culture, was dominant, jazz-influenced artists and composers, such as Utesov, Dunaevskii and Blantner, were under constant attack for their "degenerate bourgeois music." Even after the April 1932 decree, former RAPP and RAPM members continued to plant landmines around Aleksandrov's *Happy Guys*.

Utesov's third and most successful jazz show was *The Music Store* (1932), a loosely connected series of comedy skits on a day in the life of a musical establishment.[28] Utesov plays multiple roles: the store clerk Kostia Potekhin ("potekha" = fun), a visiting American jazz conductor, a naive peasant, and even arrives at the music store as a young, romanticized version of himself, whom he proceeds to parody.[29] The script for the show had been written by Erdman and Mass; the music was composed by Dunaevskii, the musical director of the Leningrad music-hall. The show was directed by Utesov and A. Arnol'd, who later played the foreign conductor Fraskini in *Happy Guys*[30]; the cast consisted of Utesov's fifteen-man jazz orchestra. In *The Music Store*, Utesov had already brought together the group that was to become the creative nucleus of Aleksandrov's film.

Apart from Dunaevskii's jazz renditions of Russian classical music and a tap-dancing horse that brought down the house, it was the script with Erdman and Mass's brand of political satire that assured the success of *The Music Store*. Potekhin lives in a large bass viol case on the premises of the music store (a reference to the housing shortage) and tells the store manager, "Please note, Fedor Semenovich, there's not a single communicating room and I have all the conveniences. Only one convenience is missing—it's impossible to live here." Blinded by the glittering instruments, a peasant mistakes the music store for Torgsin (a store selling foreign goods for foreign currency and valuables) and brings in his horse in order to sell manure, which an agronomist has told him is as good as gold, the ironic effect of Soviet agricultural propaganda. And, like a true *edinolichnik* (non-collectivized farmer), he will not part with his one horse. The store manager gives Potekhin sheet music to perform, the titles of which openly parody RAPM themes: "Danse industriale" to the lyrics of "Oh, My Ball-bearings," "The Complete Course of Historical Materialism," music by Davidenko, "The Meeting at the Steamboat Depot"—a sonatina.[31] This cacophonic piece mimicked steamboat horns, the noise of machine lathes and the "voice of the people" at a political meeting.[32] A tall son, dressed as a young pioneer, and his short father enter the store. The son treats the father as if he were a small child: "When I was born, he was twenty years old. After that he lived abroad during the whole revolution. Since he didn't take part in the revolution, I believe that fifteen years have been crossed out of his life. You're five years old—don't pick your nose!"[33]

During fall 1932, Shumiatskii attended a performance of *The Music Store* and afterward suggested to Utesov the idea of a short musical comedy film based on the show, with Aleksandrov as director. Utesov countered with a proposal to make a full-length film, with a new script by Erdman and Mass, music by Dunaevskii and lyrics by Lebedev-Kumach, then a little-known writer on the staff of *Krokodil*.[34] Shumiatskii ignored the unknown Lebedev-Kumach's candidacy and refused to consider Dunaevskii, apparently because the composer had always been a prime RAPM target. But Utesov refused to undertake the project without Dunaevskii, and Shumiatskii finally consented.[35]

After a night spent discussing ideas for the film with Dunaevskii, Aleksandrov called Erdman in Moscow at 5:00 a.m., asking him to come to Leningrad immediately with Mass. The unflappable Erdman quipped, "When the audience wants to laugh, it's no longer a laughing matter for us!" According to Dunaevskii's records, the group met at Utesov's apartment on December 1, 1932 to begin work on *Happy Guys*.[36] Erdman, Mass, and Aleksandrov continued to work on the script at the Matkachi vacation home near Petrozavodsk during the remainder of the month, and then at Abramtsevo, outside Moscow, during January.[37] The first version of the director's script, entitled *Pastukh* (*The Shepherd*), was completed by mid-March 1933.[38]

Because *Happy Guys* was originally intended as a vehicle to showcase Utesov's talents, the script retained the Kostia Potekhin character from *The Music Store*: "prostoi paren', nasmeshlivyi i s khitretsoi" ("an ordinary guy, a scoffer and sharp customer"), as Utesov describes him in a memoir,[39] a characterization indicative of the anomalous way he was to interpret the film role. However, the combination of Erdman and Mass's comic-satirical figuration of Soviet contemporaneity and Aleksandrov's cache of American comedy tropes produced a narrative entirely different from *The Music Store*. The plot of the completed film begins with Potekhin, the head shepherd of a collective farm near the Black Sea, who wants to become a professional musician and takes violin lessons from Karl Ivanovich, an elderly German music teacher.[40] Wealthy NEP holdovers Lena ("Child of Torgsin" in the film titles) and her social-climbing mother mistake Potekhin for Kosta Fraskini, a visiting Paraguayan conductor, and the acquaintance leads Potekhin to fall for Lena's charms.[41] Aniuta, Lena's maid, both idolizes Potekhin, who is indifferent to her, and has ambitions to become a singer. After Potekhin's animals wreak havoc at Lena's party and he is unmasked and ejected, Potekhin travels to Moscow where, by a series of comic coincidences, he replaces Fraskini in what becomes a slapstick music-hall performance of Liszt's *Second Hungarian Rhapsody*. A group of jazz musicians then invites him to lead their orchestra. After a monumental brawl among the musicians, which deprives them of rehearsal space in their dorm room, they are forced to rehearse in a funeral cortège and then race through the rain to make their engagement at the Bol'shoi Theatre. En route they pick up a bedraggled Aniuta, who has been discharged for outsinging Lena. Potekhin and his orchestra triumph at the Bol'shoi; Aniuta is an even bigger hit as a singer. Potekhin sees the light and declares his affection for Aniuta.

The original *Shepherd* script differed from this synopsis in significant ways and, as we will see later, throws light on the narrative discontinuities for which *Happy Guys* was criticized after its release.[42] At this initial stage, the plot of *The Shepherd* develops perfectly logically, and even gags are carefully motivated: for example, we are told that the rope with a hook by which Potekhin tethers the obstreperous Mar'ia Ivanovna to himself, and which is instrumental to the falling statue and connection gags, was left on the street by electrical workers repairing telegraph poles. Potekhin is allowed to become gradually more aware of Aniuta's looks and talent as the story progresses, unlike his sudden recognition of her singing abilities and declaration of love during the Bol'shoi Theatre finale. The early script contains plot lines, comedy routines, animation, and gags that are missing from *Happy Guys* as we now know it. Though hard to imagine, the original script aimed to pack even more plot complications, chases, and gags into the film than survive in its final, rapid-fire version.

First, consider the gags. In the early script, Lena calls three fat sisters, guests at her reception, "cows"; the metaphor later reifies as the women reappear ("these cows again," says Lena), and Potekhin drives them out with his whip exclaiming, "How can I leave them there, they'll poop in your room. Get out! Go to hell!"[43] (In the next director's script, the women promptly fall out a window.) A calf gives one of the guests a wet nudge in the neck; assuming that Lena's mother is showing affection, the guest embraces her, with predictable consequences. The gag in *Happy Guys* with the moving statue of Venus pulled on a rope by the buffalo heroine, Mar'ia Ivanovna, is extended here by adding a similarly propelled piano, which moves away just as various pianists begin to play. As part of the chase in the music-hall, Potekhin runs into a magician's dressing room where he bumps a vase that immediately produces a huge bouquet of paper flowers. Next he disturbs a top hat that disgorges twelve doves and runs to hide behind the crinoline of the magician's assistant. When she leaves the room, he jumps into a large trunk (used for the classic sawing a woman in half trick), which ejects him into the next room. The following day, the "Druzhba" (Friendship) musicians cannot rouse Potekhin for rehearsal until they stand his bed on end, thereby setting up a standard gag used by Groucho Marx in *Duck Soup*: "At that moment, when the bed assumes a vertical position, the blanket falls off and Kostia, who is fully dressed, having straightened his jacket, is the first person to walk calmly to his place in the orchestra and sit down at the drums." Finally, the funeral procession rehearsal was originally enhanced by a chase involving a painter's cradle and several timing gags: "Behind the corner rises a new eight-story building. On the sidewalk near the house stands a huge painters' cradle. The orchestra members run up to it, look around, quickly climb into the cradle and bend down to hide. The policemen run up to the cradle and stop, but don't see the musicians. Two painters turn on the motor of the winch. Looking to the sides, the policemen turn their backs to the cradle. At that moment the walls of the cradle rise, leaving the platform with the musicians on the sidewalk. The workers at the winch exclaim, 'Stop, go back, we forgot to fasten it.' The bewildered policemen again turn to face the cradle. But at that moment the sides of the cradle come down, again hiding the musicians. A worker walks up to the cradle, fastens the bottom, and at that moment the cradle with the musicians begins to move upward." Along the way, Potekhin and the musicians mistake Aniuta's singing for Lena's. The voice breaks off at the highest note, just as a rope breaks, leaving the musicians dangling from the now vertical platform. "The street. The catafalque moves along slowly. On the sidewalk stands an old man. Seeing the catafalque, he piously takes off his hat and crosses himself with a broad gesture. He lifts his arm to cross himself again, but a hat suddenly falls on his head. The bewildered old man removes the hat, lifts his arm to cross himself, but a new hat falls on his head. The same performance is repeated a third, fourth and fifth time.... The musicians climb up on the roof and then descend by the fire escape. Running out of the yard onto the street, they see the old man crossing himself with fifteen hats in his hands. Running past the old man, each of the fifteen musicians takes his hat and joins up with the catafalque, which is passing by just then in the street. The rehearsal resumes."

The *Shepherd* script also contained animation and trick photography gags that were ultimately cut from the film. Karl Ivanovich's cartoon canary stares intently at a point outside its cage, "then lifts its head and sings. Breaking off the singing, it again looks over in the same direction and again continues to sing." It turns out that the cage stands on a table by a music stand with sheet music, and the canary is reading the notes. The character of Potekhin's mentor, the pre-revolutionary German music teacher Karl Ivanovich, was more developed in the *Shepherd* script, and a trick photography gag, borrowed from Eisenstein's *Strike*, draws a sociological equal sign between them that is missing from *Happy Guys*. When Potekhin comes to borrow Karl Ivanovich's good clothes for the visit to The Black Swan, the old man shows him a photograph of a baroness in 19th century dress, the woman who "ruined my career." As Potekhin looks at the photograph, the figure becomes a living Lena, who speaks to Potekhin in a comically squeaky little voice consistent with the size of the figure. Karl Ivanovich continues, "She was a baroness, I was a teacher, and she remained a baroness and I remained a teacher.... Never indulge a woman. When Ludwig van Beethoven used to visit Emma Stiedrich, he would say, 'Respected guests, I come to you with particular pleasure because when I play here, one can hear marvellous music.'" The entire sub-plot, along with the photograph gag, was cut when the ending of the film changed to the grand finale at the Bol'shoi. A pre-revolutionary, foreign mentor who loses out in the class struggle may also not have been a politically correct model for a Stalinist hero.

The *Shepherd* script originally contained an additional major plot line, which both anchored *Happy Guys* in Soviet reality and determined the original ending of the film. Potekhin's collective farm chairman disapproves of his music making and frequently reminds him, "Don't forget that you're a shepherd." Potekhin's teacher, Karl Ivanovich, argues the opposite: "Don't forget that you're a musician," thereby establishing the classic musical comedy opposition between art and practical reality. After Potekhin's animals wreak havoc at the Black Swan hotel, they are called to account at a mock trial in which the humor is rooted in a telling analogy between animals and collective farm workers:

> Chairman: Comrades, we're faced with a sad fact: our best sire ["proizvoditel'" also means "producer" in the economic sense], Chamberlain the bull, appeared for morning exercise today in an intoxicated condition with an "attribute" on his head.

Exclamations: —A disgrace. —It's not true. —It can't be.

Chairman: Feast your eyes on this, comrades. [He points to a clearing where several milkmaids lead the staggering bull, with a cane in his teeth and a torn straw hat on his horn. The bull resists and they restrain him with difficulty.]

Chairman: Comrades, but this isn't all of it. Two of our foreign specialists, the Swiss citizen cow Zoia and the Dutch citizen cow Esther Van Dongen did not spend the night at home and appeared for pasturing with traces of lipstick on their udders, and their muzzles were powdered!

Exclamations: —Outrageous. —Be quiet. —Petty bourgeois behavior. —Listen, listen.

[The milkmaids lead the cows, smeared with lipstick and powder, with wilted flowers on their horns, along the clearing.]

Chairman: Comrades, I consider the misuse of such cosmetics disgusting even on women. But on cows it is simply unbearable. Let's go on, comrades: Fomka, a yearling ram from our herd appeared to go out to pasture disguised as a tiger.

Exclamations: There's a son of a bitch.

[General commotion. The milkmaids lead the ram covered with a tiger skin along the meadow. The sheep watching the disguised ram fall into a faint. The chairman sits down. One of the women sitting on the table stands up and addresses the meeting.]

The Woman: Comrades, the tiger is nothing. There are worse things than the tiger, comrades. Mar'ia Ivanovna, the Professor's own sister, went on a spree and didn't show up at all.

[A young milkmaid who runs in at that moment interrupts the woman's speech and whispers something in her ear.]

The Woman: Comrades, Fenia reports that Mar'ia Ivanovna has just shown up, but how, comrades—in a completely indecent state and, comrades, I'm ashamed to say, with someone's trousers.

[There is a general exclamation of surprise and an uproar. The noise of the excited crowd hides the loud and wild roar: it's the buffalo tearing along the meadow. Tied to her neck is a rope at the end of which dangle a pair of trousers.]

Chairman: Comrades, such excesses disrupt our production plan and spoil the milking.

Exclamations: Right. True...

Chairman: (Comrades, let's not gloss over things: if the cow is guilty, we'll make her answer. But, comrades, first and foremost the leadership must answer for such excesses.)[44] Head shepherd, Comrade Potekhin, respond to the criticism.

Kostia [stands]: Comrades, I blush with shame. [Kostia's face turns pink.]

Kostia: I blush with shame for myself. [His face reddens.] But I blush even more for Mar'ia Ivanovna. [His face turns crimson.]

[Kostia is upset and drinks a glass of water. The color in his face fades and disappears.[45]

...One of the collective farm workers gives an energetic speech, standing behind the table.]

Farm Worker: Comrades, if Konstantin doesn't abandon his music, he'll ruin all our music.[46] We have a collective farm here, comrades, not a circus.

Exclamation: Correct.

The Orator: We must tear this music by the roots out of our herd.

The kolkhoz plotline, doubtless concocted by Erdman and Mass, parodies collective farm workers via their misbehaving animals who drink, debauch, and show up late for work. Potekhin is called to account for their excesses since, according to established Stalinist practice, it is those in authority who are responsible and must bear the punishment for the mistakes of their subordinates. Finally, the early script parodies the language of socialist construction: the bull Chamberlain is a "proizvoditel," both sire and producer on the socialist front; cows from Swiss and Dutch breeds become "foreign specialists," a reference to the foreign engineers and other technical staff working in Russia during the twenties and early thirties; Potekhin's music must be "torn out by the roots" from the herd, a cliché of the political rhetoric of the time.

Later Potekhin makes another humorous reference to a recent Party initiative when he goes to complain to the building supervisor about the noise next door that is distracting his musicians during rehearsals in Moscow: "We're creative workers, comrade commandant. We need quiet, you understand, but there it's noise from early morning on, tararum, the devil knows what. We need socialist realism, but this turns out to be some sort of mysticism—sounds arising from nothing. Stop this outrage. Take energetic measures."

The kolkhoz line also motivates the circular symmetry of the ending in the early script. *The Shepherd* begins and ends in the South in order to effect the reconciliation of art and life that is at the heart of the show musical. After the orchestra's successful number at the Bol'shoi (Aniuta is not involved in the early script), they are invited to perform in the South with ballet dancers and a female singer—the latter to be provided by Potekhin. Aniuta, who has been keeping house for the orchestra, asks to be considered, but Potekhin, who has mistaken Lena's voice for Aniuta's, tells Aniuta that she has no talent and the girl leaves the group. Two months later, the orchestra boards a train to perform in the Caucasus. On the radio Kostia hears what he supposes is Lena's singing at an amateur concert. The orchestra members jump off the train and reach the radio station by hydroplane after unwittingly winning a boat race. Now acknowledged, Aniuta joins the group, which flies south on the newly constructed Maksim Gorky in order to be on time for their engagement. This airplane motif is an early example of Aleksandrov's inclination toward the proleptic "future in the present" in his musicals. The legendary Maksim Gorky, the largest passenger plane of its time, although written up extensively in the newspapers during the second half of 1933 as a coming marvel of Soviet aviation, made its first flight only in June 1934, more than a year after the writing of the *Shepherd* script.[47] Because the orchestra's rehearsing disturbs the other passengers, the musicians and Aniuta settle themselves outside on the plane's wings, precipitating the usual acrobatic stunts à la Harold Lloyd as the plan dives and does loops. After the Maksim Gorky flies through a black cloud of soot from a factory below, the orchestra members appear in blackface, which is later washed away by passing through a storm cloud. (This gag is repeated in the raft scene of *Volga-Volga* and with Tania's smoking samovar in *The Radiant Path*.) The orchestra and Aniuta all perform successfully and Potekhin is reunited with Karl Ivanovich, who tells him of the collective farm's plight—a shortage of workers to gather in the hay in time to make production goals. Potekhin and his troupe go to the rescue: a row of his dancers mows the hay, competing against the local farm workers. When the laborers begin to tire, Potekhin and his orchestra revive them with a lively march that "rhythmically organizes their work" and allows them to finish mowing. Art and practical existence are thus reconciled, with art playing a saving role.

The finale of *The Shepherd* reprises Lena's initial acquaintance with Potekhin on the beach, which now backfires on her politically:

> Elena: I thought you were Konstantin Potekhin, the performer.
>
> Kostia: I *am* Kostia Potekhin, the performer.
>
> Elena: But you're a shepherd.

Kostia: I'm a shepherd too.

Elena: How is that possible?

Kostia: Everything is possible in our country.

Potekhin then swims out to join Aniuta and tries to declare his love, in spite of various comic obstacles, but she understands nothing:

Kostia: You dummy. I said I love you.

Aniuta: [losing consciousness] Oh!

[She begins to sink. Kostia grabs her.]

Kostia: What's wrong with you?

Aniuta: [opening her eyes] Water.

[Kostia sprinkles water on her forehead. Aniuta smiles and snuggles up to him.

Underwater around them little fish dance and sing to the main leitmotif of our film.]

Aleksandrov planned to do this final scene with animation. Several years later, the unexploited ending was to migrate to the conclusion of *Volga-Volga*.

A secondary plot line branches out from the topic of the NEP bourgeoisie who are parodied through Lena's reception at the Black Swan. One guest puts on a record of Vertinskii songs: "A reverent hush descends. All the faces assume a prayerful expression. The young man winds up his record player and Vertinskii begins to sing. There are several dogs in the garden by the dacha. The dogs can't resist Vertinskii's sentimental wailing and begin to howl along." Singer and actor Aleksandr Vertinskii (1889–1957) was immensely popular in pre-revolutionary Russia as a performer and composer of cabaret songs about failed love affairs, cocaine addicts, and similar Silver Age topics. He emigrated in 1920, and his music came to represent both the degenerate lifestyle and anti-Soviet convictions of the NEP bourgeoisie.[48] When both the record player and his Vertinskii record are destroyed in comic accidents, the guest laments: "Now there's nothing left in my life." Potekhin is similarly in despair after leaving the reception and decides to hang himself. He throws the noose over a tree branch and sits on a large branch to sing before doing the deed. In the meantime, the man who has lost his record and hence "everything in life" appears, intending to drown himself—a parody of the Vertinskii lyrical hero. Seeing the noose, he uses it, but only succeeds in breaking the branch, throwing himself and Potekhin to the ground. "Then the man without a record player suddenly takes up the song that Kostia did not have time to finish. Kostia picks it up and together they happily sing the final couplet." This small side plot clearly illustrates both the superiority of the new Soviet music over pre-revolutionary popular songs, as well as its energizing and life-affirming effect.

The script of *The Shepherd* was read to the staff of *Komsomol'skaia pravda*, whose services Shumiatskii had enlisted to advocate and advertise his new project. Although supportive, *Komsomol'skaia's* initial response already rehearses the terms of the acrimonious debate over the film that will rage for the next year and a half, throughout production and up to the date of its official release in December 1934:

> The film will have healthy music, and not diseased and enfeebling foxtrotomania [fokstrotchina].... The entire plot is based on interestingly conceived and wittily resolved comedy situations and tricks, which are not in any way an end in themselves, but flow logically from the entire action of the film.... The purpose of the script is to make a happy film that infects you with a desire for work and building.... The editorial staff of *Komsomol'skaia pravda*...put forth a number of concrete recommendations for changing several episodes in the film. The need to avoid the danger of sliding into sheer foxtrotomania was particularly pointed out.

* * *

The controversy surrounding *Happy Guys* continued unabated in various corners of the film community throughout the spring—at the April 1933 House of Scholars script reading and discussion, at the June 5 meeting of Leningrad script writers, at the mid-June two-day discussion among the Association of Workers of Revolutionary Cinema (ARRK).[49] The topography of the battlefield was everywhere identical. The overarching question was the definition of "Soviet laughter" ("sovetskii smekh"), a vexed issue the culture was never able to resolve, ultimately because of the impossibility of satire in a perfected socialist society. The localized debate sparked by *Happy Guys* centered on the poetics of comedy as ideology or entertainment (even if justified ideologically as providing rest and relaxation to the working population), with corollary questions of undesirable foreign, chiefly American, influences and realism in the treatment of Soviet everyday life. Aleksandrov's critics were not only bureaucrats and ideologues, but also respected filmmakers—Roshal', Raizman, Macheret, and Esther Shub—who asked, "Do we have the right to 'simply laughter'?"

The newspaper account of the discussion at the House of Scholars unmasks the essential hypocrisy of Bolshevik ideological asceticism:

> During several hours the sedate hall of the House of Scholars rocked with bursts of laughter. Grown-up, serious people, who are knowledgeable about the arts, were laughing spontaneously, like children, forgetting about their adulthood, seriousness and experience.... Then the laughter died out.... The reading of *Jazz-Comedy* [*Happy Guys*] concluded. The serious people who were knowledgeable about the arts recovered their seriousness and knowledgeability. "The work is brilliantly talented," they said, "but it has no social backbone."

Aleksandrov responded, "Soviet comedy has been overly problematized, and it is no longer funny.... Our main goal is to solve the problem of laughter. And that's all!" Iurii Raizman and Grigorii Roshal' objected to the wholesale borrowing of Harold Lloyd-type situational comedy without locating it in Soviet reality: if Lloyd's comedies were inseparable from everyday American life, *Jazz-Comedy* takes place in some sort of Filmland ("Kinolandia"). Aleksandrov ended his response on a publicly conciliatory note: "My main goal as the film's director is to bind it inseparably to Soviet soil, to ground it in a Soviet way."[50]

Shortly before *Happy Guys* was scheduled to go into production, the factory cell at Potylikha, the future Mosfil'm, then still Soiuzfil'm, issued a resolution against the script which rejected the project for merely summarizing "achievements in the art of bourgeois laughter." In addition, "the episodes with thirty showgirls who catch up the production plan at the collective farm smack of intentional naiveté and border on mockery." The script was branded a political mistake of the GUKF leadership and Soiuzfil'm. The *Kino* editors responded by citing new Party policy: "the instructions of the directive organs that a film must provide rest and entertainment."[51] Shumiatskii quelled the rebellion from below, although the resentment and foot-dragging of rank and file studio workers was to continue through much of production.

The final director's script was completed and approved by late May 1933, just before *Happy Guys* went into production. Its literary epigraph, doubtless added by Erdman, makes an appeasing little bow to the enemies of the film, who had been on the ideological warpath since the public reading at the House of Scholars: "Don't look upon it as a guide, except perhaps in the sphere of the humorous. Rabelais, 1532."[52] In reality, very little in the script was altered to placate the critics. The director's script moves a step beyond the 1932–33 *Shepherd* version, providing specific technical and staffing information, paring down gags and plot complications to some degree, and expanding the role of Aniuta.[53] One, more sophisticated, gag has been added: Elena drinks raw eggs as she practices singing her scales, breaking the shells on the nose of a bust of Beethoven (replaced by Bach in the film). Both Lena and Potekhin are thus shown to be unequal to the classical tradition: Elena's singing leaves Beethoven with egg on his face, and Potekhin tries but is unable to duplicate Beethoven's monologue at Emma Stiedrich's as he faces the guests at the Black Swan: "Respected guests...as Beethoven said. Oh, yes...respected guests...no, not respected...Oh, it doesn't matter [bows casually]...hi all." (The poke at Potekhin is eliminated from the completed film.) The musicians' brawl is now worked out descriptively in ten scenes, to be edited according to the musical score. The entire airplane plot line has been eliminated, possibly because it was too difficult to film in the studio. The deletion proved to be fortuitous, since the Maksim Gorky crashed May 18, 1935 and the plane was immediately dropped as a media topic.

Aleksandrov had been searching for a Mary Pickford-type heroine to sing, dance, and act in his film.[54] By this time he had met Liubov' Orlova, in whichever version of the story one chooses to believe, and had developed a personal interest in enlarging her role in the film.[55] While in the *Shepherd* script Aniuta was merely scolded by Lena while washing the floor, now she sets the table for the reception, pours wine, and performs a separate musical number. When Aniuta is also picked up by the musicians on the way to the Bol'shoi engagement, Orlova is given yet another major performance opportunity.

On April 10, 1933, Aleksandrov contracted with the cartoonists Kukryniksy for sketches of costumes and makeup for *Happy Guys*, promising to provide photos of the actors and a catalogue of musical instruments to be used in the film.[56] At the time, Kukryniksy were already busy with another film, *The Life of Klim Samgin*. Aleksandrov never delivered the promised materials, and Kukryniksy backed out of the contract a month later amidst mutual recriminations with the studio. Aleksandrov did not like the work of the artist Kanevskii, suggested by Kukryniksy, and turned to Eisenstein for assistance.[57] Ready to help his long-time assistant, Eisenstein quickly produced approximately twenty-five sketches for the musical brawl scenes of the film.[58] Several are concrete descriptions of the fighting: a view of the room showing the placement of figures with arrows depicting trajectories; a man leaning down from atop a kettledrum beneath which lies a trapped animal; a musician holding cymbals while standing on a kettledrum; another standing upside down on the drum, playing with his head; one musician bowing on a cello with a second man sitting on his shoulders to handle the fingering;[59] a man playing a tuba, whose opening is blocked by a dish and pitcher which apparently landed there during the mayhem; a man hanging by the pants from a chandelier while playing a tambourine and drums with each bare foot and cymbal and drum with his hands. This last composition is closest to any pose actually employed in the film: the musical brawl ends with a semi-conscious man hanging in the same position in front of the window (Figs. 2–3).

The remaining Eisenstein drawings reveal a conceptualization of the brawl that has little to do with the comic routines employed in the film. In *Happy Guys*, musical instruments are transformed into weapons—an oboe is shot from the strings of a cello, xylophone keys become musical missiles. These are traditional switch gags, long used in American film comedy and cartoons. Eisenstein's vision is both more original and largely impossible to realize. As his musicians mix it up in the brawl, the functions of instruments, household objects, and human bodies are displaced upon each other

Figure 2.

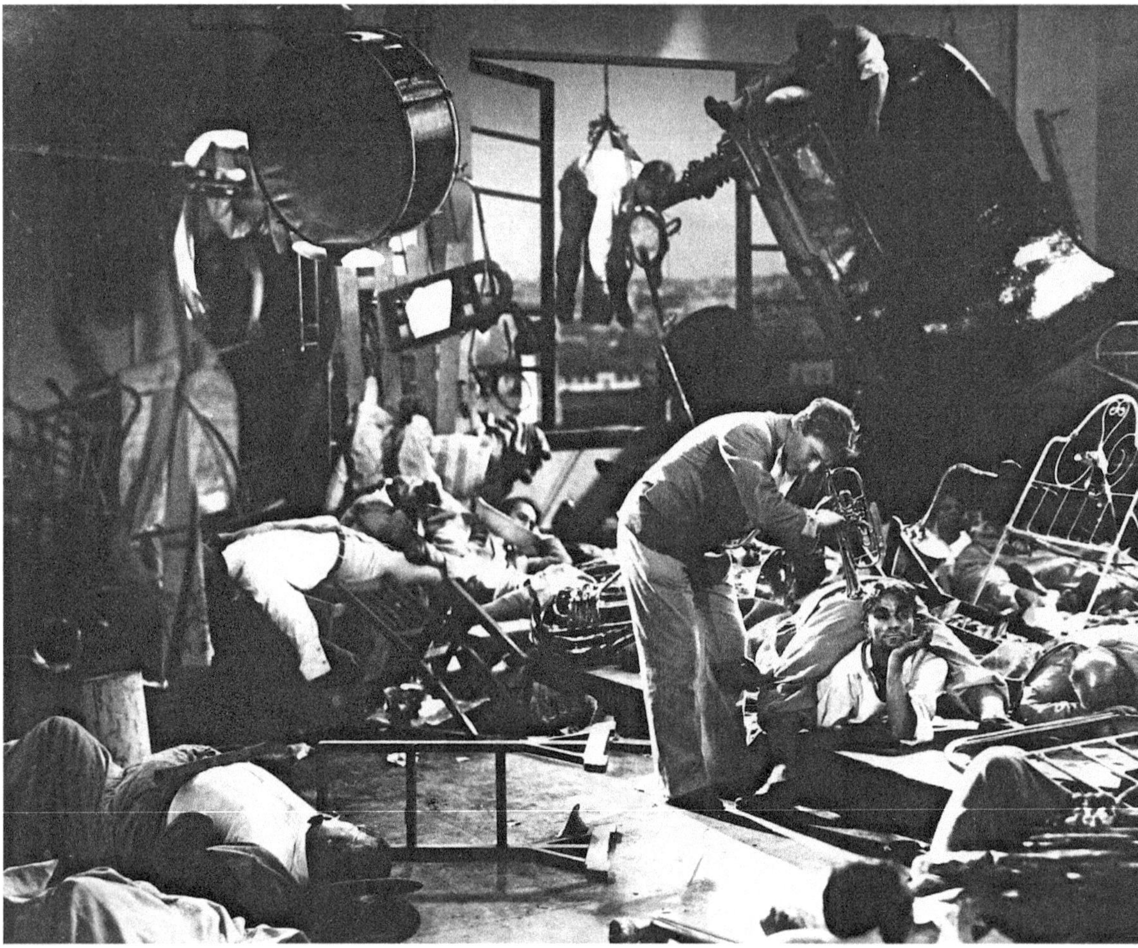

Figure 3.

metonymically, under the pressure of physical force. As in his sex drawings, Eisenstein explores the possibilities of the human body through unusual combinations of body with object. Like Disney's shape-shifting cartoon characters—Mickey pulls out his tail to make a climbing rope and later turns it into a spring for comfortable riding in *The Gallopin' Goucho* (1928)—the brawling musicians stretch and twist into fantastic figures. In Disney's *Skeleton Dance* (1929), one skeleton uses the other as pogo stick, and another plays the spine and skull of a bony pal as a xylophone. In Eisenstein's drawings, musicians more typically—and autoerotically—play their own bodies.

Musical instruments become household objects: a tuba produces steam (a metaphor for passionate performance) that heats up the teapot perched overhead; a vertically positioned trumpet morphs into a hanging lamp as the violence of the brawl forces the two into incongruous contact. As the brawl destroys their musical instruments, the musicians resort to performing on household objects: one plays the webbing of a bed frame like a harp; another performs on a three-tiered cake dish instead of a cello; and a third plays a cello, the top of which has acquired a dresser complete with mirror and candelabras. The dapper musician elaborates the grooming motif by bowing with a large hairbrush (Fig. 4).

In the press of comic violence, Eisenstein's musical instruments also metamorphose into human parts. A man plays a trumpet that encircles his neck. Together with his beard and outwardly extended glasses, its twisted stem forms a second human profile (Fig. 5). Another musician plays his body as cello and violin (Fig. 6), both the comic outcome of the brawl—one figure in the four sketches of this subject has a swollen and blackened eye—and a metaphor for the psychology of performance. The body of another musician has merged with a gramophone: the machine sits on his back, his arm has become the player arm, and the sound trumpet curves under his belly with its large flared end protruding from the rear, so that the phonograph-man also resembles a male turkey. True to type, Eisenstein lets himself go and throws in some phallic humor: a musician with a glum expression stands pigeon-toed, in his long underwear, with his hand over his crotch and upper legs.[60] His pants, which have taken on an independent existence, stand next to him. From the top of the pants protrude multiple erect horns and trumpets, one of which he touches with his hand.[61] In another drawing, a trumpeter penetrates a nude female statue from below with his instrument, while another man holds the statue steady on a table.[62]

At the end of May, Aleksandrov paid Eisenstein for eighteen completed sketches of the musical instruments which could only have served as general inspiration.[63] *Kino*, which regularly reported on the progress of the film during this time, also attributes makeup to Eisenstein, and costume design to Aleksandrov.[64] Filming was complicated by the availability of only one microphone to record music, voices, and sound effects.[65] Nil'sen's wife, Itta Penzo, recalls that Eisenstein helped Aleksandrov edit the musical brawl episode, afterwards commenting, "*Now* this resembles a real attraction!"[66]

Figure 4.

Figure 5.

Rehearsals for *Happy Guys* began June 1, 1933. For most of the summer, Aleksandrov filmed scenes from the second half of the script in the still unfinished, largely roofless, Studio One of Potylikha. According to Neia Massal'skaia, the assistant to the director, the idea for the brawl was Utesov's, and he devoted considerable time to choreographing and rehearsing the actors.[67] However, both Aleksandrov and Dunaevskii devoted a great deal of effort to constructing the episode—identifying the musico-comic possibilities of various instruments (e.g., "laughing" saxophones, playing a harp by dragging a body across the instrument, using violin bows as swords, etc.) and making detailed plans of the musical routines. Dunaevskii then composed the musical score, to which separate scenes were precisely keyed and then filmed using the playback system.[68] Aleksandrov shot more than 250 short sequences during ten working days to produce the four-minute (120 meter) musical brawl episode.[69] In later years, Dunaevskii considered this sequence from *Happy Guys* his second most technically challenging musical composition for film, after the train scene in *The Beethoven Concert*.[70]

Figure 6.

Figure 7.

During July, Aleksandrov filmed the musical brawl and adjacent scenes, such as the dormitory staircase where Potekhin complains to the building supervisor. Intourist had offered the Utesov orchestra a gig at the Metropol' for several months, which conveniently included room and board. Arkadii Kotliarskii, one of the orchestra members, recalled that lunatic summer when a bus would pick them up at 6:00 a.m. for the day's filming, they would return by 6:00 p.m., rush to perform at the Ermitazh at 8:00 p.m., and then return to the Metropol' to play the dance program at midnight. The orchestra members were sent home to Leningrad while the scenery for the Bol'shoi Theatre performance was being built. There, without asking Utesov's permission, they contracted for performances at the Astoria hotel. Utesov promptly fired 12 of the 15 musicians and asked his friends Arnol'd and Kotliarskii to find replacements. A new orchestra then returned to Moscow for filming, so that the musical brawl sequences in the film are actually a montage of two different contingents' performances.[71] Besides the 15 members of the Utesov orchestra, Aleksandrov also used additional actors and two professional acrobats in the musical brawl scenes.[72]

From early to mid-July, Aleksandrov filmed the orchestra's funeral procession scenes on the streets of Moscow (Fig. 7) while complaining about the usual traffic problems.[73] During late July to early August, he was occupied with filming the Bol'shoi Theatre performance. As usual, there were technical problems and other delays: the scenery for the Bol'shoi finale was built outside in the studio yard, but filming had to be postponed repeatedly because of rain, until the scenery eventually disintegrated and had to be rebuilt.[74] A malfunctioning moving floor, which Aleksandrov attributed to studio workers' carelessness, prevented multiple takes of some of the Bol'shoi segments.[75] To make matters worse, at some point during the summer, the newly established Kinokomissiia decided to review the *Shepherd* script. In his October 7, 1933 report to Central Committee Secretary Kaganovich, Stetskii listed previously approved scripts which had been significantly altered by the Kinokomissiia; among them was *The Shepherd*.[76] The Kinokomissiia required the elimination of the episodes with musicians and showgirls harvesting the hay because they were seen, in Shumiatskii's public retelling, as "an attempt to give the film an ideological character not typical of it as a whole."[77] Since the harvest scenes are the culmination of the kolkhoz sub-plot, Aleksandrov then removed the entire narrative line from the film. Potekhin's socialist realism wisecrack may also have been cut at the same time. For the super-vigilant Kinokomissiia, which was ideologically more orthodox than even the Politbiuro, both collective farms and socialist realism were too much sacred cows of the era to be served up for the entertainment of the masses.

In late August, the group left for filming on location by the Black Sea. Aleksandrov chose the resort town of Gagry in western Abkhazia, where he had vacationed with Eisenstein and Tisse in 1928.[78] The actors and crew settled in at the Hotel Gagripsh, and filming began on September 9 (Figs. 8–9). Aleksandrov began with the outdoor scenes

Figure 8.

near the Black Swan.[79] Erdman sent his mother a colorful description of the first day's shooting at the palatial dacha of the surgeon Fedorov:

> The professor himself is probably in Moscow at the moment, cutting people up. He's represented here by an Italian steward, whom we told that he would destroy the picture if he didn't permit filming at the dacha entrusted to his care. Without knowing the content of the film and thinking that only love scenes can be shot in such a place, the Italian graciously gives permission. While they were setting up the camera and

Aleksandrov, in a blue shirt, Mexican pants and a pith helmet, was giving instructions, the steward sat on the upper balcony and contemplated the work of the inspired artists with a benevolent smile. But then the signal sounds and, to the wild shouts of Abkhazians, a crazed herd of cows bursts onto the white, steep staircases leading to the main entrance. The animals rush up the stairs, sweeping away everything in their path, butting

e 9

> each other, bellowing, wrenching out steps and pulling out banana trees with their roots. The unfortunate Italian sees the wonderful plaster vases crack one after another and fall on the road, the railings crumble and the rose bushes being trampled. He holds his head and begins to shout some sort of earnest words in the sonorous language of Petrarch and Croce, but no one pays any attention. The filming continued for four hours, the Italian shouted for four hours, and Aleksandrov smiled imperturbably for four hours, feeling just as calm as if he were in the studio at Potylikha. During filming two cows fainted because of the heat, a third fell off a high slope and crashed down on the road, scaring the hell out of two ladies returning from the beach.[80]

For filming musical numbers, Aleksandrov used the playback system, which he had observed in the US, where it was in general use by early 1930.[81] However, his approach was still tentative: he filmed on the basis of inexact, "rough" recordings without using a full orchestra. The recordings subsequently required extensive corrections and re-recording, a hard lesson that moved Dunaevskii and Aleksandrov to proceed differently with their next film.[82] The three long tracking shots in *Happy Guys*—Potekhin's morning march, the beach panorama, and the Bol'shoi Theatre finale—were also innovations for Soviet cinema at the time. A narrow gauge railroad, along which travelled a small car with the camera, was constructed right on the beach for the extended tracking shot of seaside life. Although Kostia's march was later described by Aleksandrov and others as a continuous tracking shot of 140 meters,[83] eyewitness information and close observation of the film footage both contradict the claim. The railroad tracks for Kostia's march from the Prozrachnye kliuchi (Clear Springs) cattle farm through the village and to the seashore were actually constructed in three different locations—at the Bzyb' river gorge, in Gagry, and at the famous Gagry seaside park.[84] Careful observation reveals a montage of three segments, shot from slightly different angles: shortly after Kostia passes the vineyard, there is a splice in the trees to the second segment; after the lovestruck Aniuta spills milk on Kostia, the transition to the third segment occurs in shots of a high fence. But together, the three segments create the illusion of sustained vigor and energy in Kostia's triumphant march.

In Gagry, Aleksandrov was still considering two different endings for *Happy Guys*, both of which were filmed. The first followed the director's script: Potekhin tries to declare his affection for Aniuta amidst crashing waves and other obstacles; she faints in the water and then asks for water.[85] In a variant ending reminiscent of Disney cartoons, Lena's mother sees her daughter in the arms of a disreputable-looking type (Fig. 10) and promptly faints, falling from a cliff into the sea, which overflows its shores. The stunt was performed not by the actress Elena Tiapkina, but by Aleksandrov himself: "All of Gagry came to the shore to see the director, wearing a dress, fall from a great height into the sea."[86]

10.

By late September, the group's enthusiasm and spirit of camaraderie had evaporated. Nil'sen resented the "American director's" bad taste and self-importance, as well as Orlova's prominent position on the set. Both Nil'sen and the scriptwriters, who continued to work on dialogue in Gagry, felt they were wasting their time on a text that would only be vulgarized by the director. Nevertheless, Nil'sen recognized its potential for the culture:

> We're filming awful hack work—all the more harmful since all of it will doubtless be successful and become the style of Soviet film for a certain

> time. It's hard to imagine how far bad taste and vulgarity in every small thing can go, beginning with the composition of scenes to the choice of costumes or the acting. Although I haven't messed up yet and everything is okay with the photography, Grisha is angry at me, apparently because I prevent him from making a fool of himself in front of gullible listeners. I'm sick of this whole salon of affected gallantry. And worst of all is when a "mistress of the house" appears in the enterprise. Grisha has completely lost his head because of all his successes and apparently intends to get married after the picture is released. I'm sorry for Erdman. He's the only person I can talk to here. I'm sorry for his wasted work. A new script is being written that Grisha won't be able to manage, of course, and Erdman realizes it. He has already seen through him completely, and Mass comes straight out in conversation, "Vulgar trash," "No good at all," etc. Overall, a huge fuss. I just want to finish as soon as possible and then back to Moscow.... Although I was brought up on the front lines of the Civil War and in the whorehouses of peacetime, even for me an extended sojourn in the brilliant company of the American director is becoming more than I can stand.[87]

Even the more committed and less intellectual Utesov confessed boredom in a letter to his wife: "It's really lousy here. It rains all the time and I feel sad. The monotony is such that you don't want to go on living. Everybody is already sick of each other. Today there was a little variety. Yesterday on the set, I was battling the buffalo and pulled the muscles in my lower back. It's very painful and I'm staying in bed today."[88] But the heaviest blow to the group's morale was the arrest of Erdman and Mass on October 10. Their published and unpublished anti-Soviet fables had angered Stalin. Geladze, the local OGPU chief who had spent his evenings at the hotel restaurant socializing with the film people, was ordered by telegram from Moscow to carry out the operation.[89] Utesov, who shared a room with Mass, witnessed his arrest and wrote his wife: "I won't begin to describe the details of the arrest to you. The one thing I will say is that it took a good year off my life.... All of this is depressing for all of us and deprives us of the possibility of working peacefully."[90]

In late October, Aleksandrov wrote to Eisenstein, alluding circumspectly to the arrests and to his love affair with Orlova. Most interesting is Eisenstein's increasing distance from his former colleague and the publicly self-assured "American director's" real insecurity about his first independent film and consequent need to maintain contact with his former teacher:

Dear TEACHER!

In all my history with you I can't remember such lengthy intervals between meetings. I don't remember not hearing about you for such a long time.

When you went to Kislovodsk you left us without a hello or goodbye and we only learned from *Kino-gazeta* that you are a PROSPECTOR FOR REALISM.

We're returning to Moscow soon and don't know how to behave, for we don't know who you are at the present moment, since we haven't had any newspapers here for a long time.

Our picture is moving along at a leisurely pace to its completion (because of the weather), in spite of the catastrophes and storms breaking around it.

"Some are no longer here; others have been killed one after another."[91]

I very much want to finish it and begin to edit in order to see what doesn't work.

We've shot a lot of all kinds of stuff but "k'en sabe!"[92]

I very much want to see you and talk about a lot of things we never spoke about earlier, because when I was not responsible for the quality of the output on my own such thoughts never even occurred to me. It's all concerned with creative processes, and mainly working with live people.

I would also like to give you a lot of advice on the subject of mastering our technical equipment, since a huge number of unexpected developments, both pleasant and unpleasant, arise during actual sound recording and filming.

I would really like to know WHAT YOU'RE DOING and WHAT YOU PLAN TO DO. I. Babel' visited here and told us about you, but that's too little. By the way, he looked at the footage we've shot in the Caucasus and predicts a good film.

The weather alone is killing me now and our life, which resembles Tetlapayac, but I must say it's nicer thanks to certain circumstances about which they sing in our film song:

"...But there's love—and even better things,
And life is really very good."

In general I miss you a lot, Starshina. That's why I'm writing this letter.[93]

Figure 11.

Bad weather continued to delay filming in Gagry and the group returned to Moscow only on November 11, several weeks behind schedule. There was no question now of completing the film by the end of the year, as originally planned by the studio. Under pressure to complete *Happy Guys* as quickly as possible, Aleksandrov put the actors and crew on day and night shifts for much of the spring. Utesov was forced to cancel concerts because he was at the studio every day and evening until midnight—"otherwise we won't finish the film on time."[94] By May 22, he is much happier: "The filming is going brilliantly, and I'm coming out very well"[95] (Figs. 11-12). Aleksandrov was less than satisfied with Utesov's ideas, later blaming his difficult personality and their arguments for some of the film's defects: "I didn't always win my battles with him and [as a result] did a lot of vulgar things in my film."[96]

Throughout the autumn and winter, Aleksandrov continued to battle the studio about technical delays that halted shooting. In November, workers constructed the set for Simonov's *The Enthusiasts* (*Spring Days*), located in Studio One immediately next to

12.

Happy Guys, at an incorrect angle so that insufficient space remained to build the set according to specifications, resulting in a delay of several weeks.[97] In early 1934, the studio was 1.5 months late with a rear projection screen needed to complete Utesov's scenes in the tree and the finale showing the performers in front of the Bol'shoi Theatre audience. During the same period, shooting was delayed because the Shostkinskii factory supplied the group with defective film stock.[98] In January, Mikhail Romm complained that production of his *Pyshka* was delayed because resources and space were being diverted to *Happy Guys*.[99]

The film's interior scenes with animals were filmed in early 1934 with now legendary complications. For a month beforehand, the bull Chamberlain as well as various pigs and sheep had been acclimated to the strong studio lighting. Nevertheless, Chamberlain hurt his eyes on the very first day of shooting by staring at the lights and required medical treatment. The script also required the bull, a very sober animal, to laugh. Snuff was blown into his nostrils to make him sneeze, while baring his teeth for the camera. Wicker chairs made out of dried pasta were used to entice the goats into devouring the furniture at Lena's reception.[100] The studio was charging exorbitant fees to feed Aleksandrov's menagerie until the director threatened to transport them to the Metropol' where a salad lunch would be much less expensive.[101]

Aleksandrov had long been interested in the comic potential of anthropomorphized animals. He had filmed the episode "The Personal Cows of Empress Aleksandra Fedorovna," which was later cut from Eisenstein's *October*,[102] and was responsible for the animal scenes in *The Old and the New* (1929): the sow nursing innumerable wriggling piglets; a herd of pigs swimming the river (an idea later transferred to *Volga-Volga*); a montage of a malicious-looking turkey intercut with kulak women planning to poison the bull Tommy; and the cow's wedding from Marfa's dream, in which a cat bridesmaid wears a flower wreath, the bovine bride appears adorned with flowers, and the bull charges downhill to mate, like any eager bridegroom.[103] In Hollywood, Aleksandrov had visited Disney studios and particularly admired Mickey Mouse and Disney's other animal characters.

Training the animals to act out their comic roles presented Aleksandrov with his own comic difficulties:

> We began with the piglet. We stood him in front of a plate with cognac, stuck his nose in it and, to our surprise, the piglet lapped up the cognac with pleasure and turned into a drunk hooligan. Staggering and grunting, he walked around the table, dropping bottles, throwing plates off the table by smartly hooking them with his snout, and bravely jumped into the unknown.... We caught him on the fly, so that he wouldn't hurt himself.... Emboldened by the successful experiment with the piglet, we decided to try it on the huge bull we had chosen at the slaughterhouse. We put half

ЧУДЕСА ЗООТЕХНИКИ
Дружеский шарж худ. В. СУТЕЕВА
1929
1934
ВС
старое... и совсем новое

Figure 13.

> a pail of vodka in front of the bull and waited.... The bull sniffed it for a long time. He tried the vodka, but didn't pounce on it. Finally he began to drink the vodka, but turned out to be violent when intoxicated. He broke the rope with which he was tied, ran out into the yard of Mosfil'm and began chasing people who scattered in all directions and hid in fear. My assistant arrived on a motorcycle, the drunk bull ran after him. My assistant left his motorcycle and clambered up a tree. The bull butted the motorcycle with his horns until it fell silent.[104] (Fig. 13)

Aleksandrov then approached the renowned animal trainer Vladimir Durov who explained that bulls are proverbially stubborn animals and he might be able to do something—over the next five months. Not having five months at his disposal, Aleksandrov tried a hypnotist who stared at Chamberlain for four hours and only succeeded in working himself into a fainting fit. Aleksandrov's assistant I. Simkov then brought in a circus performer who offered to tie two of the bull's legs so that he would limp and appear drunk, but the director rejected the idea as too cruel. Finally, an elderly veterinarian suggested mixing bromide into the vodka. "The bull staggered, lay down, kept falling asleep. The task was completed. One moment of laughter had been filmed."[105]

According to the script, Utesov was supposed to ride bareback on Chamberlain in order to get him out of the room. When Utesov refused to do the tricky scene, Aleksandrov approached Orlova who recalled: "Grigorii Vasil'evich asked me to do it...and at that time, if he had asked me to jump from the seventh floor of a building, I would have done it."[106] The bull was so tall and Orlova so small that she had to climb a ladder set against his flank. For heightened comic effect, Orlova decided to sit backwards on the bull, but beat him so hard with a small broom ("venik") that the bull bucked and threw her off (Fig.14). Only after a month in Sklifosovkii hospital, recovering from a cracked vertebra, was Orlova able to return to finish filming the scene in which she quickly jumps up off the floor and pushes the bull out of the room. Rather than expose Orlova again to the bull, Aleksandrov carried her piggyback, while she beat him with the venik, then using the close-up footage to complete the episode.[107] In the episode where Orlova holds a large salad, intended for the guests at the Black Swan which is instead devoured by Chamberlain, the bull also licked her hand in passing, leaving abrasions that needed medical treatment.[108]

The scene in which Potekhin replaces a toy lamb with the real thing in order to hide the animal was filmed in January. Since there were no baby lambs available at that time of year, Aleksandrov substituted a fox terrier wearing a specially sewn sheepskin equipped with appropriate head and hooves.[109] The scenes outside the music-hall (Potekhin's arrival and later escape in the arms of the orchestra) were also filmed that winter in Studio One, which did not yet have a roof. The music-hall episodes take place during the summer, so large fans were set up to blow snowflakes out of camera range, and the actors threw off their coats only at the moment of filming.[110]

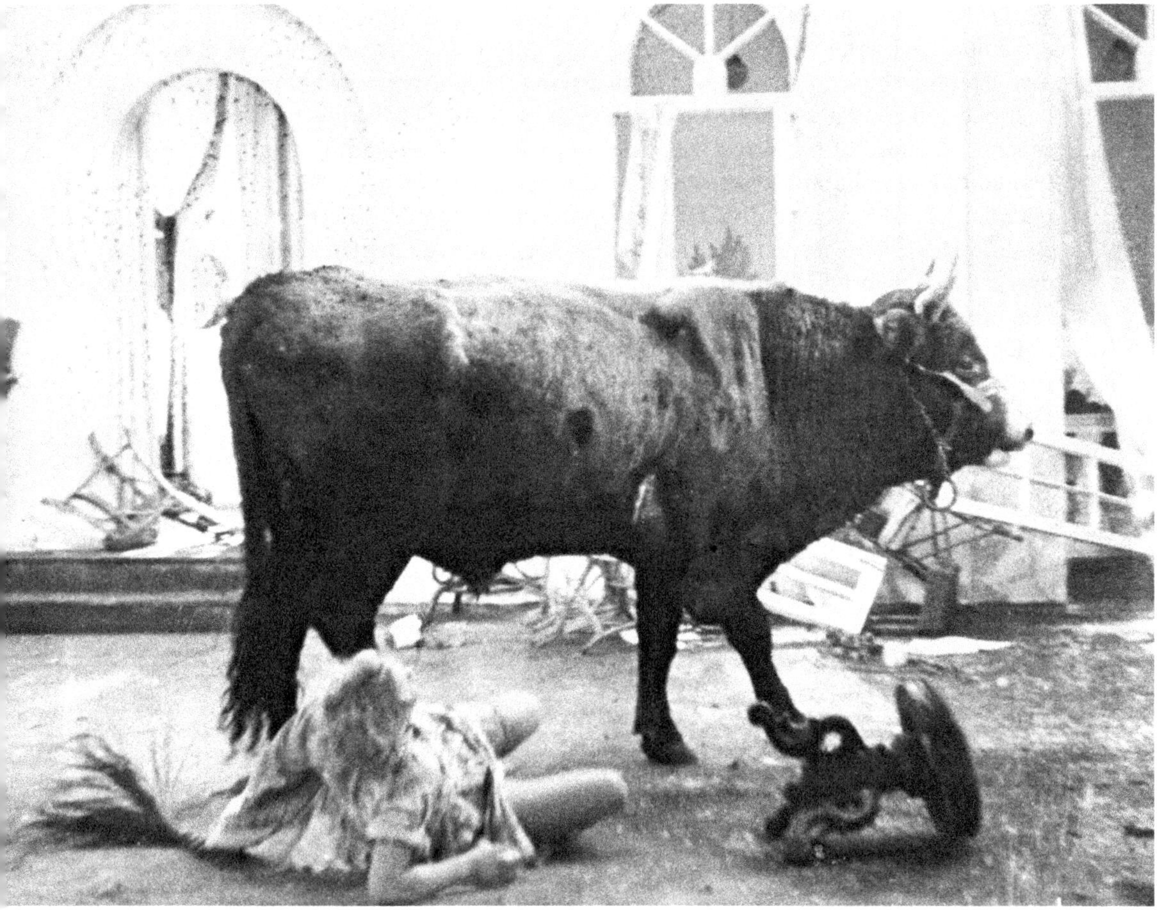

Figure 14.

Dunaevskii had finished most of the music for *Happy Guys* by mid-1933. He later recalled that composing mass songs was relatively easier in the early thirties because this was a new genre and "every new song was, in its own way, fresh, necessary and original.... Every theme was new. Consequently, the 'March of the Happy Guys,' in spite of its difficulties, was written in less than two weeks."[111] In 1938, Aleksandrov remembered the search for the film's central song: Dunaevskii would telephone from Leningrad to sing and later play different melodies to Aleksandrov in Moscow. During one of these nocturnal sessions, because of a crossed telephone connection, Aleksandrov was unknowingly treated to bad radio music instead of a Dunaevskii composition. With the telephone out of order, the frustrated director telegraphed the composer, "That's not the right thing at all!" Dunaevskii responded, "I'm leaving for Moscow." At Dunaevskii's hotel they dragged an old upright from the café up to the composer's room, and Dunaevskii played for Aleksandrov the melody that later became the centerpiece of the film.[112]

During summer 1933, several poets, including Svetlov, Saianov, and Lugovskoi, had tried their hand at writing the lyrics for Potekhin's opening song, already composed by Dunaevskii. Scriptwriter Vladimir Mass was only able to produce an apathetic love song:

> Liubov', liubov'—zolotaia zarnitsa.
> V tebe i schast'e, i bol', i beda.
> I ne uiti ot tebia, ne ukryt'sia,
> Ne ubezhat', ne zaryt'sia nikuda.[113]

That autumn, the march was filmed in Gagry using text provided by Semen Kirsanov:

> Akh, gory, gory, vysokie gory,
> Vchera tuman byl i v serdtse toska,
> Segodnia snezhnye vashi uzory
> Opiat' goriat i vidny izdaleka.
>
> A nu, davai, podnimai vyshe nogi,
> A nu, davai, ne zaderzhivai, bugai!
> Ty bud' zdorova, grazhdanka korova!
> Schastlivyi put', uvazhaemyi bugai![114]

Utesov was not satisfied with verse that was both colorless and childish and, after the group's return to Moscow, quietly solicited new material from Vasilii Lebedev-Kumach, who had written verse for an early Utesov stage show *Dhzaz na povorote* (*Jazz at the Turning Point*).[115] Lebedev-Kumach produced the now famous "March of the Happy Guys" and the lyric song "Kak mnogo devushek khoroshikh" ("How many lovely girls there are"). Utesov paid him from his own funds, and then sang the songs to Aleksandrov and Shumiatskii at the studio. The two pieces were an immediate hit. After diplomatically arranging to get his money back, Utesov revealed the name of the author, who then joined the film group.[116] Lebedev-Kumach's daughter Marina's account of events corresponds to Utesov's, and both contradict Aleksandrov's memoirs, which completely erase Utesov from the picture. In his 1976 memoir *Epokha i kino*, Aleksandrov claims to have initiated a contest in *Komsomol'skaia pravda* to supply words for Dunaevskii's melody, the notes for which were also published in the newspaper. Among the respondents was Lebedev-Kumach, who sought out Aleksandrov at the studio—and the rest was history.[117] Although there are several calls for new army and aviation songs in *Komsomol'skaia pravda* during 1933–34, there is no mention of any contest for *Happy Guys*.[118] Aleksandrov's story appears to be a fabrication based on the actuality of similar competitions.

Dunaevskii's march was re-recorded in spring 1934 with Lebedev-Kumach's new text. At that time music, dialogue, and sound effects could only be recorded simultaneously on one track. The sound recording of Potekhin's morning march required more than 500 participants—a symphonic orchestra, jazz orchestra, orchestra of folk instruments, choirs, sound effects technicians for Potekhin's dancing on the bridge, music making on clay pots, and animal imitators for the mooing of cows and bleating of sheep—all of whom directed their efforts, according to strict sequence, into one microphone.[119] This complicated procession of sounds was overseen by Dunaevskii, who always conducted his own film scores. Because Potekhin's Gagry march could not be re-shot at this point, Utesov's lip movements remained noticeably out of sync with his singing in the completed film.

The episodes requiring process shots, such as the orchestra's night ride on the catafalque, the interior music-hall scenes, Utesov's song while sitting on a tree branch, the performance in front of the Bol'shoi audience and the exterior of the theatre, were filmed during February–April 1934. Nil'sen used rear projection extensively in *Happy Guys* and was instrumental in establishing a studio for that purpose.[120] A second technical innovation was the double process shot: the music-hall stage with a small model extending its upper section was first filmed as a combination shot; next, a theatre box with spectators was added in a separate operation.[121] Thus, in the second finale of *Happy Guys*, in a long tracking shot, the camera moves back from Kostia and Aniuta on stage, passes through a theatre box with clapping audience and out a window to the street outside the Bol'shoi. Nil'sen constructed the shot by means of a series of scale models set up on an inclined ramp, along which the camera moved backwards from the stage (Fig. 15).[122] Given the state of Soviet film technology in the early thirties, not all the innovations were successful, and visual continuity in *Happy Guys* is sometimes broken because of the lengthy production period of the film: the background in the scene of Utesov singing on a tree branch noticeably wobbles; the quality of the rear projection in the scene of the Bol'shoi conductor facing the audience is very poor; Utesov suddenly

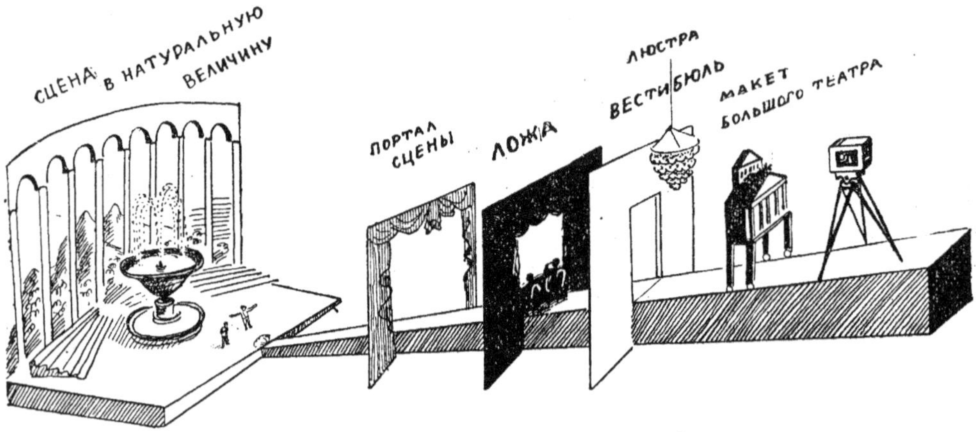

Figure 15.

develops shorter, darker hair when his violin playing for Karl Ivanovich switches to a studio shot, and his clothing sometimes changes in its details in a single episode.

In January, Aleksandrov was still planning to shoot the original *Shepherd* ending (Potekhin and Aniuta's aquatic love scene) in a specially built glass tank.[123] By spring, he had substituted another ending, which the film crew called "the finale of finales," a second, grandiose Bol'shoi performance sequence following on the heels of the first comic performance. Dunaevskii, conducting an orchestra of 150 musicians, recorded the music for the "finale of finales" on May 23.[124] *Happy Guys* was finally completed, five months behind schedule, in early June 1934.[125] On June 23, Shumiatskii, together with the editorial staff of *Komsomol'skaia pravda*, viewed a rough cut of the film.[126] His comments anticipated much of the later public criticism: the lack of a tight plot; too many unmotivated gags and musical "attractions" that weaken part two; editing that destroys the logic of the narrative (How does Kostia get to the Moscow music-hall from the collective farm? How does a newcomer become the leader of a jazz orchestra?); too many coincidences (Lena at the Fraskini concert, the catafalque knocks down Aniuta); overly long episodes, specifically the catafalque ride and Kostia's conducting at the music-hall; Utesov's "estrada" presence; poor filming in Aniuta's scene by the oak after Kostia's departure.[127] Aleksandrov deserves our sympathy at this point: the narrative discontinuities in the film are largely due to the Kinokomissiia's cuts to the script: in the eliminated kolhoz sub-plot, Kostia's playing convinces the collective farm workers to send him to Moscow to study music, thereby creating a narrative bridge between the two parts of the film. Secondly, coincidence is the standard narrative engine of comedy; to expect realistic motivation is not realistic. Finally, the film was originally built around Utesov, who had been contracted by Shumiatskii before the existence of any script. His limitations therefore become the limitations of the film.

The contours of the events relating to the prohibition and subsequent rehabilitation of *Happy Guys* remain rather fluid, mainly because of Aleksandrov's tendency to fib, exaggerate, and conflate events and chronologies for greater dramatic effect and self-aggrandizement. In his memoirs, Aleksandrov falsely places himself at an August 1934 screening of the film for Gorky and credits Gorky with subsequently organizing a Politbiuro screening at which Stalin saw the film for the first time, another misrepresentation.[128] The crucial documents that contradict Aleksandrov's story are Shumiatskii's notes on the July 13, 1934 Politbiuro screening of the film, his July 28, 1934 letter to Stalin regarding the Kinokomissiia's prohibitions on *Happy Guys* and other films, and Konstantin Iukov's notes on Gorky's viewing of the film in early August.[129]

Stalin, together with Molotov, Voroshilov, Kuibyshev, Kaganovich, Zhdanov, Ordzhonikidze, and Enukidze, saw the first two or three parts of *Happy Guys* on July 13, and viewed the entire film on July 21. In his July 28 letter to Stalin, copied to Kaganovich, Zhdanov, Stetskii, and Molotov, Shumiatskii refers to "G. V. Aleksandrov's comedy *Happy Guys*, which has been seen by you and a number of the other comrades" and makes it clear that he informed Stetskii before the June 27 Kinokomissiia screening that the film had been seen and approved by influential Party officials: "I warned Comrade Stetskii beforehand that the film had already been seen by a number of the comrades and that they had not made a single derogatory remark about it, although some of them had seen it several times. I pointed out that, on the contrary, at the screening all had seen it as a first merry comedy at which one can be entertained and relax, which rarely happens at the movies and even in the theatre."[130]

According to Aleksandrov, the nervous Shumiatskii originally planned to show only the first two parts of the film to the Politbiuro and told him to pretend that *Happy Guys* was unfinished in case the exalted audience asked to see the rest of the film. The ruse did not work, and Shumiatskii was forced to show the entire film. "However, they watched *Happy Guys* with obvious pleasure. They laughed and repeated dialogue to each other. At the end everyone fell silent, waiting to hear what Stalin would say. He approved: "Good! It's as if I've spent a month on vacation.... And take the film away from the director!" he ordered

Shumiatskii amid general laughter, "Before he ruins it."[131] Shumiatskii's notes, written immediately after Kremlin screenings, present a somewhat less colorful version of events:

> I. V.: Well, what are we going to see next?[132]
>
> K. E.: Let's have *Happy Guys.*
>
> I. V.: What kind of film is it?
>
> K. E.: It's an interesting, merry, completely musical film with Utesov and his jazz orchestra.
>
> B. Sh.: Only I don't have the entire film. It's being completed today. I can show you only the first three parts.
>
> I. V.: He's intriguing us. Let's have at least the beginning parts.
>
> L. M.: But Utesov doesn't have a good voice!
>
> Zhdanov: And besides, he's only good at criminal songs ["blatnye pesni"].
>
> K. E.: No, you'll see. He's a very gifted actor, an extraordinarily lively guy, and he sings really well in the film. It's an exceptionally interesting film.
>
> B. Sh.: We forced him to act and sing properly.
>
> L. M.: How did you do it?
>
> B. Sh.: I told him about the technical possibilities of talking pictures.
>
> I. V.: Well, if it's interesting, let's have a look.
>
> [B. Sh. narrative]: There were roars of laughter throughout the screening of this part of *Happy Guys.* Iosif Vissarionovich, Klementii Ef. [removich], Lazar' Moiseevich, and Zhdanov reacted particularly to the scene with the fish, the beach, and the exchanges: "You're so young and already a genius!" "How could he," "Habit." They really liked the march, the steamship, the roll call of the herd and so on. They began to ask who made the film and where.
>
> B. Sh.: I explained.
>
> L. M.: Was this really made here in Moscow? It's a high quality film, but people say that this Moscow factory of yours isn't a factory, but a tomb. They even talk about it often in the press.[133]

On July 21, Stalin, Molotov, Voroshilov, and Enukidze viewed the complete *Happy Guys*. Voroshilov noted that he had already seen the entire film and "laughed my head off. It was very interesting."[134] Shumiatskii's notes further record Stalin's reaction: "I.V., who had already seen its first two parts earlier, recounted the plot to the comrades who had not seen it and laughed heartily at the gags.[135] When the episodes with the roll-call began, he turned enthusiastically to Kl. Ef. [Voroshilov], saying: "This is really well thought out. But with us they try to be clever and look for the new in gloomy "restorations" and "reforgings." I'm not against the artistic development of these problems. On the contrary. But show them in a way that is joyful, lively, and cheerful." When he saw part 3—the scenes with the animals, and after that part 4—the Music Hall—and part 5—the scenes of the brawl, he laughed infectiously. At the end he said: "Good. This film provides an opportunity to relax in an interesting, engaging way. I feel the way I would after a day off. This is the first time I've had such a feeling after seeing our films, among which there have been quite good ones..."[136] Stalin praised the "good, active, and bold" acting of Orlova and Utesov, and the jazz band. "At the end, while saying good-bye, he talked about the songs. Turning to Comrade Voroshilov, he pointed out that the march would go to the masses, and began to recall the melody and ask about the words. He pointed out that songs should be distributed on phonograph records."[137]

The Kinokomissiia first screened and discussed *Happy Guys* on June 27, 1934 and, once again, the objections of more conservative and puritanical Old Bolsheviks to non-ideological comedy spiced up with American slapstick came to the fore. An additional factor was Shumiatskii's generally bad relations with the Kinokomissiia because of continuing conflicts over the approval of scripts and new films. Bubnov called the film "counterrevolutionary"; Antipov described it as "hooliganism, rotten and false to the core." Aleksandrov later recalled that Bubnov considered Potekhin's conducting of the *Hungarian Rhapsody* a mockery of Liszt.[138] Most of the Kinokomissiia members began demanding cuts in entire sections of the film. Shumiatskii would not agree, leading to a violent disagreement. In his letter to Stalin, Shumiatskii argued that the Kinokomissiia praised films which some members of the Politbiuro considered bad, among them *The Deserter*, *Revolt of the Fisherman*, and *The Accordion*.[139] The tastes of the Kinokomissiia may have been more discriminating than those of the Politbiuro, but they were also clearly weighted toward ideological and national themes.

Just before the July 25 meeting of the Kinokomissiia, Glavrepertkom, an organ of Bubnov's Narkompros (People's Commissariat of Enlightenment), which approved and censored repertoires, had blocked permission to send *Happy Guys* to the Second International Film Festival in Venice. At stake was the reputation of Soviet cinematography: this was the first international competition in which the USSR had entered films. After negotiations with Shumiatskii, only the first half of the film was permitted to leave the country; the rest (three parts) was held up at the train station. An infuriated Shumiatskii wrote Stalin: "I ask you to instruct Comrades Stetskii and Bubnov to immediately lift the clearly unfounded ban on the film *Happy Guys* and to immediately issue permission to take the film to the exhibition since all shipping deadlines have expired, and to raise the question of the Kinokomissiia's members' attitude toward GUKF and toward me personally at a meeting of the Central Committee in your presence."[140] The ban was lifted and within a week Shumiatskii had shown *Happy Guys* at a private screening in Venice.

Za Bol'shevistskii fil'm, the Potylikha newspaper, announced the completion of "*Dhzaz*" in its June 10, 1934 issue.[141] By the time the Kinokomissiia met in July 1934, *Jazz-Comedy* had become *Happy Guys* in Shumiatskii's references to the film. Mikhail Dolgopolov, the *Komsomol'skaia pravda* journalist assigned to cover the making of the film, claimed to have provided the new title.[142] Gorky could not have christened the film, as claimed by Aleksandrov, because he had not yet seen it.[143]

On August 2, 1934, after the battle in the Kinokomissiia, Konstantin Iukov, then the head of the production section of GUKF, received a call conveying Gorky's request to see *Happy Guys* and *Cabin in the Cotton*, a 1932 American film soon to be released in Russia as *The Treachery of Marvin Blake*.[144] Iukov screened the films at Desiatye Gorki, Gorky's home, the same evening. Because the writer had been meeting that day with the organizing committee for the upcoming Congress of Writers, the committee members, along with Gorky's household staff, were invited to make up the impromptu audience.[145] Gorky's curiosity about *Happy Guys* was probably piqued by Stetskii, chair of the Kinokomissiia and de facto head of the Congress organizing committee chaired by Gorky. Iukov kept a detailed record of the evening and its politics for his boss Shumiatskii:

> The first part [of the film] was shown in silence, as happens when people are seeing a completely unexpected spectacle. The episode of the animal roll-call evoked a great deal of laughter and general delight. The second part was watched in silence. The third part was very successful. The audience laughed uncontrollably, including A.M. [Gorky], A.I. [Stetskii] and the others.... After the brawl scene, A.M. commented with delight, "How they fight—wonderfully. They fight for real, without pretending." A.M. watched the rest of the film without comment, in spite of the fact that he was being provoked to comment by a whole series of remarks, coming chiefly from the representative of the Organizing Committee ("they've dragged it out," "they've gone too far" etc.). After the screening, A.M. turned to those present with the question, "Well, what do you think?" The audience responded unanimously, "It's a happy film." A.I. and others noted the talent and great skill of the director, and pointed out the excessive length of some episodes and the necessity of abbreviating the film. Then A.M. made his comments: "Talented, a very talented

film...made boldly, a happy film and extremely interesting. The talent of these people, how well that girl acts, the animals too. How did these filmmakers manage to get such wonderful animal acting? What a brawl! The people are fighting for real. This isn't American boxing; they're hitting each other honestly. I consider the brawl to be the most powerful and interesting scene. All the animal scenes are very interesting. A.M. listened to A.I.'s remarks about Potekhin's music-hall performance. A.I. was arguing the artificiality of the performance and thought it necessary to shorten it. "Why shorten it?" said A.M. "It's all happy and funny, and I don't see the need to shorten it." Comrade Kirpotin threw out a remark that this was genuine Americanism. "Yes, it's Americanism," said A.M.., "but it's our Soviet Americanism. The Americans will never dare do a whole series of episodes in such a hooliganish way as in this film. I see here pure Russian daring on a grand scale. Take the marvellous episode with the catafalque. The catafalque is one of the memorable dynamic scenes of the film. The Americans would never dare film a catafalque. It's an obligatory implement in a solemn funeral. The Americans try to reinforce respect for all sorts of cults related to the cemetery, burial of the corpse and so on. But here our Russian director took a catafalque and showed it in such a way that it's both funny and dynamic at the same time. That's art." In response to Iudin's remark that the film might exert a harmful influence, since all Soviet filmmakers might take the path of dumbing down the cinema, A.M. said, "Nonsense, this is a first, experimental comedy. It's successful, and Soviet cinema needs to make a happy film. Otherwise it's boring and wearisome. It's hard to watch *The Storm*.[146] This doesn't mean that *The Storm* shouldn't be made, but along with such films like *The Storm* and others, it's very desirable to have such lively, happy, entertaining films, and in this area Soviet cinema has done very little, and must do a lot in the future."

After watching the American film about the struggle of a tenant farmer's son with a large landowner, some of the audience voiced a preference for the American film, presumably for ideological reasons. Gorky disagreed, arguing that, "*Happy Guys* is a spontaneous film, infecting the viewer with its spontaneity. *Blake's Treachery* is sentimental in places, which is characteristic of American cinema. It's artificial and farfetched."[147] In *Epokha i kino*, Aleksandrov used excerpts from Iukov's notes to place himself at this screening and created a fictional audience of collective farm workers, schoolchildren, and hostile writers.[148] Although Gorky's opinion may have influenced Stetskii, Bubnov, and the Writers' Congress organizers, among whom were RAPP sympathizers, there is no evidence that the writer subsequently arranged another screening for the Politbiuro.

A week later, most likely on Shumiatskii's orders (given his earlier critique of the film), and despite Gorky's praise for the animal scenes, Aleksandrov agreed to: 1) cut the sacking of Lena's salon, including the animals' destruction of the furniture, Orlova riding the bull, etc., 2) shorten the catafalque episode by cutting scenes in which the vehicle circles a clock, and 3) shorten the episode of Potekhin's conducting in the music-hall by removing the middle section of the performance, the kiss, etc.[149] Fortunately the animal attack and Orlova's ride survived the scissors, but the ban on cinematic smooching, which Aleksandrov would later fight in *Volga-Volga* and which was only relaxed during World War II, had already begun.

According to a newspaper account written anonymously by Shumiatskii, at an August 5 private screening in Venice attended by the festival president, Count Volpi, and other organizers, the second part of *Happy Guys* was put on by mistake instead of *Mechtateli* (*The Dreamers*).[150] The audience was enchanted, asked to see more and applauded the film for ten minutes. The festival organizers then suggested showing *Happy Guys* on August 23, the final day of the festival, as a high point of the event.[151] In foreign newspaper reviews of the festival, most of the attention, however, went to other Soviet entries: the documentary film *Cheliuskin*, *The Storm*, and *Petersburg Night*.[152] *Happy Guys* received very positive press, but generally less publicity.[153] The Soviet and British entries together won first prize at the festival, thereby validating *Happy Guys* for Shumiatskii's purposes. The film was later released in Europe under various titles and in the US as *Moscow Laughs*, where its lack of overt Bolshevik ideology and the familiarity of the musical comedy genre made it popular among western audiences.[154] European distributors not only bought rights to the film, but published its songs and sheet music before release.[155]

But at home, GUKF, fearful of the continuing controversy in the press, postponed release of *Happy Guys* initially until November 11.[156] After the August 25 screening for the Congress of Writers, Ehrenburg, Lidin, Grebner, and Surkov criticized the film. Surkov had earlier attacked the film's mindless humor: "Yes, Soviet youth is vigorous and bubbling with life. Yes, it wants to live happily and spend its leisure time happily, but why give it the vulgarity of intermission clowning, passing it off as humor?...Why make our good, intelligent reader stupid? Why corrupt his young artistic taste?"[157] To Kaganovich's report on the writers' reactions, Stalin replied, "No, it's not a bad film, it's really happy, although superficial in its conception. It'll be fine to watch. And people will feel happy."[158] The war in the press continued all through the fall, before the release of the film, mainly between *Literaturnaia gazeta*, dominated by former members of RAPP, and pro-Shumiatskii *Komsomol'skaia pravda*.

The most interesting aspect of the debate is the inability of much of the press to take a firm position on *Happy Guys*. This was a transitional period in the cultural discourse: although the doctrine of Socialist Realism, which in its ideological emphasis was a descendent of RAPP, had been introduced at the Congress of Writers, there was still ongoing discussion about the narrowing of Soviet literature as well as a strong sense of genre conventions. On August 15, 1934, *Literaturnaia gazeta* published a largely positive review: "A magnificent zest for life makes *Happy Guys* a Soviet picture, despite all the unreality of the world reproduced in the film."[159] On November 18, *Pravda* published a mixed review that welcomed *Happy Guys* as a film based on American slapstick comedy—and justified its plotlessness by this emphasis—but criticized the lack of Soviet "local color" in the film, concluding that slapstick should be mastered by Soviet comedy but employed in a more restrained fashion than in American film.[160] On the same day, *Literaturnaia gazeta* reversed itself and went on the offensive, comparing *Happy Guys* unfavorably to *Chapaev* and attacking the lack of ideological content in Aleksandrov's still unreleased film: "*Chapaev* will sweep off our path the cardboard barricades of unideological art."[161] A few days later in a *Kino* interview, Aleksandrov answered obliquely by outlining the major impediments in making the film: the lack of any previous Russian musical comedy to serve as a model and the technological backwardness of Potylikha, which forced him to build a rear projection studio and install mercury lighting.[162] In the meantime, *Literaturnaia gazeta* had also attacked *The Counterplan*[163] and *The Storm* as lacking ideological content, defining all three films as a side line ("bokovaia liniia") of Russian cinema, as opposed to the mainstream *Chapaev*. *Komsomol'skaia pravda* and Shumiatskii then engaged *Literaturka* directly, pointing out its RAPP-like label-mongering ("enemy," "ally," "fellow-traveller") and insistence on a single general line.[164] *Literaturnaia gazeta* zigzagged back and forth in the newspaper polemic, withdrawing its criticism of *The Counterplan*, withdrawing its first, positive review of *Happy Guys*, withdrawing its theory of main and side lines of Soviet cinema, and finally withdrawing its attack on *Happy Guys*, with qualifications: "It's unquestionably a happy and skillfully done film, but it's not Socialist Realism."[165]

Meanwhile, GUKF had been preparing for the première of *Happy Guys*, originally planned for November 11, but then postponed to December 25 because of the Kirov assassination. The publicity campaign for *Happy Guys*, driven by the advertising techniques Aleksandrov had learned in the US, was phenomenal by Soviet standards. On September 19, Shumiatskii ordered that *Happy Guys* postcards and records be given production priority above all other films, even resorting to shockworker jargon: "Bear down and break all forms of resistance and vile inertia."[166] A special committee preparing the release of the film met on September 25 and October 1, and its records detail the elaborate publicity campaign: organize closed screenings in Moscow and Leningrad during October and November, especially for the correspondents of urban newspapers and factory bulletins, film distributors, editors of Komsomol newspapers and *Krokodil*; negotiate a contract with Muzizdat for sheet music (three songs and four dance melodies from the film) and supply a cover design; arrange with Tabaktrest to issue cigarettes with *Happy Guys* labels and with the Baking Trust to produce candy and cookies with the same label; have Soiuzfoto issue postcards with scenes from the film and photographs of the main characters; order slides, to be sold at the première with accompanying projector flashlights in the foyer of the theatre; order a professionally designed libretto with song texts; order records from Gramzapis' to be sold in the foyer;[167] order invitations to the première and a professionally designed program booklet; send invitations to the première to factory bulletin editors; provide photo material for the interior and exterior decoration of the theatre; order a special curtain to cover the screen and clear the sketch with Aleksandrov; hang posters and photos in movie and theatre foyers, the musical hall, circuses, hotels, restaurants, and shop windows;[168] for circulating advertising throughout the city, build an artistically designed catafalque; for the October holidays arrange a broadcast of the *Happy Guys* soundtrack, making sure to credit the source; Aleksandrov and Iukov are to develop a program for radio appearances; organize a live broadcast of the première from the movie theatre through the Dom Pravitel'stva; set up the new Shorin equipment at the Udarnik and improve the projection quality at the movie theatre; obtain a high quality copy of the film from the Leningrad laboratory.[169]

During the fall, *Happy Guys* was shown at closed screenings attended by various members of the film group. While vacationing in Sochi during September, Aleksandrov and Orlova arranged three screenings at the Sovnarkom resort home. These were attended by highly placed Party members who produced a collective review of the film, signed by more than 100 members of the audience. According to Aleksandrov's report, the "March of the Happy Guys" immediately spread among the vacationers on the Black Sea coast. By request of the audience, Aleksandrov and Orlova participated in an additional evening event at which they discussed their work on the film.[170]

Happy Guys was also shown at the Moscow Dom Kino, Leningrad Rot Front theatre, and at various student and workers' clubs during October–November.[171] Because of the initial controversy over the script of the film, Lebedev-Kumach and Aleksandrov composed an explanatory verse prologue, justifying comedy as a means of recreation which improves labor efficiency. Before screenings, Aleksandrov would read the text, singing the last two lines:

> Tovarishch zritel'
> V nyneshnem spektakle
> Geroem glavnym budet zvonkii smekh.
> Ved' Vy prishli k nam otdokhnut'—ne tak li?
> Nu, a ved' smekh vsegda byl otdykhom dlia vsekh.
> Na chas-drugoi zaboty vy otbros'te.
> Puskai segodnia pozabaviat vas
> Istoriia talantlivogo Kosti,
> Liubov' Aniuty i veselyi dzhaz.

Pust' pesnia nad "Prozrachnymi kliuchami"
Vas bodrost'iu svoeiu uvlechet,
Puskai ekran veselymi luchami
Zariadku dast dlia zavtrashnikh rabot.
I zavtra na zavode, v narkomate
Vy ulybnetes', mozhet byt', slegka,
Pripomniv dzhaz v nelepom mokrom plat'e,
Veselyi pliazh i khmurogo byka.
Lovi motiv, kotoryi ubegaet.
Pust' nashu pesniu kazhdyi zapoet—
Ved' tot, kto s pesnei po zhizni shagaet,
Tot nikogda i nigde ne propadet![172]

The reaction of the film community to *Happy Guys* was mixed. Dovzhenko noted that many western comedies had more content and ideology (bourgeois ideology, to be sure) than Aleksandrov's new film.[173] Aleksandr Macheret, who had earlier reacted negatively to the script, now saw the film as a revue with an intentionally unrealistic comic plot: "You don't take the fabula seriously and don't think about it. You enjoy yourself because of the masterful attractions. And if, from the script it was hard to imagine Utesov as a young shepherd, in the film you hear and see Utesov not as you perceive him in relation to the fabula, but in relation to his participation in a stage 'attraction.'"[174] Not surprisingly, Fridrikh Ermler's comments were the most thoughtful. He absolutely supports the film and is ready to help Aleksandrov fight for it. While criticizing Aleksandrov's lapses of taste and the poor quality of the sound, he gives high praise to the musical fabric of the brawl: "I have the impression that a man came, gave me a pill, and I've become younger.... Not many of us will risk taking Aleksandrov's road.... I contend that many of us would have neither the ability nor sufficient will to make such films." Speaking at the Leningrad Dom kino, after the assassination of Kirov and at the beginning of a wave of arrests, Ermler recognizes the saving grace of comedy: "For me, laughter is now the greatest phenomenon in life, and it seems to me that this film reminds you, dear comrades, that you are not yet as old as you want to appear. We feel some sort of load on us and don't have the strength to throw it off."[175]

The première of *Happy Guys* took place on the evening of December 25, 1934 at the Udarnik movie theatre in central Moscow.[176] Aleksandrov, Orlova, and a reluctant Dunaevskii decided to sit among the audience to hear viewers' comments. The screening was followed by the usual audience "vstrecha" (meeting) with the film group, and that night Aleksandrov and company celebrated at the Metropol'.[177]

Just as the film was being released for general distribution in January 1935, it was attacked from the new orthodox perspective of Socialist Realism for its ideological emptiness: "The director must strive for only one thing—the educative importance of laughter.... We believe that the method of Socialist Realism is compulsory for all forms, directions, genres, and shades of Soviet art.... We cannot tolerate the idea that this method is not compulsory for film comedy."[178] The fact that Konstantin Iukov, editor of *Sovetskoe kino* and Shumiatskii's assistant, actually commissioned the article so that he himself could respond in the same issue indicates the still uncanonical position of Socialist Realist doctrine. Iukov defended the film as a means of amusement and therefore rest for the population, which aids the cause of socialism. Feeling some ideological pressure nevertheless, he underscored the satirical aspects of the film, in his overeagerness pointing even to the Druzhba brawl and water-logged performance at the Bol'shoi as examples of the bad behavior of jazz musicians.[179]

The immediate and resounding success of *Happy Guys* and its music with Soviet audiences put an end—or so it seemed—to the ideological feuding over the film. In January 1935, as part of the 15th anniversary of Soviet cinema, the government awarded Aleksandrov the Order of the Red Star, Orlova was designated "zasluzhennyi deiatel' iskusstv" (Honored artist) and Utesov received—a camera.[180] At the awards ceremony, Aleksandrov wondered aloud why he had received a military decoration. Kalinin, who was aware of the battle over the film, quipped: "For bravery and daring in the battle with the difficulties of film comedy."[181] Utesov was minimally rewarded and ignored in *Pravda* and *Izvestiia* reviews of the film because of rumors that he had tried to cross the Russian-Polish border but had been stopped by the military.[182] In an April 1935 article on jazz in cinema, Shumiatskii parenthetically defended Utesov from "slanderous rumors bearing on his reputation as a Soviet citizen," and no harm came to the famous jazzman.[183] "March of the Happy Guys" was sung at the 1935 May Day parade and recorded on newsreels.[184]

Fans went to see the film repeatedly—4, 5, 6, even 25 times, according to surviving letters in Utesov's archive.[185] The texts of songs from the film were published in April 1935: "Spasibo, serdtse" ("Thank you, my heart," 25,000 copies), the march, and Aniuta's song (15,000 copies each).[186] Along with stills from the film and a gift of cologne, Orlova sent Erdman a note which underscores the paradoxes of the time—his name had been removed from the title credits, yet she looks forward to working with him again soon: "First of all, I congratulate you with the great success of our film! I hope you see *Happy Guys* soon and appraise it, in your own way.... I'm very satisfied with the picture, as much for myself as for Grisha, for you, for the whole group—our work has not been in vain.... I hope to see you soon and begin to make the film *Novye liudi* (*New People*) with you, I think about it constantly."[187] Erdman's response to Orlova has not survived; from exile in Krasnoiarsk, he sent his mother a bad review: "I saw *Happy Guys*. One rarely encounters a more incomprehensible and incoherent mishmash. The picture is stupid from the very beginning to the very end. The sound is abominable—the words don't match the lip movements. I expected a very weak work but never thought it could be that bad."[188] Years later, Aleksandrov admitted that even he had been rather surprised by Orlova's phenomenal success in *Happy Guys*.[189]

As the 5,737 distribution copies of *Happy Guys* were entertaining audiences in the Soviet Union and abroad in early 1935,[190] the RAPP diehards on *Literaturnaia gazeta* mounted an attack on Dunaevskii and Aleksandrov. The American film *Viva Villa!* had been shown at the first International Film Festival in Moscow, February 21–March 1, 1935. In a short segment of the film, peasant rebels sing part of a popular Mexican revolutionary song "Adelita."[191] On February 28, RAPP poet Aleksandr Bezymenskii published an archly sensational essay, accusing Dunaevskii of plagiarizing the *Happy Guys* march from the Mexican song:

> How awful! They're showing the film *Viva Villa!*, the tragic scenes of the peons' revolt, and the festival audience is laughing! The damned audience is making noise! They're applauding, the bastards! What? How? Why? I wasn't laughing. I wasn't making noise. At that moment I wasn't applauding. A crime was being committed in front of me.... Help! Robbers! The Mexican peasants...were singing the march from *Happy Guys*. Is this a laughing matter? The "Druzhba" orchestra members hadn't yet had a real fight when the Americans stole the song.... Comrade Dunaevskii! Comrade Aleksandrov! Why are you sleeping? The one good thing in your bad film was the music. And they stole it.... Let's forget that the shepherd Kostia's procession more than reminds you of the introductory tracking shot in the film *Congress Dances*, that in the film *The Warlike Starlings* they also shoot something resembling a clarinet out of a bow.... Several jokesters assert that YOU swiped the music from *Viva Villa!* They even say that Comrade Aleksandrov, having been abroad and specifically in Mexico (besides having a pretty good ear for music), sang something to Comrade Dunaevskii, the result of which was the march music. I'm against *Happy Guys*. But as to the music in the film, I'm no less concerned than you are. I'm upset. I'm nervous.... What if the jokesters are right?[192]

Aleksandrov and Dunaevskii responded on March 5 with letters to the editor of *Kino*. Dunaevskii explained the borrowing, pointing out that the composer of the American film had done the same: "The *Happy Guys* group, in searching for the best musical realization of the main march of the film, had recommended that I start with the Mexican folk melodies because of their unusual liveliness and accessibility. Because of stylistic concerns, in writing the march I preferred to abandon Mexican melodies but, under the influence of its amazing charm, a two-bar phrase, similar to the Mexican song that the composer of *Viva Villa!*, for his part, used in the film, entered my music." He asserted that his march had been written a year before *Villa!* appeared in Russia, and that both films had been screened at the 1934 Venice festival without arousing any untoward suspicions. Aleksandrov made similar points in his letter, also wondering whether it was chance that Bezymenskii's article had appeared on the very day Aleksandrov had received the Order of the Red Star for his work.[193]

The next day, *Literaturnaia gazeta* counterattacked with another piece by Bezymenskii fulminating about the moral purity of Soviet art and Aleksandrov's disdain for "self-criticism," and a more substantial and negative article by writer Bruno Jasieński.[194] In a public display of sour grapes, Semen Kirsanov recapped his failed collaboration with Aleksandrov during the winter of 1934, noting that Aleksandrov had played him records of Mexican music intended to be the basis of the film's songs. "Comrade Aleksandrov demanded completely apolitical texts which, to be honest, I couldn't manage. Apparently as a result of these differences, it became hard to meet or reach him by phone." Finally, Kirsanov claimed that a couplet from his material for "Aniuta's Song" had been plagiarized by Lebedev-Kumach.[195]

In the meantime, the Central Bureau of Creative Cinematography Workers had appointed a commission consisting of musicologists (Cheliapov and Gorodinskii), directors (Roshal' and Raizman), representatives of the Writers' Union (Surkov) and *Literaturnaia gazeta* (Plisko), along with the secretary of the Bureau (Krinkin), to consider the plagiarism charge. According to Dunaevskii, the commission listened to the *Viva Villa!* soundtrack three times and was unable to identify the offending passage. "The *Happy Guys* march was lying in front of them and they were waiting to be shown the relevant place. In order to save the commission embarrassment, at 1:30 a.m. we sent a special messenger to them with a collection of Mexican songs, in which this 'Adelita' was printed, and where they could find the similarity, but they couldn't find it from the film."[196] Dunaevskii was correct: the two-bar coincidence is virtually undetectable in the film. However, when one listens to "Adelita" in solo performance, it becomes obvious that the *Happy Guys* march refrain, "I tot kto s pesnei po zhizni shagaet, Tot nigde i nikogda ne propadet," nearly duplicates a passage of the Mexican song. In its report, the commission concluded that the marches in both films used musical phrases from the same Mexican folksong to produce two independent works, and that the opening tracking shot of *Happy Guys* was simply a cinematographic technique used in both Russia and the West, so that there could be no question of plagiarism.[197] I will return to the question of cinematic and musical borrowing in a later section of this chapter.

Meanwhile, the fate of Dunaevskii's music was also being decided on the street. The Leningrad Repertkom had forbidden the performance of any songs from *Happy Guys* on stage or in the schools.[198] Aleksandrov recalled that one night a downcast Dunaevskii was returning to his hotel after a public debate on the accusation of plagiarism and found the Volkhonka closed because of metro construction. He asked a policeman for an alternate route and was advised to go back and cross through the Arbat Square. The tired composer snapped: "Propadesh' tut!" ("You can get completely lost here!"). Suddenly a young female voice replied: "Ekh, grazhdanin, plokho vy zhizn' znaete: Tot, kto s pesnei po zhizni shagaet, Tot nikogda i nigde ne propadet" ("Oh, citizen, you don't know life well: he who strides through life with a song will never be lost anywhere"). Having sung the refrain to "March of the Happy Guys," the woman construction worker disappeared underground.[199] Orlova later recalled that the march was sung spontaneously at the closing session of the First All-Union Congress of Stakhanovites in November 1935.[200] Abroad, Charlie Chaplin recognized the appeal of the film for western audiences: "Aleksandrov has discovered a new Russia for America. Before *Happy Guys*, Americans knew Dostoevsky's Russia. Now they have seen great progress in people's psychology. People laugh energetically and cheerfully. This is a great victory. This makes more propaganda than the evidence of shooting and speeches."[201]

The plagiarism commission's report was accompanied by a damning article, authored by Shumiatskii, in which he outlined *Literaturnaia gazeta's* refusal to print his immediate response to Bezymenskii's accusations and the newspaper's subsequent machinations to avoid admitting its mistake.[202] Shumiatskii had sent the committee report and his accompanying article both to *Literaturnaia gazeta* and *Kino*, but only the latter published the material.[203] On March 11, he met with Stalin and Molotov, who supported his efforts on behalf of the film. Stalin defended Aleksandrov, who was being persecuted for producing the "first happy Soviet film."[204] At this point, an unsigned editorial in *Pravda*, which typically signified a directive from Stalin, put an end to the media debate over *Happy Guys*, as part of a more wide-ranging attack on both *Literaturnaia gazeta* and *Izvestiia*, the latter edited by Stalin's enemy Bukharin. The two newspapers, though differing in their arts politics, were both scolded for ignoring the 1935 Moscow film festival and for their assaults on *Chapaev* and *Happy Guys*. Although the newspapers held antithetical views on the two films, both were called to account for opposing GUKF and Politbiuro policy:

> Following the example of *Izvestiia*, Comrade Bolotnikov, the editor of *Literaturnaia gazeta*, while not covering the outcomes of the festival, devoted almost an entire page to the incorrect, harmful chatter of Comrades Kirsanov, Bezymenskii and others regarding the film *Happy Guys*.... It's time to stop this unscrupulous persecution! Like the editor of *Izvestiia*, the editor of *Literaturnaia gazeta* is notable for his tendency toward vulgar polemics, initiating them for any reason and completely without a reason. And they persist, even when their mistakes are completely obvious. Both editors have apparently forgotten the elementary rules of decency essential to Soviet newspapers.[205]

The following day, a jubilant Dunaevskii wrote Aleksandrov that he still would like to sue *Literaturnaia gazeta* for slander: "With a moral-political factor like *Pravda* behind us, one can bet that these thugs would each get a year of forced labor."[206] On March 15, a cowed *Literaturnaia gazeta* apologized to Aleksandrov and Dunaevskii in an editorial, and Bezymenskii made his excuses on the back page of *Pravda*, acknowledging the commission's decision and the wrongness of his own unfounded charges.[207] Dunaevskii noted his enemies' lack of political savvy in charging that a Soviet film had plagiarized from western, even worse—American cinema:

> I have to tell you that I didn't expect such a vile and humiliating end for our enemies. And I have to confess too that our business hit a really delicate nerve and this essentially decided everything. Those dummies, you can't call them anything else, missed the entire political social side of the question and were told off in spades, not expecting that forces they were unable to fight would rise up against them. Amen![208]

The day after Bezymenskii's mea culpa, *Kino* chided Bolotnikov for his sins and attacked the dramatist Kirshon (a former RAPP leader) for criticizing both *Happy Guys* and Il'f and Petrov's play *Pod kupolom tsirka* (*Under the Circus Cupola*) as western bourgeois art in a speech at the Writers' Union plenum.[209] Kirshon's lumping the two works together was not accidental: by spring 1935, Aleksandrov was already working on his next film— *Circus*, based on the same Il'f and Petrov play.

II. THE REVUE-LUTIONARY FILM

At the time of its release, a French critic wrote jokingly, "*Happy Guys* creates the impression that some bourgeois directors sneaked into the GUKF studios at night and secretly shot the film using a Soviet stage set."[210] Aleksandrov's film is a largely non-political show musical, whose ideological charge is carried only in the lyrics of its central march. In 1933, the Socialist Realist paradigm was not yet operative; the hero was not, as a matter of course, committed to parallel public and private tasks. In *Happy Guys*, the only "ideological" public task was entertainment. Both the mythology and method of the film are borrowed from American cinema. A star (really two) are born in *Happy Guys*, for its underlying narrative is concerned with the success of a talented underdog. The frantic pace, anarchic comedy, and cartoon devices of the film are similarly borrowed from American cinema.

After seeing *Happy Guys*, Eisenstein is said to have remarked: "Grisha has made a revue-lutionary film," an ironic pun on the film's fragmented "revue" structure, as well as its "revolutionary" status as the first Stalinist musical comedy film.[211] At the time of its completion, in an interview, Aleksandrov defined *Happy Guys* as "twelve music-hall attractions connected by a roughly sketched out plot."[212] The *Vecherniaia Moskva* reviewer immediately connected Aleksandrov's method to Eisenstein's montage of attractions, calling the film a relapse into formalism. Thirty years later, Aleksandrov added: "The film was indeed based on the principle of 'montage of attractions,' in its pure form, but it was realized on the basis of free improvisation, imagination, the search for the comic, the study of its laws and possibilities."[213] Aleksandrov thus points to Eisenstein's early theatrical ideas on "sideshow montage" as a partial model. Writing in 1923 about his production of Ostrovskii's *Enough Simplicity for Every Wise Man*, Eisenstein argued that "the school for the montageur [director] is cinema and, principally, music-hall and circus because, from the point of view of form, putting on a good show means constructing a strong programme that derives from the situations found in the play that is taken as a basis."[214] In this sense, *Happy Guys* is the descendant of Eisenstein's theatrical productions: the film serves up a series of elaborate attractions derived in a general way from the narrative. However, *Happy Guys* completely lacked the ideological glue of Eisenstein's montage theory, in which independent attractions subjecting the audience to emotional shocks derive their meaning and coherence from the overall ideological goals of the play or film.

Aleksandrov's attractions in *Happy Guys* are not justified by a political-ideological purpose. The "ideology" of the film is purely musical: the genre validates itself by advocating popular music, both jazz and popular song. The *Happy Guys* march opens with, "Legko na serdtse ot pesni veseloi" ("The heart is light from a happy song"), and at the beginning and end of the film we hear, "Nam pesnia zhit' i liubit' pomogaet" ("A song helps us live and love"), a glorification of song entirely appropriate to the tradition of musical film, and not the ideological, "Nam pesnia stroit' i zhit'" ("A song helps us build and live"), which appeared in the later published versions of "March of the Happy Guys." Every other song in the film similarly turns on matters of the heart: "Spasibo serdtse, chto ty umeesh' tak liubit'!" ("Thank you, heart, that you know how to love like this"; "Serdtse v grudi / B'etsia, kak ptitsa" ("The heart in my breast flutters like a bird"); "Ot liubvi my muchimsia" ("We're tortured by love"); "serdtse khlopochet, boitsia opozdat'" ("The heart bustles, afraid to be late"). The film was shot under the sign of Aleksandrov and Orlova's love affair, and its unmotivated optimism could not but be informed by Aleksandrov's own personality and worldview, by his personal mantra preserved through good times and bad: "Everything will be fine!"[215] The spontaneous optimism of *Happy Guys*, along with the upward trajectory of its talented but unknown heroes, typical of musical film, become its points of contact with the social egalitarianism and self-congratulatory elation of the Stalinist State after the completion of the first five-year plan.

Although critics attacked *Happy Guys* for its fragmented revue structure, the film hardly resembles the Hollywood revues of this time, such as *Paramount on Parade* (1930) and *The Show of Shows* (1929), which were essentially cinematic variety shows. To a modern audience, *Happy Guys* positions itself comfortably within the tradition of the western show musical, in which the creation of a work of art—in this case, the performance at the Bol'shoi Theatre—parallels the making of a romantic couple "both symbolically and causally related to the success of the show."[216] The classic romantic triangle (the male or female lead and an inappropriate or inadequate lover, who is abandoned for the true love) is a conventional plot motif of the earliest American musicals. In *The Broadway Melody* (1929), the hero-singer-songwriter, who is engaged to a vaudeville performer, falls for her kid sister. In *Whoopee!* (1930), a rancher's daughter abandons the sheriff to whom she is engaged for the half-breed Indian whom she loves. In *The Smiling Lieutenant* (1931), a roguish officer leaves his ladylove, the leader of an all-girl orchestra, for a mousey princess. *Happy Guys* follows the same genre conventions: in the Potekhin-Lena-Aniuta triangle, an inappropriate bourgeois lover is replaced by an initially unrecognized lower-class true love.

The opposition of classical music to jazz, and elite to popular culture, has always been part of the basic syntax of the musical because the genre validates and affirms itself by advocating popular musical forms. In the first American backstage musical, *Broadway Melody*, the conductor and director argue about whether the music should be played in a classical or popular style.[217] In American musical film, either a duel of two young performers or a generational conflict may be the vehicle for the contest between elite and popular culture. In *Love Me Tonight* (1932), Maurice Chevalier's popular singing style is opposed to Jeanette MacDonald's operatic voice. Judy Garland and Deanna Durbin's popular and operatic styles clash openly in *Every Sunday* (1936) and *Babes in Arms* (1939). In *The Jazz Singer* (1927), the conflict between traditional religious music and mammy singing is generational. Classical music may also be aligned with a comic senex character who rejects or does not understand the popular style, which is the domain of the youthful romantic couple (*The Time, The Place and the Girl*, 1946). In the end, both musical modes are either reconciled in a merger of musical styles or, where the conflict is central to the narrative, popular music invariably emerges victorious.[218]

Classical music itself is not vilified in *Happy Guys*: early in the film, Potekhin studies and plays a Beethoven piece for Karl Ivanovich with full seriousness (Fig. 16), and the classical music then modulates seamlessly into a phrase from the march, "Tot nikogda i nigde ne propadet," sung by Aniuta as she listens to Kostia's violin from the roof of a distant house. Through a symbolic synecdoche, *Happy Guys* replaces the senex with an entire antiquated class, the remnants of the NEP bourgeoisie, of which Lena is a youthful representative, thereby both furthering the comic purposes of the film and aligning the degenerate bourgeoisie with a distorted incarnation of classical music. And popular music—both jazz and the mass song—will, of course, triumph at the Bol'shoi Theatre, the citadel of elite Russian musical culture.

The tension between elite and popular culture inscribed into the syntax of the show musical also dovetailed with the orientation of the cultural milieu in which Aleksandrov had received his theatrical education. The avant-garde of the 1920s, the theatre of Maiakovskii, Meierkhol'd, and Eisenstein, rejected the realism of Stanislavskii and the Renaissance stage-box, taking art into the audience space and stylistically—into the streets. In 1921, Aleksandrov was admitted as a student to Proletkul't, where he acted in Eisenstein's productions of *The Mexican* and *Enough Simplicity for Every Wise Man*. According to Aleksandrov, the production was influenced by the theatre of "physical action": "Using theatrical clowning and Meierkhol'd's biomechanics as a starting point, Sergei Mikhailovich moved toward a blending of theatre with the circus and music-hall." The stage was transformed into a circus arena, and the action was often moved into

Figure 16.

the audience space. "The numerous acrobatic, gymnastic, and musical numbers or, as Eisenstein called them, 'attractions,' were in the end intended to convey the propaganda significance of the performance to the viewer."[219] One of the attractions was Eisenstein's first film, *Glumov's Diary*. As Golutvin in *Enough Simplicity*, Aleksandrov dressed in a top hat and tails, wore a black mask with green electric eyes, performed on the trapeze, stood on his head, and traversed a high wire stretched from the stage to the balcony, balancing with an orange umbrella.[220] While still in production, one act of *Enough Simplicity* was staged at the Bol'shoi Theatre for Meierkhol'd's jubilee celebration in 1923. In one scene, Aleksandrov conducted an orchestra of saucepans, milk cans, musical pipes ("pishchalki"), and other improvised materials. The memory of this performance informed an analogous attraction in *Happy Guys*—the jazz orchestra's scat singing in imitation of musical instruments, also performed on the Bol'shoi stage.[221] The Druzbha orchestra's choreographed brawl, which included acrobatics and slapstick routines using musical instruments, similarly traces its genealogy to Eisenstein's theatrical productions, which were constructed with clowning, gags, and acrobatic stunts. As late as 1929, before his departure abroad, Aleksandrov wrote the script for Georgii and Sergei Vasil'ev's anti-classical *Spiashchaia krasavitsa* (*Sleeping Beauty*). The film associates classical ballet with the degenerate old bourgeoisie audience, and in the end both performers in 19th century costume and the audience are routed by workers who occupy the stage, calling for proletarian art.[222]

In the establishing shot of *Happy Guys*, the opening gates of the "Prozrachnye kliuchi" animal farm signal the beginning of the performance. The making of the final show also encompasses its preliminary stages—Potekhin's music making at the kolkhoz, his conducting at the music-hall, and his rehearsals with the Druzhba jazz orchestra. As we have seen from the early scripts, the "star is born" narrative, as it relates to Aniuta, has been truncated in the film, which elides her attempts to begin a singing career in Moscow. The syntax of American show musicals includes the emergence of a new star as part of the success of the spectacle: Sally O'Neill in *On with the Show* (1929), Ruby Keeler in *42nd Street* (1933), Joan Crawford in *Dancing Lady* (1933). Although the newcomer often takes over from an incapacitated prima in these musicals, in the more streamlined narrative of *Happy Guys*, the talented Aniuta is simply called upon by Potekhin to perform, thereby assuring the success of the show. "Making a show" and "making the couple" come together during the final performance at the Bol'shoi, when Potekhin acknowledges Aniuta as both singing star and lover.

Non-hermetic genres, like the musical, animated cartoon, and comedian comedy, do not follow the classical Hollywood model, which creates an illusion of reality through narrative causality, a closed narrative structure, and uninterrupted exposition.[223] Because of their descent from episodic and composite genres, like vaudeville and the variety show, these forms allow for constant play between storytelling and showmanship, which have become codified as generic conventions. Non-hermetic genres are further marked by a more open narrative structure, narrative exposition that is derailed by actors who step out of character, "a foregrounding of [the] marks of production, essential artificiality, and a deconstruction of signifying practices."[224] *Happy Guys* displays precisely such a non-hermetic configuration.

Leonid Utesov's stage persona as a wisecracking, almost middle-aged, Jewish performer with an Odessa accent coexists in tension with his role in the film—the musically talented young Russian peasant boy Kostia Potekhin. In his rendition of "Kak mnogo devushek khoroshikh," filmed in studio close-ups as professional performance, and his clearly practiced conducting during the finale, Utesov steps out of the Potekhin role to become himself as estrada performer and band leader. In the same way, during the Bol'shoi Theatre performance, the awkward, tipsy and bedraggled peasant girl Aniuta emerges as the sophisticated and professionally confident operetta star, Liubov' Orlova. Their "Spasibo serdtse" duet during the Bol'shoi performance, partly filmed in non-diegetic close-ups of a well-dressed and well-groomed Utesov and Orlova, reveals their authentic performative personae.

As is typical of non-hermetic genres, the reality of *Happy Guys* is an artificial construct and the film does deconstruct its own signifying practices. At every step, the film tells us: this is not real and furthermore, don't take any of this seriously. The diegetic time of *Happy Guys* is problematic. Given the flourishing bourgeois enclave at the Black Swan, a number of period critics assumed that the film was set during NEP. Years later Aleksandrov asserted that the film parodied the holdovers of NEP society: "At that time, NEP people had not yet ceased to exist. Their pathetic remnants used to gather for so called 'vecherukhi,' where they unburdened their hearts in gorging themselves and getting drunk."[225] Lena, her mother and their coterie may be pretentious fools but, given their way of life on vacation and in Moscow, they are far from pathetic. Furthermore, their affluent circumstances do not correspond to the social leveling that had occurred by the end of the first five-year plan in 1932. The Black Swan episodes were filmed at the palatial dacha of a well-known surgeon, a member of the new Soviet elite, and not a former Nepman. Aleksandrov needed both the idle rich and his imaginary peasants, Kostia and Aniuta, for genre reasons that had nothing to do with the depiction of Soviet reality and everything to do with established western comedy paradigms.

Only one period critic, V. Platova, argued in the cinema industry newspaper *Kino* that realism—Socialist or otherwise—was not the point: "It is not the social status of the heroes that has independent meaning, but their beautiful, rhythmic bodies, their voices, merry songs, the skill of the musicians and dancers. Who would think of asking acrobats for historically accurate costumes or political tendencies in their trapeze exercises?"[226] At the All-Union Conference of Cinema Workers in January 1935, just after the release of *Happy Guys*, Aleksandrov explained to his colleagues that he had intended to make an eclectic film based on different Hollywood genres and using the topics and themes of American comedy:

> We wanted to try out not just the method of the musical comedy genre, but also to do each scene in a new genre. The first entrance—the parade of the leader of the troupe, the act with trained animals, the acrobatics act, the brawl act, Orlova and Utesov's lyrical songs—all of these are different genres.... In these same scenes, I wanted to study the methods of American constructions, and then and there try to do them not as in America, but to do them better. But it didn't work out everywhere because the subjects of American comedy that are being parodied are not familiar to audiences in our country."[227]

As in Proletkul't days, Aleksandrov is still conceptualizing his work in terms of circus attractions or acts: Potekhin's morning march thus becomes a "first entrance—the parade of the leader of the troupe." Within this framework, he carried out an experiment in replicating Hollywood genres, such as the musical, slapstick and comedian comedy, and the cartoon, which are all tenuously and conditionally located on Soviet soil. Aleksandrov adopted both the parodic subjects—the snobbish and spoiled rich (e.g., the wealthy widows of Marx Brothers films), Harold Lloyd's country boy seeking to make good in the city, the sanctity of death rituals, the mindless admiration of musical "geniuses"—and the methods (the slapstick and gag traditions) of American comedy, all of which inhabit *Happy Guys* with little regard for contemporary Soviet reality.

In his March 1935 article on *Happy Guys*, the literary critic Bruno Jasieński attacked the film for its imitativeness, citing a number of Aleksandrov's alleged sources: Keaton's *Go West* (1925), Buñuel's *L'Âge d'Or* (1930), Chaplin's *The Goldrush* (1925) and René Clair's *Entr'acte* (1924).[228] In the context of the director's stated goals for *Happy Guys*, Jasieński's accusations are understandable, though not completely fair, for two reasons. In *Happy Guys*, Aleksandrov draws upon the same common gag and slapstick heritage of western vaudeville and early film comedy, as did Chaplin, Keaton, Lloyd, and other screen comedians, without their being accused of plagiarism. Secondly, where Aleksandrov borrows situations, routines, and formal elements from western films, he develops them differently. For example, Potekhin's morning march in *Happy Guys* is based on the extended tracking shot cum theme song in Erik Charell's musical comedy *Der Kongress tanzt* (1931). At one point in the film, shop owner Christel drives through Vienna on her way to a suburban villa given to her by Czar Alexander I of Russia, whom she has charmed. Sitting in her open cabriolet and singing, "Das ist für einmal, Das kommt nicht wieder," she passes and greets the inhabitants of the city—waving and dancing soldiers, shopkeepers, pedestrians, children, peasants, laundrywomen, and boating couples who pick up the film's central song.[229] Yet while Aleksandrov uses the same formal elements (long tracking shot, greeting motif, passed along theme song), he employs them more dynamically, in a different mise-en-scène, and with additional comic routines (Potekhin's playing jugs and fence posts, dancing on the log bridge) for the bravura opening of *Happy Guys*, thereby setting the optimistic tone for the entire film.

In *Go West*, city boy Keaton pulls a stone from the hoof of the cow Brown Eyes, who becomes his only friend. In Chicago, Keaton's cattle cause mayhem by getting into a Turkish bath, a department store, and a barber shop, but Brown Eyes leads the herd to the Union stockyards, thereby saving the day for Keaton, who wins the rancher's daughter. In contrast, Potekhin's Mar'ia Ivanovna is a troublesome buffalo cow who causes comic mishaps when Potekhin tethers her to himself. She then leads the animals into the Black Swan, where they cause havoc in the slapstick tradition.

In *The Gold Rush*, Charlie ties a rope around his waist to keep his pants up while dancing with Georgina, but the dog at the other end proceeds to drag him around in unexpected directions. The connection device gag, in which a string links objects or people, thereby leading to a series of comic events, is a staple of the earliest comedy films.[230] Aleksandrov develops this traditional gag in the scenes with the Venus de Milo statue and the guest who throws ice water on Mar'ia Ivanovna. The connection gag also becomes a standard "redirected joke" in which the victim outfoxes the prankster:[231] as the guest prepares to throw the water to make Mar'ia Ivanovna bolt, taking Potekhin with her, Kostia attaches the rope to the guest's pants and leaves the room.

In Buñuel's *L'Âge d'Or*, the wealthy heroine enters her bedroom to find a cow lying on her bed. Completely unsurprised, she pushes the cow off the bed and out through the double doors. Buñuel's surrealist film plays with the animal in the house gag, while Aleksandrov uses it in traditional fashion, placing the cow in bed with Lena's mother to elicit hysteria and comic chaos. In the equally surrealist *L'Entr'acte*, a hearse drawn by a camel detaches from the animal and careens through the city pursued by the funeral mourners. In the end, the coffin opens to reveal a magician who waves his wand to make everyone, including himself, disappear. In *Happy Guys*, an elaborate white catafalque-carriage careens through the city as the jazz musicians rush to their première at the Bol'shoi. The funeral with jazz musicians may resemble New Orleans customs, but the catafalque-carriage, which seems exotic to modern audiences, was actually a feature of early Soviet life, in common use for the funerals of Old Bolsheviks and well-to-do citizens during the early thirties. A period memoirist recalls: "A funeral procession is slowly passing through the city center. The policeman stops traffic with his stick; trolleys, open carriages, trucks, carts freeze in place. Six horses, decorated with feather headdresses and harnessed in tandem, pull a white hearse with the coffin under a canopy—a catafalque. The torchbearers ('fakel'shchiki'), men in white clamyses and top hats, march solemnly by the sides of the catafalque.... Why 'fakel'shchiki'? They explained that at one time they carried burning torches near the coffin. In the rear is a brass band, playing a mournful march."[232] In any case, the graveyard humor of both films, laughing at socially sanctified death rituals is also a traditional feature of early comedy. In 1939, Aleksandrov recalled the inspiration for the tune switching of the funeral musicians: "I had to hire an orchestra for the funeral and the conductor asked me where they would walk—in front of or behind the procession. I asked him why he needed to know. He answered that, if they went behind, then they would barely manage one funeral, if they went in front, they would have time to get to three places.... These experienced hacks could play a funeral march as a polka. On the basis of this experience, I did the funeral march in *Happy Guys*." [233]

More significant than the search for Aleksandrov's particular sources is the fact that in *Happy Guys* he employs all the major categories of visual humor from the American comedic tradition, as practiced by Chaplin, Lloyd, Keaton, and others. Most prevalent is simple physical humor: Aniuta falls over with the fence as she spies on Kostia, sits backwards on a bull while beating it with a twig broom, clobbers a guest with a brush, and slides down a banister holding a pile of dishes; Potekhin's animals wreak havoc in the Black Swan's dining room (Fig. 17); Kostia, chased by the staff of the music-hall, accidentally opens a trap door into which Fraskini falls, loses his pants, and escapes by jumping from a second floor window.[234] The musical brawl is based entirely on physical humor: a head is banged on the piano, another is crowned with a wastebasket, a musician throws piano keys, a drum falls on Potekhin's head, and so on. When the rain-soaked orchestra members attempt to perform on the Bol'shoi stage, water spouts from their instruments. Potekhin inspects a drum by hitting it and is sprayed in the face.

Most gags, such as transformation, switch image, interpenetration of action, switch movement, employ various forms of incongruity.[235] Aleksandrov uses simple physical incongruity sparingly: the delicately built Aniuta wears huge Little Tramp shoes; a small child's small sounds in the neighboring room provoke a large reaction among the Druzhba musicians. The most frequent transformation gags in the film involve animals behaving like humans: the morning kolkhoz roll call, which the Professor, Secretary, Bureaucrat, and Chamberlain answer with incongruous mooings and bleatings;[236] the episodes of the herd's feasting and drinking in the dining room of the Black Swan. Living beings are also transformed into things: birds become musical notes,[237] a lamb becomes a toy, and a bull becomes a hat rack for a tipsy guest. Finally, an animal can be transformed into another animal: a sheep dons a tiger skin, terrifying the guests at Lena's party.

Gags based on the interpenetration of two events or narratives, a kind of visual irony, where the audience is aware of both scenarios, but the heroes are not, were a staple of early film comedy. One of the Black Swan guests sits down to feast on suckling pig without realizing that the piglet has been on a binge and is sleeping it off on a serving dish (Fig. 18). In the related switch-image gag, neither the audience nor the characters are aware of the intersecting narratives: at the outset of their acquaintance on the beach Lena understands Potekhin's loud laughter as directed at her appearance and examines the bodice of her bathing suit to make sure everything is in place. Neither she nor we know that Potekhin is being tickled by a fish caught in his swim trunks. In the switch-movement gag, the hero suddenly changes from one activity to another when surprised

Figure 17.

by an authority figure, such as the boss or his wife. In the funeral procession episode, the Druzhba musicians play traditional funeral music until the traffic cop turns away, and then switch to a foxtrot accompanied by dancing.

Verbal gags (doubtless the work of Erdman and Mass) are less prominent in *Happy Guys* and occur primarily in the dialogues of part one where there are opportunities for misunderstandings with Lena and her mother. The film exploits two categories of verbal humor popularized by the Marx Brothers: context reversal (or verbal interpenetration of meanings) and concretization of idioms.[238] In the first, each of the speakers interprets

Figure 18.

the dialogue in a different context, thereby producing humorous outcomes which are perceived mainly by the audience. When Lena asks Potekhin, whom she has mistaken for the conductor Fraskini, about his living situation, he talks about his animals, which she interprets as female rivals:

—Nas tam mnogo...gollandki, shveitsarki...

—Krasivye?

—Kto?

—Gollandki.

—Okh, shikarnye gollandki. Boka—vo boka. Glaza—vo glaza kakie!

—Vy za nimi ukhazhivaete?

—Eshche by, s utra do vechera!

—Kak by ia khotela byt' na ikh meste.[239]

Other episodes with context reversals abound: Lena invites Potekhin and his guests to enter, but he tells Lena he can't come in because he is not alone: "Ia ne odin. Menia zhdut" ("I'm not alone. They're waiting for me"—referring both to cattle and human guests); Potekhin asks Lena, who is preoccupied with his attachment to her and wonders why he keeps close to the window: "Zametno, chto ia priviazan?" ("Is it noticeable that I'm attached?") (attached to a rope and attached to her); Lena asks for Potekhin's autograph, which he protests he can't provide because he doesn't own one (signature vs. object); when Lena's mother finds out Potekhin's profession, she ask, "Prostoi pastukh?" ("An ordinary shepherd?"). He replies, "Net, ne prostoi, a glavnyi" ("No, not ordinary, the chief one") (social status vs. job title). Concretization of an idiom, the Russian "Igrat' kak sapozhnik," "to play badly," literally "to play like a shoemaker," occurs in Potekhin's dialogue with Karl Ivanovich:

—Razve eto igra? Ty dolzhen igrat', kak sapozhnik!

—Vy, Karl Ivanovich, ko mne pridiraetes'. Ia ne mogu igrat', kak sapozhnik. Sapozhnik u Vas uzhe 6 let zanimaetsia, a ia vtoroi god.[240]

Gags function in various ways in early comedy films. They may function inside or outside the narrative logic, advance the plot, delay potential resolution, produce alternate patterning, or introduce social problems.[241] In *Happy Guys*, the visual and verbal gags function largely within the narrative and agendas of musical and comedian comedy. The film's animal gags satirize the wealthy bourgeoisie both by analogy (the drunken bull and piglet) and action (the sheep-turned-tiger and cow in the bed terrify the guests). Potekhin's fruitless attempts at social integration into the bourgeoisie are demonstrated through gags, such as the fish, rope, and autograph episodes. His conducting the *Hungarian Rhapsody*, Lena's cracking eggs on Bach's nose, and the destruction of the Venus di Milo statue all parody the classical music and culture associated with the bourgeoisie, a typical paradigm for musical comedy.

In part two, the musical brawl and catafalque episodes with their multiple gags are only tenuously linked to the narrative. They are also transgressive in contesting social order and authority, which audiences living in the regimented world of five-year plans must have found refreshing. Friendship takes a beating when the Druzhba musicians disagree about musical phrasing. Their musical thinking is individualistic and intolerant, completely unworthy of the group's name, "The Musical *Collective* Druzhba (Friendship)." (We are shown the sign on their door both before and after the brawl.) The brawl quickly degenerates into cinematic anarchy, the likes of which Soviet audiences had not seen since the twenties (Fig. 19). While the catafalque episodes (from the street rehearsal

Figure 19.

through the wild ride to the Bol'shoi) satirize the excesses of both bourgeois and Soviet funeral rites, they also disturb the Soviet social order in their carnivalizing of death. During the street rehearsal-funeral procession, the musicians subvert official authority by playing inappropriate dance music as soon as the policeman turns away. A driver sleeps—or perhaps sleeps it off—in the coffin, given his vodka bottle. A transfigured Aniuta performs on the Bol'shoi stage in funeral accoutrements, among which a corpse's identification tag, a large card with the initials "PB" ("Pokhoronnoe biuro," Funeral Bureau), prominently displayed on her right shoulder is the most grotesque.[242] The catafalque ride thus mediates peasant Aniuta's death and resurrection as a singing star, and she performs, still wearing the tag and a fishnet coverlet from the catafalque.

Aleksandrov's ironic sensibility, an air of detached, good-natured mockery, pervades *Happy Guys*, and here the gags serve to deconstruct the stereotypes of romantic melodrama, persistently displacing the lyrical into the humorous. When Potekhin finishes his lyrical solo, "Kak mnogo devushek khoroshikh," the tree branch breaks, dumping him unceremoniously on the ground. Aniuta's would-be romantic conversation with Potekhin is derailed by the mosquitoes, one of which she kills by slapping Potekhin's face, thereby provoking his anger rather than affection. When he leaves and she calls after him, his name echoes ironically across the ocean. In Aniuta's following "Serdtse v grudi" solo, the tone alternates between lyrical and humorous, as she both sings and chases mosquitoes. In the finale, Aniuta and Potekhin's lyrical performance of the refrain to "Kak mnogo devushek khoroshikh," "Spasibo serdtse, chto ty umeesh' tak liubit'" slides into a humorous register when one of the musicians seconds the refrain with parodic distortions. In the final scene of the romantic plot, as Potekhin and Aniuta lean forward to kiss after the performance, the driver comes up between them, receives the kiss with a smirk, dispelling the aura of romance and causing Potekhin to spit in disgust.[243]

In the middle of the music-hall chase episodes, Potekhin makes an ironic, self-reflexive comment that reminds us not to take this diegetic world seriously: "Nu, opiat' bega nachinaiutsia" ("Well, the running is starting up again").[244] Although the introductory titles of *Happy Guys* tell us that Charlie Chaplin is not in the film, he is nevertheless present in the film's mixture of the comic and lyrical, and Aleksandrov cites him ironically through Aniuta's huge tramp shoes and holey umbrella and Potekhin's distributing flowers to ladies in the music-hall, as Chaplin does in *City Lights*. The animals' assault on the Black Swan, the bastion of bourgeois culture, by climbing the white staircase ironically quotes the storming of the Winter Palace in Eisenstein's *October*, during which the soldiers stream up the white Jordan staircase. The cartoon intermezzos of the film serve the same function by exploding diegetic reality. In the first, a cartoon clock simply marks the passage of time; however the second and third segments depict a male crescent moon, later joined by a female full moon, who dance and sing ditties about the passage of time and the search for happiness—another ironic treatment of the romantic plot of the film. Cartoon sparks fly, first when Aniuta hits an entering guest with a push broom and later when Potekhin pushes the catafalque driver into a backwards tumble on the Bol'shoi stage. The extra-diegetic graphics comment ironically on the knockabout humor of the two scenes, which pervades the cartoon world, and therefore underscores the film as fictional construct.[245]

Aleksandrov, Eisenstein, and Tisse visited Walt Disney studios in 1930. For Aleksandrov, the principles behind Disney's animation work were a revelation, which later influenced the musical choreography of *Happy Guys*: "The Disney method of filming was of great interest to us. The famous cartoonist began with the phonogram. The carefully prepared phonogram became, as it were, the carcass of the film."[246] While working on the film, Aleksandrov also had an opportunity to see Disney's latest cartoons, which were shown at a festival of his work at the Udarnik Theatre in spring 1933.[247] Although animation of some kind is present in each of Aleksandrov's musical films, the coordination of phonogram with comic kinesis is most prominent in *Happy Guys* (Potekhin's morning march, his conducting at the Moscow music-hall) and in *Volga-Volga*, Aleksandrov's return to eccentric comedy (the townsfolk's pursuit of Byvalov). Disney used music as the basis for his animation, which followed and depended entirely on the music: the movement of a figure—a step, a jump, a fall, a physical blow—corresponded to the strong beat in a measure. *Steamboat Willie* (1928), Disney's first sound cartoon, already uses the techniques Aleksandrov was to employ in *Happy Guys*. Music and movement function synthetically: figures move to the rhythm of the music, and when they are not moving, their bodies bounce and sway to the musical beat. At one point, Willie plays "Turkey in the Straw" on a trashcan, barrel, washboard, and a series of pots and pans, and then uses the bodies of animals (a goat, cat, duck, cow, and piglets) as eccentric musical instruments to produce the tune. In *Happy Guys*, even the geometric graphics forming the background for the opening film credits also pulsate in time to the music. The episodes consisting of music and movement are all synthetic, coordinating physical motion to rhythm. Aniuta sets the table in time to her theme song.[248] In the opening scenes of the film, Potekhin steps to the rhythms of the *Happy Guys* march, plays jugs and a fence, and dances on log bridges to a xylophone on the soundtrack.[249] The rhythmic coordination with ordinary activities in these episodes imitates Disney and not early thirties American musicals or revues, of which few were made between 1930 and 1932.[250] Aleksandrov even borrows the cow who paints Mar'ia Ivanovna's name in the titles with her tail from early Disney cartoons, such as *Steamboat Willie*, *Plane Crazy*, *The Karnival Kid*, and *Mickey's Follies*.

Period critics pointed to the American silent film *The Battling Orioles* (1924), directed by Guiol and Wilde and released in Russia two years later as *Voinstvennye skvortsy*, as the model for the musical brawl in *Happy Guys*. In the American film, the Orioles are former baseball players who were once notorious for their violent fights on the diamond. The now aged team leaves its retirement home to aid a young couple by fighting a group of nightclub toughs. The grand brawl that concludes the film is choreographed with several minutes of gags: an Oriole slides up and down a fire pole three times, knocking out his opponent below; another oldster sits on the shoulders of his enemy and crowns him with a chamberpot; another sticks his cane out from under a table, tripping up the younger opponents; yet another geezer makes his suspenders into a slingshot and shoots liquor bottles at the enemy. There is no synchronization with music in this silent film, and musical instruments are not used in the gags.[251] Aleksandrov was doubtless familiar with *The Battling Orioles*, but a more plausible and chronologically proximate source for the musical brawl is the early thirties cartoons he saw in the United States.

Knockabout humor, physical movement synchronized to music, and the use of musical instruments as weapons, usually in a classical music performance that goes awry, are all featured in early sound cartoons. Since these devices in early cartoons migrated from one work to another, Fleischer's *Car-tune Portrait* (1937) may serve as a compendium of classical music gags. In the cartoon, an animal orchestra's serious performance degenerates into a fight: the lion conductor throws his baton at an orchestra member; an ostrich shoots bows from the strings of a violin and is later shoved through a cello; and in the end the conductor is crowned with a drum, much like Potekhin at the end of the brawl. Aleksandrov uses these gags, among others, in the musical brawl, and the final result is far more artful than the analogous episode in *Battling Orioles*.

In his memoirs, Aleksandrov notes that Disney used classical music to achieve comic effects, citing as an example *The Skeleton Dance* (1929), which was animated to Grieg's *March of the Trolls*.[252] Disney's *Barnyard Concert* (1930) is animated to the *Dichter und Bauer* operetta overture. In *Just Mickey* (1930), the mouse hero plays "Träumerei" from the *William Tell Overture*, and *The Band Concert* (1935) is animated to sections from the same overture. The comic effect is derived from the incongruity between products of high culture and mundane activities. Because of the sharp contrasts between slow and fast tempos and their musical dramatism, Liszt's *Second Hungarian Rhapsody* and the *William Tell Overture* have become synonymous with cartoon music.[253] Whether or not there is a direct source for Potekhin's music-hall routine, Fleischer Studios had already used the *Hungarian Rhapsody* in *Fire Bugs*, a 1930 animal cartoon. Fleischer cartoons were distributed by Paramount, for whom Eisenstein and company were writing scripts while in Hollywood, so Aleksandrov must have been familiar with their work. Although the two interpenetrating narratives (Potekhin's conducting a musical performance and communicating with the beloved by gestures) are the primary source of humor in the music-hall episode, Aleksandrov also employs body humor characteristic of early cartoons. Synchronizing his movements with the *Hungarian Rhapsody*, Potekhin throws his arms up in surprise at seeing Lena, shrugs, crooks his finger in invitation, pulls up his pants, drops and retrieves a shirt cuff, pulls on a shirt sleeve, steps on and off the podium, and runs up and down a staircase to retrieve Lena's flower. In Disney's *The Band Concert* (1935), Mickey conducts the *William Tell Overture* while struggling with his long sleeves and cap, which keeps slipping over his eyes, and gyrates to harem music when ice cream gets down his neck. When a tornado carries the entire orchestra into the air, a pig loses his clothes in tune to the "Storm" section of the overture.

The cartoon visages of Chaplin, Lloyd, and Keaton, who do *not* appear in the film, as we are told in the opening titles, are nevertheless present in the comedian comedy acting of the film.[254] Unlike clown comedy, such as that of the Marx Brothers, which resists and contests the dominant social categories, comedian comedy stresses the longing for social integration. The comedian's comedy stems from mistakes and mishaps arising from efforts to conform to social roles. In the end, the clown wanders away alone from the crowd, while the crowd embraces the comedian as one of its own in the final celebration.[255] In the course of the film, Potekhin seeks integration into two opposing social groups—Lena's bourgeois circle and broader Soviet society—but his attempts to fit in with the former lead to comic mishaps. His entré into bourgeois society is engineered through the mistaken identity motif, driven by the aspirations of the ignorant rich, a staple stratum of American comedy. To please Lena and her mother, Potekhin plays his reed pipe for their guests, which precipitates the animal invasion of the Black Swan. Thinking that "avtograf" is an object, he refuses to autograph his picture for Lena, explaining that he begrudges her nothing, but just doesn't have one to give her. Potekhin's eccentric conducting of the music-hall orchestra is the comic by-product of his attempts to communicate with Lena. The finale of *Happy Guys*, Potekhin's performance on the stage of the Bol'shoi Theatre and his leading the audience in song denotes his full integration into the Soviet community. The expressive anarchy of gags in the tradition of Chaplin, Lloyd, and Keaton is ultimately embraced by the community as Potekhin and his orchestra replace waterlogged instruments with comic scat singing in the first finale of the film. Their non-normative behavior is then completely muted in the second ending.

*****

The plotline of *Happy Guys* falls into two parts separated by the chronological-geographical-causal gap of Potekhin's unexplained arrival in Moscow. Faced with overly long running time because of the songs and with official disapproval of the kolkhoz episodes, Aleksandrov decided to drop the section of the script in which the kolkhoz votes to send Potekhin to Moscow to study music.[256] Critics accustomed to theatrical realism and the "true comedy" of farces attacked *Happy Guys* for its structural defects. The modern viewer, accustomed both to the conventions of musical film and the anarchic comedy of the Marx Brothers and Jerry Lewis, is much more forgiving. The emotional trajectory of the plot is downward in the first segment: at its end, Potekhin has been rejected by Lena, while Aniuta has been rejected by Potekhin. The second segment in Moscow moves upward as both Kostia and Aniuta find fame and love. Apart from the chronological story line, the structural logic of *Happy Guys* turns on the parallel and contrast of contiguous elements.

As demonstrated by Rick Altman, the musical film genre has a dual-focus structure in which the sexual duality of the plot, driven by the male and female principals, is mirrored in the setting, shot selection, music, and dance of the film: "In the musical, chronological presentation and causal relationships alike are at climactic moments eschewed in favor of simultaneity and similarity."[257] The dual-focus narrative of *Happy Guys* is organized around the interplay of proximate semantic units, including—but also extending beyond—the relations of the male and female principals. Each segment must be understood not so much in a causal sequence but rather in relation to the segment it parallels, and the paradigm may be either contrastive or congruous and complementary. The contiguous semantic pairs of *Happy Guys* denote not only the performative simultaneity of the romantic couple but also highlight class distinctions (a fictionalized bourgeoisie vs. a socially mobile peasantry), which are in turn calibrated with the central contest between classical and popular music. Finally, the semantic pair of the film's two endings effects both localized closure and public aperture.

The opening tracking shot of Kostia's morning march functions in contrast to its syntactic pair, the long tracking shot at the beach. Potekhin's energetic, youthful pace and bravura song, along with various humorous episodes—his awakening of Karl Ivanovich, Aniuta's milk-spilling idolatry of the shepherd, her falling over with the fence as she spies on him, the shepherd's xylophonic bridge-dancing and music-making on jugs and fences—set the tone of the film. Potekhin's march song gradually incorporates his entire provincial world as he passes and greets horsemen, haymakers, villagers, apple-pickers, grape-gatherers, children, and horses. After the second editing splice of the tracking shot, the tempo of the march song speeds up and, after Kostia waves to passing villagers, a chorus performing the first stanza of the *Happy Guys* march and later the "My mozhem pet' i smeiat'sia, kak deti" ("We can sing and laugh like children") stanza enters the soundtrack. The tempo remains fast after the third splice, but Potekhin and his companions now change to a broader, energetic marching step, as they come out on the village street. The march ends with blacksmiths loudly hammering on their anvils in time with the march music as Potekhin arrives by the sea.

In the contrasting beach panorama Lena, whose extravagant garb with its excessively wide slacks and loud geometrical patterns is as complicated and outlandish as Kostia's clothing is simple and restrained, mirrors him as the lead figure in the tracking shot. However, she slinks where he marches, she is silent where he sings, and tango rhythms accompany her predation with an insistent, sultry beat—the inverse of the folksy, carefree *Happy Guys* march. The beach life of the bourgeoisie is served up with lightly ironic humor: a naked little boy in full-figure profile imitating classical statues; a large gramophone sitting on the sand; a man taking pictures with a hand camera; a woman feeding a cluster of grapes to her mate in the style of Roman orgies; foreground close-ups of the soles of large male feet, a posterior and then a series of male backs; a photographer with a large camera on a tripod, for whom Lena half-poses during her walk; two men playing chess; a toddler looking innocently into the camera; a woman frying up a meal, an older couple in wicker chairs, and several leggy women behind a Chinese umbrella who provide the transition to the episode with Fraskini. (The umbrella filling the frame is borrowed from the Odessa steps episode in *Potemkin.*) Aleksandrov's figuration of the vacationers is markedly ambivalent, falling somewhere between amused affection and light irony at the "Roman revels" of the bourgeoisie.[258] However, in their general visual and auditory figuration, the two panoramas contrapose peasant to city dweller, poor to rich, work to leisure, and energy to lethargy.

The next semantic pairing suggests the equivalence between animals and humans. At Potekhin's early morning roll-call, the animals answer to their human names, professions, and nationalities: the bull as John Bull, both chamberlain and Neville Chamberlain—the British politician and natty dresser; goats as secretaries, bureaucrats, and professors; pigs as Englishwomen (anglichanki); and cattle as Swiss and Dutch women (shveitsarki, gollandki). Aleksandrov has borrowed here from Eisenstein's *Strike*, in which czarist secret agents physically resemble their animal code names of Monkey, Owl, Fox, and Bulldog and are presented to us through montage of humans with the corresponding animals. In *Happy Guys*, Aleksandrov gives us portraits of animals whose monikers are negative or highbrow professions or double-entendres of animal breeds and human nationalities, to which they respond with incongruous bleatings, mooings, and oinkings. Shortly thereafter, while posing for a trick photo, Lena's mother substitutes her lapdog's head for her own. After Potekhin, standing outside the Black Swan, tells Lena, "I'm not alone. They're waiting for me," she unwittingly identifies the animals as guests by inviting them all in: "Zakhodite vse vmeste." But the obverse also holds true: her human guests turn out to be beasts: for every gluttonous animal, there is a gluttonous guest—the bull and cows who lap up punch and even aquarium water and the fat man who greedily cuts into a live suckling pig; the drunken bull and the drunken guest who hangs his hat on the horn of the bull. And after she faints, Lena's mother is put to bed next to a sleeping cow.

In keeping with the traditional dual-focus simultaneity of musical film, both Kostia and Aniuta are, in proximate scenes, rejected by the objects of their affection—Kostia by Lena, Aniuta by Kostia, moving them to sing parallel love songs, "Kak mnogo devushek khoroshikh" and "Pesnia Aniuty" ("Aniuta's Song").[259] Not surprisingly, both performances center around "heart" and look optimistically toward the future:

> Akh, serdtse, tebe ne khochetsia pokoia!
> Serdtse, kak khorosho na svete zhit'!
> Serdtse, kak khorosho, chto ty takoe.
> Spasibo serdtse, chto ty umeesh' tak liubit'!
> ("Kak mnogo devushek khoroshikh")

Serdtse v grudi
B'etsia, kak ptitsa.
I khochesh' znat', chto zhdet vperedi,
I khochetsia schast'ia dobit'sia.
("Pesnia Aniuty")[260]

Figure 20.

In the second, Moscow section of the film, the music-hall performance of the *Hungarian Rhapsody* (Fig. 20) and the contiguous musicians' brawl form another semantic pair. Both performances are equally stagey and minutely choreographed. Kostia's eccentric conducting of the *Rhapsody* as he tries to communicate with Lena comprises a similar pairing. Each of Kostia's comic gestures follows the Liszt musical score. In the musical brawl, each of the Druzhba musicians' movements follow Dunaevskii's jazz score. Potekhin's "original interpretation" of Liszt, which is praised by the well-heeled, pretentious, and ignorant music-hall audience, and the episode of the husband who loves his wife "even more" because of her tears of emotion during the performance (actually due to tight shoes) both serve to discredit the bourgeois elite. In the competition between classical and modern popular music that is frequently operative in musical film, the preference here is given to Dunaevskii's original jazz composition and the imaginative choreography of the musical brawl as true art. Jazz is the music of the rising class—the peasant Potekhins and Aniutas of Soviet Russia. As in American musicals of the swing era, jazz dance rhythms and high energy level mark it as the music of youth and of the future.

Lena's vocalizing in preparation for her acceptance by the Bol'shoi Theatre is intercut with Druzhba's rehearsing in a funeral procession in preparation for their Bol'shoi début. Hoping to improve her voice, Lena makes her way through a plate of raw eggs, which she cracks open on J. S. Bach's nose, or rather his bust standing on the piano. Wiping clean the nostrils of a nearby bust in metonymical sympathy, Aniuta follows as Lena repeatedly fails to complete her scales and continues to deface Bach's physiognomy with raw eggs. Since the plot of a musical is ideally conveyed in musical terms, it is not surprising that bad girl Lena cannot sing at all, and it is Aniuta who easily takes the high notes in Lena's scales. Meanwhile Kostia and his ensemble rehearse by joining a funeral procession following an elaborate carriage-catafalque through the streets of Moscow. They play Chopin's *Funeral March* until the policeman turns away, and then break into a jaunty foxtrot accompanied by lively dancing. The parallel semantic segments demonstrate that no amount of rehearsing will ever make Lena a good singer, while *any* means of rehearsal makes the Druzhba crew good musicians. Bach ends up with egg on his face: once again, classical music suffers from its association with the bourgeoisie and Chopin's *Funeral March* is displaced by a lively jazz melody.

The dual-focus first finale of *Happy Guys* affords parallel triumphs for the romantic couple: when their waterlogged instruments prove useless for anything but comic relief, Kostia persuades his musicians to play "na gubakh" ("on the lips"), i.e., to perform the *Happy Guys* march as a combination of scat singing and dancing. Summoned forth by Kostia's trumpet call, the bedraggled, tipsy servant girl Aniuta, wrapped in a coffin cover and holding the driver's hat, metamorphoses into the sophisticated, well-dressed singer Liubov' Orlova, who dons Dietrich's *Blue Angel* top hat with a confident gesture and performs Aniuta's signature song with a triumphant inflection.[261] (Fig. 21)

Figure 21.

The two finales of *Happy Guys* form a semantic pair effecting different levels of closure in the film. The first finale brings the musical comedy narrative to its conventional conclusion: Kostia, Aniuta, and friends have staged a successful performance at the Bol'shoi, during which the male and female principals are finally united as lovers. The second finale of *Happy Guys* reifies and validates the triumph of popular music in the heartland of high culture and extends its supremacy to the audience and the outside world. The contest between the two has already been introduced by the catafalque driver's question about the jazz ensemble's unpaid fare: "A kto budet platit'—Pushkin?" ("And who is going to pay—Pushkin?"). The classical tradition (Liszt) is displaced by popular music, along with an ironic jab at the ethos of Soviet industrialization, when Potekhin's musicians are introduced at the Bol'shoi as "ansambl' imeni *list*oprokatnogo tsekha" ("the ensemble of the sheet metal rolling shop"). The victory of jazz is, of course, already implicit in the first finale: the stage show is a resounding success and the formally attired Bol'shoi orchestra conductor acknowledges the popular style by leading his musicians in the first bars of "Aniuta's Song."

Throughout the narrative, Potekhin has brought carnivalistic chaos into the various worlds he inhabits, destabilizing all established orders, whether bourgeois or Soviet. The animal invasion destroys the elegant world of the Black Swan; Potekhin subverts the serious music-hall performance of the *Hungarian Rhapsody*, which ends in a chaotic chase and an offense to cultured mores, as he loses his pants.[262] Druzhba's musical brawl disrupts Soviet communal order. The subsequent rehearsal in the funeral procession and the orchestra's wild catafalque ride disturb established Soviet ritual. Disobeying the policeman during the funeral procession subverts authority. The performance with waterlogged instruments and in ragged clothing (one orchestra member wears only underpants) brings anarchic entertainment to the Bol'shoi stage, where it is victorious (Fig. 22). As the curtain goes up on the second finale, the Bol'shoi's ballerinas (a stock symbol of elite culture in the musical) applaud the performance, loudly seconded by the theatre audience. A few minutes later, the ballerinas sway and swish their tutus on stage in time to the *Happy Guys* march, replicating Aniuta's dance movements in the first finale. Classical style thus converts to the rhythms of popular music, and the reconciliation of high and low musical cultures is complete, as jazz takes its place at the center of highbrow culture.

The second finale of *Happy Guys* both integrates Potekhin's anarchic persona into Soviet establishment culture and extends the stage performance to the outside world. In parallel scenes, Utesov and Orlova now perform the *Happy Guys* march as themselves, i.e., in their own stage personae. Dressed in an elegant white suit, Utesov as professional band leader, brings his—still raggedly costumed—orchestra down an onstage staircase and sings the "Nam pesnia zhit' i liubit' pomogaet" ("A song helps us live and love") refrain of the march. Maintaining symmetry, Orlova, as experienced operetta star, leads a navy orchestra down the opposite staircase and performs the same stanza.

The stage scenery for the two finales is rather curious: a snowy mountain top is painted on the backdrop; a tall, curving colonnade borders the stage; and at center stage stands the vase-like base of an enormous fountain, which produces streams of water during the second finale (Fig. 23). The mountain, the Utesov-Orlova performance of the *Happy Guys* march, and the Bol'shoi audience's singing of the "My mozhem pet' i smeiat'sia, kak deti" ("We can sing and laugh like children") stanza, which reprises the villagers' choral singing during Kostia's march, all refer us to the opening scene of the film, which is thereby duplicated in a monumental register on the Bol'shoi stage. One of the early *Happy Guys* scripts notes that the stage decorations represent a Venetian street, so that the appearance of the ragged and bandaged musicians in this civilized setting provokes audience laughter.[263] However, the second ending of *Happy Guys*, the "finale of finales," as Aleksandrov called it, makes a stylistic shift to celebratory spectacle, to which the classical colonnade and cascading Venetian fountain now contribute monumental grandeur.

Figure 22.

Figure 23.

The second finale is thus intended to achieve an apotheosis—the integration of all participants—the performers (including sailor-musicians and ballerinas), the diegetic audience and the real audience—through the mediation of popular song and the socialist hero. Kostia's folksy march is no longer marginal; it has travelled from the periphery to take its place in the sacred space of the cultural center as mass song.[264] He himself has moved from studying Beethoven on a provincial kolhoz to directing a jazz orchestra in Moscow. Both popular genres have established themselves on an equal footing with the classical forms residing at the Bol'shoi Theatre.

Integration is achieved by both narrative and filmic means. Utesov and Orlova lead their fellow performers on stage and the Bol'shoi audience in a sing-along of the "My mozhem pet' i smeiat'sia, kak deti" stanza that continues as the camera tracks backward through the theatre. Both Orlova in her solo singing and then Utesov and Orlova in their duet of "Nam pesnia zhit' i liubit' pomogaet" use direct address, looking straight into the lens, thereby establishing contact with the extra-diegetic audience. In the early thirties, shots of applauding theatre audiences became a sine qua non of American show musicals, as a way of encouraging the viewer to identify with the spectral cinematic audience.[265] Instead of the usual camera location for recording an onstage performance (the imaginary third row center seat), Aleksandrov situates us at a greater distance, and literally in the official State box located across the hall directly opposite and above the stage. As the camera pulls back, we find ourselves among the audience sitting in the box, looking out over the shoulders of its applauding occupants. The gaze and point of view of the ruling elite and the mass audience are thus merged. In a mise-en-abîme effect, the camera then tracks back through the doors of the theatre into the foyer and out a window to the external facade of the Bol'shoi Theatre and the street. Filmic reality thus extends out into the "real" outside world, uniting both, as the melody of the *Happy Guys* march now becomes audible on the street.

*****

It was Dunaevskii's songs, which were immediately taken up by the general population, that assured the continuing popularity of *Happy Guys*. Although he had made his cinematic debut in Korsh-Sablin's *Pervyi vzvod* (*The First Platoon*, 1933), *Happy Guys* was Dunaevskii's first major commission for the score of an entire musical film. In 1938, looking back at his earliest attempt in the genre, Dunaevskii viewed the songs of the film as a musical accompaniment rather than its dynamic axis: "Although it expands along with the plot, the theme of the *Happy Guys* march and all the subsequent rhythmic and orchestral development of this theme is essentially an accompaniment in song."[266]

Dunaevskii's sometimes lyrical, sometimes raucous instrumental and song music, most of which recurs in different orchestrations and tempos throughout the film, does not yet drive the narrative, but instead functions to unify the meandering plot of *Happy Guys*. Of the major instrumental pieces, the tango accompanying the beach tracking shot, the comic banquet music, which illustrates the staggering movements of tipsy animals, and the brawl music, which does drive the action and to which Aleksandrov subordinated his editing, are special topics which occur only once. Three animal herd episodes are all connected by the same dynamic musical theme representing incremental chaos and havoc: we first hear it when Potekhin locks up his herd behind wooden doors, which they immediately break through to escape; the same theme illustrates the animal invasion of the Black Swan via the staircase, and it reappears with the renewed havoc of animal depredations after the banquet—a bull pulling on the doorbell, a cow in bed, and a sheep in a tiger skin terrorizing the guests. The jazz prologue to the film recurs appropriately in part two, the film's second beginning, as Potekhin stands in front of the Moscow music-hall. The same piece then illustrates the ensuing chase scenes within the building.

The major songs of *Happy Guys* recur with differing tempos conveying different meanings. Most prominent is the *Happy Guys* march, which opens the film in a populist mode reminiscent of its original title, "Korovii marsh" ("The Bovine March"), and accentuated by the opening bars, which resemble Mexican folk music. At the Black Swan, Potekhin performs the march again on a reed pipe in front of the NEP audience—a simple melody that contrasts to the culturally overdetermined milieu. During the first finale, Potekhin's orchestra reprises the march instrumentally as scat singing in jazz rhythm, marking this incarnation of the song as *entertainment*. In the second finale, Utesov, Orlova, and their respective bands perform the *Happy Guys* march *qua* march. The spectacle is festive and triumphant; the "Bovine March" has become a message to the nation.

The march is the only song in the film that carries an ideological payload. Dunaevskii noted that in *Happy Guys*, Lebedev-Kumach consciously pursued his own goals: "Lebedev-Kumach looked beyond the film; for him the film and its situations were only an occasion for the achievement of his own, deeply apprehended task: to give the people a new song, a patriotic, heroic, lyric, or humorous song, and sometimes one with a satirical edge."[267] Rather than following the localized plot of *Happy Guys*, the poet produced a social prescription, a code of behavior for the youth of the country that overlaid and went beyond the comedic goals of the film. The *Happy Guys* march introduced the population at large to the mass song. According to Dunaevskii, "musically this is a sprightly march with an elastic rhythm; verbally these are stanzas with patriotic content that are not bound by the plot, and are colored in lyrical tones in Aleksandrov's films."[268] Crucial too was Lebedev-Kumach's aphoristic talent, which produced memorable refrains that distilled the spirit of the era: "I tot, kto s pesnei po zhizni shagaet, / Tot nikogda i nigde ne propadet." This type of lyrical-patriotic mass song became the most popular minor musical genre of the 1930s.

In the song appendix attached to the early *Shepherd* script, the text of the march had more of an ideological emphasis than Aleksandrov was apparently willing to insert into the film at that time: the first refrain begins "Nam pesnia zhit' i liubit' pomogaet" ("A song helps us live and love"), but is replaced in the second refrain by "Nam pesnia stroit' i zhit' pomogaet" ("A song helps us build and live"). Although the second variant had apparently been proposed before the completion of *Happy Guys*, it does not appear in the film. In the opening and closing segments, Utesov and Orlova repeatedly sing "zhit' i liubit'" and, in fact, the reflexive lyric, a song about singing, is entirely natural to the musical.[269]

Lebedev-Kumach's original lyrics are primarily an encomium to the power of song, personified as a good friend who brings lightheartedness and dispels boredom ("Legko na serdtse ot pesni veseloi, / Ona skuchat' ne daet nikogda," "The heart is light from a happy song, / It never lets you be bored"), who helps in all aspects of existence ("zhit' i liubit' pomogaet," "Helps to live and love") and guides us through the minefields of life ("I tot, kto s pesnei po zhizni shagaet, / Tot nikogda i nigde ne propadet!," "And he who strides through life with a song, / Will never be lost anywhere"). It is song—not yet ideology—that unites both city and country ("I liubiat pesniu derevni i sela, / I liubiat pesniu bol'shie goroda," "Villages and hamlets love a song, / And big cities love a song"). In the final stanza used in the film, song is situated in childhood, and the opposites of childlike song-laughter and adult labor-struggle (both armed and revolutionary) are united in the character of the Russian people: "My mozhem pet' i smeiat'sia, kak deti / Sredi upornoi bor'by i truda, / Ved' my takimi rodilis' na svete, / Chto ne sdadimsia nigde i nikogda" ("We can sing and laugh, like children / In the midst of determined struggle and labor, / For we have been born into the world like this, / So that we'll never surrender anywhere"). Thus, at the end, Lebedev-Kumach moves from an encomium to the power of song, its universality and personal benefits, to a framing of song as political power, together with an infantilization of the population.

Sometime during the thirties, after the release of the film, Lebedev-Kumach added another three stanzas and refrain to the march, introducing the themes of victory over both nature and foreign enemies, thereby bringing the march closer to the invariant characteristics of his later "Song of the Motherland" in *Circus* and "Song of the Volga" in *Volga-Volga*:

Shagai vpered, komsomol'skoe plemia,
Shuti i poi, chtob ulybki tsveli,
My pokoriaem prostranstvo i vremia,
My—molodye khoziaeva zemli!

My vse dobudem, poimem i otkroem—
Kholodnyi polius i svod goluboi.
Kogda strana byt' prikazhet geroem,
U nas geroem stanovitsia liuboi.

I esli vrag nashu radost' zhivuiu
Otniat' zakhochet v upornom boiu,
Togda my pesniu spoem boevuiu
I vstanem grud'iu za Rodinu svoiu!

Nam pesnia stroit' i zhit' pomogaet,
Ona na kryl'iakh k pobede vedet,
I tot, kto s pesnei po zhizni shagaet,
Tot nikogda i nigde ne propadet![270]

The later version of the march thus sets up the hierarchical paradigm of Stalinist culture: ordinary citizens are both "masters of the earth" and potential heroes who, at the same time, permanently remain children, vastly inferior in consciousness and in their relationship to the Great Father-Leader.

The remaining three songs of *Happy Guys*, "Aniuta's Song," "Kak mnogo devushek khoroshikh," and "Tiukh-tiukh," are purely lyrical or comic and not ideological. The tempo of "Aniuta's Song" changes according to its function in the narrative. The heroine sings in waltz tempo as she sets the table because at this point the melody denotes hopeful and therefore happy love.[271] After Potekhin has rejected Aniuta at the end of part one, she repeats the song in a slower, lyrical mode. The melancholy tone temporarily switches to a jazz tempo as she jumps up to fight off mosquitoes, but ends lyrically as she catches and releases a mosquito that represents her romantic hopes. When Aniuta performs the "Serdtse v grudi" refrain of her song on the Bol'shoi stage, she has metamorphosed into a star, and the tone is triumphantly operatic.

"Kak mnogo devushek khoroshikh" is first performed in slow tango rhythm by Potekhin after his rejection by Lena, and at this point it signifies an affirmation of life and love in spite of adversity.[272] When the refrain to the song is sung by Potekhin and Aniuta during the first finale, it serves as a declaration of love between the couple. An instrumental jazz version of the song then makes a bridge to the "Tiukh-tiukh" chastushki.

At this point, the musical dramaturgy expresses the action and is more than an emotional accompaniment to the narrative. In the parallel performances of the first finale, Aniuta expresses a desire for love, "Serdtse v grudi / B'etsia, kak ptitsa, / I khochesh' znat', chto zhdet vperedi, / I khochetsia schast'ia dobit'sia" ("The heart in my breast / Flutters like a bird, / And you want to know what awaits you, / And you want to gain happiness"), which Kostia immediately answers: "Liubov' nechaianno nagrianet, / Kogda ee sovsem ne zhdesh'..." ("Love suddenly comes out of the blue, / When you don't expect it at all"). Their duet, "Akh, serdtse, tebe ne khochetsia pokoia! / Serdtse, kak khorosho na svete zhit'! / Serdtse, kak khorosho, chto ty takoe. / Spasibo, serdtse, chto ty umeesh' tak liubit'!" ("Oh, heart, you don't want peace! / Heart, how good it is to be alive! / Heart, how good that you are like this. / Thank you, heart, for being able to love like this!") then affirms their mutual affection, which is *verbalized* only after the curtain goes down on the performance: "Aniuta, ia davno khotel tebe skazat'" ("Aniuta, I've long wanted to tell you").

Dunaevskii and Lebedev-Kumach's "Tiukh, tiukh" chastushki at the conclusion of the first finale are a jazz-dance treatment of the traditional folk genre, a strategy he employed consciously to better etch his melodies into the popular consciousness and had already used in his "Russian Rhapsody" for Utesov's *Dzhaz na povorote* (*Jazz at the Turning Point*) music-hall program. The folk genre, accompanied by traditional Russian dance steps in the film, contributes meanings which are not articulated elsewhere in the narrative and ultimately belongs to the fairy tale register of the film. The repeating initial lines of each stanza have sexual overtones: "Tiukh, tiukh, tiukh, tiukh / Razgorelsia nash utiug" ("Puff, puff, puff, puff / Our iron has heated up"). Each stanza is performed by the relevant character as an ironic pendant to the romantic plot. As an outsider, the catafalque driver points out Kostia's errors: "Ty vliubilsia, promakhnulsia, / Vstretil damochku ne tu— / Ogorchilsia, oglianulsia i uvidel krasotu." ("You fell in love, slipped up, / met the wrong little lady— / You were upset, looked around and saw a beauty"). Kostia responds that one learns by making mistakes: "Kazhdyi mozhet oshibit'sia, / Ot liubvi my muchimsia / Ved' nedarom govoritsia, / Na oshibkakh uchimsia!" ("Anyone may make a mistake, / We're tormented by love / It's not for nothing they say / We learn from our mistakes!"). Confident as never before, Aniuta then asserts ownership of Potekhin: "Ne revnuiu ia k drugoi, / Da eto peremenitsia, / Vse ravno, on budet moi, / Nikuda ne denetsia!" ("I'm not jealous of another woman, / And this will change. / He'll be mine all the same, / He won't get away!").

In *Happy Guys*, the fairy tale stratum operates implicitly through selective analogies to the Cinderella story: the persecuted heroine is a servant to Lena and her mother, the social-climbing stepsister and stepmother. Even though Aniuta dresses in rough and clownish clothes, her beautiful voice attracts the "prince" outside the Black Swan, although he cannot see her and does not know the identity of the singer. It is only when she sings during the first finale that identity merges fully with voice, the glass slipper fits, and Aniuta is transformed into a princess.[273] Given their content and placement in the first finale, the "Tiukh-tiukh" chastushki also duplicate the codas or morals of Perrault's fairy tales. When Perrault ends his tales with two morals, the first typically pertains directly to the tale, while the second is either more generally didactic, or sometimes cynical. The first moral of his "Cinderella" tells ladies "you have but to be / Just as kind and sweet as she!"; the second moves on to godmothers and the usefulness of having friends.[274] The second moral of "Blue Beard" is more caustic: "...Then the husband ruled as king. / Now it's quite a different thing; / Be his beard what hue it may— / Madam has a word to say!"[275] The first "Tiukh-tiukh" chastushka refers directly to Potekhin's mistakes with women: "Ty vliubilsia, promakhnulsia"; the second is a general response: "Na oshibkakh uchimsia." However Aniuta's boasting in the third chastushka is cynical: "Vse ravno, on budet moi / Nikuda ne denetsia!" In later years, Aleksandrov gave *Happy Guys* a standard political-ideological reading, one that was equally appropriate to *Volga-Volga*: "The main idea is that Soviet power has opened all paths to great art for talented individuals from the people."[276] The unpromising hero or heroine always triumphs in fairy tales, and this pattern was appropriated by Stalinist culture to depict metaphorically the rising curve of its citizens' lives, the path to success which comes relatively easily and even miraculously.

Chapter 1 Endnotes

1. B. Shumiatskii report, *Za bol'shoe kinoiskusstvo* (Moscow: Kinofotoizdat, 1935) 184; G. Aleksandrov, "O sovetskoi kinokomedii," *Sovetskoe iskusstvo*, 4 Feb. 1939: 4.

2. Savchenko's *Garmon'* (*The Accordeon*), released a few months before *Happy Guys*, contained folk music, but the dramaturgy of the film was not influenced by the music.

3. "Party Cinema Conference Resolution: The Results of Cinema Construction in the USSR and the Tasks of Soviet Cinema," *The Film Factory. Russian and Soviet Cinema in Documents 1896–1939*, eds. Richard Taylor and Ian Christie (London: Routledge, 1994) 211–12.

4. *Kul'lturnaia zhizn' v SSSR. 1928–1941. Khronika*, Comp. S. N. Bazanov et al., vol. 1 (Moscow: Nauka, 1976) 260, 263–64.

5. For the effects of the 1932 decree on the music world and the delayed evolution of the Union of Soviet Composers, see Leonid Maksimenkov, *Sumbur vmesto muzyki* (Moscow: Iuridicheskaia kniga, 1997) 26–32.

6. "O G.V. Aleksandrove," I.O. Dunaevskii, *Vystupleniia. Stat'i. Pis'ma. Vospominaniia*, 33.

7. Boris Zakharovich Shumiatskii (1886–1938) joined the Bolsheviks in 1903, became active in underground work, and led armed revolts in Krasnoiarsk and Vladivostok 1905–07. To escape czarist authorities, he moved to Argentina with his family, returning to Russia only in 1913, when he joined the czarist army, while continuing revolutionary activities. In 1917, he was named chair of the executive committee of Siberian Soviets, then served in Blücher's division during the Civil War. He later served as chair of the Tiumen' and Tomsk revolutionary committees, minister of foreign affairs in the Far Eastern Republic, and chair of the Eniseisk regional executive committee. From 1923–25, he was the Soviet representative in Persia. In 1925, he was appointed to the Leningrad regional committee and then became rector of the Communist University of Eastern Workers. In 1930, he was named head of Soiuzkino and in 1933 became head of GUKF and vice-chair of the government Committee on the Arts.

   Shumiatskii had little artistic sensibility (his feuds with Eisenstein were legendary), but he was instrumental in developing the fledgling Soviet cinema industry. In 1935, he published the monograph *Cinema for the Millions* and traveled to the United States to familiarize himself with the American film industry. His plan to relocate Soviet studios to the South with an American-style construction plan was ultimately rejected by Stalin and he gradually lost influence. Shumiatskii was arrested Jan. 17, 1938 and charged with being a member of the czarist secret police, a Japanese and English spy, a Trotskyite, and the organizer of a group of film industry wreckers who had tried to poison the Politbiuro with mercury vapors at a film screening in the Kremlin. He was sentenced and executed July 29, 1938.

   For general biographical information, see: Boris Bagaev, *Boris Shumiatskii. Ocherk zhizni i deiatel'nosti* (Krasnoiarsk: Krasnoiarskoe kn. izd-vo, 1974). For an account of his career in the film industry, see Richard Taylor, "Boris Shumyatsky and the Soviet Cinema in the 1930s: Ideology as Mass Entertainment," *Historical Journal of Film, Radio and Television*, 6.1 (1986): 43–63; Richard Taylor, "A 'Cinema for the Millions': Soviet Socialist Realism and the Problem of Film Comedy," *Journal of Contemporary History*, 18 (1983): 439–61. For documents relating to his arrest and rehabilitation, see *Vernite mne svobodu*, editor-compiler V.F. Koliazin with V.A. Goncharov (Moskva: Medium, 1997) 162–68.

8. *Kul'turnaia zhizn'*, vol. 1, 289.

9. *Kul'turnaia zhizn'*, vol. 1, 323. In 1933, the Commission of the First All-Union Conference on Directorial Cadres was charged with developing a list of "approved directors" for the film industry, i.e., those permitted to make films during the following year. The aim was to ease politically unreliable directors out of the profession without harming already faltering production. "Uslovniki" (conditionally approved directors) were permitted to complete ongoing work before joining the category of "otsechennye" (literally, those cut off from the field) (RGALI f. 2456/1/75).

10. "Partiia proveriaet svoi riady," *Sovetskoe kino*, 3 (1933), qtd. in Peter Kenez, "Bezhin lug (Bezhin Meadow)," *Enemies of the People*, ed. Katherine Bliss Eaton (Evanston, IL: Northwestern University Press, 2002) 112.

11. Mikhail Dolgopolov, "'4 Komedii v 1 seans' ili 3 komedii za tselyi god," *Komsomol'skaia pravda*, 21 May 1934: 5.

12. Mikhail Dolgopolov, "Predatel'stvo Marvina Bleika" *Komsomol'skaia pravda*, 12 Aug. 1934: 6.

13. RGASPI (Russian State Archive of Social-political History), f. 17/114/351.

14. Films released: 1927—118, 1928—124, 1929—92, 1930—128 as compared to 1936—50, 1937—40, 1938—44, 1939—57. (Sergei Zemlianukhin and Miroslava Segida, *Domashniaia sinemateka. Otechestvennoe kino. 1918-1996* [Moscow: Dubl'-D, 1996] 6.)

15. O.V. Khlevniuk, *Politbiuro. Mekhanizmy politicheskoi vlasti v 1930-e gody*, (Moscow: Rosspen, 1996) 99.

16. *Komsomol'skaia pravda*, 15 Nov. 1933: 3 and 6 Jan. 1934: 3.

17. A.I. Stetskii, 25 May 1932 note to L.M. Kaganovich, *Letopis' rossiiskogo kino 1930-1945*, eds. A.S. Deriabin et al. (Moscow: Materik, 2007) 171.

18. S. Eizenshtein, "Samoe zabavnoe," *Sovetskoe iskusstvo*, 9 July 1932: 3, *Letopis' rossiiskogo kino 1930-1945*, 178.

19. Grigorii Aleksandrov, *Epokha i kino*, (Moscow: Izdatel'stvo politicheskoi literatury, 1976) 159.

20. Mark Kushnirov, 96-7. During 1932, Aleksandrov also filmed *Internatsional* (*The International*), a short propaganda film which showed Stalin, Mikoyan, and Bukharin observing a parade in Red Square and included workers' meetings in Germany and the US.

21. N. Shafer, "Zhit' i liubit' ili pir vo vremia chumy," *Muzykal'naia zhizn'*, 8 (1990): 11.

22. Grigorii Aleksandrov, "Kompozitor mysliashchii kinematografichno," *Iskusstvo kino*, 10 (1961): 107; Kushnirov, 97.

23. Jay Leyda, *Kino* (Princeton, NJ: Princeton University Press, 1983) 305.

24. Aleksandrov, *Epokha i kino*, 163. In newspaper interviews, Aleksandrov sometimes gives the date of the conference as 1933, as does Iurenev in *Sovetskaia kinokomediia* (Moscow: Nauka, 1964) 192, although this later date is unlikely, given the history of *Happy Guys* and Eisenstein's *MMM*. I. Frolov records the slogan in *Grigorii Aleksandrov* (Moscow: Iskusstvo, 1976) 21.

25. Aleksandrov, *Epokha i kino*, 163.

26. O. Shul'ga interview with Aleksandrov, "Ne chustvuiu sebia starshe ni na odin den'," *Sovetskaia kul'tura*, 22 Jan. 1983: 5.

27. An early article on Utesov's work for the film is Arkadii Bernshtein, "Madam s"ela vsiu moiu plenku," *Nedelia*, No. 52 (1994): 13.

28. Utesov recalled that the show had more than 150 performances. (Leonid Utesov, *Spasibo serdtse* [Moscow: Vagrius, 1999] 224).

29. For a plot summary of the show see Utesov, *Spasibo serdtse*, 220–22.

30. According to Iurii Nikulin, Arnol'd, who had a minor role in the film, contributed comic ideas during the filming of *Happy Guys*, among them putting a straw hat on Chamberlain, the bull (Iurii Nikulin, *Pochti ser'ezno*, [Moscow: Terra, 1994] 146).

31. "Muzykal'nyi magazin," RGALI, f. 3005/1/15.

32. Utesov, *Spasibo serdtse*, 222.

33. "Muzykal'nyi magazin," RGALI, f. 3003/1/15.

34. Aleksandrov later claimed that *he* had invited Dunaevskii to work on the film. See *Komsomol'skaia pravda*, No. 24 (1970): 2.

35. Utesov, *Spasibo serdtse*, 224–25. Utesov gives a shorter, slightly different account in Leonid Utesov, *S pesnei po zhizni*, ed. Iu. Dmitriev (Moscow: Iskusstvo, 1961) 161–63.

36. Minchenok, 226.

37. In Nikolai Erdman, Angelina Stepanova, *Pis'ma*, (Moscow: Ivan-PRESS, 1995), 27–28, the date is incorrectly given as 1931; L. Trauberg, "Order na samoubiistvo," Nikolai Erdman, *P'esy, Intermedii, Pis'ma, Dokumenty, Vospominaniia sovremennikov*, (Moscow: Iskusstvo, 1990) 448–49, 512.

38. An alternate title "Pastukh iz Abrau-Diurso" ("The Shepherd from Abrau-Diurso"), a play on both the Southern setting of the action and the famous brand of champagne produced at the czar's former Abrau-Diurso estate was also used. See, for example, Ia.L., "Kak vygliadit templan," *Kino*, 16 May 1933: 4. One early newspaper advertisement preserved by Utesov still used the title "Skripach iz Abrau" (RGALI, f. 3005/1/1113).

39. Utesov, *Spasibo serdtse*, 220.

40. Nikolai Erdman's father, Robert, had successfully played a German businessman in Barnet's *Okraina* (*The Outskirts*), released in 1933, and Aleksandrov offered him the role of Karl Ivanovich.

41. Lena Zhukovskaia was played by Mariia Strelkova (1908–1962), an actress from Teatr Lesi Ukrainki in Kiev. According to Neia Massal'skaia, Strelkova was not considered particularly talented, but was chosen for her striking good looks.

42. I have located two versions of the early *Shepherd* script: *Pastukh*, GFF (State Film Archive) and RGALI, f. 2806/1/166 are identical, except for a missing last page in the GFF script. The RGALI, f. 3005/1/14 version is very close in plot but has slightly more descriptive detail, as well as several additional jokes and dialogue elaborations that were apparently inserted as Erdman and Mass continued to work on the material.

43. The source of these and all subsequent quotations from the *Shepherd* script is GFF/RGALI, f. 2806/1/166.

44. RGALI, f. 631/3/212. This phrase is from a slightly later director's script.

45. Aleksandrov intended to paint Potekhin's face red by hand on the film stock in the manner of the flag at the conclusion of *Battleship Potemkin*.

46. Idiomatic: "He'll ruin everything for us."

47. The building of the Maksim Gorky was financed by contributions from the Russian people. It was fitted out as a propaganda plane with a printing press, film and photo equipment, a processing laboratory, film projector and screen, external loudspeaker ("Golos s neba"), and equipment to project light slogans in the sky. See various articles in *Komsomol'skaia pravda*, 18 Aug. 1933: 2–3.

48. Vertinskii petitioned to return to the USSR several times during the 1930s, but received permission only in 1943. He then began a second career as a singer and film actor.

49. See E. Len-a, " 'Dzhaz-Komediia'. Chitka i obsuzhdenie novogo komediinogo stsenariia," *Kino*, 16 April 1933: 3; "Proizvodstvennoe soveshchanie kinodramaturgov. Stenogamma," (5 June, 1933, Leningrad), RGALI, f. 631/2/3; E. Len-a, "Globokaia razvedka v oblast' komedii," *Kino*, 16 June 1933: 3.

50. E. Len-a, " 'Dzhaz-Komediia'. Chitka i obsuzhdenie novogo komediinogo stsenariia."

51. Anon., "O Dzhaz-komedii," *Kino*, 28 May 1933: 2. The newspaper account of the three-point resolution is much more complete than the text published in Aleksandrov, *Epokha i kino*, 174.

52. RGALI, f. 631/3/212. Erdman is listed here as the first author, as opposed to Aleksandrov in the GFF *Shepherd* script, probably because this copy of the director's script was submitted to the Union of Soviet Writers, where Erdman's name would carry more weight.

53. The script now lists footage and running time for each section, although these are not justified in any way. Apart from a listing of main characters, information is now provided on secondary roles and animation: *Crowd Scenes*: 50 male collective farm workers, 20 children, 50 female collective farm workers, 300—music-hall audience, 500—Bol'shoi Theatre audience; *Animals*: 15 cows, 10 sheep, 5 goats, 10 horses, 15 pigs. *Training*: dog, pigs, donkey, bull, female buffalo; *Animation*: (three-dimensional) 1) canary, 2) fishes, 3) swallows, 4) ram, 5) bull, 6) Graphics: 1) "a month has passed," 2) "two months have passed," 3) "many months have passed."

54. Sokolov reminiscences in the 1983 documentary film *Liubov' Orlova*, dir. G. Aleksandrov and E. Mikhailova.

55. Aleksandrov places his first meeting with Orlova at the Musical Theatre of Nemirovich-Danchenko where, upon the advice of Petr Vil'iams, the director in search of a female lead for his film went to see Orlova as the lead of *La Pericole* (Aleksandrov, *Epokha i kino*, 168). Kushnirov, who provides the fullest early biography of Orlova, names Planquette's operetta *Les Cloches de Corneville*, in which she played Serpolette, with the actual meeting backstage the next evening during her concert at the Ars cinema, (Kushnirov 45, 60–1, 99). Orlova may have glimpsed Aleksandrov earlier, when she was invited to audition for the role of Aniuta (Dmitrii Shcheglov, *Liubov' i maska* [Moscow: Olimp, 1997] 98–9). In a third version of their meeting, after being rejected for the role, Orlova arranged to run into Aleksandrov at a friend's apartment, seduced him, and was approved a few days later (Ivan Frolov, *Liubov' Orlova v grime i bez grima* [Moscow: Panorama, 1997] 60–1). Most recently, Saakov asserts that during the winter of 1932/33, the cartoonists Kukryniksy were living at the dom tvorchestva in Abramtsevo, where Aleksandrov, Erdman, and Mass were working on the *Happy Guys* script. Knowing that Aleksandrov was looking for a

leading lady, they suggested he go see Orlova in *La Pericole* (Iu.S. Saakov, *Liubov' Orlova. Sto bylei i sto nebylits* [Moscow: Algoritm, 2002] 178–79). Years later, in conversation with Rina Zelenaia, Orlova produced disastrous stills of her screen test for *Happy Guys*, and credited Aleksandrov with teaching the camera crew how to arrange attractive lighting for her face (Rina Zelenaia, *Razroznennye stranitsy* [Moscow: SMD RSFSR, 1987] 240).

56. "Kukryniksy" was the collective pseudonym, formed from the first syllable of their surnames, of the cartoonists Mikhail Kupriianov (1903–91), Porfirii Krylov (1902–90), and Nikolai Sokolov (1903–2000). Their satiric, grotesque, and naturalistic drawings on domestic and international topics, particularly the condemnation of fascism, capitalism, and western imperialism, were well-known during the Soviet era.

57. Anon., "Dzhaz-komediia vstupila v s"emochnyi period," *Kino*, 4 June 1933: 4; Kukryniksy, "Pis'mo v redaktsiiu," *Kino*, 16 Aug. 1933: 4; Darevskii, "Pis'mo v redaktsiiu," *Kino*, 22 Sept. 1933: 4.

58. The drawings are located in RGALI, f. 1923/2/1646, f. 1923/1/364, f. 2753/1/98 (photographs).

59. Eisenstein's inscription at the bottom of the drawing reveals its autobiographical source: "Ein Schweres Instrument (1853) (man muss es frühzeitig erlernen) (Dvoenie edinogo)."

60. See reproduction in Iu. Saakov, "Secha v kommunal'noi kvartire," *Iskusstvo kino*, 2 (1995): 141.

61. The variant sketch of this subject shows the man with a bandaged face, in short underpants, from which protrude his hairy legs. With one hand he tries to play the erect horn or clarinet that protrudes from his nearby pants.

62. On Eisenstein's preoccupations in his drawings, see for example, S.M. Eisenstein, *Dessins Secrets* (Paris: Éditions du Seuil, 1999).

63. 29 May 1933 receipt for 1,500 rubles. RGALI, f. 1923/1/365.

64. Anon., "Dzhaz-komediia" vstupila v s"emochnyi period," *Kino*, 4 June 1933: 4.

65. Gr. Aleksandrov, "Nam pesnia stroit' i zhit' pomogaet . . .," *Dunaevskii. Vystupleniia. Stat'i. Pis'ma. Vospominaniia*, 284.

66. Arkadii Bernshtein, "Gollivud bez kheppi-enda. Sud'ba i tvorchestvo Vladimira Nil'sena," *Kinovedcheskie zapiski*, 60 (2001): 225. Aleksandrov later told one of his students, Ivan Frolov, that Eisenstein was not involved (Ivan Frolov, *Grigorii Aleksandrov* [Moscow: Iskusstvo, 1976] 47). According to Kushnirov (98), after viewing the completed film, Eisenstein quipped, "Da, ne nashi rebiata!" ("They're not our guys!").

67. Information from Neia Aleksandrovna Massal'skaia (Interview with R. Salys, 2002). A musical brawl does not seem to have been part of the *Music Store* show, as claimed by Frolov (*Liubov Orlova v grime i bez grima*, 83); it does not appear in the script nor is it mentioned in the memoirs of Utesov's musicians.

68. Aleksandrov, *Epokha i kino*, 166.

69. G. Aleksandrov, "Veselye rebiata," *Sovetskii ekran*, 12 (1967): 20.

70. I. Dunaevskii, "O G.V. Aleksandrove," *Dunaevskii. Vystupleniia. Stat'i. Pis'ma. Vospominaniia*, 34.

71. Arkadii Kotliarskii, *Spasibo dzhazu*, (Leningrad: Khudozhestvennaia literatura, 1990) 33–4.

72. A. Savenkov, "S pesnei po zhizni," *Leningradskaia pravda*, 2 March 1983. Nikolai Pavlovskii recalls that he was offered the job after Aleksandrov saw him in a music-hall acrobatic act which included comic fight sequences (L. Iukhnevich, "Odin iz 'Veselykh rebiat'," *Ogni Mangyshlaka*, 17 Sept. 1977).

73. Anonymous untitled note in *Kino*, 10 July 1933: 3; Anonymous, "Snimaetsia 'Dzhaz-komediia'," *Kino*, 16 July 1933: 3.

74. Kotliarskii, 35.

75. Anon., "Vozmutitel'no, no fakt," *Kino*, 8 Aug. 1933: 3.

76. RGASPI, f. 17/114/365.

77. Shumiatskii's explanation in his "Trudneishii zhanr osvoen," *Kino*, 16 Dec. 1934: 2.

78. Kushnirov, 90.

79. Kushnirov (113) names the "Black Swan" number at the Foreger Theatre, a parody of the Saint-Saens-Fokin "Swan," as the source for the name of the hotel.

80. Undated N. R. Erdman letter to V. B. Erdman in Erdman, *P'esy, Intermedii, Pis'ma, Dokumenty, Vospominaniia sovremennikov*, 247–48. The editors incorrectly attribute the letter to 1931.

81. Gerald Mast, *Can't Help Singin': The American Musical on Stage and Screen* (Woodstock, NY: Overlook Press, 1987) 92.

82. I. Dunaevskii, "Moia rabota nad pesnei v kinofil'me," (draft) in *Dunaevskii. Vystupleniia . Stat'i. Pis'ma. Vospominaniia*, 378.

83. Anon., "Zheleznaia doroga na pliazhe," *Komsomol'skaia pravda*, 5 Oct. 1933: 4; N.T., "Dzhaz-komediia," *Kino*, 28 May 1934: 2.

84. A. Danel'ian, "Po sledam 'Veselykh rebiat'," *Sovetskaia Abkhazia*, 11 Feb. 1982.

85. See RGALI, f. 3005/1/44 for three photographs of this ending. Aleksandrov later said that he was unable to use this conclusion because Utesov did not have the right timing to make the episode funny. (G. Aleksandrov, "Snaiperskoe iskustvo," *Kino*, No. 24 [1939]: 3.)

86. Elena Tiapkina, "Zhizn'—tvorchestvo," *Iskusstvo kino*, 10 (1982): 84–5.

87. V. Nil'sen, 26 Sept. 1933 letter to M. M. Shtraukh, RGALI, f. 2758/1/1396.

88. Undated L. Utesov letter to E. O. Utesova, RGALI, f. 3005/1/99.

89. Vitalii Shentalinskii, *Donos na Sokrata* (Moscow: Formika-S, 2001) 431. For documents relating to the arrests, see G. G. Iagoda's 9 July 1933 letter to Stalin about the fables of Erdman, Mass, and Vol'pin in *Vlast' i khudozhestvennaia intelligentsia 1917–1953*, comp. Andrei Artizov and Oleg Naumov (Moscow: MFD, 1999) 202–3 and *Vernite mne svobodu*, 14–20.

90. L. Utesov, 18 Oct. 1933 letter to E. O. Utesova, RGALI, f. 3005/1/99. For the apparently apocryphal story of Utesov's giving his coat to Erdman or Mass, see A. Khrzhanovskii, "Iz zametok i vospominanii o N.R. Erdmana," Erdman, *P'esy, intermedii, pis'ma, dokumenty, vospominaniia sovremennikov*, 386–87.

91. Aleksandrov's "Odnikh uzh net, drugie, smotrish'—perebity" is a misquotation of Skalozub's "To starshikh vykliuchat inykh, / Drugie, smotrish', perebity," ("They're letting go some of the older people / Others have been killed one after another") from Griboedov's *Gore ot uma*. The phrase

is part of Skalozub's explanation to Famusov of the reasons for his rapid advance in the army. Aleksandrov is referring to the arrests of Erdman and Mass and, perhaps unconsciously, identifies himself with the careerist Skalozub, who is glad to have troublesome rivals conveniently out of the way.

92. "¿Quién sabe?" ("Who knows?").

93. G. Aleksandrov, 29 Oct. 1933 letter to S. Eisenstein, RGALI, f. 1923/1/1606. During 1931, Eisenstein, Tisse, and Aleksandrov shot much of *Que Viva Mexico!* at Hacienda de Tetlapayac. In the letter to Eisenstein, Aleksandrov enclosed a photograph of himself talking to Utesov and two of the camera crew by the "Prozrachnye kliuchi" gates. The verso is inscribed: Gagry 1933, Bzybskoe Ushchel'e, "Dzhaz Komediia."

94. L. Utesov, letters to E. O. Utesova, undated and 10 May 1934, RGALI, f.3005/1/99.

95. L. Utesov, 22 May 1934 letter to E. O. Utesova, RGALI, f.3005/1/99.

96. *Za bol'shoe kinoiskusstvo* (Moscow: Kinofotoizdat, 1935) 149.

97. Anonymous, " 'Tragediia' s 'Dhzaz-komediei'," *Za bol'shevistskii fil'm*, 27 (1933): 4.

98. V., "Shturmovaia gruppa," *Kino*, 16 Jan. 1934: 2; K.E., "Snabzhaiut brakom," *Kino*, 16 Jan. 1934: 3.

99. Quoted in Frolov, *Grigorii Aleksandrov*, 28.

100. Mikhail Dolgopolov, "Veselye prikliucheniia pastukha Kosti," *Komsomol'skaia pravda*, 10 Jan. 1934: 4.

101. Aleksandrov, *Epokha i kino*, 178.

102. Aleksandrov, *Epokha i kino*, 162.

103. Aleksandrov's anthropomorphized animals illustrate Marfa's symbolic sexual progress as she brings home the young bull for the collective, then dreams of the cow's wedding and mating with the bull (a substitute for her own), is sprayed by the phallic cream separator, plays out the coy seduction scene with the tractor driver, whose male potency she assimilates at the end of the film when she reveals herself as tractor driver to two village lovers.

104. Aleksandrov, *Epokha i kino*, 178–79. Some of the animal scenes were filmed in the Red Room of the Metropol' (Frolov, *Liubov' Orlova v grime i bez grima*, 235).

105. Aleksandrov, *Epokha i kino*, 180. An episode with Erast Garin as a veterinarian tending the collective's cows was shot, but not included in the film. (See photo in Erast Garin, "Avtokinografiia," *Iz istorii kino*, Vypusk 7, eds. S.S. Ginzburg et al., [Moscow: Iskusstvo, 1968] 134.)

106. L. Kudinova, "Narodnaia artistka," *Sovetskii ekran*, 5 (1967): 7.

107. Aleksandrov, *Epokha i kino*, 181. In his memoirs, Aleksandrov casts Orlova as a volunteer rider (180), but her own earlier version is more likely to be true. (Saakov, *Liubov' Orlova. Sto bylei i sto nebylits* [Moscow: Algoritm, 2002] 172). The footage of Orlova beating a galloping Aleksandrov survives and has been shown in television programs about the actress.

108. Kushnirov, 117.

109. Aleksandrov, *Epokha i kino*, 181.

110. G.V. Aleksandrov, "'Veselym rebiatam'—30 let," *Sovetskii fil'm*, No. 51 (1964): 4.

111. I. Dunaevskii, 24 Oct. 1954 letter to R. Ivanycheva, in Dunaevskii, *Izbrannye pis'ma*, 219. N. Shafer notes that Dunaevskii's *Russian Rhapsody*, composed for Utesov's music-hall program *Dzhaz na povorote*, was preparatory to the "Tiukh-tiukh" chastushki with jazz in the finale of *Happy Guys* (N. Shafer, *Dunaevskii segodnia* [Moscow: Sovetskii kompozitor, 1988] 36).

112. G. Aleksandrov, "I. Dunaevskii i V. Lebedev-Kumach," *Iskusstvo kino*, 6 (1938): 8.

113. "Love, love—golden summer lightning. / In you is happiness, and pain, and misfortune. / And I can't get away from you, I can't escape, / can't run away or bury myself anywhere." (Aleksandrov, *Epokha i kino*, 167).

114. "Oh, mountains, mountains, high mountains, / Yesterday there was fog and in my heart—anguish, / Today your snowy tracery / Burns again and is visible from afar. / Giddyap, lift your legs higher, / Giddyap, don't hold things up, Bull! / Be well, Citizeness Cow! / Pleasant journey, respected Bull!" Utesov, *Spasibo serdtse*, 226; Kushnirov, 116. In *The Shepherd*, Potekhin's morning procession was indeed called "Korovii marsh" (The Cows' March).

115. Leonid Utesov, "O druge i soratnike" in *I.O. Dunaevskii. Vystupleniia. Stat'i. Pis'ma. Vospominaniia*, 280.

116. Utesov, *Spasibo serdtse*, 227.

117. Aleksandrov, *Epokha i kino*, 167. In earlier interviews, Aleksandrov claims to have singled out Lebedev-Kumach's verse from among thirty-six responses to the newspaper announcement (G. Aleksandrov, "Veselye rebiata," *Sovetskii ekran*, 12 (1967): 20 and Grigorii Aleksandrov, "Kompozitor-kinematografist," *Sovetskii fil'm*, 1 (1975): 41). In a 1972 interview, Aleksandrov describes "hundreds" of responses and blurs the circumstances of Lebedev-Kumach's appearance: "Hundreds of poems were sent in. We suggested to Lebedev-Kumach that he write about the dreams of our young people" (G. Aleksandrov, "S pesnei po zhizni shagaet," *Molodezh' Azerbaidzhana*, 8 Jan. 1972).

118. See for example, the calls for songs or text and music for songs in *Komsomol'skaia pravda*, 2 and 5 Dec. 1933; 9 Jan. and 12 July 1934.

119. Aleksandrov, "Kompozitor-kinematografist," 41.

120. V. Nil'sen, "Transparantnyi tsekh," *Kino*, 22 March 1934: 3; Mikhail Dolgopolov, "'Chudesnyi tsekh' Sovetskoi kinematografii," *Komsomol'skaia pravda*, 28 April 1934: 4. Rear projection was first employed in Russia by Aleksandrov for his 1932 short film *The International*.

121. V. Nil'sen, "Transparantnyi tsekh."

122. See Nik. Renkov, "Izobrazitel'naia traktovka 'Veselykh rebiat'," *Sovetskoe kino*, 1 (1935): 37–42.

123. Mikhail Dolgopolov, "Veselye prikliucheniia pastukha Kosti."

124. N.T., "Dzhaz-komediia."

125. Anon. note, *Za Bol'shevistskii fil'm*, 10 June 1934: 1.

126. B. Shumiatskii, "Pis'mo v redaktsiiu," *Kino*, 22 Dec. 1934: 3.

127. B. Shumiatskii, "Trudneishii zhanr osvoen," *Kino*, 16 Dec. 1934: 2.

128. Aleksandrov, *Epokha i kino*, 183–84.

129. Boris Shumiatskii, "Moia zapis' besedy s I.V. na prosmotre fil'm 13.VII s 21 chasa do 1 ch. nochi na 14.VII.1934 g." RGASPI, f. 558, op. 11, d. 828, ll. 46-50; Nikolai Sidorov, "'Veselye rebiata'—Komediia kontrrevoliutsionnaia," *Istochnik*, 3 (1995): 72–8. Inaccurate excerpts from the letter were published in O. Iumasheva, "Kak Kostia Potekhin ne ugodil Bol'shevikam," *Ekran*, 5/6 (1993): 43. Most of the text has been published in G. Skorokhodov, "Gor'kii smotrit 'Veselykh rebiat'," *Literaturnaia gazeta*, 26 June 1974: 8. See also K. Iukov's article, "Gor'kii o kino," *Kino*, 22 June 1936. The original is in RGALI, f. 2450/2/266.

130. Sidorov, 73. Shumiatskii's notes make it obvious that Voroshilov had seen at least part of the film before July 13.

131. Saakov, "Secha v kommunal'noi kvartire," 140. This text is more complete than what appears in Aleksandrov's *Epokha i kino*. Saakov's speculation about Stalin's order to remove the collective farm sub-plot and socialist realism joke appears unfounded.

132. Shumiatskii probably kept his records with an eye to their falling into the hands of the secret police. Party officials are mostly referred to respectfully by name and patronymic: I. V. Stalin, K. E. Voroshilov, L. M. Kaganovich, but Zhdanov.

133. B. Shumiatskii, "Moia zapis' besedy s I.V na prosmotre fil'm."

134. B. Shumiatskii, "Moia beglaia zapis' besedy s Iosifom Vissarionovichem 21.VII-1934 g.", RGASPI, f. 558, op. 11, d. 828, ll. 51-2.

135. Shumiatskii's notes on who was present at this screening must be incomplete since Molotov and Enukidze had been present at the first screening.

136. Shumiatskii, "Moia beglaia zapis' besedy s Iosifom Vissarionovichem 21.VII-1934 g."

137. Shumiatskii, "Moia beglaia zapis' besedy s Iosifom Vissarionovichem 21. VII-1934 g." Stalin's remark led to an initiative to boost the distribution of audio recordings.

138. Frolov, *Grigorii Aleksandrov*, 32.

139. *Dezertir* (1933), dir. V. Pudovkin, *Vosstanie rybakov* (1934), dir. M. Doller, *Garmon'* (1934), I. Savchenko.

140. Sidorov, 74. The next day, Shumiatskii sent a copy of the letter to Stalin to Voroshilov, asking for his help and explaining that the instigator of the trouble was Bubnov, who was unhappy that the film industry had not been placed under his ministry, Narkompros (Sidorov, 75). Bubnov, who is notorious for the stalinization of Russian education, was arrested and perished, along with Shumiatskii, in 1938.

141. 10 June 1934, issue 1.

142. Frolov, *Liubov' Orlova v grime i bez grima*, 83.

143. In addition, Iukov's detailed notes on the screening at Gorky's dacha make no mention of a title change.

144. *Cabin in the Cotton*, 1932, directed by Michael Curtiz.

145. Committee members present were Stetskii, philosopher and Party activist P. F. Iudin, literary historian V. Ia. Kirpotin, historian I. I. Mints, and A. Bolotnikov, editor of *Literaturnaia gazeta*, the newspaper which later attacked *Happy Guys*.

146. *Groza* (1934), directed by Vladimir Petrov.

147. RGALI, f. 2450/2/266.

148. Aleksandrov, *Epokha i kino*, 183–84.

149. Typed note dated 10 Aug. 1934 from Iukov to Assistant GUKF director Ia. E. Chuzhin, RGALI, f. 2450/2/266.

150. *Mechtateli* (1934), directed by Vladimir Balliuzek.

151. RGALI, f.2456/1/116 and B. Shumiatskii, *Sovetskii fil'm na mezhdunarodnoi kinovystavke* (Moscow: Kinofotoizdat, 1938) 14–17.

152. RGALI, f. 2456/1/116, 117, 118, 121. *Cheliuskin* (1934), directed by Iakov Posel'skii; *Peterburgskaia noch'* (1934), directed by G. Roshal' and V. Stroeva. A brown-haired Orlova played a dancer in the second film.

153. In an interview after his return from Italy, Shumiatskii noted that the Germans and, to some degree, the English filmmakers at the festival had remarked that, in spite of the success of *Happy Guys*, comedy was not Soviet cinema's strong suit, that it should make serious films (I. Rod., "Sovetskii fil'm v Venetsii," *Komsomol'skaia pravda*, 4 Sept. 1934: 4).

154. See excerpted reviews and Charlie Chaplin's statement in Aleksandrov, *Epokha i kino*, 185–86. The film premiered at the Cameo Theatre in New York City on 21 March 1935.

155. Shumiatskii, *Sovetskii fil'm na mezhdunarodnoi kinovystavke*, 111.

156. An example of the violent controversy in the film industry is a 25 Sept. 1934 letter from an administrator, possibly Darevskii, to Iukov regarding supposed opposition to *Happy Guys*: "You have told me about the rumors reaching you that I supposedly don't like the film *Happy Guys* and that the rumors about its prohibition being circulated by someone are not being refuted by me, and what is more, are being encouraged by me. Putting aside conversations about 'like' and 'don't like,' I categorically and indignantly reject any gossip that I might have anything whatsover to do with those who disseminate malicious rumors about the prohibition of the picture. And I insist that you name the persons who are disseminating these filthy rumors. Then, in their presence, we will determine to whose benefit and with what aim this gossip about me is being disseminated. As you see, such unbearable conditions relating to me and my work have arisen that I am forced once again to earnestly ask that you accept my official request to release me from my job." RGALI, f. 2450/2/266, published in Saakov, "Secha v kommunal'noi kvartire," 142.

157. Congress of Writers record, qtd. in Boris Shumiatskii, *Kinematograf millionov* (Moscow: Gudok, 1936) 238.

158. 30 Oct. 1934, Shumiatskii notes, qtd. in *Letopis' rossiiskogo kino 1930–1945*, 294.

159. Georgii Berezko, "Veselye rebiata," *Literaturnaia gazeta*, 15 Aug. 1934: 4.

160. O. Davydov, "Iskusstvo veselogo triuka," *Pravda*, 18 Nov. 1934: 2. *Izvestiia* similarly gave general praise, but criticized the unrealistic plot and wholesale borrowing of foreign comedy devices (E. Mikhailov, "Veselye rebiata," *Izvestiia*, 17 Nov. 1934: 4).

161. Anon., "Podlinnoe iskusstvo sotsializma," *Literaturnaia gazeta*, 18 Nov. 1934: 1.

162. "'Veselye rebiata.' Beseda s rezhisserom G. Aleksandrovym," *Kino*, 22 Nov. 1934: 1.

163. *Vstrechnyi* (1932), directed by F. Ermler, S. Iutkevich, and L. Arnshtam.

164. Anon., "Chto est' 'bokovaia liniia'," *Komsomol'skaia pravda*, 27 Nov. 1934: 4.

165. Anon., "Chto est' 'rappovskii naskok'?" *Literaturnaia gazeta*, 28 Nov. 1934: 4; Anon., "Posledniaia 'Barrikada' Literaturnoi gazety," *Komsomol'skaia pravda*, 30 Nov. 1934: 4. See also the attacks and counterracks not cited in the main text: Anon., "Ve-e-selye rebiata v 'Literaturnoi gazete'," *Komsomol'skaia pravda*, 22 Nov. 1934: 4; Boris Shumiatskii, "Kto zhe liudi inskusstva v kavychkakh. Pis'mo v redaktsiiu," *Literaturnaia gazeta*, 24 Nov. 1934; Anon., "Otvet po sushchestvu," *Literaturnaia gazeta*, 24 Nov. 1934.

166. RGALI, f. 2450/2/266.

167. A limited number of records were cut using the soundtrack in the small Leningrad atelier of inventors Vladimir Zaikin and Valentin Tovstoles and technician Lidiia Abramovich (G. Skorokhodov, *Zvezdy sovetskoi estrady* [Moscow: Sovetskii kompozitor, 1986] 41).

168. Five different posters are preserved in Utesov's archive, RGALI, f. 3005/1/1113.

169. RGALI, f. 2450/2/266. The text was partially published in Saakov, "Secha v kommunal'noi kvartire," 141.

170. RGALI, f. 2450/2/266. Partly published in Saakov, "Secha v kommunal'noi kvartire," 141–42.

171. RGALI, f. 3005/1/1113 and f. 2539/1/88. At the Dom kino screening, Aleksandrov inscribed the sheet music of the march as a gift to Eisenstein: "To My Dear Teacher, who taught me something else. Grisha." (Saakov, *Liubov' Orlova. Sto bylei i nebylits*, 53).

172. Grigorii Aleksandrov, "Komediia nikomu ne nuzhna, krome...zritelia," *Sovetskii ekran*, 23 (1974): 19. See also their doggerel quatrains based on Lermontov and Pushkin, which were used for advertising (Kushnirov, 128): "Comrade viewer, / The main hero in this show / Will be ringing laughter. / After all, you've come to us to relax, isn't that so? / Well, laughter has always been a rest for everyone. / Set aside your cares for an hour or two. / May the story of talented Kostia, / Aniuta's love and the merry jazz / Amuse you today. / May the song heard over "Clear Springs" / Captivate you with its energy. / May the screen with its merry rays / Energize you for tomorrow's tasks. / And tomorrow at the factory, at the ministry / You'll smile slightly perhaps / Remembering the jazz orchestra in its ridiculous damp clothes, / The happy beach and gloomy bull. / Catch the song motif that runs away. / May everyone begin to sing our song. / After all, whoever goes through life singing / Will never be lost anywhere!"

173. Qtd. in T. Rokotov, "Smekh na ekrane," *Vecherniaia Moskva*, 16 Nov. 1934: 3.

174. A. Macheret, "Zavoevat' stratosferu smekha i vesel'ia," *Za bol'shevistskii fil'm*, 13 Aug. 1934: 1.

175. F. Ermler, "Kartina raduet," *Kino*, 16 Dec. 1934: 2.

176. Announcements of the première: "Veselye rebiata," *Komsomol'skaia pravda*, 24 Dec. 1934: 4 and V.U., "Veselye rebiata," *Izvestiia*, 24 Dec. 1934. Kushnirov is uncertain about the date and names the Khudozhestvennyi as the site of the première, describing the elaborate advertising on its facade: "Today and Every Day of the Season the Jazz-Comedy "Happy Guys." Below were two columns of text intended to arouse the curiosity of passersby. On one side was a quotation from one of Aleksandrov's public statements on the film: "The Director—Aleksandrov, The Problem of the Work—Laughter, The Theme—Liveliness, The Task—Optimism, The Form—Musical Comedy," on the other—"The action takes place in the Caucasus and later in Moscow." In the eclectic style of the time, the space between placards was decorated with alternating jazz instruments, portraits

of Orlova, Utesov, Arnol'd, and the animal actors, with a stanza from the "March of the Happy Guys" printed below (108–9).

177. Minchenok, 276-77.

178. Kritik, "O smekhe i 'smekhe'," *Sovetskoe kino*, 1 (1935): 26–7.

179. K. Iukov, "O smekhe i 'Kritike'," *Sovetskoe kino*, 1 (1935): 33, 36.

180. Utesov, *Spasibo serdtse*, 231. In November 1936, Molotov agreed to the "Znak pocheta" award for Utesov in recognition of his work in *Happy Guys*, but nothing came of the idea. (See 19 Nov. 1936 Shumiatskii note, RGASPI, f. 82/2/957).

181. Aleksandrov, *Epokha i kino*, 187.

182. Arkadii Bernshtein, "Chelovek iz dzhaza," *Rossiiskaia gazeta*, 21 Mar. 1995: 7 and Arkadii Bernshtein, "Madam s"ela vsiu moiu plenku," 13.

183. B. Shumiatskii, "Muzykal'naia kul'tura v kino," *Pravda*, 8 Apr. 1935. Utesov's orchestra used the march from *Happy Guys* as its opening number at least through the sixties (V. Maliugin, "Sud'ba odnoi kinokomedii," *Gor'kovskaia pravda*, 4 Dec. 1964). Utesov was fated to have one more difficult experience relating to the film: when *Happy Guys* was restored in 1958, Utesov and Orlova's voices were replaced by those of Vladimir Troshin and Leokadiia Maslennikova. Utesov blamed Aleksandrov for the betrayal, even though Orlova's voice had also been deleted. (See Utesov, *Spasibo serdtse*, 231 and G. Skorokhodov, *V poiskakh utrachennogo* [Moscow: Rutena, 2000] 390.) After Nikita Bogoslovskii complained about the change in a 1966 *Izvestiia* article, A.V. Romanov, chair of the government's Cinematography Committee, announced that the original soundtrack would be restored, which finally occurred in 1978 (Arkadii Bernshtein, "Chelovek iz dzhaza," 7; E. Maksimova, "I vnov'—'Veselye rebiata'," *Komsomol'skaia pravda*, 7 Feb. 1979).

184. See Zapisi Shumiatskogo, No. 26, RGASPI, f. 558, op. 11, d. 829, ll. 32-35. Simon Montefiore mistakenly cites the first stanza of the march as an example of Stalin's songwriting. See Montefiore, *Stalin: The Court of the Red Tsar* (NY: Knopf, 2004) 163.

185. RGALI, f. 3005/1/745.

186. RGALI, f. 1104/1/7.

187. RGALI, f. 2570/1/74. *Novye liudi* never materialized.

188. N.R. Erdman, 14 Feb. 1935 letter to V.B. Erdman in Erdman, *P'esy, intermedii, pis'ma, dokumenty, vospominaniia sovremennikov*, 255–56. Erdman's comment about poor postsynching refers to the new text of "March of the Happy Guys," which was superimposed on the footage filmed in Gagry.

189. V. Skuratnik, "I znachitel'no i veselo," *Sotsialisticheskaia industriia*, 17 Aug. 1974: 4.

190. Aleksandrov, *Epokha i kino*, 186.

191. The 1934 film, directed by Jack Conway, is a fictionalized biography of Pancho Villa. The salon piece "Adelita" was actually composed by Spanish guitarist Francisco Tarrega (1852–1906), but its popularity led to its being considered a Mexican folksong.

192. A. Bezymenskii, "Karaul! Grabiat!," *Literaturnaia gazeta*, 28 Feb. 1935: 4. The first account of the conflict, based on documentary material, appeared in Matthias Stadelmann, *Isaak Dunaevskij—Sänger des Volkes*, 116–25.

193. G. Aleksandrov, I. Dunaevskii, "Pis'ma v redaktsiiu," *Kino*, 5 March 1935: 4.

194. A. Bezymenskii, "Legche na povorotakh!" and Bruno Iasenskii, "O dvukh neudachnykh popytkakh," *Literaturnaia gazeta*, 6 March 1935: 6.

195. S. Kirsanov, "O pol'ze chteniia entsiklopedii dazhe maloi," *Literaturnaia gazeta*, 6 March 1935: 7.

196. RGALI, f. 2062/1/332.

197. "Zakliuchenie ekspertnoi komissii," *Kino*, 10 March 1935: 4. Musicologist N. Shafer also sees a similarity between the "Tot nikogda i nigde ne propadet" line and the folk song "Iz za ostrova na strezhen'" (N. Shafer, *Dunaevskii segodnia*, 36).

198. I. Dunaevskii, 13 March 1935 letter to G. Aleksandrov, Dunaevskii family archive, Moscow.

199. G. Aleksandrov, "I. Dunaevskii i V. Lebedev-Kumach," *Iskusstvo kino*, 6 (1938): 8–9.

200. Al. Romanov, *Liubov' Orlova v iskusstve i v zhizni* (Moscow: Iskusstvo, 1987), 114; L. Pinchuk, "Dunaevskii-kinematografist," *Iskusstvo kino*, 10 (1961): 93; G. Sveshnikov, "Pesnia o rodine," *Sovetskii ekran*, 17 (1980): 14.

201. Qtd. in I.L. Dolinskii, *Sovetskaia kinokomediia tridtsatykh godov* (Moscow: Vsesoiuznyi gosudarstvennyi institut kinematografii, 1957) 11.

202. B. Shumiatskii, "Novyi pokhod Mal'bruka," *Kino*, 10 March 1935: 4.

203. See B. Shumiatskii, 8 March 1935 letter to the editor of *Literaturnaia gazeta*, RGALI, f. 634/1/320. For more details on the polemic in the press, see Stadelmann 133–34.

204. *Letopis' rossiiskogo kino 1930-1945*, 325.

205. Anon., "Ob itogakh kinofestivalia i besprintsipnoi polemike," *Pravda*, 12 March 1935: 1.

206. 13 March 1935 letter to Aleksandrov, Iu. E. Biriukov archive, Moscow.

207. Anon., "Ot redaktsii," *Literaturnaia gazeta*, 15 March 1935:1; A. Bezymenskii, "Pis'mo v redaktsiiu," *Pravda*, 15 March 1935: 6.

208. I. O. Dunaevskii, 20 March 1935 letter to G. Aleksandrov, Dunaevskii family archive, Moscow.

209. Reprint of *Pravda*, "Ob itogakh" article with editorial comments, *Kino*, 16 March 1935: 1; Anon., "Ot redaktsii" *Kino,* 16 March 1935: 4.

210. Review in French journal *Marianna*, qtd. in B. Iasenskii, "O dvukh neudachnykh popytkakh," *Literaturnaia gazeta*, 6 March 1935: 6.

211. Slava Tsukerman quotes Eisenstein in "Veselye rebiata," Radio Svoboda program, 2002, http://www.svoboda.org/programs/cicles/cinema/russian/happyguys.asp. Accessed 10 January 2007.

212. Quoted in T. Rokotov, "Smekh na ekrane," *Vecherniaia Moskva*, 16 Nov. 1934: 3. Whether or not Aleksandrov literally meant twelve attractions is unclear. In any case, there seem to be several more than twelve in the film.

213. Aleksandrov, *Gody poiskov*, 63.

214. Sergei Eisenstein, "The Montage of Attractions," in *The Eisenstein Reader*, ed. Richard Taylor, trans. Richard Taylor and William Powell (London: BFI Publishing, 1998) 31.

215. Kushnirov, 86–7.

216. Altman, 200.

217. Jane Feuer, *The Hollywood Musical* (Bloomington and Indianapolis: Indiana University Press, 1993) 55–6, 62.

218. Feuer, 54–59.

219. Aleksandrov, *Epokha i kino*, 23–4.

220. Aleksandrov, *Epokha i kino*, 20.

221. Aleksandrov, *Gody poiskov*, 19.

222. For a plot summary of the 1930 film, which has not survived, see Aleksandrov, *Epokha i kino*, 112 and Iu. A. Fedosiuk, *Utro krasit nezhnym svetom... Vospominaniia o Moskve 1920–1930-x godov* (Moscow: Flinta-Nauka, 2003) 185–86. Eisenstein disapproved of the script for ideological reasons (RGALI, f. 1923/1/1029).

223. David Bordwell, Janet Staiger, and Kristin Thompson, *The Classical Hollywood Cinema* (NY: Columbia University Press, 1985) 3–41.

224. Steve Seidman, *Comedian Comedy: A Tradition in Hollywood Film* (Ann Arbor, MI: UMI Research Press, 1979) 54.

225. 1974 Aleksandrov interview in V. Druzhbinskii, "Ochepatka ili tridtsat' let i tri goda," *Ekran*, 9 (1995): 31.

226. V. Platova, "Ironiia i smekh," *Kino*, 16 Dec. 1934: 2.

227. Aleksandrov in *Za bol'shoe kinoiskusstvo*, 150. The sense is that Americans are parodying their own subjects.

228. Iasenskii, 6.

229. A simpler early model is Lubitsch's *Monte Carlo* (1930) in which Jeannette MacDonald sings from the window of a train and the melody is picked up by peasants in the fields.

230. Tom Gunning, "Crazy Machines in the Garden of Forking Paths: Mischief Gags and the Origins of American Film Comedy," *Classical Hollywood Comedy*, 91–2.

231. Gunning, 92.

232. Fedosiuk, 108. In Zoshchenko's "Rasskaz o bespokoinom starike," a white, horse-drawn chariot with torches arrives to collect the dead man.

233. "Tvorcheskoe soveshchanie, sozvannoe Komitetom po delam kinematografii v Dome kino po voprosu o razvitii sovetskoi kinokomedii, 16–17 noiabria 1939 goda," *Zhivye golosa kino*, 141.

234. The common trap door gag occurs, for example, in Chaplin's *Behind the Screen*.

235. Years later Aleksandrov told his VGIK students: "Funny acts are usually built on extreme contrast" (Frolov, *Grigorii Aleksandrov*, 40). The sources for the gag terminology in this section are: Dan Kamin, *Charlie Chaplin's One-Man Show* (Carbondale: Southern Illinois University Press, 1991); Noël Carroll, "Notes on the Sight Gag," *Comedy/Cinema/Theory*, 25–42.

236. This is another traditional gag: Dan Rice, the first great American clown, used his one-ring circus as a comic forum for cultural and political debate employing trained horses, pigs, and mules named Daniel Webster, Stephen Douglas, and Ulysses S. Grant (Ron Jenkins, *Subversive Laughter. The Liberating Power of Comedy* [New York: The Free Press, 1994] 171–72).

237. During a 1937 visit to Moscow, Frank Capra praised the cleverness of this gag, although the basic idea is an old one (RGALI, f. 2456/1/200). In *Hard Times*, Dickens speaks of wires as music paper and Tsvetaeva mentions sparrows instead of notes on a greeting card given to her mother in M. Tsvetaeva, "Mat' i muzyka," *Sobranie sochinenii v semi tomakh*, vol. 5, eds. A.A. Saakiants and L.A. Mnukhin (Moscow: Ellis Lak, 1994) 10–31.

238. See Peter Meijes Tiersma, *Language-Based Humor in the Marx Brothers Films* (Bloomington, IN: Indiana University Linguistics Club, 1985).

239. The humor lies in the double meanings of words:

—There are a lot of us there...Dutch ladies/cows/, Swiss ladies/cows/...
—Are they beautiful?
—Who?
—The Dutch.
—The Dutch ladies/cows/ are splendid. Sides—like this. Eyes—like this!
—Do you take care of/flirt/ with them?
—You bet, from morning to night!
—How I would like to be in their place!

240. —Is this playing? You must play like the shoemaker!
—Karl Ivanovich, you're picking on me. I can't play like the shoemaker. The shoemaker has been studying with you for six years, but this is only my second year.

241. See Henry Jenkins and Kristine Brunovska Karnick, "Introduction: Acting Funny," *Classical Hollywood Comedy*, 63–122.

242. The large card bears the initials PB for Pokhoronnoe biuro (Undertaker's office), together with representations of a bone and what appears to be a feather. For a close-up of the card, see L. Mamotova, *Shedevry rossiiskogo kino* (Moscow: Izd-vo Andreevskii flag, 2000) 152.

243. Similarly, in Disney's *Klondike Kid* cartoon (1932), Mickey and Minnie are about the kiss at the end of the film, when Pluto comes up between them.

244. Erdman himself was a lover of horseracing.

245. In the *Shepherd* script, the animal roll call includes Pat and Patashon, a reference to early Danish slapstick comedians Schenstrom and Madsen, and is another self-reflexive comment on the gags of the film.

246. Aleksandrov, *Epokha i kino*, 131. See Anne Nesbet's overview in Nesbet, *Savage Junctures. Sergei Eisenstein and the Shape of Thinking* (London: I. B. Tauris, 2007) 157–84.

247. Anatolii Volkov, "Veselye rebiata," in Mamatova, 144. According to Evgenii Isaakovich Dunaevskii, Aleksandrov told Isaak Dunaevskii that he was completely taken with the US, and especially Coney Island with its attractions (Minchenok, 247).

248. Donald Duck does the same in *The Orphan's Picnic* (1936), which imitates earlier cartoons.

249. Mickey dances on a xylophone-like sidewalk in *Mickey Steps Out* (1931).

250. *42nd Street* revived the popularity of the genre (Richard Barrios, *A Song in the Dark. The Birth of the Musical Film* [NY: OUP, 1995] 160, 274).

251. *Footlight Parade* (1933) also has a short, choreographed bar brawl, but it is not a model for the Russian film.

252. Aleksandrov, *Epokha i kino*, 130. Aleksandrov remembered the titles incorrectly.

253. The Liszt work is used in *Farmyard Symphony* (1938), *Rhapsody in Rivets* (1941), *Rhapsody Rabbit* (1946), and *The Cat Concerto* (1947).

254. According to Nil'sen's sister, Erna Solomonovna Al'pers, during the filming of *Happy Guys*, Nil'sen told the family that he was very pleased with his idea for the cartoon comedians introduction, which Aleksandrov had eagerly accepted (Interview with Rimgaila Salys, February 2002).

255. Henry Jenkins and Kristine Brunovska Karnick, 156.

256. He commented publicly on the first issue: "Our getting to know the music showed that the plot was getting longer, not shorter, since each song takes up an average of 120 meters, and in a new musical comedy this is a series of scenes. We were forced to abbreviate the plot. Then it turned out completely plotless and this is the main defect of the film" (Aleksandrov in *Za bol'shoe kinoiskusstvo*, 149–150).

257. Altman, 28.

258. A bad imitation of the Venus de Milo stands in Lena's apartments in the Black Swan. Just as the bourgeoisie is aligned with classical music, it is also associated with canonical classical art. Venus figures in three different scenes, in which Aleksandrov uses three different, progressively less voluptuous nude plaster statues in accord with the length of on-screen time—apparently a concession to the censorship. In its first, very brief, appearance near a window, the statue's breasts have large, protruberant—markedly unclassical—nipples. In the second brief scene, the statue's physique resembles that of the familiar Venus de Milo. In the third, extended episode in which Potekhin jokes about the armless statue's inability to vote on March 8, Venus is nearly breastless.

259. In the 1932–33 script, "Kak mnogo devushek khoroshikh" was entitled "Pesnia Kosti."

260. "Oh, heart, you don't want peace! / Heart, how good to be alive! / Heart, how good that you are like this, / Thank you, heart, for being able to love like this!" ("How many lovely girls there are").

"The heart in my breast / Flutters like a bird. / And you want to know what awaits you, / And you want to gain happiness" ("Aniuta's Song").

261. Eisenstein and friends met Joseph von Sternberg, the director of *Blue Angel*, during the fall of 1929 in Berlin, where he was working on the film. They visited the set, studied sound techniques and editing of sound film with Sternberg (Aleksandrov, *Epokha i kino*, 118–119). According to critic Vitalii Vul'f, he learned in the 1960s that the top hat used by Orlova in *Happy Guys* was the same one worn by Dietrich in *Blue Angel*. (http://www.v-vulf.ru/officiel/officiel-33-1.htm. Accessed 5 May 2007).

262. In losing his pants, Utesov deconstructs classic cinematic masculinity. (See John Haynes, *New Soviet Man. Gender and Masculinity in Stalinist Soviet Cinema* [Manchester: Manchester University Press, 2003] 78).

263. RGALI, f. 631/3/212.

264. On spatial mythologies in Stalinist culture, see E. Dobrenko, "Do samykh do okrain," *Iskusstvo kino*, 4 (1996): 97–102; E. Dobrenko, "Iazyk prostranstva szhatogo do tochki ili estetika sotsiial'noi klaustrofobii," *Iskusstvo kino*, 9 (1996): 108–17 and 11 (1996): 120–29; Evgenii Dobrenko, *Politekonomiia sotsrealizma* (Moscow: Novoe literaturnoe obozrenie, 2007) 553–61.

265. Feuer, 26.

266. I. Dunaevskii, "Moia rabota nad pesnei v kino," in *Pesnia v sovetskikh fil'makh* (Moscow: Goskinoizdat, 1938) 27–8.

267. I. Dunaevskii, text of radio speech, "Vasilii Ivanovich Lebedev-Kumach (Dlia radio-biulleteni MVTU, Stavropol'-kavkazkii)," RGALI, f. 2062/1/456.

268. I. Dunaevskii, "O G.V. Aleksandrove," *I.O. Dunaevskii. Vystupleniia. Stat'i. Pis'ma. Vospominaniia*, 35.

269. Feuer, 50–51. Given the chronology of their composition, the song texts must have been appended to the 1932–33 *Shepherd* script in mid-1934.

270. Stride forward, clan of Young Communists,
Sing and joke, and make smiles bloom.
We are taming space and time,
We are the young masters of the earth.

We'll grasp, discover, and attain it all,
The cold North Pole and the clear blue sky,
When our country commands that we be heroes,
Then anyone can become a hero.

We can sing and laugh like children,
Amid our constant struggle and toil,
But that's how we were born into the world,
Nowhere and never to relent!

If our enemy decides to start a battle
To take our living joy away from us
Then we'll strike up our song of battle,
And leap to defend our motherland.

A song helps up building and living,
Like a friend, it calls and leads us forth,
And whoever goes through life singing,
Will never ever fall behind.

Translation from *Mass Culture in Soviet Russia*, ed. James von Geldern and Richard Stites (Bloomington, IN: Indiana University Press, 1995) 234–35.

271. The first stanza of the song, which is directly tied to the plot, was omitted from later printed editions of the song:

Liubit—ne liubit
Dai, pogadaiu
Net—da, net—net,
Net luchshe k nemu
Sama podoidu i uznaiu.

He loves me—loves me not
Let me tell my fortune.
No—yes, no—no,
No, better to go up to him myself
And find out...

272. The song mimics the Mexican rhythms of "Chanita," which was well known in Russia at the time, as well as the intonations of the Odessa underworld. (E. Petrushanskaia, "O 'misticheskoi' prirode sovetskikh massovykh pesen," *Russian Literature*, 45 [1999]:96).

273. Orlova herself saw the role as a Cinderella story (G. Aleksandrov, *Epokha i kino*, 172).

274. "Cinderella," *Perrault's Fairy Tales*, trans. A.E. Johnson (NY: Dover Publications, 1969) 78.

275. "Blue Beard" *Perrault's Fairy Tales*, 43.

276. Aleksandrov, *Gody poiskov*, 63.

Chapter 2

Tsirk

Circus

"*Circus* is a more mature product. It's an ideological piece."
– Isaak Dunaevskii[1]

I. ORLOVA'S TROTTERS

In Aleksandrov's second musical film, Marion Dixon, an American star performing at the Moscow circus, falls in love with Russian performer Ivan Martynov, who introduces her to Soviet society. Franz von Kneishitz, Dixon's abusive manager, tries to foil the romance by revealing Dixon's secret: she has an illegitimate mulatto child. However, the circus audience welcomes the child without prejudice and Dixon remains in the land of the soviets with Martynov. The plot is based on Il'f and Petrov's play *Pod kupolom tsirka* (*Under the Big Top*), which premiered at the Moscow Music Hall on December 23, 1934.[2] According to GUKF documents, pre-production for *Under the Big Top* (the original title of the film) began October 15, 1934, so that Aleksandrov must have read the text or seen the play in rehearsal, quickly deciding on a film adaptation as his next project.[3] In the style of the times, Aleksandrov had included circus acts in his production of the opera *The Demon* during his early years in Ekaterinburg.[4] At Proletkul't, Eisenstein had his actors trained in gymnastics and acrobatics, and Aleksandrov walked the high wire and worked the trapeze in Eisenstein's production of *Enough Simplicity for Every Wise Man*. In Moscow, Aleksandrov had performed in the circus as an acrobat, so that he was familiar with the milieu, which also provided a natural venue for his love of grand spectacle.[5] Boris Tenin, who starred as Martynov in the music hall production, recalls that Aleksandrov saw the show many times and used the show's production number "Thirty Girls" in the film, adding with some irony: "He said that he was doing this [seeing the show] so as not to repeat us."[6] On November 5, Boris Shumiatskii, who was to be more directly involved in the creation of *Circus* than he had been with *Happy Guys*, and Konstantin Iukov, head of GUKF's artistic production section, approved the Il'f and Petrov screenplay for the film.[7] The GUKF and Mosfil'm leadership was so enthusiastic about the project that Aleksandrov was permitted to begin work without the usual work schedule and budget plan required by the studio, an exception that later caused production problems and delays.

The first Il'f and Petrov script, which was most likely based closely on their play, has not survived. In January 1935, Aleksandrov, Il'f, Petrov, and Petrov's brother, the writer Valentin Kataev, traveled to Leningrad for additional work on the script and its musical development with Dunaevskii.[8] Aleksandrov had his own ideas about the development of the story line and insisted that Dunaevskii be involved from the early stages of the project so that the film's music could be fully integrated with the plot. Il'f and Petrov reworked the literary script several times according to Aleksandrov's wishes, later complaining that the collaboration had been marred by serious conflicts from the very beginning: Aleksandrov had insisted upon adding elements of melodrama and "superficial glitter" to their light comedy plot, thereby destroying its plausibility and logical development.[9] The problem was that Aleksandrov had envisioned an entirely different film. He wished to correct the "mistakes" of *Happy Guys* by producing a tightly plotted work with a timely ideological message.

Tensions continued as authors and director pulled in different directions. In early March 1935, Aleksandrov sent Dunaevskii a revised script, which now included an additional comic-romantic plotline, inserted by Il'f and Petrov, about a frequently pregnant circus performer named Margarita and another male hero, Aleksandr Morisovich Dankman.[10] Dunaevskii was dissatisfied with the new version of the script and complained to Aleksandrov about the meandering plotline and boring dialogues:

> I prefer the romantic Martynov line of the earlier script, i.e., his falling in love right in front of the audience's eyes. Why was it necessary to introduce Dankman and the pregnant Margarita?... [The text] is mediocre and boring. If the authors are relying on you to stretch out their boring tale by your cinematic skill, then insist that they give you what they owe you for their author's fee: *brilliant dialogues and conversational scenes.*[11]

What appears to be Il'f and Petrov's final version of the literary script was first published in the 1961 edition of their collected works.[12] This script includes the same cast of characters as in the film except that Marion Dixon, the American circus star, carries the conventional romantic heroine's name of Alina, and Martynov is clearly a middle-aged man. As Dunaevskii had suggested, the Margarita-Dankman line has been eliminated; the remaining material (the Martynov-Mary-Kneishitz love and racial blackmail plot, the rival circus acts, the Skameikin-Raechka and talking dog sub-plots), became the dramatic kernel of the film, albeit in simpler and more conventional form, with fewer peripeties and reversals of fortune than were finally included in the film. For example, Raechka and Alina never change clothes to deceive Kneishitz as they do in the film. Instead, Alina leaves with him and then jumps off the train, leaving behind her baby, whom Kneishitz snatches up as he pursues her.[13] The Il'f and Petrov script also condenses the most dramatic elements of the plot at the end: the first "Flight to the

Stratosphere" fails and Martynov falls to the ground. Seeing Alina's concern for him, Kneishitz reveals her dark secret and is ridiculed by the circus audience. Alina then declares her intention to remain in the USSR and performs the circus act with Martynov, after which the corps de ballet dances with balloons.

A secondary plot line, concerned with Skameikin and a woman taxi driver, adds elements of slapstick comedy reminiscent of *Happy Guys*. Repeatedly foiled in his attempts to carry off Raechka, Skameikin has no money to pay the ever-increasing fare for a waiting cab and takes evasive action. He hides from the giantess of a driver in the circus cannon, only to be shot into the air, landing in her arms. He dances with her, tracing fancy steps with his feet in order to distract onlookers from her angry chokehold on his neck, until the circus director finally pays the fare. At this point, Dunaevskii and Lebedev-Kumach's music and songs had not yet been integrated into the plot: Martynov declares his love for Alina via dictated text in a Russian language lesson, and there are, as yet, no lullabies.

Il'f and Petrov's *Under the Big Top* thus remains a localized genre comedy about Soviet circus life, satirizing both the secondary characters and the political fashions of the day. The ringmaster speaks in the "disgusting head-cold voice that is the norm in the circus." Raechka is described as a "vulgar circus beauty (*krasotka*) with a grimace of happiness on her face," who is constantly chowing down, wolfing carrots intended for the animals—even without the help of Kneishitz's cakes. And Liudvig Osipovich, the circus director, speaks incorrect Russian: "Chto vy ot menia khochete?"[14]

The screenplay's satirical jabs at the politics of the day and Soviet *mots du jour*, as they bear upon circus life, are truly comic, but they would be dropped from the film as inappropriate to its ideological trajectory. In the screenplay, the circus director invites Martynov, Raechka, and the foreign performers to dine at the luxurious "capitalist" restaurant Monopol' (a play on Metropol'), while Aleksandrov has Raechka and Kneishitz lunch on the roof of the still uncompleted hotel Moskva. One of the comic sub-plots of *Under the Big Top* concerns a "captain" with his talking dog, both of whom constantly bother the director to be permitted to perform. Liudvig Osipovich rejects the dog as "petty bourgeois" because of its three-word repertoire (*liubliu*, *elki-palki*, *fininspektor*, ("I love," "damn it," "financial inspector"), which he terms "uncontemporary, not calling [to the masses], and non-mobilizing." Buka, Buzia, and Buma, a comically named writers' brigade for minor genres, have been hired to produce a new repertoire for the talking dog: "'We'll destroy the old world r-r-r, r-r-r.'—How is that bad?"; "You never have ideology in two words. Marx wrote three volumes, but we fit it all into forty pages. And he [the director] doesn't like it." Martynov is annoyed at the director's persistent attempts to persuade him to develop a new Soviet act to surpass the American star's "Flight to the Moon": "Why are you propagandizing me? What am I to you—Intourist?"[15]

Skameikin embodies the Soviet obsession with acronyms as he persuades Raechka to marry him: "Oh, we'll have a splendid life. I'm an ITR, and a member of ITS, I work for the NKPS, I have a ZR, and signed up in RZhSKT—in a word, let's go." Confused by whether he is supposed to meet the American circus star at backstage left or right, he makes an ideological joke: "What strange architecture! There where it's left, it's right, and where it's right, it's left. Downright dialectical materialism!"[16] The circus director complains about the various hats he is forced to wear ("director, mestkom, party cell, and juggler. That's okay. Today is a good day"), and walks around, reading aloud from the latest edition of the newspaper in order to adjust to the prevailing political winds, as RAPP ideological asceticism gives way to Stalin's approval of entertainment for the masses: "While the organized spectator comes to the circus to solve a series of topical questions in an entertaining form, a ballet is shoved at him, made up not of older working women, typical for our era, but of young and even beautiful women(!). We must put an end to this unwholesome eroticism." The Director asks: "Where's the ballet? They've made a fool of me again. Like an idiot, I was reading the seventh line from the top, when I should have been reading the seventh from the bottom.... The audience expects wholesome liveliness, wholesome cheerfulness, and wholesome eroticism from the circus. We aren't monks!"[17]

By late March 1935, Aleksandrov had finished his first director's script for *Under the Big Top*.[18] At this stage, he largely followed the Il'f and Petrov text, changing and condensing several episodes and taking the film even further into the realm of both performative spectacle and slapstick comedy. After Raechka informs Martynov of the Skameikin-Alina romance, Martynov refuses to appear with Alina, who has offered to replace the distraught girl. He leaves, but meets Skameikin, who untangles the romantic confusion. Martynov and Alina then begin their act, which is interrupted by Kneishitz's revelations. The audience passes her child up to Raechka, who is seated in the circus administration's box, plying him with food en route. The Soviet act is performed successfully, followed by "almost 100 frames of a brilliant circus revue, toward the end of which there are no more sweets in the administration box, and Skameikin, Raechka, and the little black boy have gotten terribly fat. In an iris shot, the black boy and a little white girl kiss. THE END."[19] Although the final kiss, a cliché of American comedy, was later discarded, its formal elements later found their way into the beginning of Aleksandrov's next film, *Volga-Volga*.

The Charlie Chaplin figure in the circus act plays a larger slapstick role in this first director's script. Charlie crawls headfirst into the cannon and his legs protrude comically; Kneishitz drags him out, feigning annoyance. Charlie then falls and leads himself by the collar out of the arena. Later he tries to extend a helping hand as Billy (Alina's stage name) is lowered into the cannon, but he can't quite reach her and instead pulls out a giant hand mounted on a stick, which she presses as she is lowered into the cannon.

This rudimentary script outlines the beginnings of Aleksandrov's visual conceptualization of the storyline. In this version, he is searching for an effective beginning: a conductor's baton raps against the podium and the orchestra, which has been tuning up, grows quiet. The conductor waves his hands; we see the orchestra box in the circus and hear the overture. The titles, framed by uniformed human figures and musical notes, then appear superimposed on a curtain. At this point in the development of the script, Aleksandrov introduces Billy's striking "portable altar in a suitcase," complete with crucifix, Madonna, Bible, electric lights, and plug, and she prays while adjusting her makeup. Billy makes her grand entrance in "the uniform of an artillery general of the George Washington era" while the horses pulling her trap sit other generals. This allusion to the American war of independence was apparently too sensitive to survive.

After the performance, Kneishitz shouts at Billy in more colorful, albeit less idiomatic English than in the film: "Hell! Daughter of a Bitch! You forget your place!" As in the Il'f and Petrov script, the circus director takes his foreign guests, Martynov and Raechka, to dinner, where the rivalry between Martynov and Kneishitz flares up openly. After dinner, the would-be lovers skate together at a nearby ice rink; the mise-en-scène here justifies the introduction of the frosted glass trick shot, as Martynov stares down Kneishitz, who has been spying on the couple. But the frost patterns do not melt into spring on Red Square; this script, like the Il'f and Petrov text, completely lacks the national address of the completed film. Here Aleksandrov envisions his finale merely as grand spectacle: Martynov and Billy descend a white staircase before performing their act, and the extended circus revue, which concludes the film, is pure entertainment.[20]

As the script underwent revisions, financial terms were also renegotiated. The preparatory period continued throughout the spring of 1935. GUKF delayed approval of high salaries for Orlova and Volodin.[21] Orlova's was finally set at 2,200 rubles for nine days of shooting per month, with 50% pay during the preparatory and rehearsal periods. Iukov wrote Mosfil'm director Babitskii instructing that operetta star Volodin be brought up to the same pay scale. Fedor Kurikhin (the Captain) was to be paid 250 rubles per shooting day.[22] Technical arrangements were also being worked out. Instead of the Agfa Pankine film stock offered to the group, cinematographer Nil'sen wrote to Soiuzintorgkino, requesting (and receiving) Kodak Super-Sensitive Panchromatic film, which facilitated shooting in lower light and was wide enough to be developed by machine.[23]

In early May 1935, Aleksandrov read a revised script at a meeting of the Central Bureau of Creative Workers and explained his working plan. By this time, he had added a May Day parade finale to the script, signaling a shift to a national register.[24] Pudovkin, Romm, Ptushko, Macheret, Raizman, Donskoi, Mar'iamov, Roshal', and others spoke at the meeting, mostly approvingly. Criticism focused on the need to emphasize the moral and economic dependence of the American star on her exploitative manager (possibly moving Aleksandrov to inject more melodrama into the film) and on the flatness of the Martynov character—a problem Aleksandrov was never able to resolve. As insurance against the resistance of Moskovskii kinokombinat workers, who had hindered work on *Happy Guys* for ideological reasons, Aleksandrov also gave his presentation at Potylikha.[25]

Filming began June 13, 1935, still without a finalized script or general plan, and continued until July 14, when work was halted in order to produce a new script and a formal general plan, which were submitted to GUKF on July 22 and 23 respectively.[26] According to GUKF records, the metro, train station, café, and Marion's dressing room episodes, as well as bits and pieces of the entrance march, moon waltz and several other scenes totaling fifteen usable minutes, had been shot before the mid-July halt.[27] Nil'sen was abroad from May 21 to August 18, 1935 with Shumiatskii's group[28]; these fragmentary episodes were probably filmed by his student, assistant cameraman Boris Petrov.

Aleksandrov later stated that he had parted ways with the scriptwriters long before filming began.[29] In his first script, completed March 1935, Aleksandrov had already dropped Il'f and Petrov's secondary Margarita plot line. On May 13, 1935, three days after Aleksandrov's public reading of his director's script, he and the writers informed the copyright office that, because of creative disagreements, Il'f and Petrov would not be named as authors of the screenplay, although they retained their right to authors' fees. In a second letter, Il'f and Petrov reminded Mar'iamov, the director of Mosfil'm's Third Studio, that they had retained the right to include their names in the film credits as authors of the screenplay, to be decided after their viewing the rough cut of the film.[30] Nevertheless, five days later, in an interview for *Moskovskie novosti*, Aleksandrov still described the film as "an eccentric comedy based on a scenario by Il'f and Petrov. I expect it to be a real side-splitter."[31]

Just after the première of *Circus*, Aleksandrov explained the break with Il'f and Petrov as caused by stylistic and genre discord: "In working on *Circus*, there arose a battle with the script. We eliminated from the script those witticisms and situations which would perhaps make an impression in the theatre, but are inappropriate for cinema. The conflict began with the announcer's substandard rejoinder in the script: 'Chego vy khochete?'"[32] Aleksandrov's general comments in the same article also illuminate the major course corrections that had taken place in May and July 1935: The aim of the film is "to reflect...a significant idea—racial equality and international solidarity...When compared to *Happy Guys*, in *Circus* we retreated in the direction of melodrama. This helped us demonstrate a complicated idea in a more convincing way. We were afraid that the genre of light, eccentric comedy would not be able to accommodate significant social context, and switched to melodrama. *Circus* is not a comedy, but a melodrama with comic scenes."[33]

Aleksandrov's admission of "retreat" in the battle for Soviet comedy is clearly disingenuous: the Bolshevik topos of confessing shortcomings became *de rigueur* under Stalin, and often averted serious ideological attacks. Furthermore, we will see that Aleksandrov's treatment of melodrama is highly ironic, that is to say—comic.[34] Aleksandrov's confession was apparently motivated by Stalin's pronouncement on the film, which was conveyed with some irony by Dunaevskii during an informal May 1937 talk at the Music Studies Research Institute: "Let it be known to you that our country's greatest and most authoritative critic has declared that he considers *Circus* to be a good picture, but considers it a retreat, a running away from our positions, and he considers *Happy Guys* to be courageous."[35]

Shumiatskii, with Nil'sen, Ermler, Trauberg, Shorin, and several other film workers, was traveling abroad during the summer of 1935, researching the western film industry as part of his proposal for a "Soviet Hollywood," but approved the script changes upon his return.[36] During the spring or summer, upon the recommendation of Eisenstein, Aleksandrov also brought in the writer Isaak Babel' to sharpen up the dialogues of the film.[37] The May and July script changes were set forth concretely in Mosfil'm's subsequent letter to Il'f and Petrov:

> It would be a mistake to assume that the disagreements regarding the literary script were caused by the personal wish of Aleksandrov, the director, to make certain changes. Actually, there occurred a different situation. General instructions on correcting the script were issued by the studio directors and, since you did not consider it possible for you to accept them, Aleksandrov carried out the directors' instructions and made corrections to the script on his own, about which you were notified. The disagreements were submitted to Shumiatskii, the Head of GUKF, Aleksandrov completely shared Mosfil'm's point of view, and its correctness was later reaffirmed by Shumiatskii...The script dialogues and character traits, and the emphasis of the plot line have changed, but this has strengthened the film. The main idea of the film is the internationalism of all Soviet peoples; the lack of racial prejudice in the USSR has become the main theme of the film. It is no longer cluttered up with the foreign currency problem, which has ceased being relevant, while your script gave it too much space and, in fact, the Soviet cannon act, one of the central motifs of the work, was developed because of the economics of foreign currency.
>
> Certain traits in the Raechka and Skameikin characters, which discredit these essentially positive heroes of our Soviet circus, have been eliminated. In the script they were completely undeservedly and unjustifiably given a trait that can be called stupidity. We have largely freed ourselves of this.
>
> In the interests of stylistic clarity we deleted the scenes with the pregnant Margarita, Aleksandr Morisovich, that did not, incidentally, influence the development of the action and cluttered up the plot. Similarly, we could not agree to retaining such lines as "khochete," "what—pregnant again," "fininspektor," "where can I find an idiot" and so on. We consider them unacceptable in a film and are surprised by your statement that

> their deletion "decreases the elements of comedy." Instead it decreases the bad comic acting.... At the same time the new episodes included in the picture—Mary and Raechka's changing clothes, the wall newspaper, Mary's participation in the performance, the kidnapping of the child, the finale (the lullaby and parade)—have strengthened the development of the story line, since the plot in the second half of the script had noticeably gone downhill.[38]

As the Mosfil'm letter suggests, the seventh and final revision of the script[39] was motivated by two concerns: the desire to improve dramatic action and to elevate a localized plot to a higher register—the grafting of egalitarian-nationalist ideas onto the carcass of a slapstick genre comedy. The plot of the second half of the film was indeed improved by Raechka and Mary's identity change and Skameikin's comic escape with her Jimmy, which exculpates Mary from the negative of irresponsible child abandonment. Furthermore, because muddleheaded comic characters had become a problem for writers and directors with the implementation of the doctrine of Socialism Realism in 1934, buffoonery had become problematic. Positive heroes could not be stupid and therefore comedy—whether slapstick or satirical—gradually waned in Soviet cinema in spite of a succession of conferences on the topic, beginning in 1936.

The elimination of substandard language (the notorious "Chego vy khochete") and other slang in the film was the studio's reaction—or overreaction—to Gorky's campaign for the purity of the Russian language. In late 1933, targeting Panferov's collectivization novel *Bruski* (*Whetstones*), Gorky had attacked RAPP theories on the development of a proletarian language, which would replace the bourgeois language of classical Russian literature. In his February and March 1934 *Pravda* articles, "O boikosti" and "O iazyke," the writer opposed proletarian writers' introduction of phonetic spellings, thieves' slang, obscure dialect words, and crude authorial neologisms into the literary language.[40] Il'f and Petrov's slang expressions were now considered to be a poor model for Soviet audiences.

Years later, in 1949, Aleksandrov began to blame Volodin, who played the circus director in the film, rather than Il'f and Petrov, for insisting on "Chego vy khochete?" According to Aleksandrov's later retelling of events, Gorky finally settled the argument during a chance meeting by insisting that comedy must create, not destroy.[41] Nevertheless, in 1935 Aleksandrov allowed Volodin to continue to accompany his lines by frequent spitting, a stock comic device from early Disney cartoons such as *The Chain Gang* and *Pioneer Days* (both 1930), but hardly a model of good manners for Soviet audiences.

The national address of the film, the figuration of the USSR as the land of racial equality and internationalism of its peoples, was largely the work of Boris Shumiatskii, who personally suggested the first of the two finales—the lullaby of Soviet peoples in the circus—during the spring of 1935.[42] We will see how this line was integrated into the film through its music. The ideological augmentation of the script also led Aleksandrov to write the melodramatic prologue of the film in which Mary and her baby barely escape an American lynch mob, thereby justifying her fear of exposure throughout the film.[43] The May Day parade of 1935, the first to be formally choreographed (by Igor' Moiseev) and also filmed by Soiuzkinokhronika for distribution throughout the Soviet Union, had been a public relations success and was followed on June 30 by the parade of *fizkul'turniki*. By integrating footage from the actual May Day parade, Aleksandrov's second finale on Red Square further enhanced the national address of the film, opening out the spatially localized internationalism of the first ending in the circus to the reality of the national celebration of racial equality and the international solidarity of workers.

*****

Aleksandrov's group worked intensively from August through the fall of 1935. Mary's song and dance number on the cannon was filmed during September.[44] In November, Mosfil'm planners reported to GUKF that 64% of the film had been completed. The "new circus," meaning the Soviet acts (the staircase and rotating tower numbers), introductory poster scene, the cupolas of the old and new circuses, various backgrounds, the circus prop room, episodes with the Lincoln car in which Kneishitz rides had not yet been filmed. The re-filming of several sets and the editing and finalizing of the soundtrack remained to be done.[45] According to Sergei Stoliarov (Martynov), Nil'sen reshot Orlova's close-ups in soft focus in order to minimize her age: at 34, she was ten years older than her male partner.[46] Costumes for the film were made by Nadezhda Lamanova, the most fashionable dressmaker of the period.[47]

At the end of January 1936, finally filming was completed.[48] Aleksandrov worked on editing during the next two and a half months. After corrections and additions, *Circus* was submitted to GUKF on May 15, 1936. The film had been in production for 19 months and was 760,000 rubles over budget.[49] But production delays and budget overruns, exacerbated by the technical innovativeness of *Circus*, were the norm in the poorly organized and underfunded Soviet industry. Both Aleksandrov and Z. Iu. Darevskii, director of the second unit at Mosfil'm, wrote explanatory letters to the studio newspaper. Aleksandrov cited other commitments by the main characters as the primary reason for delays: initially two months of filming were lost because Massal'skii (Kneishitz) and Komissarov (Skameikin) were in Leningrad with the Moscow Art Theatre troupe and Stoliarov was on tour with the Red Army Theatre. After their return to Moscow, scheduling problems continued because actors' commitments in four different theatres conflicted with the work schedule set by the studio.

Parts of three major sections of the film (Mary's room, the old and new circuses) had to be reshot because the soundtrack had not been synchronized. Sets were not built on time, e.g., "Novyi manezh" (The New Arena) was delivered 45 days behind schedule. Because of the group's experimentation with new technology, process shots in the circus arena episodes took longer than expected. The group was unable to check its work for two–three days after filming because the studio possessed only one viewing room. Sloppy work by the developing lab, such as overdeveloped film and perforations, necessitated nine days of reshooting. Little Jimmy's illness caused further delays. But Aleksandrov particularly blamed the absence of Stoliarov, who was busy completing work in Dovzhenko's *Aerograd*, for the cancellation of the May Day parade episode with 10,000 extras. As a result, a special indoor set had to be built at Mosfil'm for the finale on Red Square. In the end, this set was not used in the film.[50] According to Orlova, the cast was placed at the front of a group of fizkul'turniki and actually marched in the May Day parade.[51] Finally, Aleksandrov mentions—but only in passing—his own and artist Grivtsov's unclear directions for sets, such as the staircase and pandus (Aleksandrov's name for the rotating tower), that also caused delays.[52]

An official report provides more detail: when, after the construction of the pandus, Aleksandrov increased the number of girls, borrowed from the Technicum of Circus Art,[53] from 20 to 60, the structure had to be rebuilt. Technical planning for the "Novyi manezh" set began only a few days before construction was due to begin, and a careless truck driver then broke the wind machine for the parachute episode. Both circumstances forced a halt to filming for 20 days.[54] Darevskii's letter repeats most of problems enumerated by Aleksandrov, but it particularly emphasizes the poor technical organization and staff shortages at the studio, which delayed the construction of sets, and Grivtsov's inaccurate drawings, which created confusion among the film crew.

After viewing the rough cut of the film, now titled *Circus*, on March 10, 1936, Il'f and Petrov wrote to Mosfil'm on the same day, summarizing their earlier disagreements with Aleksandrov: the director's changes to their screenplay, which they had already modified several times according to his wishes, resulted in the introduction of dialogues which were "stylistically unpleasant for us"; a significant reduction in comedy elements and a significant increase in melodrama, with a loss of balance between the two; an emphasis on external splendor and excessive embellishment, which detracted from the verisimilitude of the film and clear plot development; the replacement of their "precise and clear anti-fascist prologue" with a less significant introduction; a change in title and the names of several characters. "Having seen the almost completed film, we stand by our earlier decision. In spite of a number of brilliant cinematographic achievements (particularly the superb photography), the film suffers from precisely the defects we had feared." Il'f and Petrov requested that their names be removed from the credits, all newspaper ads, and other advertising texts.[55] In the end, the popular writers' inflated egos blinded them to the difference between themselves as authors of the screenplay and Aleksandrov as author of the film. This proud gesture cost them the screening royalties for *Circus*, which apparently then accrued to Aleksandrov as sole author.[56] A week later Sokolovskaia, the deputy director of the studio, replied to Il'f and Petrov's letter with a polite but firm rebuff, which attributed the script changes to the studio's initiative, rather than to Aleksandrov, and defended the revisions as improvements to the film.

Shumiatskii had his own accounts to settle with the authors of *One-Story America* and was not inclined to intervene on their behalf. In 1934–35, the ambitious GUKF chief had proposed to Stalin and the Politbiuro the construction of a "Soviet Hollywood" or *kinogorod* in the south with a population of 25,000 and 22 studios, where the abundant sunlight and mild climate would facilitate efficient production.[57] During summer 1935, Shumiatskii had visited European and US film studios, gathering information for his project, and developing a proposal to build the *kinogorod* with American technical assistance and to initiate joint productions.[58] Beria, who feared that the construction of a *kinogorod* in Sukhumi would sap the budget of his Georgian fiefdom, apparently persuaded Il'f and Petrov, after their return from the US, to write a letter to Stalin arguing against the project on the basis of their American experiences.[59] Shumiatskii defended his project to Stalin at a March 9, 1936 film screening in the Kremlin and in a March 27 letter. Stalin and Molotov eventually chose the Crimea as the site, but the proposal for a *kinogorod* in the south was ultimately shelved, as Shumiatskii was increasingly criticized for not meeting planning goals and lost ground in his power struggle with his superior, Committee for Arts Matters chairman Kerzhentsev.[60]

Aleksandrov was given significantly more resources to make his second major film. He had a co-director, I. Simkov, and chief cameraman-cinematographer Vladimir Nil'sen was assisted by second cameraman Boris Petrov and their assistant, V. Pereslavtsev.[61] Aleksandrov boasted to the press that 750 people had worked on the film.[62] *Circus* was mostly filmed at the Potylikha studio, except for a few animal act scenes shot at the Solomonskii Circus,[63] and the restaurant set (Kneishitz and Raechka's meal and dance), constructed on the roof of the unfinished hotel Moskva. Much of the studio filming was carried out at night because of scheduling conflicts and delays, and the relative quiet of the night hours.[64]

Circus was Aleksandrov's most stylistically imaginative and tightly structured film—in this sense the polar opposite of *Happy Guys*—largely due to his collaboration with Vladimir Nil'sen, who had just returned from the US with a thorough understanding of American production practices and technology, which Aleksandrov then adopted with the aim of completing most of the creative and technical planning for the film in the pre-production stage. In its organizational methods, including the extensive use of preliminary drawings and storyboarding and new techniques in process photography, *Circus* was the most innovative Soviet film of its time.

Nil'sen was faced with depicting the daytime, non-performative circus world: "Has anyone ever thought what that same circus looks like in daytime, when the sun's rays that struggle through the narrow cupola windows fall in soft patches on the empty and partly darkened arena? Has anyone observed the dark circus stables during the day that remind you of a zoo, or the backstage area during rehearsals?"[65] For aspects of the pre-revolutionary circus, such as Liudvig Osipovich's bicycle act, Nil'sen and Petrov researched documentary photo materials at the Leningrad Circus Museum. In their search for the visual figuration of Marion Dixon and the other characters, they observed modern circus rehearsals and became acquainted with performers.[66] Nil'sen and Petrov's article on the making of *Circus* illustrates, via a series of frames from the film, Dixon's evolution from a "vulgar circus performer," masked by a dark wig, hood, and heavy makeup, her artificiality exaggerated by extreme chiaroscuro lighting, to the relatively unadorned, kindly blonde woman in street clothes and stylish hat under soft lighting, and finally to the "woman who has realized her place and her rights in the land of the soviets"—a hatless, brightly illuminated, and very determined-looking Orlova.[67]

During pre-production, the entire film was mapped out in 640 frame drawings of each shot. The Vasil'evs and artist Makhlis had done the same in *Chapaev*, and Eisenstein taught this method at VGIK,[68] but the practice was not common among Russian directors. In his notes on the Hollywood studios he visited in June 1935, Nil'sen observed that *Blue Angel* director Von Sternberg, by then at Columbia, who acted as both cameramen and director for his films, also worked from preliminary drawings.[69] Nil'sen clearly recognized the creative and practical advantages of composing a film in this manner and advocated the method for *Circus*.

After an initial rehearsal and the director's explication of an episode, the artist Luchishkin produced draft sketches of each shot. After the second rehearsal, the artist made final drawings of the composition of each shot, showing the placement of figures and lighting. Drawings were transferred to film and shown to the actors on an Alloscope projector before shooting the episode. Aleksandrov also adopted American-style storyboarding as an organizational tool. The frame drawings were photographed and glued onto large storyboard sheets, along with sketches of the set. The storyboard, kept by a script girl, recorded scene number, actors, footage, time, music, sound effects, camera angles, number and quality of takes, and instructions for editing and film development.[70] Aleksandrov also used a microphone which could be heard throughout the studio and had a telephone connection to his lighting technicians. After the completion of filming, *Iskusstvo kino* printed a detailed, unsigned account of one shooting day. Although clearly intended to show Aleksandrov in the best light and to deflect administrative criticism of scheduling lapses, the description also gives a sense of the difficult working conditions at the Potylikha studio. (See Appendix A).

As cinematographer for the film, Nil'sen devoted the most attention to composition, camera angles, lighting, and special effects. Before beginning work on *Circus*, he wrote: "In this film, I am trying to outline a way of resolving the dynamic composition of a frame. I want to find techniques of dynamic filming that, in planning the mise-en-scène, may perhaps help liberate me from the moribund stasis of the fixed tripod."[71] In a detailed article for *Iskusstvo kino*, he defined his guiding principles for each frame as clarity, simplicity, and expressiveness. The first two were achieved when the formal elements of a frame were strictly motivated by plot. In searching for expressive composition, he had come up against a number of formal problems, of which the most difficult were long shots in which the rounded shape of the circus arena had to be inscribed into the quadrangular proportions of the frame.[72]

As a result of his American experience, Nil'sen was able to employ different types of process photography and mechanical constructions to solve complex spatial problems. The 30-meter high interior of the circus was simulated by combining a life-size set extending to the last amphitheatre row with a 1.5-meter model of the remainder of the building. For Orlova's "Moon Waltz" number, Nil'sen devised a rotating carousel on which the camera moved together with the actress.[73] For Volodin, Popova, and Karlin's "Miracle of 1903" act, Nil'sen attached their bicycles to a rotating floor so that the actors could perform the number without physical risk or extensive rehearsals. Skameikin's flower fight with the lions was filmed using three different kinds of process and trick photography: rear projection for close-ups; for medium and long shots—a camera angle that hid the internal bars in the single cage holding both Skameikin and the lions, and a small model of cage bars placed directly in front of the lens, and lined up with the cage bars, creating the illusion that the actor was in the cage with the animals[74] (Fig. 24). Nevertheless, Skameikin's horsewhipping of the lions with a bouquet of roses had to be filmed with the actor in direct proximity to the animals. Dressed in Skameikin's clothes and a wig, the well known lion tamer Boris Eder substituted for Komissarov in the dangerous episode.[75] For Martynov and Marion Dixon's flight scenes, Nil'sen used the transparency (*transparant*) method he had developed with N. N. Agokas in 1933: chemically treated positive footage of the circus background was placed in the camera in front of blank negative film. The actor was then filmed in the episode, providing a realistic composite image.[76] Nil'sen filmed the actors' jumps from the train at Kiev train station in Moscow, parts of the bicycle number, and the Chaplin clown's tricks at a slower speed (10–14 frames per second) in order to speed up the action under normal projection. Hanging tracks for the camera were constructed for action shots, which became easier to film when, toward the end of work on *Circus*, the studio finally acquired an American crane with a 2-meter extension.[77]

More than in any other of his films except *The Radiant Path*, Aleksandrov edited artistically with match cuts on sound and image, and here again Disney's cartoon continuity, a single musical phonogram linking changing episodes, may have been an influence. Sound bridges are used in parallel editing: the whistle of a man impatiently awaiting the beginning of the Stratosphere act becomes the whistle of the train on which Kneishitz and company intend to leave Moscow. The whistle of a policeman whose attention is attracted by the passengers running from the departing train becomes the bridge back to the circus through the whistle of the man in the audience. Trick shots facilitate radical changes of setting: the globe of the Southern Railway caboose becomes the balloon-globe of the Russian circus act; as Martynov stares coldly at Kneishitz, the frosted glass graphics, which gradually melt, facilitate the shift from the circus dressing room to a panorama of Red Square; Martynov's cartoon wings in the hotel love scene become part of his actual cartoon on the wall newspaper at the circus.

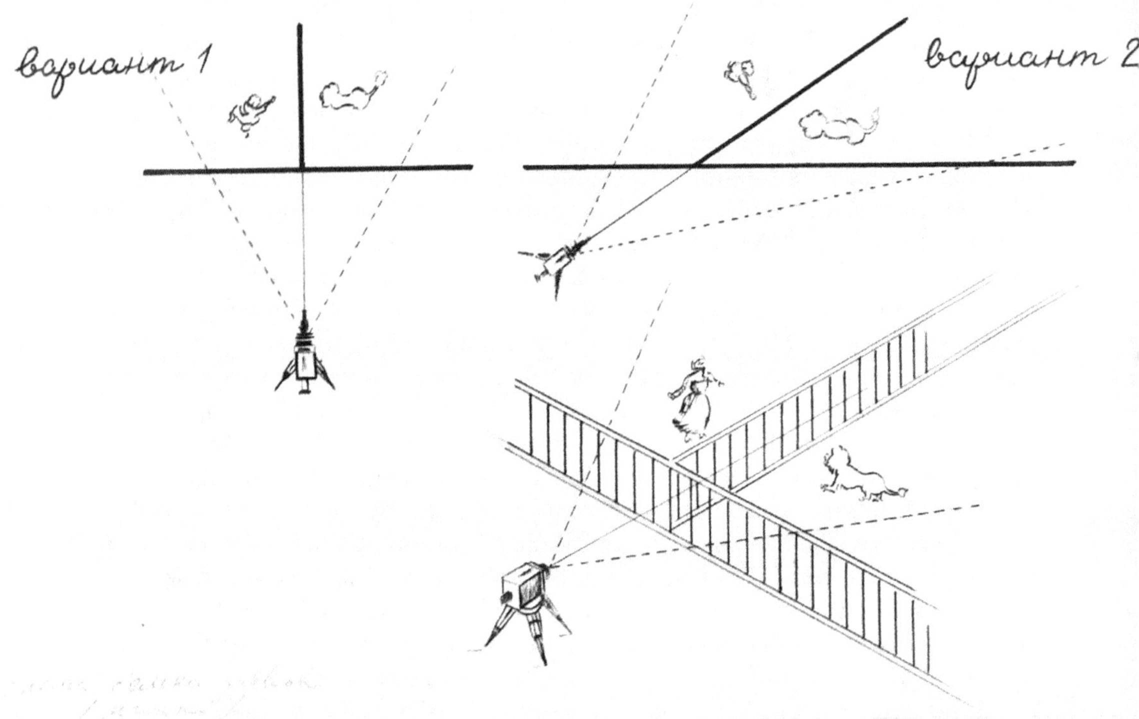

Figure 24.

*****

Early progress on the film was hindered by casting changes. In the first 1935 director's script, Aleksandrov had noted down his initial choices of actors: Orlova for Billy Florens; Kurikhin, Arnol'd, and Tiapkina, all of whom had acted in *Happy Guys*, were chosen for the roles of Capt. Borneo, Kneishitz, and the female taxi driver; comic actor Erast Garin for Skameikin; operetta star Vladimir Volodin for Liudvig Osipovich; Evgeniia Pyrialova for Raechka; and D. Pokrass for the circus orchestra conductor.[78] The Martynov and little Jimmy roles had not been cast at this point. By early May 1935, a contract had been signed with N. Berezovskaia for the role of Raechka.[79] In the end, Moscow Art Theatre actors Pavel Massal'skii and Aleksandr Komissarov were selected for the roles of Kneishitz and Skameikin. Ever conscious of the latest thematic trends, Aleksandrov picked actors and staff from two recent aviation films. Evgeniia Mel'nikova, who had just appeared in *Aerograd* and *Letchiki* (both 1935), replaced Berezovskaia as Raechka. Sergei Stoliarov had played a handsome, square-jawed, calm, and capable pilot in *Aerograd*, and Aleksandrov selected him, without a screen test, for the "New Man" role of Martynov. Georgii Grivtsov, who had been the artist for *Letchiki*, was also hired for *Circus*. Aleksandrov needed a mulatto baby for Marion Dixon's child, and found one-and-a-half-year-old Jimmy Patterson, the son of an American black who had married the Russian theatre artist Vera Aralova.[80]

The filming of *Circus*, with its child and animal actors, foreign characters, acrobatic acts, mechanical constructions, and special effects, was an adventure and a challenge for Aleksandrov and the film crew. As always, Orlova approached her role in a professional manner, preparing meticulously and bearing adversity with good humor. The prologue to *Circus* was shot on a set built at the Sukogo (now Solnechnaia) train station outside Moscow. During the filming of Marion Dixon's escape with her black infant (a doll) from the lynch mob, Orlova tripped and fell on the slag underlying the tracks, bloodying her knees and tearing her skirt and stockings in front of a crowd of spectators. Without losing her presence of mind, the actress got up, put herself in order, and remarked with a wry expression: "Is the *baby* alive?"[81]

Orlova recalled that the Marion Dixon role required extensive linguistic preparation:

> I have never been to America or seen an American circus, but I have seen visiting American performers in our circuses. I have also read books and have seen many American films from which I formed a picture of Marion Dixon's character. However, to be a circus performer in the film, I had to do trapeze exercises and learn to juggle in real life, according to the demands of the role.
>
> I decided to speak only Russian, but with an American accent. For this I got acquainted with an American woman who spoke Russian badly and made a long study of her errors in pronunciation, leading her into pronouncing precisely those words that I had to speak in the film.[82]

Various doubles replaced Orlova for the more dangerous stunts in the film. Acrobat Aleksandra Vorontsova performed the high trapeze exercises; acrobats Gusarova and Litvinenko doubled for Orlova and Stoliarov in juggling burning torches on the pandus and staircase.[83] Nevertheless, Orlova had her own share of painful and unpleasant experiences. During an eight-hour shift filming the "Moon Waltz" scenes, she was strapped into a bicycle seat that revolved around the circus arena, precipitating an attack of vertigo, nausea, and weakness associated with her Ménière's disease.[84] For the "Mary's Song" number, Orlova had to dance on a glass plate 75 centimeters in diameter atop a four-meter high cannon.[85] The lights within the barrel of the cannon, which were on throughout the song and dance number, brought the glass plate to a white-hot heat. Because she knew that Aleksandrov avoided too many retakes due to a shortage of imported film stock, Orlova completed the scene as planned by sitting down on the glass plate to sing her concluding couplets, and then dove straight into the safety net around the cannon without waiting for a ladder. Skin peeled off, along with her burned tights, and retelling the story in later years, she joked: "For two days afterward I sat on the toilet in eagle position."[86]

During the summer of 1935, Aleksandrov found his "Flight to the Moon" cannon act at Sokol'niki Park, where three young Kharkiv inventors entertained crowds by shooting a "human torpedo," athlete Vera Buslaeva, 18–20 meters into the air from a six-meter cannon. The trajectory of the cannon proved to be too high for the Potylikha studio ceiling, and the inventors returned to Kharkiv to build another model with the help of the local airplane factory. Orlova had hoped to do the stunt herself, but the inventors feared the risk to the inexperienced actress, and Buslaeva performed the stunt for the cameras.[87]

Filming Jimmy Patterson was a time-consuming undertaking because the boy was two years old at the time—not yet old enough to play his role upon command. When the plot called for him to cry, Pavel Massal'skii frightened him with terrible faces; when Jimmy was supposed to laugh, Aleksandr Komissarov, whom the boy liked, stepped in to put him in a good mood.[88] The film crew had to wait until Jimmy fell asleep in order to shoot the lullaby episode, playing the soundtrack quietly and using hand signals to communicate. If something wakened him, Jimmy would not fall asleep again that night and the shift had to be cancelled.[89]

Animal episodes presented their own difficulties and dangers. Aleksandrov recounts:

> Growling in fear and looking back confusedly at the bright lights, a reddish bear tries to run backstage. After reluctantly juggling a globe, the sea lion suddenly snarls and resolutely moves out of camera range. It takes considerable effort to lure him back. The little monkey that was supposed to shoot off a revolver was frightened by the sound of the shot, took off up along the trapezes, and hid in the huge corridors of the building, forcing the director's assistant to spend a good hour searching for him.[90] Liuba, the sea lioness, escaped from the studio, hid on another set, and Durov himself was unable to get her out of there for a long time.[91]
>
> Boris Petrov, the cameraman, was busy checking the condition of the scenery and readiness of the extras for the scene in which the "madly brave" Skameikin…tames half a dozen lions with the aid of a bouquet of flowers. Petrov was completely preoccupied with his work and was giving orders standing in direct proximity to the steel cage in which Boris

> Eder was rehearsing the kings of the jungle. For some reason, the figure looming near the cage irritated one of the predators. It stuck a clawed paw through the iron bars and tore the cameraman's jacket to pieces, leaving bloody marks on the inattentive Petrov's body. The trainer's warning shot saved him from more unfortunate consequences.[92]

Following Charlie Chaplin's economical practice in *his Circus*, Aleksandrov replaced most of the live audience around the arena by mannequins. Years later, he recalled an embarrassing episode: irritated by the unnatural appearance of a mannequin, he ordered it to be carried further away from the camera, to which the powdered and rouged "doll," a Mosfil'm extra, replied: "Why have me moved—I can do it myself."[93]

*****

With *Circus*, Dunaevskii perfected a close collaborative relationship with Aleksandrov that produced three successful musical comedy films. Aleksandrov and Orlova provided the support, admiration, and friendship that the emotionally hungry Dunaevskii always needed to produce his best music. When the couple once asked him how he managed to write wonderful melodies like "The Moon Waltz," he replied: "Just love me and my work, please. All the rest is up to me. That's the way I'm made."[94] Both Orlova and Vladimir Volodin recall that Dunaevskii worked with them on their songs, willingly adjusting the music to their vocal range.[95]

Aleksandrov was himself an amateur musician who was familiar with American musicals from his travels in the US and Europe. Dunaevskii, naturally, preferred to work on musicals, but more significant for the film was Aleksandrov's recognition of the importance, even primacy, of musical dramaturgy in the genre. After the success of *Happy Guys* and its songs, Aleksandrov was prepared to give Dunaevskii more creative control, bringing him in at an early stage of script development:

> Not a single syllable in the script is written before the musical plan has been developed. And this is the reason for my musical achievements.... It's necessary because this is a continuation of what exists in the West and in America, but what we haven't had here.... If you had seen the rough cut of the film *Circus*, you would tear your hair. Such scrupulous rhythmical elaboration of a picture is typical of Aleksandrov alone. He elaborates the theme musically with perfect virtuosity. I'm convinced that if "Song of the Motherland" had been given to Timoshenko, he would have buried it.... Aleksandrov uses all the possibilities of not only the central, but also the secondary theme. He himself is very musical, he's a dilettante, but he listens very closely to any kind of musical instructions.

> In Aleksandrov's pictures, the music is composed before filming. Seventy percent of the music was written before shooting *Circus*.... This complicates my work because I have nothing from which to push off. I am the creator of the rhythm, the emotional tone, and the dynamic, and together with Aleksandrov, we deal with all of it. This gives Aleksandrov what he's searching for. He's looking for the rhythm, the right musical development.[96]

As the men worked on the musical plan of the film, Aleksandrov shortened and altered the literary script in order to highlight the music.[97]

Blessed with a sensitive internal timepiece, Dunaevskii enjoyed the challenge of time constraints in composing for the movies, and here too Aleksandrov gave him creative license:

> I've achieved such precision that I can, without looking at the clock, say how many seconds [a piece] runs. I myself conduct the film and the precision I achieve disconcerts all the directors: I can rehearse something 6 times and make it fit exactly all 6 times.... Aleksandrov is a very kind person. We don't bargain with each other, we meet each other half way: 5 seconds or 10 seconds doesn't matter, and if I have the desire to elaborate some phrase and give it a more finished character, he always cooperates.[98]

Instead of the draft recordings used in *Happy Guys*, Aleksandrov and Dunaevskii opted for a finalized soundtrack that would drive the visual conceptualization of *Circus*: "The recording is the only emotional-semantic factor in constructing the film. Everything that has been put into the recording must be manifested visually."[99] Aleksandrov was careful to harmonize sound with image through editing: in the "Moon Waltz," strong beats correspond to editing cuts; in the circus finale, Marion Dixon and Martynov descend the staircase in perfect step with the music.

While Dunaevskii once described his work on *Happy Guys* as his "first love,"[100] his approach to *Circus* was more that of an experienced and rational inamorato. As he thought about various musical designs for the film in early 1935, he also began to formulate the principles that were to govern his work in cinema during the rest of his career: the general population is most receptive to songs that resemble the national melos; song motifs must be sufficiently simple and accessible to be remembered by audiences after they leave the theatre; the composer's task is to: 1) produce a central song, then develop the musical design of the film based on symphonic elaboration of its material; 2) compose situational musical leitmotifs for major characters; and 3) make extensive use of illustrative music that conveys the central plot peripeties to the viewer. Dunaevskii's letters to Aleksandrov set forth his initial discoveries; a lecture to colleagues in 1937, a year after the release of *Circus*, summarized his creative method.

> I'm constantly thinking about the music, and must say that it's indescribably painful. I'm analyzing thoroughly all the ways of doing the musical design, and reaching a conclusion that overturns existing concepts. We must take the road of a musical legacy after the picture. We must go the route of a good motif that permeates the film and is *accessible to the ear*. There isn't one, I'm searching for it. We need simplicity. There isn't any!... I need to construct the music in such a way that departing viewers would sing what we needed them to sing.... Our pictures must leave after themselves phrases and anecdotes, songs, situations, and so on. This should be their artistic-agitational power. The text must therefore be honed like a blade! The verse striking and clear! The music easily assimilated! The flow of the action (montage) simple and persuasive![101]
>
> My consciousness is in complete ferment. An analysis of my musical work, and not only mine, has shown me that our population does not absorb any melodies that do not correspond to the national sound perception to which its ears are accustomed. Please pay maximum attention to these comments as they hold the key to the correct musical path. Just check—wherein lies the power of "Kostia," "Schastlivyi put'" ("Happy Journey")? All of these Polish tangos? Some of the German foxtrots? Their strength is a commonality of melodic construction, their internationality! Why does the broad population *here* not sing the wonderful American and English blues songs and foxtrots? Because they're not ours! Their entire architectonics, rhythmics, and intervals are foreign to our ears![102]

In later years, Dunaevskii was often criticized for borrowing musical motifs from 19th century urban folk songs and romances, and musicologists made a game out of identifying the sources of his most recent mass song. When a colleague asked him about echoes of Verstovskii's 1835 folk opera *Askol'dova mogila* (*Askol'd's Grave*) in "Song of the Motherland," Dunaevskii explained his strategy for the present and his hopes for the future:

> I think that a song must be close to what is current among the people. I disregard all sorts of remarks in this connection. For example, they say that there's a similarity between "Kakhovka" and the song "Umer bedniaga v bol'nitse" ("A Poor Fellow Died in the Hospital"). So what if he died—I think it's very good that the songs are similar in their interpretations.

> But if you move away from this path, then you lose accessibility. Our average listener, who has been introduced to mass culture, will, in the end, demand more complex combinations, which means that the mass song will also rise to a higher level. How many cadences do you have in a mass song—a maximum of 4 variants. If you include a complex cadence, the song won't be sung. That's why I'm not afraid of these things being pointed out and think it's right for the mass song to remain within the limits of accustomed sounds.[103]

Before and during his work on *Circus*, Dunaevskii formulated his musical method in composing for the cinema:

> My task is to create a central song for the picture and then, taking the song as a starting point, I create the musical design of the film. Next, I'm in favor of the widespread use of illustrative music, which conveys to the viewer in an accessible form all the main plot peripeties, and third, I employ the method of very close association to the contents of the theme. I don't like what doesn't reach the viewer and doesn't elevate the picture, and, conversely, I like that which presents it better to the viewer. Those are my three precepts.... If in *Circus* Mary sings the "Moon Waltz" in her act, then her melodramatic tribulations are subsequently accompanied by this motif, perhaps elaborated somewhat. My practical working method begins with the preparation of material for the main characterizations. I wouldn't say that this is a system of leitmotifs, but rather a system of leitmotif situations.... I wouldn't say that "The Moon Waltz" is Mary's leitmotif. Her entire situation is accompanied by this waltz. When some employee pulls down the last posters, the "Moon Waltz" often sounds there. This isn't a characterization of her, but a characterization of her circus situation.[104]

Dunaevskii himself always conducted during recording sessions.[105] His work on *Circus* led him to abandon symphonic seating and develop his own orchestra arrangement.

> I believe that it [the orchestra] should be placed in the following way: first violins, then woodwinds at a four-meter distance, and the brass ten meters away. I don't use kettledrums at all. Drums can only be used with a muffler. I'm against transitions from one group of instruments to another. I object to this categorically because one form runs into the other, and you a get a total mish-mash…I use only six first violins,

> four violas, and two double basses sitting at the microphone and, in all cases, a tuba. I don't use kettledrums because they drown out the fortissimo.[106]

Dunaevskii worked on the music for *Circus* from January 1935 through March 1936, composing six songs and fourteen instrumental pieces for the film.[107] He began with "Mary's Lullaby," which progressed with great difficulty, leading to his epiphany regarding the Russian national musical vocabulary as the necessary melodic language of the new mass song. Initially he defined his vision of the lullaby as "Kostia's song plus nobleness plus poignancy,"[108]—in other words, the accessibility and directness of the *Happy Guys* song "Kak mnogo devushek khoroshikh" combined with the noble and touching image of Marion Dixon as downtrodden Madonna-mother. Dunaevskii composed "Mary's Lullaby" on the model of Negro spirituals but later realized that the song would not live outside the film:

> You can write a thousand wonderful pieces and not achieve mass appeal! Consequently, I'm coming to the conclusion that "The Lullaby" won't be sung, no matter how much you foist it on the audience. You need some sort of clever maneuver, a magic trick, to make the American woman sing something "American" that nevertheless remains on *our soil*. Of course, I don't intend any "Russianisms" for the American, nor do I intend any Americanisms for the Russians either. So that's what I'm working on now, and I beg your pardon in advance if this work doesn't bring me the speedy outcome we would all like to see.[109]

In 1937 Dunaevskii remarked that, although the initial versions of his songs were usually accepted right away by directors, he was forced to produce five versions of "Mary's Lullaby," of which Aleksandrov chose the worst one for the film.[110] Dunaevskii and Lebedev-Kumach tried to bring the song closer to Russian audiences by mixing English and Russian lyrics, but in the end, Dunaevskii's prediction was correct: the lullaby never became a popular hit.[111]

The music for Mary's dance on the cannon and her post-flight circle of the arena was originally planned as a single western-style composition in the manner of a Strauss waltz. Dunaevskii composed the lyrical "Moon Waltz" with its ascending development and exclamatory figure at the end of phrases with some difficulty, working through several variants together with Aleksandrov. Lebedev-Kumach did not work with Dunaevskii and Aleksandrov during the creation of the song but provided lyrics later for the finalized melody.[112] In the cannon episodes, as originally filmed, Orlova performed a few ballet steps (arabesques and *battements en pointe*) atop the cannon, and then flew to the moon, all to the tune of the slow "Moon Waltz." In September 1935, Aleksandrov decided to jazz up the cannon scenes with the addition of a new American-style song and a lively dance number. Dunaevskii, who was experienced in jazz composition from his music-hall days, produced "Pesenka Meri" ("Mary's Song"), a version of the "Moon Waltz" melody with a different rhythmical foundation and in the stride-piano style, and Lebedev-Kumach thought up the jaunty "digi-digi-du" lyrics right in the studio.[113] As a result, when the earlier and later footage were edited together, Orlova performed her jazz dance in high heels but entered the circus ring, flew out of the cannon, and circled the arena in ballet slippers.

The "Moon Waltz" never plays in its entirety in *Circus*. Fragments of the song, some with different lyrics from the published version, are used to highlight Mary's situation.[114] Mary's final circus performance originally included another song, "Ia tantsuiu s pechal'iu v glazakh" ("I dance with sadness in my eyes"), which was replaced by a repetition of "Mary's Song," sung in tragic tempo.[115] Judging by earlier versions of the second lullaby, the circus finale of the film was originally planned as a unifying passed-around song among Mary and the other primary and secondary characters. The second, "International Lullaby," was initially not at all international but was composed with all Russian-language lyrics, along with comic couplets by Raechka and Skameikin about children and family. When the lullaby became international, with Shumiatskii rocking the cradle, Ukrainian, Uzbek, Georgian, and Yiddish lines were added and the Russian text was significantly abbreviated.[116]

"Song of the Motherland" was not part of the original musical plan for the film. Initially, Dunaevskii had planned a standard lovers' duet for the piano scene in Mary's hotel room.[117] The composer and director only gradually came to the fusion of the love plot with a national-ideological message through "Song of the Motherland," and only then did Dunaevskii elaborate the song symphonically throughout the musical design of the film.

> A curious thing happened with the film *Circus*. We were not thinking of any "Song of the Motherland." We had Mary, the circus performer, and the Russian performer Martynov, a good Soviet guy. The idea of assimilating Marion to the Soviet way of life through a song appeared much later. There was no "Song about My Motherland," there was only the theme. Martynov is sitting and playing, and suddenly the idea came to us: why show love through a kiss; let's do it through a song. This was Aleksandrov's idea, but it was discredited by the turning of the frame, when they're standing over the piano. But then the sound of the song and their motionless faces—that's done well. After that, the finale had to be different. At the beginning, they announce that she has a child and run her out of town in disgrace. The lullaby was my idea; the question was whether to end it in the circus or carry it out onto the square to show that she was in the Soviet family. Then we got the idea of creating a march and we included Mary's lullaby.[118] Take the scene where she writes

> the letter. She begins: "Dear Martynov," crosses it out and writes "My Dear," then crosses it out again, and writes simply "Petrovich." The song is playing all the time, while she decides her fate once and for all.... Let me say that in Aleksandrov's films a number of scenes have been dictated by me. The entire finale of the film *Circus* is my work.[119]

Mary and Martynov's love scene by the piano is silent, their emotion signaled only by agitated breathing. As they recognize their Lacanian ideal selves in the mirror reflection of the piano, professional singer Daniil Dem'ianov performs "Song of the Motherland" in a majestic, elevated baritone,[120] signaling the displacement of the plot line from a romantic to a national register. Thus Aleksandrov's original idea of expressing only the couple's love via the song was replaced by an ideological imperative, necessitating a public and global rather than private and localized circus finale. Secondly, the march tempo needed for "Song of the Motherland," when sung on Red Square, then evolved backward to the same song, again in march tempo, as the musical background to Mary's love letter to Martynov, thereby undermining the letter's purely personal impulse.

Because Stoliarov was unable to sing, Aleksandrov himself performed the song Martynov teaches Marion in the film. Dixon's diversional but masterful piano variation on "Song of the Motherland" was recorded by Dunaevskii himself,[121] a professional performance that begins the transmutation of song into national anthem. Naum Shafer's account of the original Mary-Martynov piano scene, as it existed before the restoration of *Circus* in 1970, throws further light on the shift in musical register that, in effect, subsumed the love affair to an ideological conceptualization of the film more akin to the folk musical. In the original version of *Circus*, Martynov responded to Mary's plea, "Poi, Petrovich!" ("Sing, Petrovich!") with the lines, "Esli by ia umel pet! Kak by ia spel!" ("If I knew how to sing, how I would sing it!"), which were deleted from the restored film.[122] Responding directly to the New Man's fervent wish in the 1936 version of *Circus*, Dem'ianov's stately, professional off-screen rendition of the song elevates "Song of the Motherland" to a national register. At this juncture, Mary's love for the circus performer Martynov assimilates to the New Man's politics, thereby justifying the elaboration of the idea of ethnic-racial equality throughout the remainder of the film. Martynov's reaction to the black baby is similarly elided: he does not hear—or pretends not to hear—Jimmy's crying in Dixon's hotel room. Toward the end of *Circus*, he is momentarily shocked by Kneishitz's revelations and turns to stare at Dixon, but his surprise is immediately superseded by the "International Lullaby."

The story of the composition of "Song of the Motherland" has become the stuff of legend, fraught with half-truths and contradictions. Attuned to the increasing State emphasis on nationalism and patriotism rather than proletarian internationalism, Aleksandrov suggested the song topic to Dunaevskii and Lebedev-Kumach, and Dunaevskii named it "Song of the Motherland" even before the lyrics had been written.[123] According to A.

Sokhor, Dunaevskii brought an early version of the song to show his colleagues at the Leningrad Union of Composers. After playing "Song of the Motherland," which they liked, he asked them to sing it back from memory. They began well, but then lost the melody, leading Dunaevskii to remark that the song still lacked the necessary simplicity and vividness, and therefore needed more work.[124]

Lebedev-Kumach had initially envisioned a song without a refrain, instead repeating the final two stanzas. After seeing the full verse text, however, Dunaevskii pointed to the initial four lines, saying, "This is the refrain," and adjusted the melody accordingly.[125] The melody of "Song of the Motherland" was clearly influenced by the folk songs of the "volzhskaia vol'nitsa" (Volga Cossack freemen). Both the main text and the refrain have a broad, rolling, stately melody, and the refrain displays the ascending melodic progression characteristic of Volga songs, such as "Iz-za ostrova na strezhen'" ("From behind the island to the river").[126] Dunaevskii has left the fullest account of the evolution of the song:

> "Song of the Motherland" was first created as music, and Lebedev-Kumach composed the lyrics for the most part. At first the music arose with a broad and drawn out melodiousness, in a slow movement, and was then modified to a march, according to the demands of the film. The first contours of "Song of the Motherland" were created during the summer of 1934 [1935][127] at Orlova's old apartment, in the now half-collapsed little house in Gagarinskii Lane in Moscow. At that time Orlova was not yet such a celebrity and lived with her parents in an extremely modest old Moscow apartment.
>
> I was sitting at the piano (also old), on my left was Aleksandrov, on the right—Lebedev-Kumach. When the melody appeared, everyone started singing it at once. We yelled and screamed and rejoiced at the happy find. Prompted by the music, Lebedev-Kumach found a first line on the spot. The line began: "Khorosha strana moia rodnaia" ["Beautiful is my native land"]. But I told him that the broadness of the music demands not "khorosha" but "shiroka" ["broad"]. And everyone agreed on that. We were all young and passionate. I was 34, Aleksandrov was 31, Kumach—36. It was a wonderful time, those were wonderful years.[128]

In later years, possibly to magnify his cinematic achievements, Aleksandrov muddied the waters by claiming that the composer, lyricist, and director had worked through thirty-six variants of the song (the exact number varied in different retellings), amidst arguments and quarrels, before arriving at the canonical version. In addition, Aleksandrov transferred to *Circus* his 1938 story of the garbled song for *Happy Guys* that Dunaevskii had played for him over the telephone from Leningrad.[129] In a contemporary letter, Dunaevskii directly contradicted Aleksandrov's story: "Of course, Aleksandrov, over the radio, talked about

36 times just to be witty. It's not true! It was precisely 'Shiroka strana moia rodnaia' that came out amazingly naturally and easily, and had few corrections. (For example, at first it was 'khorosha strana moia rodnaia'.)"[130] Although Dunaevskii does mention the change in the lyrics of the first line, which he himself suggested, he is referring generally to the ease with which he composed the melody. Orlova's 1939 account of Lebedev-Kumach's work on "Song of the Motherland" is more credible than Aleksandrov's later mythmaking: "The poet never spared his authorial pride if it was necessary to work again and again on one and the same song.... While working on "Song of the Motherland," he composed thirty variants and—not content—redid it once more, stopping at the thirty-first."[131] Thus, Aleksandrov's later, hypertrophied version of the evolution of "Song of the Motherland" pertains only to the search for the appropriate *words* for the song.

Here Lebedev-Kumach followed both his own intuition, as well as the director's wishes. Dunaevskii's melody inspired Kumach to write lyrics reminiscent of Volga folk songs, such as "Vniz po matushke, po Volge" ("Down the Mother Volga"), which often conjoin the broad expanses of country and river with individual freedom: "Ot Moskvy do samykh do okrain, / S iuzhnykh gor do severnykh morei, / Chelovek prokhodit kak khozain / Neob"iatnoi Rodinoi svoei. Vsiudu zhizn' privol'no i shiroko, / Tochno Volga polnaia, techet." ("From Moscow to the very borderlands, / From the southern mountains to the northern seas, / Man passes as the master / Through his boundless Motherland. / Everywhere life flows freely and broadly, / Like the brimming Volga").[132] Aleksandrov also wanted "words that would contain a maximum of generalization, like "The Internationale."[133] Kumach responded with: "Nashe slovo gordoe—"tovarishch"— / Nam dorozhe vsekh krasivykh slov. / S etim slovom my povsiudu doma, / Net dlia nas ni chernykh, ni tsvetnykh" ("Our proud word—"comrade" / Is dearer to us than any beautiful words. / We're at home everywhere with this word / For us there are no black or colored peoples"). Two models, then, both familiar to Soviet audiences—the Volga folk song and the revolutionary song/hymn—provided the verbal template for "Song of the Motherland."[134]

*****

GUKF officials saw the rough cut of *Circus*, minus part of the soundtrack and the circus acts, on March 10, 1936. Their report praised the film, but identified three problem areas to be corrected: 1) because the plot was minimal, the chronological sequence should be maintained, so as not to confuse the audience; 2) because of the music, minimal plot, and interpolated episodes, rhythmical precision should be maintained and prolix episodes eliminated; and 3) complete the ending, i.e., the Kneishitz line, lullaby, and parade. Further detailed remarks provide an insight into the extent of Shumiatskii's creative control over films: 1) in Mary's escape scene, the crowd chases her too long—shorten it; 2) Kneishitz should be called an "artist," not "colonel" [evidence of GUKF's ignorance of American circus parlance]; 3) shorten Mary's dance on the cannon to improve the episode and make it more proper [evidence of Bolshevik Puritanism]; 4) slightly shorten the lions episode; 5) shorten the first lullaby—although it sounds very pleasant, it is too drawn out; 6) shorten Kneishitz and Mary's [should be Raechka's] dance on the restaurant roof to avoid showing the empty restaurant, or else delete [the episode was filmed atop the unfinished Moskva hotel]; 7) reshoot the panning shot with the lullaby in different languages, making it shorter, smoother, and with more effective character types, so that the ideologically correct conception of this scene resounds with all artistic force; 8) re-record Kneishitz's words when he uncovers Mary's shame to the audience to preserve his usual foreign accent [Aleksandrov did not or was unable to make the change]; 9) the Kneishitz line is not finished; the studio administration and the director should think through a new variant for the conclusion of the Kneishitz line so that his disgraceful behavior (transferring to Soviet territory an unethical attitude toward a woman, a comrade, and a human being) receives not only social censure, but also retribution [during the lullaby, Kneishitz is prevented from reaching Jimmy by two military men and is followed out of the circus building at the end by two policemen, suggesting impending arrest]; and 10) make *the time clearer* in the film, especially in the final episodes occurring just before May 1.[135] (In the completed film, a close-up of Mary's hotel room desk calendar shows April 29; later the night-time illumination on Red Square forms a "May 1" figure.) Aleksandrov finally completed the changes on April 16 and the film was approved by May 19.[136]

The première of *Circus* on May 23, 1936 was conjoined with the opening of the outdoor movie theatre "Gigant" (Giant) within the Zelenyi teatr (Green Theatre) at the far end of Gorky Park, a showpiece of Soviet recreational culture. The première was preceded by a week of intense publicity in the newspapers. As with *Happy Guys*, Aleksandrov arranged for western-style advertising in the city: a plywood effigy of Marion Dixon in full plumage, accompanied by "gerls," the muted Soviet variant of showgirls, was affixed to the tall bell tower of Strastnoi monastery in the center of town. The construction was decorated with electric lights and could be seen from as far away as the Nikitskii Gates.[137]

Circus premiered in ideal circumstances. Gigant, which seated up to 20,000 spectators on wooden benches, was the largest movie theatre in the Soviet Union. For the première, it was equipped with a three-story high screen of 170 square meters (25–27 meters were typical) and a 400-watt foreign sound system instead of the usual 8–10 watts.[138] According to a period journalist, the program began at 9:00 pm, with Shumiatskii, Aleksandrov, and other officials seated at an onstage presidium table. Speeches by the head of GUKF, by Betti Glan, director of the park, and Aleksandrov, who described the filming of *Circus*, preceded the screening, after which the actors, wearing their costumes from the film, put on a show for the audience. Antimonov (the circus ringmaster) introduced the performers: Orlova sang, accompanied by Dunaevskii; Volodin, Otto (the "Chaplin" assistant in the film), and Villi Karlin performed the 1903 bicycle routine; Kurikhin (Capt. Borneo) performed with his dog; Otto did Chaplinesque tricks with a cane; the actors and a choir sang "Song of the Motherland." After a cartoon intermission, at 1:00 a.m. the audience was treated to a special edition of Soiuzkinokhronika, filmed by Roman Karmen, with excerpts from the three earlier speeches.[139]

The première also had its bad moments: because the advertising posters for *Circus* in front of the Zelenyi Theatre mentioned only Orlova and Stoliarov, Moscow Art Theatre actors Pavel Massal'skii and Aleksandr Komissarov took offense, refusing to participate in the post-screening program. Stoliarov supported them and also refused, thereby provoking official displeasure.[140]

Aleksandrov's original plans for *Circus* had been so grandiose and at the same time—fluid, and he had filmed so many extra takes that, instead of the allotted 20,800 meters of positive stock, Mosfil'm was left with 88,369 meters of footage, which the studio decided to exploit for a silent version of *Circus* and a children's circus film.[141] The silent version, needed for the older equipment in outlying areas of the country, was constructed from unused takes of *Circus* footage and submitted to GUKF on July 25, 1936.[142] During late summer 1936, Simkov, Aleksandrov's co-director, wrote a script titled "Little Black Jim," for a children's film that varied the *Circus* plot: Jimmy, who was happily ensconced in a circus children's home run by Skameikin, is kidnapped by Marion Dixon's brother, Reginald.[143] As the basis for the new work, Simkov cobbled together material from unused takes of *Circus*, to be augmented by some additional filming. However, Sokolovskaia, Darevskii, and Aleksandrov rejected the script because of poor dialogue, and the studio halted production, fearing that the 200,000 ruble expense of additional filming would not guarantee quality.[144] In November, Aleksandrov himself was considered for the project, but Usievich informed his boss that the director was on vacation and would have to begin work on a new film after his return.[145] Simkov was returned to the project and produced the short, two-part *Nash tsirk* (*Our Circus*), a potpourri of circus acts (dogs on the high-wire, a balancing bear, the Chaplin clown bumbling through trapeze routines with the acrobats, performing lions, and the 1903 bicycle act), edited together from unused *Circus* materials and unified by humorous and instructive verse commentary.[146]

A record one million people saw *Circus* during the first two weeks of its run in Moscow theatres; by 1939, it was the most popular of all Soviet films, having been seen by forty million viewers.[147] In 1937, *Circus*, along with eight other Soviet films, was awarded the Grand Prix at the International Exhibition in Paris. In a controlled show of tolerance, *Sovetskoe iskusstvo* published a long negative letter about the film from one V. Belinskaia, accompanied by a formal response from Shumiatskii, and a column of excerpts from mixed reviews by other readers.[148] Belinskaia's rather querulous letter does point out the excessive melodrama, the awkward heaviness of the Soviet "Flight to the Stratosphere," when compared to Marion Dixon's act, Stoliarov's mediocre acting, and other defects of the film, which Shumiatskii either admitted or was not able to rebut in his response.

Professional critics Balázs and Zel'dovich praised *Circus* in a special July 1936 issue of *Iskusstvo kino*. Balázs argued for the end of traditional Bolshevik asceticism: glamorous spectacles are appropriate in the land of the Soviets because they reflect Russia's new social reality.[149] Aleksandrov, Dunaevskii, and Orlova were all awarded the newly instituted Stalin Prize, first degree, in 1941.

Dunaevskii's score for the film was criticized—from the perspective of original musical composition rather than the film musical—for imitative, bravura circus music and overly repetitive waltzes and foxtrots,[150] but professional criticism did not interfere with the tremendous popular success of his music. Mary and Martynov's march from their "Flight into the Stratosphere" act became a popular item in radio programs, and a generation of mothers sang their children to sleep with the "International Lullaby."[151] As advance publicity, the text and music of "Song of the Motherland" were published in the newspapers a month before the release of *Circus*[152] and the song was broadcast over the radio. As a result, some provincial viewers assumed "Song of the Motherland" to be a folk song inserted into the film, thereby proving Dunaevskii's thesis about the successful mass song.[153]

Since the lyrics of "Song of the Motherland" were linked to the new Soviet constitution, which was discussed in the media and adopted in 1936, the song immediately gained official status as the music for celebrations in honor of the constitution.[154] With its memorable melody and patriotic message, "Song of the Motherland" very quickly became a second national anthem, like "America the Beautiful" in the United States. Lebedev-Kumach recalled hearing the song performed by 100,000 people at the opening of Sokol'niki Park in 1937.[155] The following year, women pilots Osipenko and Grizodubova reported singing "Song of the Motherland" to keep their spirits up after crash-landing in the taiga.[156] Before the war, the song opened programs of All-Union Radio; during the war, it was sung by soldiers going into battle, preceded announcements of the commander-in-chief's orders, and was used by partisans to check the identity of parachutists found in their territory.[157] During the post-war years, Radio Moscow began its 6:00 am broadcasts with its call sign, the first line of "Song of the Motherland."[158]

The song remains a recognized cultural sign in post-Soviet Russia: in Tverskaia Station, the Moscow metro system has advertised itself with a panorama of the Kremlin bearing the caption, "Ot Moskvy do samykh do okrain." The ad turns on the use of a widely recognized signifier whose significance has shifted from political-ideological to geographic-commercial. In Zel'dovich's *Moskva* (2000), the Russian hero, disguised as an orthodox Jew, performs "Song of the Motherland" as pastiche, but for modern audiences the musical quotation comments ironically on New Russian society. In *Okkupatsiia* (2003), Orlova and her performance in *Circus* are iconic for the opposing sides, Russian and Belorussian combatants. In post-Soviet films on the Stalin era, "Mary's Song" and Orlova's performance on the cannon have become emblematic of the paradoxes of the era, the high spirits of acquiescing members of Soviet society and the misery of the

Gulag: in *Zashchitnik Sedov* (1988), the hero sees Orlova's dance on the cannon at a provincial movie house and laughs at the episode as a respite from the day's labors—advocating for men arrested as wreckers during the purges. In *Koma* (1989), the wife of a prison camp officer gives a rousing performance of Orlova's song and dance routine against the background of prisoners' Gulag existence. Ganshin, the hero of *The Inner Circle* (1991), screens the episode for Stalin. Glasha in *Come and See* (1985) performs the song and dance in the woods to distract the hero, Floria, as they are under attack by Germans during World War II.

Looking in on the set of *Circus*, just as Dunaevskii and Lebedev-Kumach were working on "Mary's Song" and Aleksandrov was devising dance steps, the ironic Eisenstein astutely dubbed them all "Orlova's trotters" ("Orlovskie rysaki").[159] The film was indeed Orlova's vehicle, establishing an ideal of *femina sovietica* and making her the reigning superstar of Soviet cinema. On June 3, 1936, shortly after the première of *Circus*, as one of the country's prominent women, she was asked to speak over the radio in support of the impending abolition of legal abortion.[160] Crisscrossing the country with concerts, she was besieged by crowds of admirers in every city.[161] Her concert in Cheliabinsk elicited an engraved piston ring from local workers with the famous refrain from the *Happy Guys* march, "Nam pesnia stroit' i zhit' pomogaet" and the dedication: "To the artist L. Orlova from the Stakhanovites of the piston ring department of the foundry shop, Cheliabinsk Tractor Factory. Dec. 20, 1936. 12,314 pieces—a record after your concert."[162]

II. THE SPECTACLE OF IDEOLOGY

The storyline of *Circus* is more logical and unified than that of *Happy Guys*, and in its cinematography this is Aleksandrov's most innovative film. *Circus* was a more polished product, although Aleksandrov now and forever abandoned the exuberant zaniness of *Happy Guys*. It was also one of the first films to embody the grand style (*bol'shoi stil'*) of High Stalinism through both myth and circus spectacle. A 1933 article in *Sovetskoe iskusstvo* comments disapprovingly on the anomalous position of the circus among the Soviet arts: a typical program still consists of a series of independent acts by individual artists, instead of a unified performance; the performers themselves—not the director—determine content, music and presentation; performances emphasize skill and technique over content.[163] Of all the popular arts, circus thus remained the most independent at a time when cultural uniformity—socialist "unified performance"—was in the ascendant, thereby allowing Aleksandrov a certain artistic license in creating his world under the big top. By setting his film in the circus world, which he knew and liked, Aleksandrov was able to infuse Soviet reality with the western pageantry, glamour, and showmanship he admired, while pressing spectacle into the service of ideology. At the same time, he deftly located the social problems mentioned in the film—racism, physical abuse of women, prejudice against illegitimate children, capitalist exploitation of talent—in the West.[164]

Circus differed radically from *Happy Guys* in its over-determined topicality. Shortly after its release, Aleksandrov and Nil'sen explained their conscious design: "From our point of view, the film *Circus* is above all a Soviet film in which today's environment, saturated with energy and optimism, plays a large role. Every detail of the film, even one that is perhaps insignificant by itself, must to some degree reflect the present day of our Soviet land."[165] Both explicitly through the script and implicitly in the mise-en-scène, the film presented a comprehensive inventory of Soviet beliefs, initiatives, achievements, and hopes at the beginning of High Stalinism.

The 1935 May Day and Physical Culture parades, the first to be choreographed by Moscow artists with formal production numbers in march rhythms, created the template for subsequent ritualized celebrations of Soviet success.[166] *Schastlivaia iunost'* (*A Happy Youth*), the documentary film chronicling the Physical Culture parade, had been released in 1935. Aleksandrov called his pandus production number with showgirls clad in exercise outfits "a physical culture review in the 'new circus,'"[167] and *Circus* itself concludes with the grand spectacle of a May Day parade led by the jauntily marching cast, all attired in impeccable sport whites of *fizkul'turniki.*

The topicality of *Circus*'s themes is validated by newspaper accounts of the decorative leitmotifs of various Moscow squares for May Day 1936: "The design of Red Square follows the theme 'Long live the international proletarian May 1st holiday!' A sculpture—an international group of workers with red flags—is being erected on the square."[168] Pierre Herbart, who witnessed the 1936 May Day parade, particularly noticed the tableau vivant of a black man carrying an immense red flag that streamed behind him, snapping in the wind, "above the young faces raised toward the Lenin mausoleum."[169] The design for Sverdlov Square emphasized children's interests. Large panels on the Lenin and Historical Museums depicted the achievements of the Red Army. Mayakovsky Square was decorated with aviation motifs devoted particularly to "stratonauts" and parachutists. The design of Komsomol Square emphasized railroads and transportation.[170]

Circus consciously elaborates on all these subjects of the moment, several of them motivated by the new constitution, which had been presented for public discussion in 1935.[171] Jimmy, Marion Dixon's black baby, is welcomed into the land of racial equality that stands opposed to the racist politics of both Nazi Germany and the US, as personified by Dixon's manager, Franz von Kneishitz. In 1935, the press trumpeted a new initiative: "the special care of the Soviet government for children and mothers" through increased subsidies for nurseries, kindergartens, and new school construction.[172] By the end of *Circus*, Dixon with Jimmy in her arms is elevated to the perception of Madonna with child, and the audience amply demonstrates its affection and care for children in the circus lullaby episode. Dixon's illegitimate black baby now belongs to her bourgeois past, and she forms a new and proper Soviet family with Martynov, symbolically configured in the often reproduced shot of the trio on the circus stairs (Fig. 25). As a foreign performer who joins the Soviet circus, Dixon affirms the international solidarity of all workers. At the beginning of the film, Martynov, a trained sharpshooter, has just returned from service in the Red Army, wearing medals on his Stalin-style military jacket.

Eight hundred airplanes had participated in the 1935 May Day parade.[173] In July 1935, Stalin and members of the Politbiuro attended a large demonstration of parachute jumping at the Tushinskii airport, and the first all-union rally of parachutists occurred on August 16.[174] Russian aviators were competing with foreign pilots in the race to conquer "the stratosphere," a term much in the news: "Gliders Fly to the Stratosphere," "A Flight to the Stratosphere."[175] Aleksandrov also named the Soviet circus act "Flight to the Stratosphere"; in the pandus production number, the girls' tank tops were emblazoned with airplanes; in another scene, their hands mimic propeller blades. After her flight, Orlova descends to earth in a parachute, and miniature parachutes spell out "The End" of the film. Polar exploration was another indicator of Soviet success linked to aviation. "Dixon" thus functions in two registers, both as a typical American surname and as the site of a research station and Arctic settlement built up during the early thirties.[176]

The new Moscow metro had opened May 15, 1935, and Nil'sen was the first to include it in an entertainment film: "We wanted to show the splendid architecture of the Okhotnyi riad station, highlight the dynamics of the powerful escalators, reproduce the unique lighting of the station, even in insignificant transitional shots."[177] In the process of incorporating the pléiade of topical themes for 1935 May Day decorations into *Circus*, Aleksandrov failed to include only the folk arts. The May Day celebration had concluded on May 2 with a radio concert of folk songs performed by the newly created Theater of Folk Arts.[178] The folk melos was, of course, to become the subject of Aleksandrov's next film, *Volga-Volga*. Nevertheless, in approving the musical score for *Circus*, he was already sufficiently savvy to accept Dunaevskii's reading of popular musical tastes, which drove the composer's work on "Song of the Motherland" with its underlying folk melodies.

Stalin's notorious 1935 dictum, "Life has become better, comrades. Life has become more joyous," was intended to signal an improvement in the general standard of living, initiating a discourse of abundance, which engendered a concomitant celebration culture. Food ration cards had been eliminated in September 1935 and *Pravda* now ran a special column devoted to new consumer goods. Living well was no longer anti-Bolshevik: *Circus* explicitly situates the luxurious new Hotel Moskva, where Marion Dixon resides, in close spatial proximity to the centers of power, Red Square and the Kremlin's Spasskaia Tower, whose brand new stars, encrusted with precious stones, Aleksandrov was the first to record on celluloid.[179] The Kremlin tower outside the hotel window now "stands as a guarantor of the good life."[180]

In *Circus*, the official discourse of plenty characteristic of high Stalinism is specifically coded as Art Deco through mise-en-scène and quotation of American and European models. In *Happy Guys*, only the fictional Moscow music-hall had been decorated in the

Figure 25.

Art Deco style, complete with the multiple grand pianos of American musical film. But in *Circus*, Aleksandrov also adopted the gender assumptions of Art Deco into the film and attempted to reconcile western style with the vocabulary of totalitarian representation through visual analogies: modernist elements of the Art Deco frozen fountain are congruent to the Palace of Soviets; the female body functions as architectural building block or bio-tile in both the cinematic frozen fountain and in the human iterations of the Palace of Soviets at physical culture and May Day parades.

In his 1936 review of *Circus*, film critic Béla Balázs defended Aleksandrov's extravagant concluding production number (the rotating wedding cake topped by the film's star, Liubov' Orlova, and decorated with posing "gerls": "We have no reason to develop ascetic tastes. We don't intend to let bourgeois art have a monopoly on glitter and beauty."[181] The 1925 Paris Exposition Internationale des Arts Décoratifs et Industriels Modernes, from which Art Deco takes its name, showcased western industrial modernity *precisely as glitter and beauty*, affluence and consumerism, as expressed through the Art Deco style dominating all aspects of exposition design, from the architecture of pavilions to the contours of furniture and smaller consumer goods, such as jewelry and toiletries, and disseminated throughout the western world by the exposition and, later, Hollywood cinema, which heavily influenced Aleksandrov.

Art Deco or Style Moderne, often termed the "skyscraper style," is characterized by a classical, streamlined, geometric visual practice associated with the machine age and urban life. The imagery of Art Deco was broadly inclusive and eclectic: "It was drawn from the ancient past—classical features from ancient Greece and Rome, as well as from Egypt and Asia. It was drawn from the distant future—with images from the world of Buck Rogers. It was drawn from contemporary views of the 1920s, 1930s, and 1940s—twentieth-century visions of machines, jazz, and speed."[182] In its representation of modernity, Art Deco incorporated the Futurist love of the machine, Cubist geometricism, Expressionism's penchant for distortion, and Art Nouveau's rhetoric of whiplash curves. Beyond its attachment to the ancient and the primitive, including Native American art, Deco courted the exotic—the art of Japan, China, and the South Seas.[183]

Because Style Moderne emphasized the decorative arts, it rapidly gained mass appeal and its visually striking aesthetic was adopted into American cinema via set and costume design, even the blocking of figures within the film frame. (Typical examples are *Top Hat* [1935] and *Swing Time* [1936].) In *Circus*, Aleksandrov frames *his* vision of Soviet modernity in exactly the same stylistic language, metonymically associating it with the nexus of power, the Kremlin and Red Square. Dixon's hotel room with its balcony and French doors, through which blows a gentle spring breeze, its artistically arranged cut flowers, its grand piano and sectional sofa are reminiscent of 1930s American high society films. The décor of the hotel room is elegantly minimalist. An Art Deco chandelier, a curvilinear window treatment and two large floor vases with just three elegantly arranged flowers in each (an Oriental influence) are obvious examples.[184]

Marion Dixon herself favors Art Deco clothing: a floor length, high necked evening gown with simple lines (in the scene of her rejection of Kneishitz and writing to Martynov), hats with low brim, cocked to one side (while teaching Raechka performance postures) and Garbo, Dietrich, and Hepburn's man-tailored pants suits (in Raechka's visit to Dixon at the Hotel Moskva). In the "Song of the Motherland" episode at the piano, the design of Dixon's dress with its densely frilled high ruff encircling the neck is the same as Eleanor Powell's in the 1936 musical *Born to Dance.* Art Deco also indulged in a rage for exotic ostrich feathers, often depicted on popular chryselephantine (bronze and ivory) statuettes. Such feathers form Dixon's outré headdress in the "Flight to the Moon" act, the headdress in turn parodied in American comedy fashion by the Chaplin clown who sticks it onto the opposite end of his anatomy.[185] In the Soviet "Flight to the Stratosphere" act, the stylized cannon mounted on a car has streamlined Art Deco lines (unlike Kneishitz's klutzier capitalist cannon), and Dixon and Martynov wear helmets with Art Deco lines—all meant to convey the speed of the modern age (Fig. 26).[186] Finally, the Negro spiritual on which Mary's lullaby to Jimmy is based represents the shadow presence of American blacks in Art Deco culture—strongly aestheticized in the influence of African art and jazz and therefore distanced.

In her recent book *Designing Women* and two earlier articles on Busby Berkeley films, Lucy Fischer has demonstrated the ways in which, for Art Deco, the female figure was a highly charged cultural site and a veritable fixation of its iconography, articulated via statuettes, figural lamps, glass shadow plaques, ashtrays, candy dishes, candlesticks, powder jars, perfume bottles, in advertising, and, of course, film.[187] In her first circus performance, the "Flight to the Moon" act, Marion Dixon is constituted as sexual object—and quite properly so. After all, this is a capitalist show. Her body language and dress are suggestive: swaying hips form the body into an S-shape that draws attention to the female figure; her long white dress has a contrasting dark bra-like bodice section, emphasizing the bust. She also wears a very short-skirted dance outfit that concentrates its spangles on Dixon's breasts, and the dance on the cannon displays her legs at eye-level to the audience.

Karina Dobrotvorskaia has written about the black and white image fields with traditional valorization for good and evil operating throughout *Circus.*[188] From the perspective of visual aesthetics, it is also the case that black and white were favorite Art Deco color combinations, familiar to us from the mise-en-scène of Berkeley films with black Bakelite or glass floors and white figures or furniture (e.g., in *Gold Diggers of 1933* and *Dames*) and the interiors of unrenovated White Castle restaurants. Dixon makes her first circus appearance in the short, dark wig of an Art Deco vamp, popularized by Lulu from Pabst's *Pandora's Box* (1928).[189] Similarly, a dark-haired Garbo, Art Deco's iconic incarnation of the dangerously sexual woman, as "La Brunna" in *The Torrent* (1926), was the *risqué* foreign female of the same mold and therefore acceptable to American audiences because the girl next door would never behave that way.[190]

Figure 26.

Initially and, of course, superficially, Marion Dixon is figured as the same sort of dangerous foreigner. But as she looks at Martynov's picture after her first performance, Dixon half removes her dark wig, revealing her blonde hair, the beginning of her transformation from vamp into *femina sovietica* (Fig. 27). At her final performance, she rejects the wig in disgust. Offstage, the blonde Dixon eschews stage makeup and dresses modestly, albeit fashionably. Dixon's *true* persona is thus coded as light and positive from the outset, as a kinder, gentler incarnation of the iconic Marlene Dietrich, although Dixon must undergo a further transformation as she joins the great Soviet family.[191]

The rotating tower production number of the first finale, occurring in the localized space of the circus, celebrates the successful resolution of the Dixon-Martynov love relationship, as Dixon sings, "...joy, you are with me, / My happiness is near." As circus performer and woman in love, attired in a flowing chiffon dress, she sings and sways atop the terraced tower. However, the second finale of *Circus*, which opens out into the public space of Red Square, shifts to a national-ideological register requiring a more contrastive coding. With the sound of a cymbal clap, as if in a big top magic act, the circus performer who is *personally* committed to Martynov as lover metamorphoses into an *ideologically* committed, sexually sanitized, white-clad *fizkul'turnitsa*. Aleksandrov legitimates and inscribes western spectacle and Art Deco aesthetics into Soviet culture by locating them in proximity to Red Square (the center of the State) and within the Soviet circus (Dixon's concluding pandus number). But at the end, he also presents the transformation of Dixon from richly attired circus star into *fizkul'turnitsa*, a traditional icon of the era which did not clash with the ideal of a good life. The two hypostases of woman are mediated and reconciled through Dixon's physical prowess as circus performer.

The black and white semiotic patterning throughout the film also actualizes Dixon's active and unlawful sexuality. In spite of her name, Marion/Mary is not virginal, and doubly guilty—with her black lover and mulatto baby—through miscegenation. Furthermore, Dixon's present abusive relationship with the dark-haired, black-garbed Von Kneishitz can hardly be platonic. The fascist Kneishitz also defines Jimmy's blackness as ugly, citing his kinky hair, flattened nose, and turned-out lips. Even though Soviet society is presented as racially tolerant, unlike Germany and America, the carnivalistic aspects of the film, which Aleksandrov adopted from American cinema, nevertheless coexist in tension with this professed ideal. The cinematic blackface performance tradition, which migrated to Hollywood from the minstrel show and vaudeville, encouraged white caricature of black culture. In a stock American comedy routine, Skameikin codes Jimmy's black skin as soiled when he tries to clean the boy off with a handkerchief after their subway trip: "Uh-oh, how black you are! How dirty I've gotten you!" Skameikin's joke thus plays on the ironies of a black actor in blackface, originally a form of self-parody required of black performers in post-Civil War minstrel shows.[192] The conclusion we draw from Skameikin's comic fussing over Jimmy is that soiled white skin can be cleaned up, black skin cannot. The circus director's closing speech on tolerance, which the ideologically orthodox

Mosfil'm administration objected to as frivolous, is comically absurd in its outlandish exaggeration, thereby undermining the ideological seriousness of the message: "Have as many [children] as you want—black ones, white, red, blue ones, if you like, pink ones with stripes, dappled greys, go right ahead." Although the tolerant circus audience refuses to condemn Dixon's past and accepts her black baby, Aleksandrov makes it clear that her future lies with Martynov, the Soviet New Man, who is of course white.

Figure 27.

Aleksandrov created Marion Dixon on the model of Helen Faraday, Marlene Dietrich's heroine in Joseph von Sternberg's 1932 film *Blonde Venus*, another Art Deco product, from which the Russian director also borrowed narrative and visual motifs. In *Blonde Venus*, Dietrich plays a German performer who marries an American chemist and settles down to happy family life in the US, but she returns to the stage to earn money when her husband needs treatment for radiation poisoning. At a nightclub, she meets a millionaire playboy, with whom she begins a torrid affair during her husband's treatment in Germany. When the husband returns earlier than expected, Helen must flee with her small son to retain custody. Victimized by the American legal system, pursued by the police and a vindictive husband, she travels from city to city, taking odd jobs that spiral downward into prostitution. Nevertheless, husband, wife, and son are reunited—in a highly ambiguous way— at the end of the film.[193]

Like Marion Dixon in Russia, Helen Faraday is a foreigner in the United States. During the production number that marks her return to the stage from private life, she dons an enormous Afro-style blonde wig, thereby assuming a sexualized performance persona (like that of black-wigged Dixon in the capitalist circus act) that also references the eroticism of her extramarital affair. *Blonde Venus* stereotypically, albeit ironically, defines active female sexuality as primitive blackness and animality. In the "Hot Voodoo" nightclub act, Helen emerges from a gorilla suit and sings her desire, amply illustrated by the dancing African native women who surround her:

> Hot Voodoo, black as mud,
> Hot Voodoo in my blood.
> That African tempo has made me a slave.
> Hot Voodoo, dance of sin,
> Hot Voodoo, worse than gin.
> I'd follow a caveman right into his cave.

As a fallen woman and therefore unfit mother, Helen must flee from city to city to retain custody of her small son. Following the Sternberg model, Aleksandrov himself wrote the parallel opening scene of *Circus* in which Dixon, carrying Jimmy, flees a Southern lynch mob enraged by her liaison with a black man. Like Helen, who impulsively begins an affair with a millionaire playboy (her nightclub act simultaneously coding Eros as black), Marion Dixon succumbs to her passion for a black man. In puritanical and intolerant American society, both women suffer persecution and abuse as the price of sexual liberation. Ultimately both discard their unlawful sexuality, returning to their true selves as devoted mothers and wives, sublimating Eros within family life, and in the case of Dixon, within the demands of the State (Fig. 28).

If Dixon's subaltern position in the capitalist circus act is signaled by her propulsive ejaculation into the sky by the phallic cannon, after doing a little dance on it (a staging of male fantasies) and then by the ropes with which Kneishitz controls the crescent moon on which she circles the arena, Dixon is figured as Martynov's equal in the stratosphere act as they descend the staircase side by side in unisex jumpsuits and helmets. Instead of being lowered into the cannon, she now steps energetically into the chamber through a side door. Nevertheless, the *continuation* of the Soviet performance, the lengthy production number with the rotating wedding cake decorated with "gerls" duplicates the objectification of the bourgeois "Flight to the Moon" act and the gender assumptions of Berkeley's Art Deco cinema with equal and even greater gusto.

:e 28.

The images of a human figure on a tower-shaped edifice in *Circus* (Dixon on the cannon, Dixon atop the terraced tower) resonate in two stylistic registers for a student of the Soviet 1930s: the American musical film and the strongly vertical "grand style" of Stalinist architecture, first defined by Boris Iofan in his project for the Palace of Soviets.[194] Aleksandrov was in Europe and Hollywood during the early years of Busby Berkeley's success in Eddie Cantor vehicles such as *Whoopee* (1930), *Palmy Days* (1931), and *The Kid from Spain* (1932), and he was clearly familiar with Berkeley's 1933 *Footlight Parade*, whose "By a Waterfall" production number he imitates in *Circus*. Aleksandrov even follows the usual *topical* sequence of the major production numbers in Berkeley's three classic 1933 films (*42nd Street, Footlight Parade*, and *The Gold Diggers of 1933*): first number features sexual suggestiveness (Dixon's performance on the cannon); second, the abstract-geometric number (the equivalent Soviet number with its bio-patterning in the propeller and rotating tower scenes); third, social commentary (the multi-ethnic circus lullaby and Red Square parade).[195] In fact, *Footlight Parade* concludes with the same type of military-patriotic number as *Circus*. The Shanghai Lil number ends in Berkeley's favorite display of synchronized military marching, complete with American flag, FDR, and eagle. *Circus* concludes with the patriotic, quasi-military marching of a May Day parade.

Berkeley's own aesthetics are grounded in the international Art Deco style of the 1920s and '30s, which the European-trained architect Iofan also knew well. One of the most popular visual metaphors of Art Deco was the "frozen fountain," made famous by its use in the 1925 Paris Exposition's entrance gate, the Porte d'Honneur. The fountain was a favorite motif in skyscraper designs, such as the Empire State and Chrysler buildings, exterior decorations, even jewelry, and ultimately became a worldwide symbol of the Style Moderne.[196] Berkeley brought the frozen fountain to life and expressed the industrial imperative of Art Deco in the rotating terraced tower decorated with showgirls of the "By a Waterfall" production number,[197] and Aleksandrov borrowed the same mechanized construction, which he called a "pandus," (a technical term for "ramp," from the French *pente douce*) for the final production number of *Circus* (Fig. 29). Possibly the Russian director also had industrial imperatives in mind in a world of five-year plans, but in *Circus*, the pandus actually rotated by man-power—studio workers exerting muscle in their hiding place underneath the wooden construction.[198]

Both Art Deco and the musical, with its inevitable chorus line, were fixated on the female figure constructed as a geometrical abstraction.[199] The rotating fountain of "By a Waterfall" illustrates Berkeley's geometrical organization of bodies and space that articulates the aesthetic code of Art Deco: seated on the fountain, bathing suit-clad girls spread their legs in v-shapes (integrated into patterns by an overhead shot); in another scene they sit swinging their legs from side to side in patterned unison. Several women, their arms raised to display their figures, are posed atop the fountain. A related architectural design of the era is the cylindrical tower with a female figure posed on the

Figure 29.

top (as is Dixon on the cannon in the "Flight to the Moon" act), an actualization of the woman on a pedestal metaphor.[200] Whether figured as Madonna or whore, the female figure is on display.

Unlike Berkeley's production numbers that create an impossible geography divorced from the narrative logic of the film, Aleksandrov's more extended pandus number, though imitating Berkeley's rotating fountain, is sutured into the plot as a circus performance and musical expression of Dixon's union with Martynov. Aleksandrov's "gerls" wear fairly revealing period sports outfits with airplane-emblazoned tank tops. Dixon again dances with her hips on a tower, as in the "Flight to the Moon" act, but in the pandus production number, Aleksandrov's appropriation of Art Deco aesthetics, while folding into itself Berkeley's geometrical routines, also borrows from Art Deco's artistic figuration of the female body.

An enormously popular Art Deco *objet* during the late twenties and thirties was the chryselephantine sculpture, most often depicting a dancing female figure on a raised pedestal.[201] The chryselephantine figures were based in dance and theatre (initially both Ballets Russes and jazz influences) and came, in turn, to influence cinema aesthetics. In the American film *Hollywood Revue of 1929*, there is even a *tableau vivant* of the female figures posed in niches.[202] Dixon's dance performance posed atop raised structures is similarly reminiscent of the chryselephantine figures, usually mounted on columnar or ziggurat-like bases.

Experimental illumination was integral to Art Deco interior design: illuminated glass panels in walls, mantelpieces of diffusing glass lit from within, wall niches lined with panels of diffusing glass to highlight the sculpture or vase within the niche. Lamps with bases of female nudes holding up illuminated globes or cylinders were pervasive in the mass market between the two world wars. "Similar to these lamps were those in which a metal figure was placed before a sheet of glass lit from behind with a concealed bulb. When the lamp was on, the female figure was illuminated in silhouette—emphasizing her corporeal outline."[203] When Dixon dances atop the pandus, her transparent chiffon dress with pendant sleeves frames her figure, which is silhouetted by strong backlighting in the manner of these widely manufactured Art Deco plaque-lamps (Fig. 29).

The entire Soviet production number following "Flight to the Stratosphere" employs abstract visual effects: the girls manipulate ropes in S-patterns and form light patterns by juggling torches in the darkened arena; in a cut to another set, the girls are massed together, imitating airplane propellers with their hands; light bulbs strung over the pandus describe circle and star motifs; the girls kneel sideways on the pandus, forming patterns with bodies and raised arms. Just as in Berkeley's extravaganzas, Aleksandrov's women are passive, manipulated as bio-tiles, their identities subsumed in a single, abstract, totalizing design. The figuration of Dixon here is no different from that of the "Flight to the Moon" number, and her union with Martynov, as celebrated in the pandus number, codes female sexuality as passive.

As the pandus number begins, statues of naked male and female athletes are seen at the bottom of the staircase, supplying a sexual subtext to the scene. After the collective torch juggling, Mary throws Martynov two burning torches (little teases), but then male vitality ignites female sexual energy as Martynov runs up the staircase with the torch to "ignite" the waves of electric light descending from the staircase which then, in turn, brightly illuminate the pandus decorated with showgirls, who then assume suggestive poses. In a kaleidoscopic overhead shot the girls spread their legs in v-shapes à la Berkeley, and then, as the camera angle changes, assume a classical, half-kneeling profile pose with a raised arm, thrusting forward the body, highlighting torso, legs and arms, and finally lie flat on their bellies (Fig. 29). The sculptural poses here are clearly borrowed from Art Deco's iterations of Greek art.[204] The celebration of female sexual energy continues as the girls run along the edges of the rotating pandus and descend the staircase with Radio City Rockette kicks, to the repeated leers of the circus director and ringmaster.

*****

For some time both during and after the making of *Circus*, Grigorii Aleksandrov had been preoccupied with incorporating the Palace of Soviets into a representation of Soviet modernity in film. He was still talking about it in July 1936, relevant to the early planning for *Volga-Volga*:

> We expect to begin our film at the source of the Volga and then, while traveling with our heroes, show the Volga-Moscow canal with its best architectural structures and new Moscow, the new Moscow port and perhaps the Palace of Soviets embankment, together with this grandiose and majestic building. The technology of modern process photography will allow us to show the Palace of Soviets at its actual location and the way it will appear in its completed form.[205]

In the end, even with Nil'sen's skill in devising ingenious process shots, Aleksandrov's plan for the proleptic Palace proved to be impossible.

Socialist Realist architecture was a highly eclectic phenomenon. Underlying the accreted neo-classicism of the Palace of Soviets are Iofan's initial, functionally modernist designs. In fact, his "Worker with a Light" preliminary sketch and modernist entry for the open competition (both 1931) rather resemble the figuration of Dixon on the cannon.[206] Iofan's 1933 competition entry has a fully rounded, terraced design (Fig. 30), and the final 1934 design for the Palace of Soviets published in *Pravda* included a rounded and terraced tower that still recalled the contours of the frozen fountain, now surmounted by a monumental human figure.[207] If the final designs for the Palace of Soviets were increasingly classicized, it is worth noting that Art Deco had also developed a classicized design for public buildings, especially in the United States.[208] The Palace of Soviets design (tower edifice with human figure) became paradigmatic for Soviet architecture and was, of course, repeated in the more rectilinear and classicized tower of the Soviet pavilion topped by Mukhina's *Factory Worker and Collective Farm Laborer* at the 1937 Paris Exhibition.

Given the strong tendency of Soviet visual culture toward schematicized abstraction, the terraced, vertical frozen fountain with human top ornament, as employed by Aleksandrov in the pandus act—and here differing from Berkeley's use of multiple female figures atop his constructions—was also familiar to Russian audiences, inscribed in visual memory as *Soviet* image through the contours of the Palace of Soviets, which were insistently advertised in the media. Both figures atop elevated edifices are on display; both have pride of place. Both structures display the ascending, terraced, vertical thrust against the force of gravity that held symbolic significance as the "skyscraper style" for

Figure 30.

Soviet as well as American architects. The American Claude Bragdon wrote: "In a true skyscraper, it seems to me that the lines should sweep unbrokenly upward to express the engineering fact of vertical continuity and the poetic fancy of an ascending force in resistance to gravity—a fountain." [209] The contours of the Palace of Soviets were replicated in human form in countless May Day and Physical Culture parades, either with a representation of the leader as top ornament or with a parade participant.[210]

Many genre films, of which the musical is one example, attempt to mediate and reconcile or resolve the vexed issues facing their societies. In accord with the normalizing syntax of the musical, capitalist and Soviet visual constructions, pandus and Palace, are thus *reconciled* in Aleksandrov's film. The first part of the Soviet "Flight to the Stratosphere" number was intended both to surpass the "Flight to the Moon" act and to signify sexual transcendence, as Martynov soars on the Cupid wings he first wore in the circus *stengazeta* (wall newspaper) cartoon. In the second part of the Soviet production number, Aleksandrov reconciles entertainment and the body politic, first via the visual links between the upward, pyramidal thrust of the pandus completed by a single human figure and the contours of the Palace of Soviets and second, through the bio-patterning of the female body as building block of a larger structure in both the pandus number and the analogous human iterations of the Palace of Soviets during Soviet celebrations. Here the lexicon of Art Deco dovetails with that of totalitarian visual representation (the individual as part of the body of the State) in a way that Aleksandrov adroitly exploits in *Circus*.[211]

Finally, like both Art Deco's "skyscraper thrust" and Socialist Realist architecture's upward imperative, the spatial semiotics of *Circus* move along a strongly vertical axis, with the attendant traditional valorization of high and low, providing throughout the film a kind of rhythmical formal harmony. During her initial performance, Dixon dances atop the cannon and flies to the circus ceiling, to her dreamland of love and peace, as described in the words of her "Moon Waltz":

> The moon is high above,
> The stars shine far away.
> They fly away from sorrows and troubles
> To that blue, blue light
> Where there are no tears, no pain.
> The moon is high above.
> It hides tears far away.
> Blue peace enters my heart in a light stream.

Afterward, in her dressing room, she is thrown to the floor by the abusive Kneishitz but then lifted up by Martynov. Her hotel room is on an upper floor and, thanks to the camera, proximate to the sacred center of Red Square. The verticality of the "Flight to the Stratosphere" act and pandus production number expresses both sexual and national transcendence, which is temporarily grounded by Kneishitz's revelations. Dixon then falls even lower as she escapes backstage and faints on the straw-covered floor of a holding room for circus animals. Kneishitz emerges onto the scene at the lowest point in the arena. As Jimmy is rescued from him, the child is lifted higher and higher in the stands. In a scene mirroring the audience's cradling of Jimmy during the international lullaby, Dixon is then lifted and carried to the circus staircase by Martynov. In the second finale of the film, the vertical hierarchy is transferred from localized and personal (the circus arena) to national and mythic space. Dixon's pedestal is trumped, as it must be, by the hierarchical Great Family with the invisible leaders now positioned atop the mausoleum and above the marchers on Red Square. The concluding scenes of the film recapitulate the dynamic vertical axis of the film as balloons rise up from the documentary footage of marching crowds and then descend to the ground as parachutes emblazoned with the letters spelling out "The End."

As a genre film, the Soviet musical typically strives to reconcile entertainment with social imperatives. In *Circus*, Grigorii Aleksandrov brings the Art Deco aesthetic of western cinema, art, and architecture to the land of the Soviets, demonstrating that, in the proper ideological context, even bourgeois luxury and entertainment can be redeemed and integrated into socialist society.

*****

The plot architectonics of *Circus* are more conventional and linear than those of *Happy Guys*: a prologue in the American South; the exposition in the various circus acts and Dixon's first performance; the complication of love and the need to develop the Soviet circus act; the struggle to overcome obstacles to love and to the show; the climax of the show itself and reunion of the lovers; the denouement of the first, localized ending and the second, spatially extended finale. In addition, the well-worn plot devices of the misdirected love letter and mistaken identity drive the action of the second half of the film.

In *Circus*, the semantics of the circus plot overlay the syntax of the show musical, combined with elements of the folk musical in its Stalinist iteration. In accord with the conventional paradigm, making a show (the development of the Soviet circus act "Flight to the Stratosphere") parallels the making of a couple identified with differing cultural (and ideological) values: the American artiste Marion Dixon and the Soviet performer Ivan Martynov. Taken in its entirety, the Soviet act ("Flight to the Stratosphere" plus the pandus production number) can be read as a celebration of national achievements in aviation (propellers, parachutes, high altitude flight), the electrification of the country (the elaborate illumination of the pandus), and finally, symbolic architecture (the Palace of Soviets and pandus congruences). Elements of the folk musical, in which the making of the couple parallels the formation of a community at the local and national levels, enter the plot in mid-film, as Martynov teaches Marion the patriotic "Song of the Motherland." Later, as Marion writes her love letter to Martynov, "May 1" appears in lights behind her on Red Square. Although the romantic plot of *Circus* is thus connected to the political-ideological messages of homeland, racial equality, and international solidarity that dominate the latter half of the film, contemporary critic N. Aduev immediately identified the "defect" of *Circus*: the motivation for Marion's break with Kneishitz and her decision to remain in the USSR is not ideological, but personal—her love for Martynov, as elaborated by Marion's declaration to Kneishitz after Martynov's accident. The ideological motives of racial equality and internationalism only surface *after* her decision to remain in Russia.[212] In reality, *Circus* simply follows the established syntax of the musical—the axiomatic primacy of the making of the couple that drives the making of the show and formation or unification of a community.

The circus as a metaphor/microcosm of the world has a long pedigree in cinema, including Chaplin's *The Circus* (1927) and Tod Browning's *Freaks* (1932) through Fellini's circus films and Wim Wenders' *Wings of Desire*. Aleksandrov borrowed the enslaved heroine motif from Chaplin's film in which the father is the villain, as well as several comic routines. Charlie enters the lion cage by mistake; to impress the girl, he later braves another lion, but is then frightened by a kitten. Skameikin finds himself in the lions' cage by mistake, but the new lion tamer later faints at the barking of the Captain's terrier. Charlie knocks out a rival and kicks sawdust all over him. Skameikin pistol-whips the lions with a bouquet of roses and then shows dominance by kicking sawdust at them. Aleksandrov actualizes the circus-world metaphor at the beginning of the film through the emblem of the Southern Railway car on which Marion escapes the Sunnyville lynch mob. The globe displaying the United States spins to reveal the landmass of the USSR and then descends to a Soviet circus arena to enter the performance: a seal balances the globe on its nose, a bear balances on a barrel with the same image, Durov family performers throw the globe to performing dogs and a clown. The change to playful circus music at this point defines the Soviet world as happier and more carefree than the violent American South.

The backstage plot alternates with circus acts, songs, and other performances which, through parallel editing, not only guarantee a brisk tempo but just as importantly, mirror and comment on the peripeties of the plot. Marion Dixon's "Flight to the Moon" act[213]—the song and dance on the cannon that propels her to the moon, the lyrical "Moon Waltz," and flight around the arena on a trapeze controlled by ropes from the ground—metaphorically rehearses her predicament as objectified female, sexualized and enslaved by patriarchal western culture. Mary's frenetic jazz song and Charleston atop the cannon appropriate the jerky rhythms of a marionette and, in fact, puppet master Kneishitz not only supervises Marion's circus act—she is announced as performing "under his direction" ("pod rukovodstvom")—but also literally controls the ropes of her trapeze swing throughout the performance. The phallic cannon of sexual transcendence propels Mary to the moon, where she sings a dream of escape from earthly travail and oppression. It is only after the performance that both Marion and Kneishitz reveal their true selves: the fragile, vulnerable blonde under the black vamp wig and the physical weakling and degenerate, screened by a pneumatic chest.[214] At the moment Martynov becomes conscious of his love for Dixon, he sprouts cartoon Cupid's wings, and his flying is similarly a metaphor for sexual transcendence.

When Fred Astaire teaches Ginger Rogers a set of dance steps, he also teaches her to love and falls in love himself. When Martynov teaches Marion Dixon "Song of the Motherland," a song about love of country, he follows the same paradigm. The initial failure of the Soviet stratosphere act mirrors the setback in their love affair as Kneishitz forces Dixon to leave the arena. In the hotel room, her lullaby, which passes into the "Moon Waltz," signals the temporary unattainability of her dreams of love. Skameikin's reading of Dixon's note, the switch gag (kissing Raechka's hand while speaking Marion's name), and Raechka's slapping Skameikin until he "understands" is intercut with the so-called Soviet-Roman gladiators acrobatic act. Their human tower comments on the precarious balancing act of love relationships, and the comedic music of the act seeps into the Skameikin-Raechka dustup. After the aggressive Raechka repeatedly slaps and subdues Skameikin, he displays compensatory male bravado by repeatedly swatting the lions with a bouquet of roses, chasing off the predators (announced as "kollektiv khishchnikov" by the ringmaster), only to faint at the sudden barking of Capt. Borneo's little dog.

Marion Dixon's last, lackluster performance reflects the seeming failure of the love affair. Captain Borneo's act, the conventional man with trained dog, unexpectedly reverses to a dog with a trained man who picks up the correct playing card on command. The balance of power between Dixon and Kneishitz, the master-servant relationship, reverses in the same way when Dixon announces, "The Mary you knew is no more," and rejects the evening gowns and furs that have bought her acquiescence. Kneishitz then becomes the weaker party, dropping to his knees to beg for her love, and subsequently never really regains his power over Dixon. The 1903 "chudo tekhniki" (miracle of technology) and Capt. Borneo's act return us to the traditional pre-revolutionary circus, providing an ironic comment on the idea of progress in its Soviet iteration.[215] The 1903 bicycle act, which was the technological marvel of its time, ironizes over both the contemporary "Flight to the Stratosphere" act and Soviet technological achievement: a scene with Skameikin and Jimmy at the Okhotnyi riad metro station with its modern escalators is intercut with the bicycle act, as the performers' ditty on the soundtrack links both scenes. The song itself, which expresses reflexive joy, seconded mechanically by the repetitive pedaling melody, must repeat, just as the performance itself is repeated, parodying the topos of obligatory Stalinist optimism: "Chudakov my vidim chasto / Tselyi vek oni v slezakh, i vzdykhaiut ezhechasno… Akh! Akh! Akh! / My takikh ne uvazhaem, / Vse pechali—chepukha / Tselyi vek my raspevaem… Akh! Akh! Akh! /

Ves' vek my poem / Vse poem, vse poem, / Zria slez my ne l'em…" ("We often see strange people / They're forever in tears and sigh hourly... Oh! Oh! Oh! / We don't respect such people, / All sorrows are a trifling matter / We forever sing gaily Oh! Oh! Oh! / We sing all our lives / We keep singing and singing / We don't shed tears without a reason…").

The success of the show "Flight to the Stratosphere" (the Soviet cannon is mounted on a car—much more modern) parallels the now successful love of the couple, whose cultural values—domestic and foreign, capitalist and communist—have been reconciled. The sexual transcendence of flight is now melded with national transcendence, just as Martynov's cupid wings have been replaced by the wings of Icarus. Dixon and Martynov make their entrance as equals, dressed in unisex aviators' jumpsuits, capes and Flash Gordon helmets, and descend the grand staircase to the rhythm of "Song of the Motherland." Symbols of Soviet air power abound, from propellers on the showgirls' tank tops to their imitation of whirring blades in front of a triangular bank of propellers to the stratospheric rocket itself. The glorification of military might is paradigmatic for the folk musical, as in Busby Berkeley's synchronized marching and flag waving in *Footlight Parade* (1933) and the battleship number of *Born to Dance* (1936). In the Soviet instance, feats of aviation, such as the rescue of the Cheliuskin crew, also signify communication and unity between the center and the marginal areas of the Motherland.

During the show, as Skameikin and Kneishitz struggle over the possession of Jimmy, a dog with a rifle on its shoulder sits upright behind the child, and a monkey fires Kneishitz's revolver. Both animal acts undermine the melodramatic seriousness of the human struggle—an important aspect of Aleksandrov's treatment of the plot, as we will see later. The Berkeleyesque extravaganza that follows the successful flight celebrates the union of Dixon and Martynov. Atop the pandus, Marion sings the making of the couple ("…radost', Ty so mnoiu, / blizko schast'e moe" ["…joy, you are with me, / my happiness is near"]), which is again frustrated by Kneishitz's racial-sexual revelations.

The "International Lullaby" of the first ending, in which Russians, Ukrainians, Jews, an Uzbek, a Georgian, and a black American expatriate participate, is typical of the folk musical's passed- around song that creates community in the localized space of the circus.[216] Just as in *Happy Guys*, Aleksandrov then extends his spectacle to the outside world. The apotheosis of the second ending, the parade "performance" on Red Square that blends into documentary footage of a May Day parade, extends the folk musical's syntax of community to the reality of the entire nation.

Differing from the structure of *Happy Guys*, the paradigmatic dual focus of the musical is diminished in *Circus* because the Dixon character is clearly the narrative center of the film, and Orlova is its dominant performer. While there is a lovers' duet at the piano, the customary parallel songs and scenes are missing. Nevertheless, the dual focus still manifests itself in secondary oppositions underlying the male-female duality: the homegrown hero vs. a foreign heroine; communist vs. capitalist ideologies; Martynov's ethic of socialist collectivity vs. Dixon's focus on individual life experiences;

social stability and order vs. chaotic passions and deviation from conventional norms of morality (Dixon's past). The American folk musical paradigm of the wandering male who is tamed by the civilizing female and endows the community with his energy and spirit is reversed as Marion Dixon abandons her peripatetic ways and endows the concluding communal celebration, the May Day parade, with *her* energy. Like the American folk musical, *Circus* concludes with the reconciliation of the opposing values attached to the primary couple through their successful union, accompanied by the reaffirmation of patriotism and community.[217]

Altman argues that the folk musical typically displays a more genuinely evil villain than the show musical, providing a touch of melodrama, along with the reassurance that evil can be overcome.[218] With his racist views on miscegenation (paralleling and alluding to the rise of National Socialism in Germany) and abusive relationship with Dixon, Kneishitz embodies the sociopolitical evils of the bourgeois world. Evil is overcome as his blackmailing of Dixon fails, and he is followed out of the circus by two Soviet policemen. Altman notes that the tragic syntax of the first wave of American musicals (1928–30), initiated by Jolson's *The Singing Fool*, was often expressed by a plot highlighting "the plight of the child caught between quarrelling parents or abandoned by a dissolute mother."[219] In *Circus*, Jimmy is both illegitimate and the victim of racial prejudice: Kneishitz reproaches Dixon with Jimmy's kinky hair, thick lips, and flattened nose, and he frightens the child to tears. To Aleksandrov, who could easily have seen the early tragic musicals during his stay in Hollywood, the melodrama of the early scenes of *Circus* may therefore not have seemed as contrary to the laws of the genre as it did to Russian critics of the film.

Aleksandrov's dramatic prologue was intended to justify Dixon's fear of exposure by Kneishitz: Dixon and her black baby barely escape a Southern lynch mob by clambering onto a passing train.[220] Although she fears the dangers of the "Flight to the Moon" act (illustrated by her use of the ingenious religious makeup kit), Dixon dreads the revelations about her past even more. However, within the body of the film, melodrama turns into farce after Dixon's first conversation with Martynov in the dressing room, and melodramatic motifs are consistently undermined by ironic-comedic treatments. The animated materialization of Martynov's frosty gaze on the window as he stares angrily at the eavesdropping Kneishitz is a highly aestheticized and not fully serious treatment of the men's rivalry. Warmth pervades Martynov's dressing room, but Martynov's gaze freezes Kneishitz out, excluding him from the space Martynov shares with Dixon. As the window frost melts, the warmth of Martynov's room translates to mild spring weather on Red Square. With his dark hair and mustache, black top hat, long cloak and intense gaze, Kneishitz is as much an inflated image of the melodramatic villain as his pneumatic vest. After setting the intrigue in motion by giving Skameikin Mary's letter, Kneishitz dramatically wraps himself up in his cloak and dissolves into thin air—a parodic comment on the conventional figuration of the cinematic villain. The "performance" of Skameikin's floor fight with Kneishitz over the revolver alternates with circus performance—the pandus production numbers. Moreover, the struggle resolves itself comically as a monkey named "Sniper" shoots off the coveted gun. During the fight, Jimmy stands watching from a corner, but his supposed distress is undermined by the comic pose of the circus animal behind him: a dog sitting upright on its haunches with a rifle over its shoulder. Throughout the film, melodramatic action is repeatedly contravened by secondary images that tell us not to take any of this seriously.[221]

The Chaplin clown in *Circus* functions as both slapstick performer and servant. As a diminished Charlie, he provides only simple physical humor throughout the film (pratfalls, clowning with the audience, and cane tricks during the circus act; a collision with a pole when leaping off the train) and serves both Kneishitz and Dixon offstage, pumping up the manager's vest and bringing Dixon her makeup kit. Aleksandrov had met Charlie Chaplin during the early thirties in Hollywood and remained friends with him throughout Chaplin's life, visiting him regularly in Europe during his and Orlova's trips abroad. Throughout his career, Chaplin had struggled with studios over creative and financial control of his work. The Chaplin figure in *Circus* thus embodies Aleksandrov's view of genius in bondage to capitalist society: the timid, quiet Little Tramp of *Circus* is Chaplin himself, the humiliated artist forced to serve the almighty dollar.[222] The diminished Chaplin figure stands in the same economic relation to Kneishitz as Dixon, and the cinematic Little Tramp evokes the same pathos offstage as the abused American circus star.[223]

The serious lovers of *Circus* are paralleled by the secondary pair of Raechka and Skameikin, who both provide comic relief and function as temporary impediments to the successful making of the show (Raechka's weight gain causes the failure of the Soviet act in rehearsal) and the successful outcome of the primary love affair (Skameikin's infatuation with Dixon). Liudvig Osipovich, the circus director and Raechka's father, fulfills the traditional senex role—the crusty but well-meaning establishment figure who is initially hostile to the primary romantic couple for financial reasons.

*****

Dunaevskii affirmed that the musical plan for *Circus* had been worked out before the script was written and that 70% of the musical score had been composed before the film went into production.[224] As noted earlier, *Circus* signaled a change in strategy: from now on, Dunaevskii would compose music for the film around a memorable central song, and all important songs repeated instrumentally throughout the film. The major music of *Circus* always defines the situation or circumstances of a character, with one melody modulating into another as a character's situation changes. Along with the pomp and glamour of Marion's profession, the "Entrance March" conveys her anxiety about both the dangerous stunt and her own life situation. In their music and lyrics, both "Mary's

Song" on the cannon and the "Moon Waltz" signal her dreams of escape and peace: "Ia iz pushki v nebo uidu / Digi-digi-du, digi-digi-du…Meri verit v chudesa / Meri edet v nebesa. / Prygnut' v nebo ne legko / Zvezdy ochen' daleko / Meri, v nebo uletai / Do svidaniia, gud bai. / Ia lechu, khello, gud bai!" ("I'm off into the sky from a cannon / Digi-digi-du, digi-digi-du…Mary believes in miracles / Mary is going to the heavens / Jumping to the sky isn't easy / The stars are very far / Mary fly to the sky / Do-svidaniia, good-bye. / I'm on my way, hello, good-bye!"); "Khodit mesiats vysoko, / Svetiat zvezdy daleko… / V etot sinii, sinii svet, / Gde ni slez, ni boli net, / Uletaiut ot pechalei i ot bed… / Khodit mesiats vysoko… / Priachet slezy gluboko. / V serdtse svetloi rekoi / Vkhodit sinii pokoi." ("The moon is high above, / The stars shine far away… / They fly away from sorrows and troubles / To that blue, blue light / where there are no tears, no pain. / The moon is high above… / It hides tears far away. / Blue peace enters my heart in a light stream"). The "Moon Waltz" repeats instrumentally, underscoring her situation, her dream of happiness and peace, as Mary cries on her dressing room floor and looks at Martynov's photo and poster. Skameikin sings the first line of the waltz he associates with the foreign star in nonsense syllables (la-la-la), as he waits for his rendezvous with Dixon. The melody also plays on the soundtrack as Mary's poster, literally her face, is torn down at the end of her contract. In the pandus production number, the "Moon Waltz" melody, now accompanied by different lyrics, expresses her happiness, i.e., her altered circumstances: "Vse tak svetlo, mir tak khorosh… / Radost', ty so mnoiu…blizko schast'e moe." ("Everything is so bright, the world is so beautiful… /Joy, you are with me…my happiness is near").

After Mary's confrontation with Kneishitz, in which he derides Jimmy's ugly features, Mary sings in English and broken Russian a lullaby, based on negro spirituals, seeking tranquility and well-being for her black baby: "Spi, mai bebi, sladko, sladko. / Spi, mai mal'chik, slip, gud nait. / Vse igrushki, vse loshadki / Vse lozhitsia, zasypait. / Noch' uzhe prishel k tebe v okoshechko, / Nuzhno zasypai, khot' nemnozhechko, / Spi, mai mal'chik, spi, mai mal'chik / Ai, baiu, baiu, bai, bai..." ("Sleep my baby, sweetly, sweetly. / Sleep my little boy, sleep, good night. / All your toys, all your horsies / All are going to bed and falling asleep. / Night has already come to you in the window, / You need to fall asleep, at least for a little while. / Sleep my little boy, sleep my little boy / Oh, rock-a-bye, rock-a-bye, bye-bye…). The lullaby then passes directly into a stanza of the "Moon Waltz," reiterating Mary's predicament and her longing for peace: "Khodit mesiats vysoko… / Priachet slezy gluboko… / Esli b mne dostat' rukoi / Vash serebrianyi pokoi / Zvezdy ochen' daleko..." ("The moon is high above… / It hides tears far away… / If only I could reach your silver peace with my hand / The stars are very far away…"). The "International Lullaby," which closes the circus plot, resolves Jimmy's situation musically by promising the black child unlimited opportunity in the land of the soviets: "Son prikhodit na porog. / Krepko, krepko spi ty. / Sto putei, sto dorog / Dlia tebia otkryty." ("Sleep comes to your doorstep. / Sleep very, very soundly. / A hundred paths, a hundred roads / Are open to you").

Like the "March of the Happy Guys," the lyrics of "Song of the Motherland" move the song beyond the narrative confines of the film and into the realm of cultural myths and their spatial elaborations. The terms "Rodina" and "Rodina-mat'" had disappeared from official discourse during the internationalist 1920s, but reappeared by the mid-thirties as an expression of the link between the biological and great Soviet families.[225] "The stability and relative economic security of Soviet society, as well as the pressure exerted by mass culture, encouraged the population to identify with the system. But the most permanent support of Stalinist society, one that weathered the purges and privations of the war, was the sense of pride and participation in Stalinist society shared by differing segments of the population."[226]

Following a major paradigm shift in cultural geography during the mid-thirties, "Song of the Motherland" defines the Motherland through a dialectic of largeness with unity, whether referencing geographical expanses, social issues, or human emotions: "*Shiroka* strana moia rodnaia, / *Mnogo* v nei lesov, polei i rek! Ia drugoi takoi strany ne znaiu, / Gde *tak vol'no* dyshit chelovek; "Chelovek prokhodit kak khozain / *Neob"iatnoi* rodinoi svoei. / *Vsiudu* zhizn' *privol'no* i *shiroko* / Tochno Volga *polnaia*, techet. / Molodym *vezde* u nas doroga, / Starikam *vezde* u nas pochet."; "Nashi nivy *glazom ne obsharish'*, / *Ne upomnish'* nashikh gorodov; "S etim slovom my *povsiudu* doma... Eto slovo *kazhdomu* znakomo, / S nim *vezde* nakhodim my rodnykh."; "S *kazhdym* dnem vse radostnee zhit'."[227] The Motherland is boundless, but one. Everywhere is Here. This model of unity presupposes the union of opposites: "Ot *Moskvy* do samykh do *okrain*, / *S iuzhnykh gor* do *severnykh morei*"; "*Molodym* vezde u nas doroga, / *Starikam* vezde u nas pochet"; "Kak *nevestu*, Rodinu my liubim, / Berezhem, kak laskovuiu *mat'*." The Motherland is defined by a "new-found benevolence of uncharted spaces." City and countryside, center and periphery, are no longer opposed in official discourse as they were during the 1920s. Aviation and exploration have conquered space, and the boundaries of cultural geography are expanded to the very margins of the country. Conflicts now arise when outsiders attempt to violate this outer boundary:[228] "No surovo brovi my nasupim, / Esli vrag zakhochet nas slomat'." When Martynov sings the refrain ("Ot Moskvy do samykh do okrain...") for Dixon, the quatrain is accompanied by a long shot of Red Square, thereby linking center to the rest of the Motherland, which is not shown at all. New Moscow, the focus of economic investment and grandiose construction projects, such as the metro system, becomes representative of the entire country, a source of national— and not only Muscovite— pride.[229]

The melodic movement of "Song of the Motherland" consolidates the significance of geographic expanses in the song. In the three eight-line stanzas, the musical progression is rising and incomplete because it is unresolved. In contrast, the melody of the four-line refrain ("Shiroka strana moia rodnaia...") is *stable* and affirmative rather than rising, thereby highlighting the importance of its lyrics. Geographic expanses give rise to freedom ("Gde tak vol'no dyshit chelovek"), opportunity ("Molodym vezde u nas doroga"), social justice and cohesiveness ("Starikam vezde u nas pochet"; "Nashe slovo gordoe—'tovarishch' / Nam dorozhe vsekh krasivykh slov…Net dlia nas ni chernykh, ni tsvetnykh, / Eto slovo kazhdomu znakomo, / S nim vezde nakhodim my rodnykh."); and indirectly—personal happiness, paraphrasing Stalin's words: "S kazhdym dnem vse radostnee zhit', / I nikto na svete ne umeet / Luchshe nas smeiat'sia i liubit'." The model of largeness-unity is further heightened by spatial and psychological maximalism: "Ia *drugoi takoi* strany ne znaiu. / Gde *tak* vol'no dyshit chelovek"; "Ot Moskvy do *samykh* do okrain"; "*Nikto na svete* ne umeet / *Luchshe nas* smeiat'sia i liubit'."

In the masculine, patriarchal discourse of Stalinist culture, *Rodina-mat'* remains a passive feminine image: "Chelovek prokhodit *kak khozain* / Neob"iatnoi rodinoi svoei" ("Man passes as the master / Through his boundless motherland"). In totalitarian societies, both sexual love and its energy (libido) and the incest taboo (the mother) are typically sublimated into love of country, which must also be protected. During the Red Square finale, the film enacts this paradigm through the figure of Marion Dixon, who is both private mother and lover, as well as the foreigner who has been assimilated to Mother Russia and toward whom Martynov turns as he sings, "Kak nevestu, Rodinu my liubim, / Berezhem, kak laskovuiu mat'." ("We love our Motherland like a bride, / We protect her like a tender mother").

Happy Guys began with a brilliant jazz overture rather than its famous march. In *Circus*, however, Dunaevskii systematically engraves the central song in audience memory, beginning with the overture. As the movie poster for *Happy Guys* is pasted over with the *Circus* poster, the Mexican-sounding introductory phrase of the "March of the Happy Guys" slips into an instrumental rendering of the line "Tak vol'no dyshit chelovek" from "Song of the Motherland," followed by a choral rendition of the song accompanying the introductory credits of the film. Although the musical bridge implies continuity between the two projects, the effacing of the visual image underscores Aleksandrov's abandonment of foreign slapstick comedy for a more serious musical genre in a national register.

Only parts of "Song of the Motherland" are used in the film: the four line refrain beginning "Shiroka strana moia rodnaia…," the first quatrain of the first stanza "Ot Moskvy do samykh do okrain", and the entire third stanza, beginning "Nad stranoi vesennii veter veet." These are the verbally memorable sections emphasizing geographical expanse, freedom, motherland, joy of life, and resistance to military aggression. Omitted are more localized references to the Volga river and two topics emanating from the new constitution—the rights of the elderly and racial equality.

Initially, "Song of the Motherland" defines Martynov's happy situation as a Soviet citizen and later comes to represent the same for Marion Dixon. As Martynov faces down—or rather, freezes out—Kneishitz through the window, the "Moon Waltz" modulates into "Song of the Motherland," as sung by Martynov to Mary, signaling the change in her situation from capitalist subservience to Soviet independence ("Chelovek prokhodit, kak khozain"). As noted earlier, in the following piano scene, individual love is parsed through love of country, again mediated by the central song. This movement is reinforced visually: as we hear Martynov singing the patriotic song, the camera slowly pulls back from Red Square (the metonymical representation of Motherland) on which three trucks spell out "Mai" in white letters for the May 1 holiday and the same letters appear on the roof of a building near Dixon's hotel. The pattern is repeated as Marion writes her love letter to Martynov while a choral rendition of the first quatrain plays on the soundtrack. "Song of the Motherland" in march tempo accompanies the performers' grand entrance in the Stratosphere act because of the significance of aviation to the State. In the first ending of the film, after Liudvig Osipovich's declaration of welcome for children of all stripes in the USSR, the instrumental "baiu-baiu" of Mary's lullaby on the soundtrack passes into her exalted rendition of "Song of the Motherland," thereby resolving Jimmy's situation by relocating him musically to the Soviet family. As Marion removes her dark wrap to reveal a white sports outfit, a cymbal clap signals (in the manner of a magic show) her transformation to Soviet citizen, and the tempo of "Song of the Motherland," now performed chorally, shifts to that of a military march, which continues to the end of the film.

Unlike *Happy Guys*, *Circus* is also ideological in its conscious construction of masculinity and femininity. While decrying racism, the color significations of the film reinforce white, Northern European stereotypes. The rise of modern European nationalism and notions of bourgeois respectability at the turn of the 18th and 19th centuries was accompanied and complemented by a Greek revival. Like European masculinities, that of the Stalinist hero derives from the classic ideal of Greek beauty described by J. J. Winckelmann in his *Geschichte der kunst des Altertums* (1774). Supple, muscular, and harmonious figures became the symbols of masculinity, the nation, and its youth. Like the flag, the national anthem, and the official coat of arms, the ideal of classical beauty was co-opted by European nationalisms in an attempt to provide masculine and feminine national stereotypes. [230] According to Winckelmann, a restrained and calm masculinity was naturally connected to national defense: "The quiet and repose of the body reveals the lofty and harmonious spirit of him who braves the greatest dangers for the sake of justice, who provides for his country's defense and brings peace to its subjects."[231] Like the newly rediscovered sculpture of Laocoon, the masculine hero was expected to display calm in the face of unbearable pain.[232]

In *Circus*, Ivan Martynov is figured as precisely this Aryan physical type—tall, muscular, square-jawed, and blonde. His first appearance in the film confirms his recent military service and unerring marksmanship. When not performing, he wears uniform garb, a Stalin jacket with cavalry trousers and high boots. Whether in public or private space, whether marching in a parade, sitting in a circus loge, or at the piano, Martynov's bearing is military, a return to the pre-revolutionary officer's body language: straight back, expanded chest, and erect torso that does not bend, even when seated.[233]

Martynov is calm, self-controlled, and a man of few words, which are also characteristic of the Socialist Realist hero who has achieved consciousness. His first greeting to the perpetually harried and angry circus director is, "Hello, and let's not be upset." As a circus performer and athlete, his physical prowess is a given. Martynov's profession also serves to underscore his courage: the circus poster Dixon finds on the floor of his former dressing room advertises him as "the pinnacle of human bravery and courage ("predel chelovecheskoi khrabrosti i otvagi"), and he refuses a safety rope during the rehearsal for the Stratosphere act. His stoic denial of pain and trauma after his fall (he eventually loses consciousness) is yet another demonstration of virility.

The native template for Martynov's masculinity is, of course, the folkloric Russian knight or *bogatyr'*—the super-sized human specimen, protector of the innocent and oppressed, and guardian of the nation's borders who serves to legitimize the Soviet government through historical continuity. Sergei Stoliarov embodied the type so successfully that, as the Stalinist hero merged with the traditional fairy tale hero, he subsequently spent most of his film career as literal *bogatyr'* in the films *Vasilisa prekrasnaia* (*Vasilisa the Beautiful*, 1939), *Kashchei bessmertnyi* (*Kashchei the Immortal*, 1944), *Sadko* (1952), and *Il'ia Muromets* (1956). The swarthy Kneishitz is Martynov's opposite in iconic masculinity: he is physically underdeveloped, nervous, temperamental, and generally out of control, as shown by his shouting and physical abuse of Dixon. These traits in the *German* entrepreneur-villain are precisely those—physical weakness, nervousness, lack of self control— attributed by the National Socialists to Jews and homosexuals.[234]

In the role of Marion Dixon, Liubov' Orlova was able to merge European standards of feminine beauty and glamour (her vaunted resemblance to Marlene Dietrich) with the ideal Soviet heroine. At the beginning of the film, the vamp is Dixon's stage persona and a reminder of her dark past. Offstage and in street clothes, she is an elegant, fashionably dressed, and cultured woman—much like period photos of Orlova herself. The sophistication of Orlova's heroine is acceptable not only in a foreigner, but more importantly, as the personification of the ideals of an emerging middle class in Stalinist Russia. Clothes make the (wo)man in *Circus*, for Dixon's transformation into Soviet citizen is marked by changes of costume. In the hotel room episode, Kneishitz throws at Marion, covering her, the expensive gowns and furs with which he has bought her professional co-operation and, most likely, sexual acquiescence. Her transformation begins as she throws off the extravagant clothing exclaiming, "The Mary you knew is no more!" And the bridge between the first finale, which confirms Dixon's place in the Soviet circus family, and the second (Red Square) ending, which confirms her place in the Soviet social hierarchy, is marked by her change into the sports attire of a May Day participant (Fig. 31).

From the outset, in her offstage persona Dixon, as a "good" foreigner, displays some of the traits of the impulsive, straightforward, and slightly naïve 1930s Soviet heroine. By nature, she is a kind and sincere woman who generously advises Raechka on the

Figure 31.

fine points of performance. With Martynov at the piano, she earnestly tries to sing the difficult foreign words of "Song of the Motherland" and later writes a love letter to him on impulse. During her final circus performance she cannot hide her despair at losing him, but naively takes no action. Instead, it is the cunning Raechka who devises the scheme of escaping Kneishitz's clutches. Because Dixon must ultimately become part of the Soviet Great Family, her metamorphosis is mediated through a subcategory of the *femina sovietica*: she is transformed into an energetic, confident *fizkul'turnitsa*.

The body language of foreigner vs. Soviet citizen is contrasted in Dixon's two circus performances. The sinuous body movements, flirtatious blowing of kisses, throwing a rose to an admirer, and coquettish hand waving are replaced in the Soviet act by the upraised arm of a military commander or orator, a military salute, and synchronized marching down the circus staircase. Marching in the Red Square parade, the body language of both Dixon and Martynov—erect bearing, head thrown back, arms held at the side—displays the restraint of the thirties hero, ultimately modeled on the gravity of the Leader himself.[235]

Kissing, like fanny-slapping, is reserved for the comedic lines of the narrative. The spotlight catches Raechka and Skameikin in the act at the beginning of the film because the plot will chronicle the peripeties of their subsequent misunderstandings. During the piano scene, Martynov pulls away and runs to another room instead of kissing Dixon. When Dixon saves the day by stepping in for Raechka during the performance, the circus director kisses her—but only as part of a standing joke begun earlier with Martynov: "on behalf of the management, on behalf of the mestkom, on behalf of the Ministry of Finance." Angry at his daughter's lateness for the première of the Stratosphere act, the circus director swats Dixon, dressed in Raechka's clothes, on the rear. After Marion's decision to remain in Russia and replace Raechka in the new act, she loosens up and mimics the peasant-vulgarian as *she* swats Liudvig Osipovich in return to get his attention.

For Aleksandrov, the transition from the pomp, pageantry, and pathos of the Hollywood musical to the Stalinist grand style and spectacle was a natural one. The successful musical—and especially the folk musical—expresses the ritual values of a society that coincide with the ideological values of the producer, in this case the Soviet State, so that Stalinist myths and their visual elaborations enter *Circus* naturally as a function of the genre. Aleksandrov's musical was perhaps the first Soviet film to give full and direct expression to the core myths of High Stalinism. Like many Socialist Realist heroes, Dixon undergoes a painful rite of passage as part of her path to consciousness and incorporation into Soviet society. Her arrival in the Soviet Union may be seen as separation; learning about Soviet society in Moscow under Martynov's tutelage expresses the transition. Dixon suffers initiation, regression into chaos, and symbolic death via Kneishitz's public revelations regarding her illicit past. At one point he tells Dixon, "This city has driven you mad!" Madness is not excluded from the death-experience of the initiate. Traumatized by the public exposure of her past, Dixon runs away from the circus arena and literally faints from shame and horror. By forming a proper family with Martynov, she transforms her formerly illicit and dark sexuality into a healthy, wholesome femininity, figured by the white sweater and skirt of the *fizkul'turnitsa*. She is resurrected into the great Soviet family in the Red Square finale of the film. Her sexual "spontaneity" is first stabilized and made passive within the family unit and then transformed into consciousness and subsumed to the state patriarchy during the second finale.

In a scene intercut with the international lullaby, Martynov finds Dixon offstage, prostrate in a pile of straw intended for the circus animals (an elephant stands nearby), and carries her back to the arena, cradling her passive figure in his arms. In the first ending, the formation of the private family is simultaneous with acceptance into the multi-ethnic family of the circus audience. Personal integration is then superseded by incorporation into the great Soviet family in the second finale as Dixon enters the sacred space of Red Square and participates in a May Day parade. But sacred space is simultaneously real-world space. Through the use of documentary footage, Aleksandrov signals our departure from the fictional world of the musical out into the actual space of the USSR. In formal terms, the device is laid bare through the differing grain of film stock. As a parade participant, Dixon the private individual is subsumed to the collective body of the State as figured in the marching masses and choreographed locomotives of the future, Palace of Soviets towers, and other human bio-constructs of May Day parades. In formal terms, her integration is effected through the superimposition of the actors' figures onto footage of the marching May Day crowds. Both visually and melodically, the Red Square finale brings to the foreground the connection between sports and military preparedness. Dressed in the garb of *fizkul'turniki*, the actors end the film marching and singing, "No surovo brovi my nasupim, / Esli vrag zakhochet nas slomat'" ("But our brows will contract in a stern frown / If any enemy tries to break us"). By 1936, the Soviet government was promoting physical culture programs for women, and one of the functions of sports in the Soviet Union was physical fitness for military preparedness.[236]

The repeating comic motif of understanding vs. not understanding, present from the early scenes of the film, is similarly recalibrated as it reaches resolution on Red Square. In the early dressing room scene of *Circus*, Dixon tells Martynov in broken Russian that she doesn't understand the language. He responds that it doesn't matter ("eto nichego"), which will ultimately prove to be true: linguistic incompetence is not an obstacle to esoteric understanding. Subsequently the motif is varied in the personal spheres of work and love relations. As Dixon shows Raechka how to hold herself during a performance, chin up, back straight, she asks: "Do you understand?" When the jealous Raechka repeatedly slaps Skameikin after reading Mary's note, he exclaims, "Raechka, I don't understand—for what?" She slaps him again, asking, "Now do you understand?" and he finally does.

During her visit to Dixon's hotel room, Raechka affirms Martynov's love for Dixon: "You are everything, absolutely everything to Martynov, do you understand?" Marion responds ungrammatically in the negative, "Ne ponimaesh." Raechka continues, "He loves you, do you understand? Stay, do you understand?" Finally, during the parade on Red Square, Raechka glances up and nods toward the mausoleum as she asks Dixon, "Now do you understand?" Dixon answers in the affirmative, albeit ungrammatically ("Teper' ponimaesh."), but her linguistic incompetence does not impede true understanding. The motif has been recalibrated from individual apprehension of everyday reality (language and human relations) to a higher, metaphysical level—the understanding of Stalinist discourse by the now ideologically conscious heroine.[237] The leader-godhead toward whom Raechka's words and nod are directed remains unseen, for he preserves sacred status by limiting access to his person in the semi-profane medium of cinema and frivolous musical comedy genre.[238] During the May Day reenactment of revolutionary events in the film, the dead leaders Lenin and Marx are resurrected through their images on flags; Stalin, the living leader, and Klim Voroshilov, People's Commissar for Defense, appear on parade posters, but not in person.

Chapter 2 Endnotes

1. Stenogramma, doklad Dunaevskogo v Muzykal'nom nauchno-issledovatel'skom Institute (May 7, 1937).
2. Il'ia Il'f, Evgenii Petrov, *Sobranie sochinenii*, vol. 3 (Moscow: GIKhL, 1961) 539. The Music Hall was located in the building of the present Tchaikovsky Hall on Triumfal'naia ploshchad'. Martynov was played by Boris Tenin, Alina (Mary in the film) by V. Tokarskaia, Raechka by Maria Mironova, the circus director by A. Zrazhevskii, Skameikin by Sergei Martinson, Capt. Sirotkin (later Capt. Borneo) by V. Lepko. (G. Ostrovskii, *Odessa. More. Kino* [Odessa: Maiak, 1989] 44; Boris Tenin, *Furgon komedianta. Iz vospominanii* [Moscow: Iskusstvo, 1987] 174). In his memoirs, Tenin underscores the professional circus acts included in the play (174–75).
3. *Proizvodstvennyi plan glavnogo upravleniia sovetskoi kinematografii na 1936 god* (Moscow: Kinofotoizdat, 1936) 37 and RGALI, f. 2450/2/1518. Aleksandrov told Saraeva-Bondar' that he and Orlova attended the première of *Pod kupolom tsirka* and immediately decided to make a film based on the play (A. M. Saraeva-Bondar', *Dunaevskii v Leningrade* [Leningrad: Lenizdat, 1985] 75). Frolov locates the inspiration for the film in Aleksandrov's response to the March 1935 Plenum of the Writers' Union Board, which called for greater cooperation between literature and arts professionals (Frolov, *Grigorii Aleksandrov*, 61). Although Aleksandrov always knew which way the political wind was blowing, documentary evidence shows that he had already decided on the project the previous fall.
4. Anon., "Neuviadaemyi Tsirk," *Kinomekhanik*, No. 5 (1986): 1.
5. G. Aleksandrov, "Printsipy sovetskoi kinokomedii," *Iskusstvo kino*, 5 (1949): 16. Aleksandrov was trained by the circus acrobat Rudenko, in whose group he participated as an extra. (Golikova, 47).
6. Tenin, 174.
7. RGALI, f. 2450/2/1518.
8. Saraeva-Bondar', *Dunaevskii v Leningrade*, 95.
9. Il'f and Petrov, Mar. 10, 1936 letter to Mosfil'm Director, RGALI, f. 2450/2/1518.
10. Sokolovskaia, Mar. 17, 1936 letter to Il'f and Petrov, RGALI, f. 2450/2/1518.
11. I. Dunaevskii, Mar. 13, 1935 letter to G. Aleksandrov, Dunaevskii family archives, Moscow.
12. Il'f , Petrov, vol. 3, 476–512. The source of the printed text is RGALI, f. 2450/2/1515.
13. Alina's abandonment of the child underscores the fact that her love for Martynov and not the racial issue is the prime motive in her decision to remain in the USSR.
14. Il'f, Petrov, vol. 3, 480, 479, 478.
15. Il'f, Petrov, vol. 3, 477, 482, 495.
16. Il'f, Petrov, vol. 3, 480, 503.
17. Il'f, Petrov, vol. 3, 501, 505.
18. Zakliuchenie GUKF-a po khudozhestvennomu zvukovomu fil'mu "Tsirk," RGALI, f. 2450/2/1518.

19. RGALI, f. 2450/2/1516.
20. RGALI, f. 2450/2/1516.
21. "Iz pis'ma produssera t. Darevskogo," *Za bol'shevitskii fil'm*, No. 13/14 (1936): 2.
22. K. Iukov, Apr. 11, 1935, Jun. 7, 1935 memos to Babitskii, RGALI, f. 2450/2/1518.
23. V. Nil'sen, Apr. 16 [1935] note to GUKF planning department. RGALI, f. 2450/2/1518. Nil'sen added that "Soiuz-Izokhrom" stock was acceptable for the silent version of the film.
24. Anon., "Tsirk," *Za bol'shevitskii fil'm*, No. 18/19 (1935): 3. The studio newspaper calls the film *Tsirk* at this early stage, although the Il'f and Petrov title, "Pod kupolom tsirka," continued to be used elsewhere.
25. S., "Pod kupolom tsirka," *Kino*, May 10, 1935.
26. Bliumenfel'd (assistant to the director of KhPO) and Zel'dovich, inspector-consultant, undated typed sheet addressed to K. Iukov, RGALI, f. 2450/2/1518.
27. Bliumenfel'd and Zel'dovich.
28. *Letopis' rossiiskogo kino 1930–1945*, 337, 346.
29. G. Aleksandrov, "Uspekh metoda," *Kino*, May 28, 1936: 3.
30. RGALI, f. 1821/1/16, publ. in Aleksandr Deriabin, "Kto s kem possorilsia? Iz istorii fil'ma 'Tsirk'," *Kinovedcheskie zapiski*, 45 (2000): 153–54.
31. G. Aleksandrov interview in *Moskovskie novosti*, May 18, 1935, qtd. in Jay Leyda, *Kino. A History of the Russian and Soviet Film* (Princeton, NJ: Princeton University Press, 1983) 308.
32. Aleksandrov, "Uspekh metoda." Standard Russian would be "Chto vy khotite" (What do you want?). The line was actually spoken by the circus director, Liudvig Osipovich.
33. Aleksandrov, "Uspekh metoda."
34. Several years later, in 1936, Aleksandrov wrote that the stubborn opposition of studio workers to *Happy Guys* also influenced his choice of genre in *Circus*. (G. Aleksandrov, "O sovetskoi kinokomedii," 4.)
35. Stenogramma, doklad Dunaevskogo v Muzykal'nom nauchno-issledovatel'skom institute (May 7, 1937).
36. RGALI, f. 2753/1/20. In his biography of Dunaevskii, D. Minchenok attributes the change directly to Stalin, who tells Shumiatskii: "Il'f and Petrov also write that a person can only be happy here. All of your people have been going to America. (Stalin meant Eisenstein, Tisse, Aleksandrov, Il'f, Petrov.) But it would be good to make it so that people came here from America, and wanted to stay as well. That's what we need. What do you think, comrade Shumiatskii?—I think that this is a very valuable addition. And that's what I will tell comrade Aleksandrov—answered the head of GUKF." (Minchenok 318). While Stalin may indeed have given instructions to change the direction of the film during 1935, Minchenok's chronology, which places the conversation after February 1936 and after Il'f and Petrov's trip to the US to gather material for *One-story America*, is contradicted by the documentary evidence.
37. Aleksandrov, *Epokha i kino*, 190. Upon Stalin's orders, Babel' and Pasternak were belatedly sent to the International Writers' Congress in June 1935.

38. Deputy Director of Mosfil'm Sokolovskaia, Mar. 17, 1936 letter to Il'f and Petrov.

39. In explaining production delays, Darevskii stated that the director's script had been redone seven times because of Aleksandrov's arguments with Il'f and Petrov. ("Iz pis'ma produssera t. Darevskogo," *Za bol'shevitskii fil'm*, No. 13/14 [1936]: 2). He is, in fact, referring to all versions of the screenplay and script, beginning with the first Il'f and Petrov effort, approved by Shumiatskii in November 1934.

40. On Gorky's efforts, see G.I. Shkliarevskii, *Istoriia russkogo literaturnogo iazyka. Sovetskii period* (Kharkiv: Vyshcha shkola) 1973, 36–45.

41. In the same article Aleksandrov also cited a character's incorrect, though comic, way of holding a pen which supposedly provoked a storm of protest from schoolteachers (G. Aleksandrov, "Printsipy sovetskoi kinokomedii," 14–15).

42. Boris Paramonov heard this from Aleksandrov during a 1967 conversation. (Boris Paramonov, "Liubov' Orlova v SSSR i v Amerike," Radio Svoboda broadcast, http://www.svoboda.org/programs/rq/2002/rq.020602.asp. Accessed Sept. 15, 2005). By June 13, 1935, when Dunaevskii signed a contract for several *Circus* compositions, "National Lullabies" were already listed. (RGALI, f. 1104/1/7.)

43. This replaced an earlier "anti-fascist prologue," written by Il'f and Petrov, which has not survived. See their March 10, 1936 letter to the director of Moskovskaia kinofabrika, RGALI, f. 2450/2/1518. The GUKF resolution on *Circus* states that "during final editing of the film, GUKF had to sharply abbreviate various episodes of a melodramatic character as unrelated to the idea and genre direction of the film. All the same, some things were not deleted." (RGALI, f. 2450/2/1518).

44. Minchenok, 301. Aleksandr Tsfasman was the pianist (Saakov, *Liubov' Orlova. 100 bylei i nebylits*, 28).

45. Danil'iants and Shul'ga, Nov. 21, 1935 memo to V. A. Usievich, A. M. Bliumenfel'd, and G. B. Zel'dovich. RGALI, f. 2450/2/1518.

46. Kirill Stoliarov, *Rodovye sny* (Moscow: Algoritm, 2001) 36.

47. Nadezhda Shamina, "Ee primerki zakanchivalis' obmorokom," *Gazeta.ru*, Oct. 14, 2001, http: www.gzt.ru/rubricator..gzt?id=2000000000003958. Accessed Apr. 12, 2003.

48. Reported in *Komsomol'skaia pravda*, Jan. 28, 1936, qtd. in Aleksandr Deriabin, "Kto s kem possorilsia? Iz istorii fil'ma 'Tsirk,'" 149.

49. "Zakliuchenie GUKF-a po khudozhestvennomu zvukovomu fil'mu 'Tsirk,'" RGALI, f. 2450/2/1518.

50. See the photograph in *Iskusstvo kino*, No. 11 (1996): 124–25. The actors are wearing their costumes from the film (flying suits from the circus act and street clothes) rather than the sport-whites of the *Circus* finale.

51. Saraeva-Bondar', *Dunaevskii v Leningrade*, 107.

52. G. Aleksandrov, "Prichiny zaderzhki filma 'Tsirk,'" *Za bol'shevitskii fil'm*, No. 13/14 (1936): 2.

53. Anon., "Tsirk," *Kino*, Apr. 22, 1936.

54. Danil'iants and Shul'ga memo to Usievich, Bliumenfel'd, and Zel'dovich, Nov. 21, 1935 in RGALI, f. 2450/2/1518.

55. Il'f and Petrov, Mar. 10 1936 letter to the Director of Moskovskaia kinofabrika, RGALI, f. 2450/2/1518.

56. See the conversation with Valentin Kataev in Frolov's *Liubov' Orlova v grime i bez grima*, 104–5 and A. Bernshtein, "Gollivud bez kheppi-enda," 227.

57. Minchenok, 302; *Letopis' rossiiskogo kino 1930–1945*, 345, 386.

58. *Letopis' rossiiskogo kino*, 348.

59. "Iz pis'ma I. Il'fa i E. Petrova I.V. Stalinu o poezdke v SShA, ne pozdnee 26 fevralia 1936 g," *Kremlevskii kinoteatr 1928–1953. Dokumenty*, comp. K. M. Anderson et al., ed. G.L. Bondareva (Moscow: Rosspen, 2005) 302–05.

60. B. Shumiatskii, "Moia kratkaia zapis' besedy s Ios. Vis. na prosmotre 9 marta 1936 goda," RGASPI, f. 558, op. 11, d. 829, ll. 94–6. "Dokladnaia zapiska B.Z. Shumiatskogo I.V. Stalinu o pis'me I. Il'fa i E. Petrova, 27 marta 1936 g," in *Kremlevskii kinoteatr*, 312–14. In April 1936, Shumiatskii was criticized by the Central Committee's Kul'tprosvetrabota department for fulfilling only 38% of the annual plan; in June he was attacked for inadequate film preservation (*Letopis' rossiiskogo kino 1930–1945*, 399, 408). In August, Kerzhentsev complained to Molotov about Shumiatskii's insubordination. Molotov had received a number of other reports about Shumiatskii's behavior and wrote on Kerzhentsev's memorandum: "Comrade Shumiatskii must be brought into line." (*Letopis' rossiiskogo kino 1930–1945*, 419.)

    Frolov reports another story referring to the earlier stages of work on *Circus*: "They say that, in the course of a conversation with Shumiatskii, the director began complaining to the chief cinema boss that the authors were interfering with his work and finding fault with trifles. 'Well then, cross them out completely,' Shumiatskii supposedly replied, thereby resolving all questions." (Frolov, *Liubov' Orlova v grime i bez grima*, 106.)

61. Nil'sen enumerated other important staff members in his "Vyrosla tekhnika—vyrosli kadry," *Za bol'shevitskii fil'm*, No. 21 (1936): 2.

62. Aleksandrov, "Uspekh metoda."

63. Interview with Konstantin Pavlovich Massal'skii, Feb. 16, 2002.

64. G. Aleksandrov and V. Nil'sen, "Kak my snimali 'Tsirk,'" *Komsomol'skaia pravda*, Jun. 21 1936.

65. V. Nil'sen and B. Petrov, "Kak my snimali 'Tsirk,'" *Iskusstvo kino* (July 1936): 43.

66. Nil'sen and Petrov, "Kak my snimali 'Tsirk,'" *Iskusstvo kino*. 43.

67. Nil'sen and Petrov, "Kak my snimali 'Tsirk,'" *Iskusstvo kino*, 43–4.

68. I. Vano, "Organizatsiia tvorcheskikh protsessov," *Kino*, Aug. 23, 1935: 3.

69. RGALI, f. 2753/2/7.

70. G. V. Aleksandrov and S. Luchishkin, "Khudozhnik v kino," *Kino*, Jun. 11, 1936: 3; Vano 3.

71. V. Nil'sen, No Title, *Kino*, Jan. 4, 1935: 5.

72. Nil'sen and Petrov, "Kak my snimali 'Tsirk,'" *Iskusstvo kino*, 44.

73. The construction diagrams, notes on lighting, and photos of American scenes in Nil'sen's archive attest to his major contributions to all visual aspects of *Circus*. (See RGALI, f. 2753/1/4 and 2753/1/31.)

74. Nil'sen and Petrov, "Kak my snimali 'Tsirk,'" *Iskusstvo kino*, 44–6.

75. O. Af., "Tsirk," *Kino*, Oct. 5, 1935: 2.

76. V. Nil'sen, "Kak snimalsia 'Tsirk,'" *Izvestiia*, May 16, 1936: 4.

77. Nil'sen and Petrov, "Kak my snimali 'Tsirk,'" *Iskusstvo kino*, 46.

78. "Pod kupolom tsirka. Rezhisserskii stsenarii," RGALI, f. 2450/2/1516. Nil'sen's wife, Itta Penzo, claims that Aleksandrov offered her the role of Raechka, but the angry Nil'sen, who despised nepotism in the film industry, demanded that Aleksandrov choose between him and his wife in the film (Arkadii Bernshtein, "Vozvrashchenie iz nebytiia," *Sovetskaia kul'tura*, Apr. 18, 1989: 6).

79. Anon., "Tsirk," *Za bol'shevitskii fil'm*, No. 18/19 (1935): 3.

80. According to a newspaper report, Jimmy's great-grandfather was a Virginia slave who had lost the use of one hand after being thrown into a stove as a child by his owner's angry wife. The great-grandfather had worked on a plantation all his life but ended up in prison in his old age for protesting the destruction of his apiary by the owner's children. Jimmy's grandfather, Archie Patterson, was a housepainter, who died young; his grandmother was a laundress. Jimmy's father, Lloyd Patterson, graduated from a Negro college, but was unable to get an engineering job in the US and had arrived in the USSR in 1932 with a delegation of black performers. Jimmy and his mother were evacuated to Sverdlovsk during World War II. Lloyd Patterson remained in Moscow, working as a journalist and foreign language radio announcer and was killed during the war. Jimmy graduated from the Riga Nakhimovskoe Uchilishche, studied at the Leningrad Naval Academy, and served as an officer of the Black Sea fleet. He began to write poetry during these years and later enrolled at the Gorky Institute of World Literature in Moscow. Patterson has published several poetry collections. (See Anon., "Ego sud'ba," *Pionerskaia pravda*, Jul. 8, 1947; E. Potapova, "Stal moriakom i poetom," *Ural'skii rabochii*, Mar. 18, 1978; Anon, "...Ia Vas svoeiu mamoi nazovu," *Rabochaia gazeta*, Feb. 11, 1982; Anon., "O sud'be poeta Dzhemsa Pattersona," *Novoe vremia*, No. 50 [1994]: 46).

81. Kushnirov, 145–46. In the overhead shots of the lynch mob pursuing Dixon, Aleksandrov borrowed from Eisenstein's *Strike*.

82. L. Orlova, "Zritel' i akter sovetskogo kino," *30 let sovetskoi kinematografii*, ed. D. Eremin (Moskva: Goskinoizdat, 1950) 378. See also L. P. Orlova, "Chuvstvo radosti nashego schastlivogo vremeni," *Za bol'shevitskii fil'm*, No. 22 (1936): 4.

83. S. Kurepov and I. Fridman, "Shurochka Vorontsova," *Sovetskaia estrada i tsirk*, No. 3 (1978): 27; Anon., "S"emochnyi den' gruppy rezhissera G. Aleksandrova. "Tsirk"," *Iskusstvo kino*, Jan. 1936: 43.

84. Kushnirov, 145.

85. Iia Savvina, "Faina Ranevskaia rasskazyvaet," *Iskusstvo kino*, No. 10 (1982): 81.

86. Kushnirov, 144.

87. V. Dolganov and Iu. Sirochenko, "Pushka dlia Liubovi Orlovoi," *Sovetskaia kul'tura*, Dec. 15, 1983: 8; E. Zvonitskii, "Attraktsion dlia kinozvezdy," *Sotsialisticheskaia industriia*, May 25, 1986; Boris Vilenkin, "Kak streliali Liubov'iu Orlovoi," *Komsomol'skaia pravda*, Apr. 15, 1994: 16.

88. Dzhems Patterson, "Tsirk," *Sovetskii ekran*, No. 17 (1967): 18.

89. Nil'sen and Petrov, "Kak my snimali 'Tsirk'," *Iskusstvo kino*, 45.

90. O. Afanas'eva, "Tsirk," *Kino*, Sept. 28, 1935: 2.

91. G. Aleksandrov and V. Nil'sen, "Kak my snimali 'Tsirk'."

92. Aleksandrov, *Epokha i kino*, 200–01.

93. Aleksandrov, *Epokha i kino*, 201.

94. A. M. Saraeva-Bondar', *Siluety vremeni*, ed. E.F. Kuznetsova (St. Petersburg: s.n., 1993), 197.

95. V. Volodin, "Vstrechi s obrazami Dunaevskogo," *I. O. Dunaevskii. Vystupleniia. Stat'i. Pis'ma. Vospominaniia*, 256.

96. Stenogramma, doklad Dunaevskogo v Muzykal'nom nauchno-issledovatel'skom institute (May 7, 1937).

97. G. Aleksandrov, "Pesnia o rodine," *Sovetskaia kul'tura*, Jan. 26, 1973: 4.

98. Stenogramma, doklad Dunaevskogo v Muzykal'nom nauchno-issledovatel'skom institute (May 7, 1937).

99. *I. O. Dunaevskii, Vystupleniia. Stat'i. Pis'ma. Vospominaniia*, 378–79.

100. Stenogramma, doklad Dunaevskogo v Muzykal'nom nauchno-issledovatel'skom institute (May 7, 1937).

101. I. Dunaevskii, Mar. 13, 1935 letter to G. Aleksandrov, Dunaevskii family archives, Moscow.

102. I. Dunaevskii, Mar. 30, 1935 letter to G. Aleksandrov, Dunaevskii family archives, Moscow. "Kostia" refers to "Kostia's Song" in *Happy Guys*. "Schastlivyi put'" was performed by Utesov in the music hall.

103. Stenogramma, doklad Dunaevskogo v Muzykal'nom nauchno-issledovatel'skom institute (May 7, 1937).

104. Stenogramma, doklad Dunaevskogo v Muzykal'nom nauchno-issledovatel'skom institute (May 7, 1937).

105. The music for *Happy Guys* and *Circus* was recorded in the Potylikha studio; there were no separate sound studios at the time. Konstantin Massal'skii recalls being taken to the *Circus* recording sessions as a small boy, because his mother, as assistant to the director, had nowhere to leave him. At one point, he turned in his chair, making a scraping sound, causing the very focused Dunaevskii to shout, "Take the child away!" (Feb. 16, 2002 interview with K.P. Massal'skii).

106. Stenogramma, doklad Dunaevskogo v Muzykal'nom nauchno-issledovatel'skom institute (May 7, 1937).

107. RGALI, f. 2062/1/127. He was paid the maximum GUKF honorarium of 15,000 rubles (GUPKhF, Nov. 29, 1939 letter to I. Dunaevskii, RGALI, f. 2062/1/577).

108. I. Dunaevskii, Mar. 13, 1935 letter to G. Aleksandrov, Dunaevskii family archives, Moscow.

109. I. Dunaevskii, Mar. 20, 1935 letter to G. Aleksandrov, Dunaevskii family archives, Moscow.

110. Stenogramma, doklad Dunaevskogo v Muzykal'nom nauchno-issledovatel'skom institute (May 7, 1937). Dunaevskii added that the first part of the lullaby in the film was originally meant to be the refrain.

111. Lebedev-Kumach's original text for the lullaby was longer, with more direct references to Mary's predicament, e.g., "in the strife," "sleep, my sorrow":

Sleep, my darling, bud' muzhchinom
Ochen' krepkim in the strife
Be a hero, smelym synom
Spi, moi mal'chik, sleep my life.

Vse igrushki, vse loshadki,
Vse lozhitsia, vse zasypait.
Sleep, my sorrow, sladko-sladko
Spi, moi mal'chik, Sleep! Good night!

Sleep, my darling, spi moi milyi.
Sleep, my little, malen'kii moi.
Baby nado mnogo sily
Spi, moi mal'chik. Sleep, my boy!

Noch' uzhe prishel k tebe v okoshechko,
Nu-zhe zasypai khot' nemnozhechko
Sleep, my baby, Spi, moi milyi
Baiu, baiu, bai-bai.

(RGALI, f. 1104/2/5).

112. I. Dunaevskii, Jan. 25, 1953 letter to K. V. Anisova and E. Strel'nikova, in *I. Dunaevskii. Izbrannye pis'ma* (Leningrad: Muzyka, 1971) 184. Early titles were "American Waltz" and "Star Waltz." T. Egorova notes the influence of Glinka's "Fantasia Waltz" on the Dunaevskii work, and sees "Moon Waltz" as a model for Khrennikov's "Pesnia o Moskve" ("Song about Moscow") in Ivan Pyr'ev's *Swineherdess and Shepherd* (Tatiana K. Egorova, *Soviet Film Music. A Historical Survey*. Trans. T. Ganf and N. Egorova [Amsterdam: Harwood, 1997] 42). Dunaevskii talked about his indifference to Glinka's music, but N. Shafer has traced his influence in Dunaevskii's work. (See N. Shafer, *Dunaevskii segodnia*, 59–72.)

113. Saraeva-Bondar', *Dunaevskii v Leningrade*, 105–06.

114. Published text:

Lunnyi val's

V ritme val'sa vse plyvet,
Ves' ogromnyi nebosvod.
Vmeste s solntsem i lunoi
Zakruzhilsia shar zemnoi,—
Vse tantsuet v etoi muzyke nochnoi…

V ritme val'sa vse plyvet,
Ves' ogromnyi nebosvod.
Vse tantsuet, skol'zia,
Uderzhat'sia nel'zia—
V ritme val'sa vse plyvet!...

Svetiat zvezdy daleko
Vse i prosto i legko...
Etoi pliaskoi goluboi
Zarazhaetskia liuboi,—
V ritme val'sa my zakruzhimsia s toboi!

V ritme val'sa vse plyvet,
Ves' ogromnyi nebosvod,
Vse tantsuet, skol'zia,
Uderzhat'sia nel'zia—
V ritme val'sa vse plyvet!...

115. "Ia tantsuiu s pechal'iu v glazakh"

Ia gliazhu na druzei i podrug
Schast'em glaza ikh goriat.
Lish' odna ia tantsuiu, moi drug,
Slezy tumaniat moj vzgliad.

Ia tantsuiu s pechal'iu v glazakh,
Ved' so mnoiu ne ty, a chuzhoi,
Vzor utopaet v slezakh.
Ty ushel, ty ushel, ty s drugoi!
Vialost' v rukakh, gorech' v ustakh,
Shutit' ne zastavit' sebia.
Ia tantsuiu s pechal'iu v glazakh,
Bez tebia, bez tebia, bez tebia!

Liudi i tantsy i dzhaz
Mne tebia ne pomogut zabyt'.
Slezy struiatsia iz glaz,
Ikh nikak ne uniat' i ne skryt'.
Vialost' v rukakh, gorech' v ustakh,
Shutit' ne zastavit' sebia.
Ia tantsuiu s pechal'iu v glazakh,
Bez tebia, bez tebia, bez tebia!

(RGALI, f. 2062/1/126).

116. Early version of the "International Lullaby":

Final'naia kolybel'naia

Son prikhodit na porog
Krepko-krepko spi ty
Sto putei
Sto dorog
Dlia tebia otkryty.

Vsë na svete otdykhaet,
Veter zatikhaet,
Nebo spit,
Solntse spit
I luna zevaet.

Spi, sokrovishche moe
Ty takoi bogatyi,
Vse tvoe
Vse tvoe
Zvezdy i zakaty.

Vse usnulo, moi malyshka,
Lastochka i myshka,
Diadi spiat,
Teti spiat
Spit v berloge Mishka.

V tselom mire net teplei
Dlia tebia zashchity.
Sto dorog
Sto putei
Dlia tebia otkryty.

Samolety i mashiny,
Skazki i kartiny,
Vsë tvoe,
Vsë tvoe,
Gory i ravniny.

Chto zavtra rano vstat'
Solnyshku navstrechu,
Nado spat',
Krepko spat'
Milyi chelovechek.

Kuplet direktora

Spiat medvedi i slony
Diadi spiat i teti
Vse vokrug
Spat' dolzhny
No ne na rabote.

Kuplet Raechki i Skameikina

Raechka: Kol' ne liubite detei,
Ne sozdat' semeiki!

Skameik.: Akh, rodis'
Poskorei
Molodoi Skameikin!

[RGALI, f. 1104/2/5]

Another variant in RGALI, f. 2062/1/126 primarily differs in Raechka's couplet:

Ia khochu troikh detei
Dlia moei semeiki.
Da rodis' poskorei
Molodoi Skameikin.

117. N. Shafer, "Odna iz samykh velikikh pesen," *Sovetskaia muzyka* (Oct. 1987): 11.

118. Dunaevskii must be referring here to the second, "International Lullaby," which he had originally planned as a Russian lullaby. (See preceding paragraphs.)

119. Stenogramma, doklad Dunaevskogo v Muzykal'nom nauchno-issledovatel'skom institute (May 7, 1937).

120. N. Shafer, "Odna iz samykh velikikh pesen," 13.

121. N. Shafer, "Odna iz samykh velikikh pesen," 13.

122. Shafer also notes that N. Trakhtenberg, the director of the *Circus* restoration, *lengthened* the Red Square finale by doubling the footage of the actors marching on Red Square and superimposing the images on additional documentary parade footage (Shafer, "Odna iz samykh velikikh pesen," 15). The effect, of course, is increased emphasis on the Red Square finale.

123. Aleksandrov, *Epokha i kino*, 194; Saraeva-Bondar', *Dunaevskii v Leningrade*, 96.

124. A. Sokhor, "Pesnia o rodine" I. O. Dunaevskogo (Moscow: Sovetskii kompozitor, 1960) 9–10.

125. I. Rozanov, "V.I. Lebedev-Kumach," *Literaturnaia ucheba*, No. 11 (1938): 64–5.

126. Sergei Bugoslavskii also points to the influence of "Vniz po matushke, po Volge," "Utes Stepana Razina," and the urban lyrical song "Bystry, kak volny." (Sergei Bugoslavskii, "Master kinopesni," *Pesnia v sovetskikh fil'makh*, [Moscow: Goskinoizdat, 1938] 21).

127. More likely, the lyrics were composed during the summer of 1935, after the script was reworked with a national emphasis. (The first Il'f and Petrov screenplay was approved only in early November 1934.) The Mosfil'm artistic council approved the melody of "Song of the Motherland" (without the lyrics) in April 1935 (Saraeva-Bondar', *Dunaevskii v Leningrade*, 100). Dunaevskii himself dated the song "Rodina" July 19, 1935. (See "Tsirk" II papka," RGALI, f. 2062/1/127.)

128. I. O. Dunaevskii, Jan. 25, 1953 letter to K.V. Anisova and E. Strel'nikova, 184.

129. See for example, Aleksandrov, *Epokha i kino*, 195 or G. Aleksandrov, "Pesnia o rodine," *Sovetskaia kul'tura*, Jan. 26, 1973: 5.

130. I. O. Dunaevskii, Jun. 27, 1954 letter to B. Ia. Kolesnikov, I. O. Dunaevskii, *Izbrannye pis'ma*, 209–10.

131. G. Zel'dovich, *Liubov' Orlova* (Moscow: Goskinoizdat, 1939) 18.

132. The more folksy instrumental case of "neob"iatnoi rodinoi svoei" ("through his vast motherland") was later replaced by a more formal "khozain / neob"iatnoi rodiny svoei" ("master of his vast motherland").

133. Rozanov, 62.

134. On the eve of the release of the film, the song did not win in a Leningrad contest, apparently because Dunaevskii was not viewed as a composer of patriotic songs (Shafer, "Odna iz samykh velikikh pesen," 15). According to Orlova, after the release of *Circus*, Lebedev-Kumach was inspired by Stalin's November 1936 speech on the new constitution to write an additional stanza to the song:

    Za stolom nikto u nas ne lishnii.
    Po zaslugam kazhdyi nagrazhden.
    Zolotymi bukvami my pishem
    Vsenarodnyi Stalinkskii zakon.
    Etikh slov velichie i slavu
    Nikakie gody ne sotrut:
    Chelovek vsegda imeet pravo
    Na uchebu, otdykh i na trud!

    "No one is unnecessary at our table. / Each is rewarded according to his services. / In gold letters we write / The national Stalin law. / No number of years will erase / The grandeur and glory of these words: / Man always has a right / To study, rest and work!"

    Orlova's 1939 account was conventionally hagiographic. Stalin's words even miraculously cure Lebedev-Kumach: "The entire country listened with excitement to the wise words of the leader. The poet was sick that day. Listening to the speech, I suddenly decided to call him: 'Vasilii Ivanovich, is your radio on, are you listening?' 'Yes, my illness has disappeared completely,' replied Lebedev-Kumach. 'I'm listening and am afraid to miss a word.' The most wonderful thing was that immediately after the speech, even before the tubes of the radio receiver had cooled, the poet sat down at his desk and wrote new stanzas for "Song of the Motherland." (Zel'dovich, *Liubov' Orlova*, 18–19). Orlova recalled that, although her concert programs had been passed by the Moscow censors, she experienced some unpleasantness in Odessa with the local censors for omitting the stanza at a concert, having given the excuse that it was not part of the film version. (Skorokhodov, *V poiskakh utrachennogo*, 407.)

135. "Zakliuchenie GUKF po prosmotru chernovogo montazha fil'ma "Tsirk"." RGALI, f. 2450/2/1518.

136. Anon., "Tsirk," *Zvezda*, Apr. 17, 1936; Saraeva-Bondar', *Dunaevskii v Leningrade*, 107.

137. Kushnirov, 147–48.

138. S. Garin, "Zelenyi teatr," *Krasnaia gazeta* (Jun. 4, 1936). A photograph in *Kino* of the film being screened at the Gigant Theatre gives an idea of the enormous size of the complex (*Kino*, May 28, 1936: 3).

139. A. Azarin, "Shiroka strana moia rodnaia," journal source and date not available, RGALI, f. 2753/1/30; Saraeva-Bondar,' *Dunaevskii v Leningrade*, 110.

140. Stoliarov, *Rodovye sny*, 38. Stoliarov's son claims that his father, at the time of the making of *Circus*, had a conflict with Aleksandrov that the actor refused to discuss, even with his family, in later years (41). Kirill Stoliarov also claims, rather dubiously, that one consequence of the conflict was his father's conscious abandonment of Soviet hero roles for less advantageous fairy tale-bylina parts. Yet another explanation for the absence of several actors is given in Arkadii Bernshtein, "Gollivud bez kheppi-enda," 227. To further confuse matters, Saraeva-Bondar' states that all the performers were present (Saraeva-Bondar', *Dunaevskii v Leningrade*, 112).

141. "Zakliuchenie GUKF-a po khudozhestvennomu zvukovomu fil'mu "Tsirk"," RGALI, f. 2450/2/1518.

142. Anon. announcement in *Za bol'shevistskii fil'm*, No. 28, Aug. 11, 1936: 3. Before approving release of the film, GUKF again demanded that the long shot of Kneishitz and Raechka in the empty rooftop restaurant be deleted, and that "priamo po dekretu" in an intertitle about "black, white, and blue little boys" be expunged as vulgar. The silent version apparently included somewhat different visuals from the sound version: GUKF required the removal of "the second close-up of the child in the cradle, since the audience can see that the boy's skin is an unnatural color and he is wearing dark brown socks." Usievich (deputy director of GUKF) and Krinkin (inspector-consultant) Aug. 7, 1936 memo to Babitskii, director of Mosfil'm, RGALI, f. 2450/2/1518.

143. "Negritenok Dzhim," RGALI, f. 2450/2/1517.

144. "Protokol soveshchaniia po prosmotru detskogo varianta '*Tsirka*'," Sept. 30, 1936, RGALI, f. 2450/2/1518.

145. Usievich and Kil'gast, Nov. 23, 1936 memo to GUKF, RGALI, f. 2450/2/1518.

146. RGALI, f. 2450/2/1517. GUKF authorized release of the film in June 1937 in 100 copies after "inappropriate" scenes (foreign words on the cannon and close-ups of the apparently Jewish woman performer in the 1903 bicycle act) were removed (Utkin and Zel'dovich memo of Mar. 26, 1937; Usievich Jun. 22, 1937 memo to Tov. Mikhailov, Upravlenie kinofikatsii, RGALI, f. 2450/2/1518.

147. B. Shumiatskii, "Za sovershenstvo masterstva," *Iskusstvo kino* (July 1936): 38; "Tvorcheskoe soveshchanie, sozvannoe Komitetom po delam kinematografii v Dome kino po voprosu o razvitii sovetskoi kinokomedii, 16–17 noiabria 1939 goda," *Zhivye golosa kino*, 136. The film was distributed in 250 prints, a larger than average number for the period (Anon., "Tsirk," *Vecherniaia krasnaia gazeta*, May 22, 1936).

148. V. Belinskaia, "Redaktoru 'Sovetskogo iskusstva'," "O fil'me 'Tsirk' and Boris Shumiatskii, "Otvet nashim korrespondentam," *Sovetskoe iskusstvo*, Jul. 11, 1936: 3; "Pis'ma chitatelei," *Sovetskoe iskusstvo*, No. 33, 1936: 9.

149. B. Balash, "Novoe reshenie temy," *Iskusstvo kino*, (July 1936): 42.

150. G. Polianovskii, "Skvoz' prizmu tsirkovogo attraktsiona," *Kino*, Jun. 11, 1936.

151. Kushnirov, 138; Stanislav Babaev, "Kolybel'naia," *Kul'tura*, Mar. 6, 1993.

152. Sokhor, 12.

153. Gr. Aleksandrov, "Nam pesnia stroit' i zhit' pomogaet...," *I. O. Dunaevskii. Vystupleniia. Stat'i. Pis'ma. Vospominaniia*, 287.

154. Sokhor, 13.

155. Rozanov, 62.

156. Karen Petrone, *Life Has Become More Joyous, Comrades. Celebrations in the Time of Stalin* (Bloomington: Indiana University Press, 2000) 54.

157. Sokhor, 13–14. The song was performed in English in *The North Star* (1943), the story of the Nazi invasion of a Ukrainian village. The screenplay was written by Lillian Hellman.

158. A stanza reputedly sung in the Gulag was: "Shiroka strana moia rodnaia, / Mnogo tiurem v nei i lagerei, / Ia drugoi takoi strany ne znaiu / Gde b tak zverski muchili liudei." (Semen Badash, "V. I. Lebedev-Kumach – poet i plagiator," http://www.seagullmag.com/oarticle.php?id=668. Accessed Sept. 18, 2007). Iurii Saakov has an amusing account of Aleksandrov and Valentin Kataev's unrealized plan for a sequel to *Circus*, set thirty years after the events of the original film. (Iu. Saakov, "Kompromat na Kneishitsa," *Iskusstvo kino* (March 1998): 73–77.

159. Saraeva-Bondar', *Dunaevskii v Leningrade*, 106. During the fall of 1935, Aleksandrov's film crew was in socialist competition (sotsdogovor) with Eisenstein's *Bezhin lug* group during pre-production. (R., "Pod kupolom tsirka," *Kino*, Sept. 17, 1935: 3). Eisenstein had a high opinion of Nil'sen's abilities and regarded his work for Aleksandrov as a temporary detour from more serious filmmaking: "Kislovodsk, 2/XII/35. Dear Volodia, I was happy to get your letter, both as such and for its contents. Of course, your place is with us, if you haven't turned into a complete whore working the street.... Although, in this case too perhaps we'll straighten you out somehow. *I would like it to be serious now.* [...] After *Circus* you will probably stabilize once and for all, and will be able to do work that interests you. Of course, work isn't work, but craziness without creative problems and prospects." (RGALI, f. 2753/1/40). By "stabilizing," Eisenstein is referring to Nil'sen's work on *Circus* as a way of erasing his shady political past. (See biographical information in the next chapter.)

160. The draft of the new law was announced May 26, 1936. Mark Kushnirov reproduces extracts from Orlova's speech in which she comes out in favor of motherhood, since "life has become happier and more joyous," but tries to justify exceptions to the ban on abortions in special career circumstances, clearly referring to her own situation: "Just as in everything else, there should be no sense of doom (obrechennost') in the item about abortion. There are many independent women in our Soviet society, many professions in which women compete successfully with men... Pregnancy tears a woman away from her work, perhaps at the very moment when she is completing a colossal project or is preparing for a heroic flight or is completing work on a big acting role on which she has spent several years of her life, and perhaps, at this most important moment of her life, and her public and political biography, she is forced to throw everything up and lose a year's time.... In such cases let a woman have a child somewhat later. In such exceptional cases let her be permitted an abortion. Let women know that the law is not fate." (qtd. in Kushnirov, 155).

161. See for example, Kushnirov's description of her post-*Circus* tours in Leningrad and Odessa (Kushnirov, 148–50).

162. V. Vol'fovich, "Dragotsennoe kol'tso aktrisy," *Muzykal'naia zhizn'*, 7 (1984): 25. In May 1937, *Pravda* even published "Kol'tso," Viktor Gusev's doggerel description of the event. (Viktor Gusev, "Kol'tso," *Pravda*, May 1, 1937: 4). Orlova responded with a letter of thanks and pride of

accomplishment: "I am proud that, through our art, I and many of my comrades may be useful to our country in its achievements and victories!" (Liubov' Orlova, May 2, 1937 letter to V. Gusev, RGALI, f. 2177/1/78).

163. M. Imas, "O tsirkovom predstavlenii," *Sovetskoe iskusstvo*, 11 (1933): 1.

164. See Beth Holmgren, "*The Blue Angel* and Blackface: Redeeming Entertainment in Aleksandrov's *Circus*," *The Russian Review*, 66 (January 2007): 5–22.

165. G. Aleksandrov i V. Nil'sen, "Kak my snimali 'Tsirk.'"

166. B. Malkin, "Oformlenie fizkul'turnogo parada," *Sovetskoe iskusstvo*, Jul. 5, 1935: 1.

167. G. V. Aleksandrov and V. S. Nil'sen, "Kak my snimali fil'm," *Moskovskii ekran* (May 1936): 5.

168. Anon., "Stolitsa gotovitsia k pervomu maia," *Vecherniaia Moskva*, Apr. 20, 1936: 2.

169. Pierre Herbart, *En U.R.S.S.* (Paris: Gallimard, 1936):82.

170. Anon., "Stolitsa gotovitsia k pervomu maia."

171. The 1936 constitution guaranteed equal rights to all Soviet citizens, irrespective of nationality and race (article 123) and equal rights for women, with provisions for maternity leave and child care (article 122).

172. Anon., "Zabota o detiakh nashei rodiny," *Pravda*, Jul. 10, 1935: 1; Anon., "Prekrasnoe budushchee raskryvaetsia pered nashimi det'mi," *Pravda*, Aug. 16, 1935: 8.

173. Anon., "Pervoe maia na Krasnoi ploshchadi v Moskve," *Pravda*, May 4, 1935: 2.

174. Anon., "Vchera na Tushinskom aerodrome," *Pravda*, Jul. 13 1935: 1.

175. Anon., "Planery letiat v stratosferu," *Komsomol'skaia pravda*, May 12, 1936: 4; M. Postolovskii, "Reis v stratosferu," *Izvestiia*, May 8, 1936: 4.

176. K.I. Sal'nikov, "Listaia starye gazety," (http://dikson.net.ru. Accessed Apr. 16, 2006). In May 1936, after a 9:00 am screening of *Circus*, Aleksandrov and his co-director Simkov, together with women parachutists, met with the audience to discuss assistance to mothers and the repeal of the abortion law. Litvakova from the US gave a speech about the oppression of blacks in that country. (Anon., "Zritel' o Tsirke," *Vecherniaia Moskva*, No. 130 [1936]).

177. V. Nil'sen and B. Petrov, "Kak my snimali 'Tsirk,'" *Iskusstvo kino*, 44. In spite of Soviet claims of independent achievement, the specifications for construction of the escalators were bought from an English firm (M. Egorov, "Kak my stroili metro," *Nezavisimaia gazeta* [May 13, 1995]: 4).

178. Anon., "Stolitsa gotovitsia k pervomu maia," 2.

179. The hotel, which housed shockworker delegates invited to the November 1935 Congress of Stakhanovites, was completed only in 1937. The first Kremlin star, constructed of metal and decorated with a hammer and sickle formed from precious Ural stones, was mounted on the Spasskaia Tower October 25, 1935 (*Bol'shaia sovetskaia entsiklopediia*, ed. A. M. Prokhorov, vol. 13 [Moscow: Sovetskaia entsiklopediia, 1969]):374.

180. Katerina Clark, "Socialist Realism and the Sacralizing of Space," *The Landscape of Stalinism. The Art and Ideology of Soviet Space*, eds. E. Dobrenko and E. Naiman (Seattle: University of Washington Press, 2003) 13.

181. B. Balash, "Novoe reshenie temy," *Iskusstvo kino*, (July 1936): 42. The following discussion on Art Deco in the film has been published in Rimgaila Salys, "Art Deco Aesthetics in Grigorii Aleksandrov's *The Circus*," *The Russian Review*, 66 (January 2007): 23–35.

182. Richard Striner, *Art Deco* (NY: Abbeville Press, 1994) 7.

183. Lucy Fischer, *Designing Women. Cinema, Art Deco and the Female Form* (NY: Columbia University Press, 2003) 16–18.

184. For Art Deco floor vases, see *Encyclopedia of Art Deco*, ed. Alastair Duncan (NY: E.P. Dutton, 1988) 121–122.

185. The film *Fashions of 1934* comments on the obsession: its rip-off designer-hero pushes ostrich feathers to his clients because he has made a deal with an American breeder (Fischer, *Designing Women* [2003], 70). Marion Dixon in her feathers—and not her flight suit or white sports outfit—was the most popular image from *Circus* in thirties fan postcards. In fact, I was unable to locate any postcard reproductions of her Soviet incarnations.

186. For relevant Art Deco images, see Victor Arwas, *Art Deco* (NY: Harry Abrams, 1992): Tamara de Lempicka, *Autoportrait*, 184; Cassandre, *Nord Express*, poster 216; R. Lalique, *Victoire*, glass car mascot, 242.

187. Lucy Fischer, "The Image of Woman as Image: The Optical Politics of *Dames*," *Film Quarterly*, 30 (Fall 1976): 2–11; Lucy Fischer, "Designing Women. Art Deco, the Musical, and the Female Body," *Music and Cinema*. Eds. James Buhler, Caryl Flinn, and David Neumeyer (Hanover, NH: Wesleyan University Press, 2000) 295–315.

188. Karina Dobrotvorskaia, "'Tsirk' G. V. Aleksandrova." *Iskusstvo kino*, 11 (1992): 28–33.

189. Dobrotvorskaia, 31.

190. Fischer, *Designing Women* (2003), 95.

191. Several critics have commented on Aleksandrov's creation of the Orlova star persona in the image of Dietrich, and Marion Dixon's initials as a mirror of Dietrich's (see, for example, Dmitrii Shcheglov, *Liubov' i maska* [Moscow: Olimp, 1997] 146). On Orlova's lifelong dislike of the star, extending to cutting Dietrich out of group photos, see Kushnirov, 152–153.

192. Susan Smith, *The Musical. Race, Gender and Performance* (London: Wallflower Press, 2005) 5–6.

193. Sternberg insisted on the reconciliation of Helen with her husband, which also pleased the censors, because the reiteration of the story of the couple's meeting as a bedtime story for their son establishes a parallel between the beginning and ending of the film, and marks the love story as fairy tale, thereby giving the ending a dissonant quality that precludes closure (Lea Jacobs, *The Wages of Sin. Censorship and the Fallen Woman Film, 1928–1942*, [Madison: The University of Wisconsin Press, 1991] 93–94).

194. On the history of the project, see Sona Stephan Hoisington, "'Ever Higher': The Evolution of the Project for the Palace of Soviets." *Slavic Review*, 62 (Spring 2003): 41–68.

195. On Berkeley's thematic sequence, see Gerald Mast, *Can't Help Singin'. The American Musical on Stage and Screen*, 123–24.

196. See the Porte d'Honneur and Edgar Brandt's bronze frozen fountain for the Cheney Brothers store in New York in Striner, 23 and 38. The motif was also popular in metalwork; for Art Deco jewelry with the fountain motif, see Sylvie Raulet, *Art Deco Jewelry* (NY: Rizzoli, 1985) 128, 145.

197. My source for Berkeley and Art Deco in this section is Lucy Fischer, "Designing Women. Art Deco, the Musical, and the Female Body" (2000), 295–315.

198. Anon., "S"emochnyi den' gruppy rezhissera G. Aleksandrova. 'Tsirk,'" *Iskusstvo kino* (Jan. 1936): 43.

199. Fischer, "Designing Women. Art Deco, the Musical, and the Female Body" (2000), 301–02. On a staircase, Skameikin ogles the chorus girl-ballerinas' legs, a stock comic scene in backstage musicals.

200. See for example, *The Great Ziegfeld* (1936) and *Broadway Serenade* (1939).

201. See Ferdinand Preiss's *Charleston Dancer* and *Autumn Dancer* in Arwas, 143–44.

202. Fischer, *Designing Women* (2003), 147.

203. Fischer, *Designing Women* (2003), 143. See plaque-lamp of *Suzanne* in Arwas, 249.

204. See the female figures in Jean-Baptiste Gauvenet, Sèvres Vase (Arwas, 6) and Cross and Cross, Elevator Doors, City Bank Farmers Trust Building (*Encyclopedia of Art Deco*, 17).

205. G. Aleksandrov, "Nasha tema—rastsvet iskusstva," *Iskusstvo kino* (July 1936): 18.

206. For illustrations, see *Naum Gabo and the Competition for the Palace of Soviets, Moscow 1931–1933*, Eds., Helen Adkins et al. (Berlin: Berlinische Galerie, 1993) 172 and Hoisington, 52.

207. See reproduction in Hoisington, 60. Compare the rounded Deco curves of the BBC Broadcasting House in Striner, 41.

208. See reproduction of the Nebraska State Capitol (Striner, 86).

209. Claude Bragdon, *The Frozen Fountain*, reprint of 1932 ed. (Freeport, NY: Books for Libraries press, 1970) 16.

210. See Vladimir Paperny, *Architecture in the Age of Stalin. Culture Two*. Trans. J. Hill and R. Barris in collaboration with the author (Cambridge: CUP, 2002) 88 and Rodchenko's 1936 fizkul'turniki parade photo (http://www.photographer.ru/pictures/1556.jpg . Accessed Mar. 19, 2006).

211. Gerald Mast also points out the affinity of Berkeley's geometric abstractions with the Nazi cult of beauty. "By a Waterfall" was a great favorite with Adolf Hitler, "whose own visual propaganda reduced human beings to visual fragments of awesome architecture and mythical abstraction." (Mast, 134).

212. N. Aduev, "'Tsirk,'" *Kino*, Jun. 4, 1936, 4.

213. Such acts were popular as far back as Jules Verne's novel *De La Terre à la Lune*. (1865) in which the Baltimore Gun Club builds a gigantic cannon which shoots a projectile carrying three men to the moon. In 1902, George Méliès made the first science fiction film, *Le Voyage dans la Lune*, based on the Verne novel and H. G. Wells' *First Men in the Moon* (1901). In the fourteen-minute Méliès feature astronomers, housed in a giant shell, are launched from a cannon to the moon. The film includes a scene of a goddess sitting on the crescent moon.

214. According to Rina Zelenaia, she provided the idea for the vest. Zelenaia had used an inflatable bust in a 1920s cabaret act, which she afterward deflated and put in her pocket, to the amusement of fellow actors. Zelenaia related the story to Orlova, thereby giving Aleksandrov the idea for the pneumatic vest (Skorokhodov, *V poiskakh utrachennogo*, 135–36).

215. Richard Taylor, "The Illusion of Happiness and the Happiness of Illusion: Grigorii Aleksandrov's *The Circus*," *The Slavonic and East European Review*, 74 (October 1996): 615.

216. The lullaby was performed by Aleksandra Panova, Pavel Geraga, Lev Sverdlin, Solomon Mikhoels, and the American actor Wayland Rodd of the Kamernyi Theatre, who often played Othello. After the assassination of Mikhoels in 1948, his Yiddish lullaby was cut from the film. In 1966, in preparation for the thirtieth anniversary of the release of *Circus*, Aleksandrov located an early print of *Circus* in Czechoslovakia and restored the scene to the film (Saraeva-Bondar', *Siluety*, 204).

217. Critics have pointed to Ernst Lubitsch's *Ninochka* (1939), in which a Soviet KGB agent chooses to remain in Paris after she falls in love with a French aristocrat, as the western response to *Circus*. (M. Turovskaia, www.svoboda.org/programs/Cicles/Cinema/Circus.asp. Accessed May 7, 2005). O. Bulgakova points out that Greta Garbo, as Ninochka, parodies the quasi-military gestural codes of High Stalinism in the film. (Oksana Bulgakova, *Fabrika zhestov* [Moscow: Novoe literaturnoe obozrenie, 2005] 222.)

218. Altman, 289.

219. Altman, 210.

220. The diagonal overhead shot of the running crowd is an Eisensteinian treatment.

221. The critic Zel'dovich explains Aleksandrov's ironies as a recognition that Mary's secret and Kneishitz's evildoing cannot be taken seriously in a tolerant and egalitarian Soviet society (G. Zel'dovich, "Tsirk," *Iskusstvo kino* (July 1936): 39.

222. Dobrotvorskaia, 30.

223. Like the reborn Dixon, the Chaplin clown marches in the studio version of the Red Square parade at the end of the film.

224. RGALI, f. 2062/1/332.

225. Petrone, 54.

226. James van Geldern, "The Centre and the Periphery: Cultural and Social Geography in the Mass Culture of the 1930s," *New Directions in Soviet History*. Ed. Stephen White (Cambridge: CUP, 1992) 62.

227. The full translation of "Song of the Motherland" is as follows:

    Broad is my Motherland
    It has many forests, fields, and streams!
    I know of no other country like it,
    Where man breathes as freely.

    From Moscow to the very borderlands,
    From the southern mountains to the northern seas,
    Man passes as the master
    Through his boundless Motherland.
    Everywhere life flows freely and broadly,
    Like the brimming Volga.
    All roads are open here to the young,
    Everywhere the old are honored.

Your eyes can't take in all our fields,
You can't name all our cities,
Our proud word—"comrade"
Is dearer to us than any beautiful words.
We're at home everywhere with this word,
For us there are no black or colored peoples,
This word is familiar to each of us,
With it everywhere we find our own.

A spring wind blows over the land,
With every day life becomes more joyous,
And no one in the world knows how
To laugh and love better than we do.
But our brows we'll contract in a stern frown
If an enemy tries to break us.
We love our Motherland like a bride,
We protect her like a tender mother.

228. Van Geldern, "The Centre and the Periphery," 65–66.

229. Van Geldern, "The Centre and the Periphery," 64.

230. George L. Mosse, *Nationalism and Sexuality. Respectability and Abnormal Sexuality in Modern Europe* (NY: Howard Fertig, 1985) 16.

231. Wolfgang Lepmann, *Winckelmann*, qtd. in Mosse, 14.

232. Mosse, 14.

233. Bulgakova, *Fabrika zhestov*, 208.

234. Mosse, 173. On the foreign "other," see Josephine Woll, "Under the Big Top. America Goes to the Circus," in *Insiders and Outsiders in Russian Cinema*, eds. Stephen Norris and Zara Torlone (Bloomington: Indiana University Press, 2008), 68–80.

235. Bulgakova, *Fabrika zhestov*, 271. Orlova attained true star status after *Circus*. She was able to tour the country with concerts; the number of peroxide blondes in the country increased and, of her thousands of fans, two women stalked her to the end of her life (Shcheglov, 145).

236. Hoffmann, David L. "Bodies of Knowledge: Physical Culture and the New Soviet Man," Igal Halfin, *Language and Revolution: Making Modern Political Identities* (London: F. Cass, 2002) 280.

237. Orlova recalled that she and Mel'nikova (Raechka) thought up the concluding "Teper' ponimaesh'?" after seeing Stalin and the other leaders on Red Square. (Orlova, "Chuvstvo radosti," 4).

238. In reality, the May Day demonstration was one of the few public events at which privileged Soviet citizens were able to see and be seen by Stalin and the political elite (Petrone, 25).

Chapter 3

Volga–Volga

"When Igor' Vladimirovich Il'inskii was introduced to Stalin at a reception, Stalin joked: 'Hello, Citizen Byvalov. You're a bureaucrat, and I'm a bureaucrat, we'll understand each other. Let's go have a chat'—and led him to a table."
– G. Aleksandrov, *Epokha i kino*, 208

"The famous sapper and hero of Spanish events, Colonel Sorin, writes that, having returned to Moscow in the summer of 1938, he couldn't understand the happy insouciance that filled the air and in which everyone—both those at the bottom and those at the top—immersed themselves. No one wanted to listen to his warnings...His bitterness, pain, and sense of insult finally concentrated itself on a giant advertising board, inviting people to the Metropol' movie theatre. A female face, carefree, tousled blond locks, a comic grimace, a captain's cap, dashingly tilted to the side. Liubov' Orlova."
– Kushnirov, 179

I. THE LONG RIVER JOURNEY

Several days after the première of *Circus*, Grigorii Aleksandrov's second musical film, on May 23, 1936, the director spoke at Dom pechati about his next project: "Our group has now been set an enormous task—making an eccentric comedy based on the material of folk art. This material is fairly powerful and vivid, but at the same time difficult in terms of drama...The film about folk art that we are making for the twentieth anniversary of October will no doubt be better because our successes are the successes of our system of labor. It will also be better because it will be based entirely on Soviet material."[1] With *Volga-Volga*, Aleksandrov moved away from the most obvious American borrowings of *Happy Guys*, as well as from the foreign plot elements of *Circus*. *Volga-Volga* begins in the northern hinterland, in the fictional provincial town of Melkovodsk. The action soon moves to the northern tributaries of the Volga and to the Volga itself,

Russia's central and quintessentially national river, concluding with a grand finale in Moscow. Strelka, a local mail carrier, wants to take her group of folk singers and dancers to the Moscow Olimpiada, hoping to perform a song about the Volga that she herself has composed. She and her boyfriend, the accountant Alesha, quarrel over their contrasting musical tastes. Byvalov, the careerist head of the local musical instruments factory, supports Alesha's classical music group. Hoping to gain a transfer to Moscow, Byvalov transports the group down the Kama River on the rickety paddlewheeler *Sevriuga* (*The Sturgeon*), while Strelka's group is forced to take the overland route to meet up with a sailboat owned by local lumberjacks. After many comic mishaps, the two groups join forces as they travel down the Volga on a modern steamship. In Moscow, Strelka's song wins the Olimpiada competition, Byvalov is disgraced, and the romantic couple is reunited.

In the July 1936 issue of *Iskusstvo kino*, Aleksandrov made obeisance to his political mentors: Repertkom's Mlechin had given him the idea of using folk art material, and Party official V. Furer had been providing (unspecified) practical assistance in the creation of the script.[2] In a 1937 discussion with fellow musicians, Dunaevskii, not without some irony, made it clear that the assignment had come from Stalin himself: "*Volga-Volga* will also be a significant event but, due to a directive from above, we are returning to the method of *Happy Guys*. Let it be known to you that the greatest and most authoritative critic of our land has declared *Circus* to be a good film, but he considers it a concession, a retreat. He considers *Happy Guys* to be daring and demands that the jubilee film be written along the same lines, and so *Volga-Volga* will be an eccentric musical comedy."[3] According to Aleksandrov, Stalin had not liked the melodramatic excesses of *Circus*: "We were set the task of making a comic film without lyrical and melodramatic digressions."[4]

Scholars of personality cults have argued that, after the secularizing Enlightenment and French Revolution, rulers no longer derived their legitimacy from God, but rather from the people. "As Claude Lefort has pointed out, the center of society was no longer only filled by a monarch's body, appointed by divine right, but also by popular sovereignty—a highly unstable and ambiguous concept."[5] A feature of the Stalin cult, which had coalesced into a system of signs by the mid-1930s, was, therefore, the leader's personal relationship with the People, who legitimized his rule, for whom he labored, and whose will he carried out. The mid-1930s are also characterized by a shift in social relations from 1920s horizontality in which all citizens, regardless of talent and merit, merged anonymously in striving toward the collective goal to a more vertical hierarchy in which the individual was encouraged to excel professionally in the public eye as stakhanovite, aviator, or kolkhoz activist. Although still part of a collective society, now framed more inclusively and nationalistically as the "The People," the individual was encouraged to fulfill his or her personal potential while also acknowledging the support of the system.

Always politically agile, Aleksandrov took up the latest official initiatives focusing on the potentialities of the Folk: the new constitution approved in December 1936 gave equal representation to all citizens, including the previously neglected peasantry, and encouraged the development of individual potential, both of which the director tied together neatly in a July 1936 article:

> The new Constitution of the Soviet State realistically guarantees every citizen the opportunity to develop in himself all his talents and fulfill all his best aspirations.... In making a film essentially about big people, we begin it from so-called little people; and it is these little people, under the influence of the surrounding environment, with the attention of the Party toward them, with the assistance of the government, who grow into the big people of our time, traveling from a small, provincial Volga town and reaching the capital as heroes. With this film we want to show that in our country, all the opportunities have been created to grow any talent of every person, to develop it to the highest degree.[6]

During the early thirties, the government had begun to encourage *samodeiatel'nost'* (amateur arts activities). An All-Russian Conference of Regional Amateur Arts House Workers was held on June 16, 1930 in Moscow. On December 9, Narkompros established the State Board of Amateur Arts Activities.[7] But the *samodeiatel'nost'* phenomenon took center stage during the 1935–36 cultural revolution that replaced Leninist-Trotskyite internationalism with Stalinist national Bolshevism, emphasizing *narodnost'*—the creative powers of the Folk, the artistic merits of the national epics, as well as Russia's glorious historical past.[8] The January–February 1936 official attacks on Dmitrii Shostakovich in *Pravda* established a stylistic of simplicity, accessibility, and realism, supposedly embodied in both 19th century classical music and in the folk melos, in place of the naturalistic cacophony of modernist music.[9] The village culture that had been destroyed by collectivization was to be resurrected in folk amateur arts activity. The Theatre of Folk Arts was opened with much fanfare in March 1936, its programs filmed and disseminated nationally by Soiuzkinokhronika.[10] And, of course, "bodryi, zhizneradostnyi" (lively, buoyant) folk performance—to use the stereotypical epithets of the era—provided the perfect musical accompaniment to Stalin's 1935 dictum: "Zhit' stalo luchshe, tovarishchi. Zhit' stalo veselee."

In his Dom pechati speech, Aleksandrov complained that he could not find a suitable scriptwriter for the film and that he and his colleagues might be forced to write the script themselves.[11] Nevertheless, in June 1936, while still in the preliminary planning stage, Aleksandrov contacted playwright and co-author of the *Happy Guys* script, Nikolai Erdman, then living in exile in Tomsk, and invited him to participate in the project. Erdman was overjoyed, though cautious about his prospects: "I'm very excited about Aleksandrov's proposal to work on a script for the twentieth anniversary of October. The only thing I'm afraid of is that it may simply end up as talk."[12] Meanwhile, with funding from Mosfil'm, Aleksandrov and Nil'sen spent the summer of 1936 traveling in Georgia,

Azerbaidzhan, Abkhazia, and Adzharistan, studying the *samodeiatel'nost'* of these areas in preparation for the jubilee film, which was to feature performers from the various republics. Their co-authored *Pravda* article describing the trip reveals the documentary inspiration of several comic episodes in the *Volga-Volga* script. Logging workers in remote areas were poorly supplied with musical instruments and lacked sheet music: "In the Urals, we heard a tall lumberjack with a blonde beard sing touchingly: 'Ia nesposobna k grusti tomnoi...' ('I [feminine] am incapable of languid melancholy...'). In response to our bewildered question as to why he had chosen an aria that was so unsuitable for a male, he replied in a simple-hearted way: 'There isn't any sheet music. We sing what we have.'"[13] On the Volga, Aleksandrov and Nil'sen had observed female barge-loaders performing Pushkin's "Rusalka" to music of their own composition. These entered the first *Volga-Volga* script as fisherwomen who sing the Pushkin text while dancing with nets that ensnare Byvalov. A truncated version of the episode survived as part of the town talent show that pursues him in the film. Finally, the *Pravda* article attacked both bureaucrats who actively opposed amateur activities and those who waited passively for talented performers to come forward, as does Byvalov in the first script.[14]

By early summer, Aleksandrov had conceptualized only visual spectacle for the film: folk performances by Olimpiada winners, shots of the Volga-Moscow canal, of new Moscow construction, of the new Moscow port, and even a Palace of Soviets, to be created by special effects. As yet, he had no real plot for his nameless film beyond the performers' journey from the northern reaches of the Volga to Moscow.[15] On September 26, 1936, Aleksandrov, Nil'sen, the artist Grivtsov, and chief administrator Brukhlis left Moscow on the yacht *Sviiaga*, rented for them by Mosfil'm, taking the river route to the Urals. The purpose of the trip was to acquaint the group with local life and folklore, to complete a literary script, and choose shooting locations (Fig. 32).[16] By this time, Aleksandrov was able to be more specific in interviews about the storyline of *Volga-Volga*, as the film was now titled:

> My film begins somewhere in a small town, ...by a shallow river. The town's only asset is a handicrafts industry. The manager of the local industry says that here "reka melkaia, ryba melkaia i liudi takie zhe—melkie" ("the river is shallow, the fish are small and the people are just the same—shallow"). He dreams of being transferred to Moscow or to a major construction project. He doesn't notice the things the people of the town live for. He has contempt for cultural life, *samodeiatel'nost'*, the artistic creations of his "craftsmen." But this life continues and when the Volga waters, which have risen due to the construction of the Volga-Moscow canal, reach the shallow river, the level of life rises too; it bursts out and transforms the everyday life of the little town, and sparkles in all its colors. And now these real people, who have constantly developed

Figure 32.

> and created, go out onto their deep-water river, along the Volga, along the canal—to Moscow for the twentieth of October celebration. They bring with them their songs, their folk dances, their joy and a wealth of art, and as they travel, they are joined by more and more ships, so that after they have moored in Moscow, by the Kremlin, together they can all report to the great leader about their happiness.[17]

Aleksandrov's précis highlights the central spatial mythologies operating in *Volga-Volga*. The river journey uniting periphery and center is part of the mid-thirties "Rodina" nexus, the shift in cultural geography elaborated earlier in "Song of the Motherland," the country's unofficial national anthem. During the 1920s, and especially during the cultural revolution, the center was opposed to the rest of the country, whether rural or boundary lands. The margins of the country were considered wild and savage, a hostile environment to be conquered by socialist heroes. By the mid-thirties, the line of demarcation between "us" and "them" had moved outward to the boundaries of the USSR, which now had to be protected from external enemies. The margins of the country were also being charted by aviators and explored by scientists for their natural resources. Social legitimacy was concentrated in the centre not as a monopoly, but as a point of distribution. Moscow remained the center, but now metonymically represented—rather than opposed itself to—the rest of the country. The reconstruction of the capital, especially its new metro system, thus became a source of pride for the entire country: "Elevating Moscow elevated the entire Soviet Union."[18] The Moscow-Volga Canal, which opened in July 1937, gave the capital a new port with access to five seas and solved the city's critical shortage of drinking water. (The water carrier's couplet "Bez vody i ni tudy i ni siudy" ["Without water you're up the creek"] thus resonated with contemporary audiences.) At the same time, the canal, which linked the Moscow River to the Volga, connected the capital to the rest of the country via the main transportation artery of European Russia. In *Volga-Volga*, continental Moscow is filmed as another "Venice of the North" as the Melkovodskites approach the Khimki port on steamers and small boats travelling on broad canals.

In interviews on the film, Aleksandrov stressed the importance of knowing the country in its entirety: "Every Soviet citizen should know his homeland, and the task of Soviet filmmakers is to show our country in their films. We love our homeland. We know that, amidst its vast expanses, there is no corner without an intense creative life."[19] "When we were working on the song about the Volga, we were thinking about our entire country and took the Volga as a symbol of our homeland...While creating comic situations...we nevertheless wanted to make our film in such a way as to show our country at the same time: the beauty of our homeland, its natural riches, its dense forests, and vast expanses. To show the new visage of our country that is expressed with extraordinary vividness in such a magnificent structure as the Moscow-Volga Canal."[20]

Within the myth of infinite socialist progress, Aleksandrov thus unites socialist construction and culture, neatly connecting the ballyhooed Moscow-Volga Canal construction project to folk performance via the metaphor of physical and cultural "elevation": the rising water level of the Volga's tributaries provides folk artists with an outlet to the greater world. The Melkovodskites make the journey in mythic time: although six-day intervals are marked by titles on the rotating paddle wheel, we do not have a clear sense of how many days have passed. They make the paradigmatic journey from the periphery to the sacred center, transferring from crude and antiquated vessels to the luxurious steamship *Iosif Stalin* as they near Moscow. This scene at "Bol'shaia Volga," the entrance to the canal, mimics conventional Socialist Realist compositions in which Stalin appears in the foreground, sometimes with other worthy Soviet citizens, with a bust or statue of Lenin in the background, thereby establishing Stalin as Lenin's legitimate heir. Examples are Aleksandr Gerasimov's *Stalin's Speech at the 16th Party Congress* (1935), Shegal's *Leader, Teacher, Friend* (1937), and the many profile medallion portraits of the leaders. In the *Volga-Volga* scene, Merkurov's Lenin statue stands high above the canal, while Stalin is metonymically present below via his mechanical double, the namesake steamship—the camera focuses twice on the inscription "Iosif Stalin"—and the two are linked via the child prodigy Tolia's playing "Song of the Volga" as accompaniment to the visuals.[21] Strelka and company negotiate the mythic space of Soviet modernity with its yachts, aquaplanes, and underwater divers, arriving at the sacred center, the Olimpiada stage, which metonymically represents the entire country—decorated with flags and coat of arms, and populated by peoples of all nationalities in native costume. In this public space, the Melkovodskites profess unity and ritual joy to the Leader, validating themselves through performance as "big little people" who are one with the country.[22]

*****

From Moscow, the film group traveled to Gorky and then down the Volga to Kazan' and up the Kama to Perm' and the rivers Vishera and Chusovaia, stopping en route to meet local performers and attending four large amateur performances.[23] During the early autumn expedition, Aleksandrov and Nil'sen together wrote the first version of the *Volga-Volga* script. On September 30, 1936, while in Gorky, they sent Darevskii, the administrative supervisor of the film, the first installment—a poorly typed twenty-page manuscript entitled "The outline of a plot."[24] Their accompanying note asked Darevskii to forward a copy of the manuscript to Vladimir Usievich, Shumiatskii's second in command at GUK, and requested that neither Darevskii nor Sokolovskaia, the deputy director of Mosfil'm, publish this incomplete working material. Aleksandrov and Nil'sen noted that they planned to continue writing during the expedition and produce a finished literary script by the end of their trip, adding, "Heartfelt thanks for the wonderful working conditions. Every day brings us a huge number of observations."[25] Vladimir Nil'sen's archive contains two other relevant manuscripts from this time: an early, fragmentary script, mostly in the hand of Nil'sen, and the full 1936 typescript that continues the two earlier mss.[26] Judging from the plot summary Aleksandrov gave reporters when the expedition returned to Gorky on October 26, this initial version of the script had been completed by the end of their trip.[27]

This first *Volga-Volga* literary script displays the general contours of the amateur performers' picaresque journey from the provincial town of Kamyshev to the Moscow Olimpiada, though with differing adventures than in the completed film, together with a number of characters, episodes, and gags that survived into the completed film. Kamyshev is most likely modeled on the old Volga town of Kamyshin, which was to be the site of one of eight dams and navigable locks, part of a grand Volga development project.[28] Strelka, the accountant Rybkin (later Trubyshkin in the film), and the town's amateur groups, as well as the bureaucrat Byvalov, are already present in familiar guise. The grounded ferry-raft, the telegram shouted across the river, the herd of pigs' escape from the ferry, the Lotsman (river pilot) who recognizes the shallows as he lands the *Sevriuga* on them ("Here's the first shoal!"), the lumberjacks who sing female parts because of a dearth of sheet music, Strelka's faint and cry for water in the aquatic love scene with Alesha (an episode that had been cut from *Happy Guys*), the paddle wheel marking elapsed days,[29] and the woman swimmer whose distance record is ruined when she is fished out of the water—all are present in the first version of the script.

Notwithstanding these surviving episodes and motifs, the *Volga-Volga* story as written by Aleksandrov and Nil'sen carried a radically different satirical charge, embedded in a tangled and labyrinthine plot, from the final film version. Multiple subplots complicate the primary narrative: Rybkin's plan to build a lock on the local river, with its attendant gags; Byvalov and the theatre director's Sviatoslavskii's unsuccessful talent search, together with the townspeople's pursuit of the director to demonstrate their talents; the romantic triangle of Rybkin, the manicurist Golli (Holly) and the director Sviatoslavskii; a barber who performs experiments in freckle removal; and a 117-year-old elder who dreams of becoming a professional dancer. In this early script, Byvalov already opposes the *samodeiatel'nost'* movement, but plays a minor role during the journey to Moscow, which includes both the loss of the *Sevriuga* and a passing steamship, *The Tourist*, to fire, as well as meetings with a series of Olimpiada delegations of various nationalities.

Byvalov, the local factory boss, a bureaucrat and careerist, is a stock comedy character familiar to Russian audiences from the time of Kapnist, a type that continued to be a convenient target during the Soviet era. However, in the character of theater director Sviatoslavskii, Aleksandrov and Nil'sen take aim at the major cultural figure of the preceding decade—Vsevolod Meierkhol'd. This first script parodies Meierkhol'd's cult status, his advocacy of avant-garde art and disdain for "massovost'" (an orientation toward popular culture), and, in a general way, his marital problems. The theater director's name, Igor' Sviatoslavskii, an ironic allusion to the hero of Russia's medieval classic, *The Tale of Igor's*

Campaign, immediately elevates him to mock epic status. Like Meierkhol'd's name change at the age of 21, Sviatoslavskii is an assumed name, taken to escape alimony payments—a poke at Meierkhold's highly serious conversion to Russianness and orthodoxy, and his abrupt abandonment of his first wife, Ol'ga Mikhailovna Munt for Zinaida Raikh.[30] Like Prince Igor' Sviatoslavovich, who fought the Polovtsy and lost, since the early thirties Meierkhol'd had also been engaged in an epic—and losing—battle with the Stalinist authorities to preserve his theatre and ultimately—his own artistic vision.[31]

Sviatoslavskii's first conversation with Byvalov identifies them both as marginalized members of the Soviet establishment:

> Director: Sergei Aleksandrovich, what on earth made you leave such an important post for some sort of local industry in such a hole?
>
> Byvalov: A misunderstanding, I'm sitting it out temporarily. I wrote Sergo [Ordzonikidze]; I'm waiting for his summons by telegram.
>
> Dir.: It's nice here!
>
> Byv.: A backwater, the river is shallow, the fish are small, the people are shallow...but what brought you here? How is the theatre managing without you?
>
> Dir.: It's not the theatre without me, I'm without the theatre. I'll stay here for a while; maybe we can sit it out together.[32]

Later, in response to Byvalov's complaint about the *samodeiatel'nost'* movement ("What do they tear people away from work for? They're not going to become artists anyway") and his plea for help in identifying local talent, "the director lets loose with a long tirade about 'genuine art' and so-called 'folk creativity'":

> Dir.: Art is—Sarah Bernhardt, it's—Coquelin, it's Eleonora Duse. Art is—Shakespeare! We never had a Russian Shakespeare. Pushkin—that's not bad, but Gogol'—that's crude. For a hundred years, the mayor walked on the level floor of the stage—and this meant nothing in the plane of art. I was the first to try to refine and elevate Gogol'; I built grandiose structures on the stage. For the first time in the history of the Russian theatre my mayor worked on the trapeze and spoke from the ceiling![33] And no one understood me! On the contrary, they had the impudence to ask me—do I understand! But I answered that I was not the one who had to understand, they had to understand me—a creative individual!

Byv.: Well and then what?

Dir.: Nothing, they took away my theatre.

Continuing his speech, the director talks about his contempt for what is called *samodeiatel'nost'* and folk creativity: "Nothing has ever come of it and never will. Talent is an innate quality of the chosen. A popular orientation is ruinous for art. Such rare individuals as Sarah Bernhardt..."

Pravda's January 28, 1936 "Sumbur vmesto muzyki" ("A Muddle instead of Music") editorial overtly attacked Shostakovich's *Lady Macbeth of the Mtsensk District*, although the real target was the avant-garde, formalist art of Vsevolod Meierkhol'd: "This is music built on the same principle of rejection of opera, as leftist art's general rejection in the theatre of simplicity, realism, the intelligibility of an image, the natural sound of a word. This is a transfer into opera and music of the most negative traits of 'meierkhol'dovshchina' in multiplied form."[34] The "Baletnaia fal'sh'" ("Ballet Falsity") editorial, which appeared nine days later, criticized the kolkhoz ballet *Svetlyi ruchei* (*Clear Stream*, libretto by Lopukhov and Piotrovskii, music by Shostakovich) for its distance from the folk tradition, thereby injecting the *samodeiatel'nost'* movement into the discussion: "There are gold-leaf 'paysans' who have jumped off a pre-revolutionary candy box, who portray 'joy' in their dances, which have nothing in common with the folk dances either in the Kuban' or anywhere else. Not long ago, on this same Bol'shoi Theatre stage, where dolls made up 'like collective farmers' show off, real collective farmers from the North Caucasus demonstrated the marvelous art of folk dance."[35] The articles signified the beginning of Committee for the Arts chairman Platon Kerzhentsev's campaign against Meierkhol'd and his theatre, which culminated in Kerzhentsev's 1937 article "Chuzhoi teatr" ("An Alien Theatre"), the closing of Meierkhol'd's theatre in January 1938, and the director's arrest in 1939.[36]

But during the spring of 1936, Meierkhol'd was still mounting a vigorous defense. In his March 14 speech, "Meierkhol'd protiv meierkhol'dovshchiny," the director defended himself by admitting errors of form, such as the slanting floor in his production of *The Inspector General*, but he also affirmed the need to experiment in order to arrive at true art. He turned the tables on his accusers by locating "meierkhol'dovshchina" in the work of his former students-epigones and threatening to become a crotchety critic of their plays, thereby distancing himself from the odious phenomenon bearing his name.[37] Soon afterward, in his March 26 speech at the Assembly of Moscow Theatre Workers, Meierkhol'd attempted to deflect accusations of decadent western influences by discovering folkloric elements in his productions of *The Forest, The Death of Tarelkin* and *The Mandate*, while not forgetting to underscore the importance of cross-fertilization between *samodeiatel'nost'* and professional theatre.[38] In April 1936, Kerzhentsev dealt another blow to the theatre, pointing out the lack of contemporary Soviet plays in its repertoire: "In the repertoire of a theatre that, from the first days of the Revolution, stood beside the Revolution, there is not a single proper Soviet play. This is the theatre's greatest error."[39] In 1923, Aleksandrov had himself performed on the trapeze and walked the highwire in one act of Eisenstein's *Enough Simplicity for Every Wise Man*, performed for Meierkhol'd's jubilee celebration at the Bol'shoi Theatre. But on the heels of the spring 1936 campaign against Meierkhol'd, Aleksandrov turned the director's trouble to advantage by writing into the *Volga-Volga* script a parody of Meierkhol'd and his modernist aesthetics that also foretold the closure of his theatre.

The first version of the *Volga-Volga* script begins with a shot of a homemade music stand on which a hand places a music notebook with "Volga-Volga" inscribed on the cover. As the hand turns the pages, the names of actors and their roles appear, as well as the notes for the main melody of the film. In the background, we hear an orchestra tuning up; on the page entitled "The Overture" appears the shadow of the conductor. A hand picks up an office pen on the music stand, pricks itself on the nib, throws the nib out of the pen, and bangs the pen on the stand like a conductor's baton. As the orchestra plays the title melody, the camera tracks back, revealing the conductor Alesha Rybkin. Rybkin's orchestra practices early in the morning, before work, playing the melody "The Bad Road," which Strelka also sings as she rides her old scooter over the crooked logs of a swamp road. She collides with a driverless horse-drawn cart in which sits the director Sviatoslavskii under an umbrella, complaining: "I'm a muscovite and am not obligated to know how to manage a horse." Strelka gives Rybkin an official letter notifying him that his calculations have been confirmed: "The lock will be built and the entire region will thereby join the Volga Basin system. The local river will become navigable." In town, she drives up to a closed barbershop bearing a slogan punning clumsily on "March of the Happy Guys": "He who strides through life clean-shaven will never be lost anywhere." She climbs through the window, awakening the elderly barber, who dons a black skullcap and gold-rimmed glasses and turns into a perfect academician. He has received a package with remedies and ointments for lifting freckles and is prepared to experiment on her. But Strelka is afraid, so he decides to try it out first on a client. Next, Strelka drives up to an old hut and gives a vigorous old man a rejection letter from an arts school that only accepts students under the age of sixteen: "Your age exceeds the norm by 100 years." The old man is despondent: "There's nothing more for me to do. Now I'm going to die." The ferryman (Strelka's father) strands the ferry on some shallows, thereby preventing Strelka from delivering a telegram to Byvalov. She shouts the telegram's contents across the river to Byvalov, but her voice is drowned out by a herd of geese. Sviatoslavskii throws stones at the geese, which then attack him, and trips over a herd of piglets, whose squealing causes the pigs on the ferry to jump off and swim to shore. The ferry lists to one side, breaks free, and moves downstream. After it is stopped, Strelka hands Byvalov the telegram of invitation to a competition of amateur artistic activity. Meanwhile, the barber talks to an important-looking bearded client intent upon sending Byvalov, whom he considers unreliable, to the barber's decontamination unit. The client, who turns out to be the caretaker, then fixes his apron and takes up his broom, opining: "I think that a resolution of a general meeting of Osoaviakhim members is needed in this matter. Well, see you; it's time for me to sweep the street."[40]

Byvalov is displeased to see the letter authorizing the lock. An old accountant praises Rybkin's courage in challenging his superior, and Rybkin responds: "Soviet people are proud people. And the accountants' tribe must not be less proud than all of them!" The humor here is a play on the clichéd "stalinskoe plemia" ("Stalin's tribe"). Byvalov asks Sviatoslavkii's help in identifying local performers, suggesting that the townspeople be invited to audition for the director. Sviatoslavskii's negative reaction ("You'll ruin the whole thing. You'll scare off *samodeiatel'nost'* that way. No announcements. You have to catch folk art unawares.") leads to a series of comic mishaps, as the director secretly searches for "talents": the lock workers chase him away; Byvalov is caught spying on Strelka and the laundresses rehearsing the ballet *Rusalka*, and the girls entangle him in a fish net. The director pursues the manicurist Niura, who has taken the name "Golli"—Aleksandrov and Nil'sen's nod toward Boris Shumiatskii's *kinogorod* project[41]. The director asks her name:

—Golli [Holly]

—From where?

—Excuse me?

—That is, from what?

—From the word Gollivud [Hollywood]. It's a city.

—Oh, in the Crimea!

—No, no! In America! The *kinogorod.*

While the barber uses hot compresses to remove Sviatoslavskii's freckles (he loses his beard instead), the director makes a date to meet Golli that evening in the same monastery cemetery where Rybkin, the barber, and Golli are rehearsing an anti-fascist play. The director spies on them and is seized by the barber and caretaker, who addresses politically charged lines from the play to Sviatoslavskii-Meierkhol'd: "I'll plunge a dagger into your dog's heart! You're an agent of the Comintern! For the last time, are you for us or against us?" In the end, for all their pains, the two talent spies, Byvalov and Sviatoslavskii, get a beating from the townspeople.

The next day, Byvalov prints a poster announcing auditions for the talent competition, at which Strelka, Rybkin, and their collective are rejected by Byvalov and Sviatoslavskii. The director agrees to audition Golli at 7:00 am the next morning in order to avoid gossip.

That evening, though pleading illness, Sviatoslavskii is roused from bed by elderly Dr. Moritz, who applies to the director's back cupping glasses, which the doctor proceeds to play like a xylophone with wooden sticks, in Marx Brothers fashion, accompanied by his wife on the guitar. A slapstick scene follows: the director tries to get up, Moritz hits him with a xylophone hammer, Sviatoslavskii rises again, breaking a glass. Moritz tells his wife: "Put on the spare 'la.' Oh, if we lived in America, we'd be millionaires!" This is followed by a musical number to the beat of Sviatoslavskii's pulse.

The director's morning rendezvous with Golli in a former church, with Rybkin spying behind a saint's statue, serves up a slapstick mistaken identity routine: from behind the statue, Rybkin tickles the director's cheek; Sviatoslavskii then passionately kisses Rybkin's extended hand and tries to kiss Golli, who slaps him, while Rybkin delivers a blow on the ear from the opposite side. Thinking that he is seeing a comedy audition, Byvalov accepts Golli for the competition.

The next day, Byvalov and Sviatoslavskii go to the lock to bathe, where Rybkin and his orchestra are rehearsing in a tied-up rowboat. When the ferryman, carried away by their musicianship, opens the gates of the lock too quickly, the rowboat is left hanging in the air like a hammock. Byvalov and the director then float by under the boat and are showered with falling mud from its bottom. An acrobatic number follows when the musicians realize their situation, panic, and capsize the rowboat.

By a sign marking the border between Europe and Asia, Strelka sings "The Echo," her farewell to her native region before leaving on the *Sevriuga*. Meanwhile, the 116-year-old Sergei Ivanovich, who has been rejected by the arts school, prepares to die:

> Sergei Ivanovich casts a fading glance over the cloudy fall sky, the tops of trees with yellowed leaves and his old house. The old man sighs heavily, "Oh, earth!" With a stiffening hand, he scoops up a handful of earth, kneads it, looks at it, and regretfully throws it back. A little girl addresses a boy in a whisper, "Is he going to die now?" "Quiet, you," says the boy. Two old men quietly enter the yard and sit down by the dying man. "How are you doing, Serezha?" asks one of them. "I'm dying," says the old man in a weak voice. "There's nothing more for me to do. I've danced out my time. This is my 117th year." The scene then switches to the orchestra's haircuts en masse at the barber shop, after which we are returned to the old man, who is still in the process of giving up the ghost: "The dying old man's yard. The little girl asks the boy again in a whisper, "Has he died already?" The boy: "Not yet. Look, he's breathing." The old man slowly opens his eyes and looks around at those encircling him. Many people have gathered around him. The old man: "What I haven't finished doing, my descendants will finish." He then asks his fifty-year-old son, thirty-year-old grandson, and two great-grandchildren to sing a

> last song for him. Strelka, who is passing by, hears the singing and comes into the yard. "The old man: "Well, farewell. I'm dying." Strelka runs up to the old man. "What are you saying, Sergei Ivanovich. How can this be, we nominated you for the competition today. You're supposed to perform the main act. You're going to Moscow!" The dying elder arises from his sickbed and asks for his boots. The little girl grabs the old man by the pants and asks in bewilderment, "Grandad, Grandad, when are you going to die?" The old man (angrily): "No time now! Get out from underfoot" and dances out the gates.

This episode parodies the death scene at the beginning of Aleksandr Dovzhenko's *Zemlia* (*Earth*): an aged friend comes to pay a last visit to the family patriarch, Grandfather Semen, who lies on the ground surrounded by his family:

> —Are you dying, Semen?
>
> —I'm dying, Petro.
>
> —I see. Well then, go ahead and die.

After eating one last pear, the old man lies back with the words "Well, farewell. I'm dying" and gives up the ghost. His grandson, the young Komsomol member Vasyl, comments laconically: "He liked pears."

Soon after its release in 1930, *Earth* was attacked by *Pravda* and *Izvestiia*, where Dem'ian Bednyi criticized the film as a kulak picture—unnatural, cynical, sexually degenerate (because of Natalka's nude scene), and politically misguided in not highlighting the social conflicts of collectivization in the countryside.[42] Dovzhenko's next film, *Ivan* (1932), was criticized for its Ukrainian nationalist subtext; the director was quietly removed from his administrative positions at Ukrainfil'm and forced to move to Moscow to avoid arrest.[43] Only with the release of *Aerograd* in late 1935 had the filmmaker managed to rehabilitate himself so that Dovzhenko's lyrical paean to peasant life was an easy mark for Aleksandrov's more "progressive" figuration of provincial life in *Volga-Volga*.

Strelka misses the departing *Sevriuga* because she has run off to pull Rybkin's letter, in which he changes his name to please Golli, from the mail. Sviatoslavskii, who has stowed away on the *Sevriuga* to escape alimony payments, dons Strelka's costume and then Golli's dress with predictable comic complications. Meanwhile, Strelka pursues the group in a canoe and faints while crossing the rapids. At the confluence of the Chusovaia and Kama, the *Sevriuga* lands on the first shoal. They are saved by lumberjacks, who have been waiting two weeks for a boat to the competition and now board the *Sevriuga*, which also picks up the unconscious Strelka. Rybkin, who was previously romancing Golli, now falls for Strelka, who loses her freckles under the barber's compress. As

Rybkin is about to declare himself, the nearby passenger steamer *The Tourist* explodes and bursts into flame after colliding with an oil barge. The *Sevriuga* passengers come to its aid, Rybkin behaves heroically and, when the fog lifts the next morning, Rybkin and Strelka are in the water, providing the mise-en-scène for the "Water!" comic routine. The Kamyshev group is picked up by the Volga German delegation on the "Al't-fater," which has been waiting to meet up with the Bashkirian delegation; both groups perform their musical numbers. The *Sevriuga* manages to reach Gorky, where the Sormovo workers take them on a new streamlined steamship, which arrives first and becomes the contest headquarters. Soiuzkinokhronika then appears to film the Kamyshev group, but Strelka asks them to show footage of other amateur performances instead. On the sail of a passing yacht, they project the performances of Georgian, Abkhazian, and Armenian folk groups. At a banquet on board the steamship, Strelka reports on the arrival of the flotilla. The script concludes: "The anchors fall with a heavy rumbling. Goblets are raised, toasts are made, and a banquet song resounds mightily. For our great and talented country and the genius of free humanity—STALIN."

During late November and December, Aleksandrov and Nil'sen were busy with a prestigious assignment—filming and editing Stalin's speech on the new constitution at the 8th Congress of Soviets.[44] Erdman completed his term of exile in Tomsk on October 19, 1936 and returned to Moscow to join in the work on the *Volga-Volga* script. He was, however, refused a Moscow residence permit and moved to Kalinin during February 1937, where the collaboration continued.[45] "Aleksandrov and Nil'sen would come to me with the outlines of episodes and together we finished writing the script. They took the lyrical line of the script, I took the satirical parts, particularly the episodes connected with the character of Byvalov."[46] The second version of the *Volga-Volga* literary script, now co-authored with Erdman, was submitted to the studio February 2, 1937.[47] Two days later, Shumiatskii, eager to advance the film, which had been planned for the twentieth anniversary of the Revolution, had already scribbled "Give a resolution" on the title page of the typescript. It is clear from this document, as well as the two subsequent revisions of the director's script, that Erdman was responsible for transforming Aleksandrov and Nil'sen's rambling and overloaded story into a viable comedic script.

This second version of the literary script established the general plot outline that is familiar to us in the completed film. Erdman performed major surgery on the Aleksandrov-Nil'sen script, amputating a number of secondary plotlines and comic digressions. He streamlined the plot by combining the Sergei Ivanovich and caretaker characters and by dropping the centenarian dancer's near-death experience; he eliminated the Sviatoslavskii, Golli, and barber characters, along with their attendant episodes, such as the director's monologue on his artistic credo. He also cut the talent search, the romantic triangle of Sviatoslavskii, Golli, and Rybkin, Rybkin's name change, the freckle removal experiments, Sviatoslavskii's boat adventures, the fire on *The Tourist*, and the ending with Soiuzkinokhronika. Also deleted was the entire lock line, from Alesha's proposed project to the comic water scenes with the stranded rowboat. The gags relating to Sviatoslavskii, such as the geese attack and his pursuit by town "talents", were transferred to Byvalov, who becomes the satirical nexus of the plot. Whether for technical or ethical reasons, or both, Erdman also eliminated the Meierkhol'd and Dovzhenko parodies.

Erdman's ironic humor is evident in a series of newly added episodes: Byvalov's "top secret" shouting scene, "untalented" Strelka's demonstration of the town's talents to Byvalov, and the townspeople's expanded pursuit of Byvalov to display their talents. Byvalov's office staff click abacuses and type in tune to a melody; the restaurant waiter sings the menu; the policeman plays "nightingale" on his whistle; and the caretaker dances. Erdman also introduces the water carrier character, whose horse is trained to stop at every bar, and transforms the ferryman (originally Strelka's father) into the braggart Lotsman. Erdman even winks ironically at *Volga-Volga*'s composer: "Noticing Byvalov, Rybkin makes a sign and the orchestra begins to play a frisky march. —'And what is this?' shouts the angry Byvalov. —'Dunaevskii,' answers Rybkin. —'Stop this outrage,' says Byvalov."[48]

Erdman reworked and elaborated the second half of the plot, the journey from Kamyshev to Moscow, into crosscutting scenes based on the rivalry between the two amateur groups led by Strelka and Rybkin. He motivates the rivalry by introducing the debate over the superiority of classical vs. popular music in the lovers' quarrel:

> Strelka and Rybkin are walking along the river bank. They dream about going to Moscow together. They've been attracted to each other for a long time and the upcoming trip promises them much joy. They begin to discuss the repertoire of their performances. Because of this, sharp disagreements arise between them. Rybkin, a partisan of classical music, believes that only a classical repertoire can be taken to Moscow. Strelka, an advocate of happy folk dances and songs, defends the light genres. The disagreements pass into a quarrel. Strelka maintains that art must be happy. Rybkin, on the contrary, demands seriousness and profundity in art. Strelka asks Rybkin whether he really never feels like dancing and singing. "But are you really never sad?" asks Rybkin in response. Each of them denies having such feelings. After quarreling to the point of utter and total disagreement, and calling Strelka a "happy fool," Rybkin leaves. Now alone, Strelka bursts into tears and sings a sad song. Rybkin, who hasn't gone far, sneaks up and listens to her singing, smiling sarcastically. "Aha!" he shouts triumphantly when Strelka finishes singing. "So you're never sad?!" Embarrassed, Strelka tries to say something to justify herself. "You're a liar to boot," says Rybkin scornfully. In her bewilderment, Strelka can't find the words to answer. Putting his hands in his pockets, Ryblin walks off proudly and disappears at the turn in

> the road. Strelka remains standing in a stupor. Regaining her senses, she runs after him. On the road she sees Rybkin, who is walking along whistling and dancing, exhilarated by his victory over Strelka. "Aha!" shouts Strelka. "So you never enjoy yourself?" Rybkin is stunned and freezes, completely stupefied. "Liar," Strelka shouts at him and goes off in the opposite direction. The collective of circle members splits apart because of their leaders' quarrel.

This stylistic conflict cum battle of the sexes repeats the conventional dual-focus narrative strategy of musical comedy film that Erdman had already exploited in *Happy Guys*. During the river journey, Erdman has the two groups battling each other via simultaneous performances of waltz and folk dance music that confuse dancers on both ships:

> Rybkin resumes the rehearsal of the waltz. The girls in tutus continue their dance. "How are we worse than them? Let's rehearse too," says Strelka, and begins to rehearse a comic folk dance. The parallel sounds of the orchestras throw off the performers. The ballerinas in tutus dance *lezginka* steps, while the *lezginka* dancers switch to a classical *pas* with a lift. Attempting to outplay each other, the orchestras play louder and louder and are thrown off too.

Next, competing folk and classical choral groups create a cacophony that frightens nearby wildlife and the travelers on a passing steamboat:

> Holding their hands over their ears, the passengers run off in different directions. Only one imperturbable man in horn-rimmed glasses remains sitting calmly in his chair. "Who is that?" a passenger asks the captain. "A music critic," answers the captain. "What is all this?" they ask the critic. "The usual argument between light and serious genres," answers the critic.

Although the conflict here is between traditional classical and popular repertoires (Beethoven, Liszt, Tchaikovsky vs. folk songs, variety, mass songs), both of which were officially acceptable because of their relative melodic simplicity and accessibility, Erdman does not miss the opportunity to comment on the 1936 campaign against Shostakovich's modernist music. In the script, the cacophony of competing music is described in the language of the January 1936 *Pravda* editorial: "The musical muddle rumbles on for a few moments." Through the words of the music critic, Erdman, who loved working for the music hall, provides a commonsense perspective on "difficult" vs. "light" repertoire: each style has its own rightful place in the world of music.

By using the device of Strelka and Rybkin's personal-professional quarrel, now magnified by Byvalov's support for Rybkin's classical orchestra (typical of old-guard characters in musical comedy) and his refusal to board Strelka's group on the *Sevriuga*, Erdman is able to shape the plot through crosscutting between the separate river adventures of the two groups, followed by a series of comic misunderstandings when the groups join up. Strelka and company take the difficult Chusovaia route, borrowing a boat from courting couples in a fishing village, and boarding the lumberjacks' sailboat at the mouth of the river. Their adventures motivate several planned songs: "Song about the Future" near the echoing cliff, and "Govorlivyi" and "the warming up number" after shooting the rapids. Strelka's group passes the *Sevriuga*, only to fall behind as the wind dies down. Both vessels are then grounded on shoals and later pulled off.

In late 1936, Aleksandrov was still unsure about the musical content of *Volga-Volga*, telling the press that the film would include folk songs, such as "Volga, Volga, mat' rodnaia," but the axial composition would be a "welcoming banquet song."[49] In this script, however, Erdman first introduces the crucial motif of Strelka's song: she goes to the *Sevriuga* to collect the group's baggage and shows Rybkin her composition, which precipitates another quarrel: "'Don't be ridiculous, what can you write? A real Beethoven in a skirt!' 'An accountant in music,' shouts the offended Strelka, and jumps into the boat." That night they go to each other's boats to apologize, missing one another en route. In the dark of Rybkin's cabin, Strelka has a comic encounter with a bear that she takes for Rybkin. On the sixth day of the trip, the *Sevriuga* sinks near Gorky in a storm, and Strelka's sheet music floats away on the Volga. Byvalov and the two groups continue the trip on the Sormovo factory ship while Strelka goes on alone in a small boat. From passing ships come individual bars of her song, which together make up the entire melody. Upon arriving in Moscow, the Kamyshevites go off to search for Strelka, who clambers onto a floating stage bearing the town name. Dismayed, she finds herself before the Olimpiada audience. The conclusion is typical Aleksandrovian political spectacle: looking up at a giant portrait of Stalin, Strelka gains the determination to sing, and is soon joined by the townspeople, and then other delegations. Her song projects outward, gaining universality, and uniting all spheres of life under the Leader: "On the Red Army's amateur performers' ships, the melody turns into a song about the Red Army; on the ships where the banquet is held, it is sung as a Soviet banquet song; kolkhoz collectives interpret the song as a hymn of the fields. The Sormovo workers sing it as a factory song, and all of them together sing a song about the genius of humanity—the great Stalin." At this point, the script lacks the concluding Olimpiada scenes, and the finale would yet prove to be problematic for Aleksandrov.

On February 5, 1937, Elena Kirillovna Sokolovskaia, the deputy director of Mosfil'm, called a meeting to discuss the second literary script.[50] Present were Aleksandrov, Nil'sen, Darevskii, and Erdman. Sokolovskaia criticized the plot, primarily on grounds of genre slippage and the downgrading of Byvalov's role: the comedy begins with Byvalov and ends with an apotheosis "addressed to the Soviet land and to Comrade Stalin." The criticisms were that this was an "illegitimate motif" for the genre; they had already been criticized for mixing genres in *Circus*. Byvalov disappeared from this version of the script, and Sokolovskaia felt he should be involved in making Strelka and Rybkin quarrel. Finally, the finale of the previous script had obstacles, but it was now simply a search for Strelka.

Instead of answering Sokolovskaia directly, Aleksandrov summarized the latest version of the still unfinished plot, which now began with the iris shot of Strelka and Alesha kissing (Aleksandrov again mentioned Cherkasov for the role) and has an episode in which the aged caretaker does poorly in the judging until it is revealed that the other dancers are thirteen-year-old boys wearing beards. Aleksandrov also voices doubts about the lack of social conflict in the plot, which Erdman had elaborated according to the classical paradigm of the musical. Instead, Aleksandrov wants to return to the social satire of bourgeois types, as in *Happy Guys*:

> What is bothering us? We have said that if the argument had been about a social question, we would have written a script in five hours. We're worried that the argument is about tastes regarding the music and we're afraid that this will not excite the Soviet viewer, because this is a very relative, indefinite theme. She ends up with a group of classical musicians, she doesn't like the way they hold their instruments, the way they hold the sheet music, etc. All of this could be made funny. If she had ended up in a bourgeois house and didn't like it there, and she had started to redo everything her own way, this would be much more interesting and valuable.

Erdman responded to Sokolovskaia with a proposal to bifurcate the conflict, with the main accent on bureaucrat Byvalov's opposition to both groups of amateur performers:

> It would be much more exciting if the argument were between Strelka and Rybkin on one side, and with Byvalov on the other. Byvalov is pursuing an incorrect policy and there would be satirical notes. Byvalov spoils everything, but they overcome the obstacles he places before them—then it will be more interesting to laugh. And what's more, in the finale the viewer absolutely must be concerned about who will turn out to be right. There can also be an argument between Strelka and Rybkin, but the main argument must be between them and Byvalov.

Sokolovskaia agreed and Erdman's strategy was adopted for subsequent versions of the script.

In order to make the twentieth anniversary deadline, Aleksandrov then proposed that part of the preparatory work, such as booking the film crew's steamboat and construction of the *Sevriuga* and the sailboat, run simultaneously with writing the director's script, due March 1. The preparatory period (casting and song rehearsals) would coincide with Erdman's completing the dialogues and Dunaevskii's the music by April 1. Remembering his experiences with *Happy Guys* and *Circus*, Darevskii refused to proceed without an approved script. As a compromise, Sokolovskaia agreed to take a revised director's outline to GUK on March 1, and Aleksandrov agreed to complete the montage script by April 1.

The revised script was submitted on March 3, 1937.[51] Several more scenes were added or expanded, most of which are marked by Erdman's wit rather than Aleksandrov's slapstick routines. Byvalov's male secretary is changed to a fire chief, allowing jokes about the lack of tall buildings in the town. In describing the town's talents to Byvalov, Strelka notes that Fed'ka, who has returned from army service, "spews out all of Pushkin by heart," an ironic reference to the media blitz surrounding the 1937 centenary celebration. During the forest trek to catch up to the *Sevriuga*, Strelka's group comes to the stone obelisk marking the divide between Europe and Asia. She exclaims, "Shape up, gang, we're marching into Europe!" This politically charged scene was cut from the film during editing. On the raft, the lumberjack Vasilii now tells his companions to get off his instrument—a log with two hammers. The xylophone-log needs to be tuned; he scolds an old man for sitting on the basses: "This isn't a grand piano—it's a delicate instrument." At this point, Erdman introduces Byvalov's "thanks to my sensitive leadership" ("blagodaria moemu chutkomu rukovodstvu") speech, poking fun at a conventional epithet applied to the Soviet leadership: "Tovarishch Zhdanov, chutkii, rodnoi—pomogi" ("Comrade Zhdanov, dear sensitive one, help me").[52] Byvalov also admires the Kama scenery: "What nature! Exactly like the wallpaper!" (Shiskin's *Morning in a Pine Forest* is reproduced on the wallpaper of the ship's lounge). After Rybkin observes, "All we need is a bear," a huge brown bear climbs on board, followed by a gypsy with a tambourine.

> Gypsy: Here's the problem. Before we used to go around with bears, but now we've settled on the land. In a kolkhoz. It's harvest time, everyone is working, but he can't do anything. He's a creative worker.
>
> [Heaving from one foot to the other, the bear performs his act.]
>
> Byvalov: So what do you want from us?
>
> Gypsy: Take him with you. He's no use to us and he'll come in handy to you as artists.... Farewell Toptygin![53]

This scene, which ironizes over the uselessness of "creative workers" to Soviet society, as well as the frivolity of *samodeiatel'nost'* at harvest time, was ultimately cut from the film. The slapstick "vertical log" routine on the *Sevriuga* is added to this script, and Rybkin's musicians write down Strelka's song on Byvalov's notepaper (important to later plot development), but the song itself does not yet figure in early episodes of the script. Both groups now board the steamboat *Volga-Moskva*, which takes all Ural delegations to the capital. Upset by Rybkin's jeers that passing delegations already know her song, Strelka jumps overboard. Abjuring apotheosis in the new, conventionally romantic ending, Aleksandrov uses the Strelka-Rybkin "Water!" fainting scene to reunite the lovers, as Strelka's song is heard from the approaching ships of other delegations.

On March 8, the Mosfil'm leadership issued a report on the script and then met with Aleksandrov, Nil'sen, Iudin (the assistant director), and Briantsev (the chief administrator) the following day.[54] Mosfil'm approved the script, subject to further changes. The administration required that the text (1000 frames) be abbreviated to 400 (dispensable scenes were enumerated); the musical plan must be completed. To resolve the Byvalov, Strelka, and Rybkin lines, the finale must be redone. The Strelka-Rybkin plotline should be resolved through "the triumph of the folk song," which then becomes Rybkin's symphonic work.[55] The underwater love scene, which trivializes the ending, must be deleted, substituting a festive finale, "but without turning it into an 'apotheosis.'"[56]

Most interestingly, the depiction of the townspeople must be altered. Never far beneath the surface, as always, was the vexed issue of Soviet satire and its mutable boundaries. "It seems to me that there's a danger that the provincial town depicted in the script may turn out to be a gorod Glupov," observed Darevskii, referring to Saltykov-Shchedrin's *History of a Town* (1869-70), a satiric historical chronicle of the town of Glupov (Stupidville). Sokolovskaia preferred to marginalize the eccentric characters: "It should be done in such a way that everything happening is in the background of the town's life. The town lives its own life. The town is a normal, good Soviet town and this kind of story plays out in it."[57] However, Aleksandrov's comedic practice, based primarily on slapstick and visual gags from American cinema, necessarily presupposed a certain stupidity and gullibility in the Kamyshevites that had already been evident in the earliest version of his script. In addition, Erdman's own experiences in Eniseisk exile had provided him with plenty of humorous material on provincial life. The Folk that had been elevated in such a simplistic way after 1935 were brought down to earth in Erdman's Kamyshev simpletons. Adding to the problem, Erdman's deletion of the lock theme from the storyline removed Aleksandrov and Nil'sen's original justification for the idiocy of the inhabitants of Melkovodsk, whose cultural and intellectual level was to be raised by contact with the outside world and Moscow, the center. Instead, the new, streamlined plot simply *magnified* their idiocy. Nevertheless, the Mosfil'm leadership saw Erdman as essential co-author of the work in progress. Darevskii suggested that the Mosfil'm report and March script be sent to GUK for approval, "with the idea that Aleksandrov and Erdman would now work in parallel." Sokolovskaia agrees, "The conclusion should be sent to Erdman and he should be summoned here as soon as possible."[58]

Aleksandrov accepted most of the studio's criticisms, objecting obliquely to Mosfil'm's strict textual supervision by citing the value of actors' ad hoc contributions, which preclude any finalized script. He responded to the demand to attenuate the "gorod Glupov" effect by insisting on the importance of the townspeople's pursuit of Byvalov as critical to the plot:

> In an eccentric comedy, much of its success will depend on the actors and my work with them. Even those sentences that have been written down cannot be considered obligatory for the comedy. When we work with the actors on the characters, a whole series of abbreviations and additions will arise. We should be trusted in this regard. If we're not free here, it will be impossible to make a funny film. If we decide that we can begin work on the basis of this script, then we need to study the characters now, together with the six main actors. Il'inskii will think his through. Shtraukh will add his touches, and Orlova too. I believe that working with them will add a great deal and, by the time of the montage script sheets, we'll have a clear picture.
>
> In the panoramas of the town, where there are a lot of balalaikas, we want to have a suite of all the popular folk songs, so that each person plays one phrase, each instrument plays for a second, and this needs to be illustrated visually with something. I object to the musicians' playing for themselves. It would be better if they put pressure on Byvalov, if they force him to acknowledge that they are talented people. When we have the music, this will be clear. If they listen passively, and don't launch an offensive, the theme of the offended town will be lost. When he says that there are no talents in the town, the town gets offended at this person.[59]

After inquiries by the studio, GUK approved the Mosfil'm report on March 17 and set the date for submission of the director's script as March 27.[60]

On March 30, 1937 a local paper reported that Aleksandrov and Nil'sen had arrived in Kalinin the previous day "and may possibly travel to other towns of the region in order to choose the on-location shots for filming."[61] However the most important reason for the trip was clearly revision of the script with Erdman. Nil'sen's archive contains a cut and pasted version of the March 3 script with handwritten inserts, mostly by Erdman, added to the March typescript.[62] Except for the finale, recorded in a separate notebook in Nil'sen's hand, it is Erdman who revised the March script, expanding dialogues and adding new scenes, especially for Byvalov, inserting descriptions of the mise-en-scène, numbering scenes (twice, in blue and orange pencil), and dividing the script into parts. To the earlier text ("The young people are sitting on a cart loaded with hay. The cart stands on a ferry. The ferry, which is filled to overflowing with passengers, pushes off from the steep riverbank"), Erdman adds "pulling back from the camera, the ferry reveals the opposite bank of the river, on which is located a picturesque old Urals town"). The fire chief has been replaced by Byvalov's secretary, Zoia Ivanovna, who is more useful to the development of the storyline.

Strelka now tells Rybkin that the song was composed by an unknown Dusia, thereby finally integrating the central song into the beginning of the script. Byvalov becomes more prominent throughout the second half of the script through additional scenes with the bear. As the *Sevriuga* takes on water in the storm, Byvalov runs up to the sailor untying a lifeboat. "Sailor: 'Wait, citizen. Women escape first.' Pushing his way through the crowd, which is running around in a panic, Byvalov, wearing Strelka's coat, runs up while tying her scarf on his head. Byvalov shouts: 'Women go ahead,' and jumps into a boat." The bear jumps in after him. The lifeboat is sighted later: "A boat with a bear and a figure in Strelka's clothes is moving toward the sailboat. Voices: 'It's Strelka! Honest to God, it's Strelka.' The caretaker shouts: 'Strelka-a-a!' Byvalov, wearing Strelka's scarf and coat sits in the stern like a hypnotized person. Hearing the shouts from the sailboat, he smiles helplessly and bends forward, trying to take an oar. The bear growls. Byvalov assumes his previous position. The boat floats along with the current."

In the conclusion, recorded by Nil'sen, with a few corrections by Erdman (here it is impossible to determine authorship), Strelka, who is now on the steamboat, goes to change before revealing herself as composer of the song. Meanwhile, the Olimpiada staff on the top deck ask Byvalov to find the author, leading to the scenes with one, two, and ten performing Dusias. Strelka jumps into the water, followed by Rybkin, to whom she confesses her authorship. He almost passes out, sinking under the water. Strelka pulls him up by the hair, and a double version of Aleksandrov's favorite "Water!" routine follows:

> Strelka: What's wrong with you?
>
> Rybkin: I feel faint! Water!

Rybkin refuses to allow Strelka to reveal herself as composer of the song:

> Strelka: What business is it of yours?
>
> Rybkin: Fool! I love you.
>
> [Strelka then faints and asks for water.]

An expanded conclusion follows. Rybkin and Strelka are fished out of the water, they return to the Olimpiada competition on the steamboat in sailor costumes, and Strelka performs her song.

> Chairman (leaning over to Byvalov): You're right, Comrade Byvalov, there are wonderful people in your Kamyshev!
>
> Byvalov: Are you talking about me?
>
> Chairman: No, I mean Dusia.
>
> Byvalov: Oh, Dusia. I've got as many of those as you want!
>
> Chairman: I envy you! It's interesting to work with such people!
>
> Byvalov: A remarkable coincidence! I was just thinking about that myself!
>
> [To the sound of a song, the ships approach the Kremlin.]

The April 1937 typescript, which Aleksandrov and Nil'sen submitted to the studio, included Erdman's contribution and the new ending, along with the notations for songs (not yet completed by Dunaevskii): the water carrier's couplets; cooks' song; Neapolitan march; Svistopliaska (Whistle-dancing) during the townspeople's pursuit of Byvalov to demonstrate their talents; the "Triumphal March" from *Aida* played by Rybkin's orchestra outside Byvalov's one window vs. "Volga-Volga", the as yet non-existent theme song, played by Strelka's group at the opposite window, with Byvalov running back and forth to close all windows; Schubert's "Musical Moment" during the trip; "Ol'ga's Aria" sung by the lumberjack; "Komsomol Road Song" as Strelka and the lumberjacks approach the sailboat on the Kama; "March from *Aida*" as the *Sevriuga* passes the becalmed sailboat; "The Waltz" for the Lotsman's "dancing" with the wheel; "Lotsman's Song" when he joins the sailboat; "Lyrical variant of Volga-Volga" sung by Strelka on deck at night; Strelka's song performed by various delegations on the river. Aleksandrov's pre-Dunaevskii idea of the theme song is recorded in one couplet:

> Ia tebia pokidaiu nadolgo,
> Ueezhaiu v drugie kraia.
> Do svidaniia krasavitsa Volga,
> Do svidaniia podruga moia.[63]

Mosfil'm approved the script on April 15, 1937, noting that the plot had been tightened by the deletion of attractions and melodramatic elements; its length had been reduced to 667 frames. During the preparatory period and by May 5, Aleksandrov and Nil'sen were instructed to provide montage sheets with the following emendations: demonstrate more clearly through the dialogues the essence of the argument between Strelka and Rybkin; change Rybkin's surname to something less disparaging[64]; include amateur performances of workers and kolkhoz farmers (at present only the representatives of secondary professions—water carrier, caretaker, lumberjacks—are in evidence); delete the bear episode and improve the scene of the Lotsman on the barge with M1s.[65] Usievich approved the April script on behalf of GUK on May 3, adding further instructions: improve [i.e., tone down] dialogues like Strelka's "And Fed'ka, after he came back from the army, spews out all of Pushkin by heart"; "Hold the bike. As now, he says, wise Oleg prepares to take revenge, he says, on the unreasonable Khazars"; achieve "greater satirical wit in the situations exposing the shady sides of life and the concrete exponents of bureaucratism."[66] The bear episodes, including the one which referred pointedly to the marginalization of creative workers, and Strelka's rendering of Pushkin (a disrespectful treatment of classical Russian literature in the changed cultural climate after the banning of Dem'ian Bednyi's *Bogatyri* in November 1936) were ultimately cut from the film, although Aleksandrov initially refused to give them up, preserving the episodes in late versions of the script.

Avenarius's official May 10, 1937 evaluation for GUK criticized the excessive number of primitive slapstick scenes (pouring water on Byvalov, his tripping on a pig), occasionally poor dialogue, and lack of character continuity (Byvalov's secretary disappears in later episodes). Once again, officialdom is concerned with the gorod Glupov effect: "Lively, merry, buoyant Soviet amateur activities develop in an archaic, seemingly pre-revolutionary environment: a raft-ferry, a water delivery nag, Byvalov seems to be a tyrant-village policeman or mayor."[67]

During April and May, Aleksandrov and his assistants were occupied with assembling the cast and approving costumes and scenery. Orlova was cast as Strelka and Volodin as the Lotsman.[68] GUK noted that Kurikhin was busy in Pyr'ev's *Bogataia nevesta* (*The Rich Bride*) and instructed the studio to find someone else for the water carrier character.[69] Aleksandrov had also considered I. A. Liubeznov for the Byvalov role, but the actor was busy playing a similarly villainous bureaucrat in on-location filming of *Bogataia nevesta*.[70] Igor' Il'inskii was not Aleksandrov's first choice for Byvalov, which later became Il'inskii's signature role. The director first chose Maksim Shtraukh and cast Il'inskii as the less important Alesha Rybkin.

Il'inskii had been a popular comic actor in 1920s films such as *Aelita*, *The Cigarette Girl from Mossel'prom*, *The Tailor from Torzhok*, *Mary Pickford's Kiss*, and *The Feast of St. Iorgen*, but with the tightening of state control over the film industry, he had fallen under an ideological cloud. He was publicly criticized in August 1936 for his lovable NEP ne'er-do-wells: "What constant characteristics have been evident in Il'inskii's screen roles to date? All of them were petty-bourgeois, shallow people, good for nothings. What was his main problem, his error and his tragedy as an actor? He was fulfilling an unnatural assignment—trying to attract the audience's sympathy to negative, repulsive, and parasitic social types by his special dramatic talent, energy, charm, and merry acting."[71] There had also been a creative failure: in 1936, Il'inskii had both acted in and directed *Odnazhdy letom* (*Once in Summer*), a mediocre comedy based on Il'f and Petrov's *The Golden Calf*. He had played both a charlatan-magician and the Komsomol hero, Teleskop, in the film. Il'inskii's portrayal of the bumbling but likeable young hero may have motivated Aleksandrov's initial casting decision. But Il'inskii had also acted the outré role of the pretentious bureaucrat Pobedonosikov in Meierkhol'd's 1930 production of *The Bathhouse*, so that he was suitable for the homologous Byvalov role and, in the end, his extraordinary performance in *Volga-Volga* revived his faltering career.[72]

Short but informative descriptions of secondary characters, for use in hiring, were compiled by Aleksandrov's assistant, K. Iudin. For example, Byvalov's secretary, played by Mariia Mironova, is described as a large woman of the Russian type, tall, 35–37 years of age, a "Cerberus" and constant hanger-on of her boss, a lover of the arts who had once studied in a provincial ballet school and had been dropped because of incompetence. She believes the cause was jealous rivals and considers herself an unrealized talent. During the trip to Moscow, she intends to show herself in all her glory.[73] By late May 1937, GUK had approved the slate of actors we see in the film as well as set designs and costumes.[74]

Shooting in the studio began in early June with episodes in Byvalov's office and reception room. By this time, the soundtrack for all the major songs and most dance numbers had been recorded. As always, production was plagued by delays in set construction, costume preparation (lace-up boots for Byvalov were nowhere to be found), and lack of adequate transport for the actors.[75]

For the Volga expedition, Mosfil'm had rented and refitted the steamship *Pamiat' Kirova* as a floating film studio equipped with editing equipment, sound equipment supported by 150 batteries, a small indoor studio, photo lab, costume and makeup rooms, projection room, and repair shop.[76] Flying a red pennant with the film's name, the film crew of sixty left Moscow for Gorky on June 20. The three month expedition took them along the Oka, Volga, Kama, and Chusovaia rivers (Figs. 33–34). Aleksandrov began filming the raft-ferry scenes on the way to Gorky. (The raft-ferry itself had been constructed on the deck of the Kirov.) The *Sevriuga* and *Lesorub*, which had been built at Krasnye Baki on the Vetluga River, were delivered in Gorky along with four truckloads of equipment for stunts.[77] The barge with M-1 cars and Caspian launch (*kater*) scenes were filmed in Gorky.[78] A few crowd scenes using workers from the Sormovo factory were also shot there, and the sailboat scenes at the end of the film were completed with the help of the Dinamo yacht club.[79] On June 16, raw footage was sent to Moscow for developing and screening by studio administrators and then returned to Gorky for editing.[80] On July 6, the film crew headed north, filming on the Kama near Sarapul, and then near Perm', at the mouth of the Chusovaia, beginning in mid-August.[81] The expedition then split into two sections; one group of actors went up the Chusovaia to film on rafts. In September, filming of the

Figure 33.

Figure 34.

raft-ferry episode continued near the village of Krasnaia Sputka, which is visible at the beginning of the film, and completed in the fall on the Volga-Moscow canal.[82] On the return trip, the dock, departure of the *Sevriuga*, and *Sevriuga* on the shallows episodes were shot on the Volga, and the Lotsman's dance was filmed at Zhiguli. Even on the quiet Kama, however, Aleksandrov was unable always to film with synchronized sound because of the constant river traffic.[83] E. P. Nesterov, the sound technician for the film, noted that an outdoor scene was sometimes located a kilometer from the recording equipment, forcing him to string cables through the air, on boats, and even under water.[84] Aleksandrov made sure the expedition generated good publicity for the film. The actors gave concerts in Gorky and Perm' and met frequently with local people during the trip. In remote areas, inhabitants heard about the expedition's route by radio and turned out to offer help.[85]

After twice screening rough footage sent back from the Volga expedition during the summer, Shumiatskii grew increasingly anxious. His first letter from July 16 was optimistic and friendly, but nonetheless expressed misgivings:

> Grisha, Volodia,
>
> We've just watched the part of the film *Volga-Volga* brought by Comrade Darevskii. I haven't thought through its evaluation thoroughly yet, but am making use of the opportunity to give instructions of a *preliminary*, so to speak, nature.
>
> 1) I have misgivings—don't the attractions create an understated and slowed-down tempo and rhythm? In this film, the montage development of frames and episodes must proceed without potholes, and through the development of the dramaturgy and humoresques.
>
> 2) Try to avoid and fear worse than fire (compositionally and tonally) uncoordinated frames. You should definitely conserve important film, but in this instance, one has to conserve sensibly.
>
> 3) I don't want to dampen your enthusiasm, but I must warn you of the need to arrange the stunts in an *increasing* degree. In the frames I've seen, somehow I haven't even noticed their presence. My misgivings come from this: will they be concentrated only in the attractions. Such a structure works objectively against the wholeness, movement, rhythm, and tempo of an honest film comedy (without lyrical and melodramatic mushiness).
>
> And in conclusion, a friendly wish: shoot even *better*, *more vividly* and, the main thing, *more quickly*.[86]
>
> Greetings to L. P., I. V., Vl. Serg., Serg. Iv., and Comrade Tutyshkin. Greetings to the entire group.
>
> —B. Shumiatskii

A typed note, hinting at another level of concern, was added for his secretaries: "In the letter to Aleksandrov and Nil'sen, I forgot to add one more thing to my comments: it's that 'the action of the film *Volga-Volga* takes place almost exclusively on sailboats and primitive vessels. In the film, you must definitely show contemporary navigation, show its wealth and the newest technology.'"[87]

On August 11, Shumiatskii and G. B. Zel'dovich wrote a more formal—and more negative—evaluation of additional new footage they had been sent, criticizing the acting of the lumberjacks as overdone and the scenes with the policeman as "not precise." They complained further about Olenev's delayed reaction to the soot pouring out on the policeman, the absence of human life in the nature shots, and the failure to carry out "our previous instructions about showing contemporary navigation in the film." Furthermore, it is obvious that Strelka is not actually playing the accordion and the policeman should not be shown with a weapon, since he is off-duty. Finally, they noted that "the material has been printed with a very gray cast. The technical sector must check the condition of the negative."[88] Shumiatskii's close personal supervision during filming indicates the importance of a successful comedy to his official agenda. While the script, with its hero-masks, pulls toward parody, Shumiatskii insists on a maximally positive enculturation of the storyline (the showcasing of Soviet shipbuilding) that also pretends to realism (the policeman's gun), and displays a doctrinaire aversion to mixing genres (comedy and melodrama in Strelka's quarrel with Alesha) in response to Stalin's earlier criticism of *Circus*.[89]

On August 9, 1937, while Aleksandrov and Nil'sen were filming on the Volga, Darevskii sent Zel'dovich two copies "of a *Volga-Volga* script with montage elaboration," adding that the ending had not yet been completed.[90] Toward the end of September, the film crew returned to complete work in Moscow. Byvalov's jumping into the launch on the way to the Olimpiada and the girl marathon swimmer episode were filmed at the end of the month on the Khimki reservoir.[91]

*****

Cinematographer Vladimir Nil'sen was arrested on October 8. During a three-day Mosfil'm meeting later in the month, devoted to the studio's "wreckers," Aleksandrov confessed to a lack of watchfulness and to being under Nil'sen's "hypnotic" influence, which also led him to accept "counter-revolutionary lampooner Erdman" to work on the film.[92] Nil'sen's arrest served as a warning to the film community. He was a logical target because of his years abroad and his criminal record with the NKVD. A case was also being prepared against Boris Shumiatskii. Nil'sen had been his main ally in the failed *kinogorod* project, traveling with him in 1935 to study the film industry in Europe and the US and co-authoring a study of American film studios. The young cameraman had a checkered past: in 1923, he had illegally crossed the Soviet border at Brest with a friend,

Aleksandr Kogan, changed his name, and made his way to Germany. Eisenstein, who met him at the German première of *Potemkin*, immediately recognized his talent and convinced Nil'sen to return to Russia. He returned with the MOPR delegation under a false passport in the name of Vladimir Nil'sen. He then worked on *October* and *The Old and the New* as Tisse's assistant. In 1929, he accompanied Eisenstein on location to the Finnish border. After the latter's departure, Nil'sen was invited to a political meeting of Soviet and Finnish young people held on the border and then accepted an invitation to visit a nearby Finnish village, once again illegally crossing the Soviet border.

Upon returning to Moscow, he was arrested, spent three months in Butyrki prison and was sentenced to three years in exile. Initially, Nil'sen and his wife, Itta Penzo, lived in Niandom, north of Vologda. There, he was able to find work as a projectionist and continue to write articles on film technique. Next, Nil'sen was sent to Kudymkar in the Komi-Perm' district of the Urals, where he taught electrical engineering. Then in 1932, his term of exile was commuted so that he could work on *International* with Aleksandrov and Tisse. His next major assignment was *Happy Guys*. Using the money earned on *Circus* and in order to give other family members more living space, Nil'sen and his wife had taken a room at the hotel Metropol', where he was arrested. He was charged with spying for Germany and planning a terrorist act against the government during a May Day parade.[93]

Boris Petrov, Nil'sen's assistant cameraman, completed filming on *Volga-Volga*, and his name appeared in the credits as chief cameraman. After the release of the film, the Mosfil'm newspaper *Za bol'shevitskii fil'm* ran two articles on its cinematography. Neither mentioned Nil'sen's work on *Volga-Volga* or—directly— his arrest; Petrov and second cameraman Pereslavtsev were simply praised for bringing the film to successful completion. Nil'sen's teacher, Tisse wrote: "An extraordinarily complicated task fell to the lot of comrades B. Petrov and V. Pereslavtsev—entering a film that had been begun, i.e., when the tone of the entire film had already been set."[94] At the end of October 1937, the Al't-fater scenes (later cut) and the torpedo boat were filmed by Tisse himself, working with Iudin.[95] During October through December, Petrov completed the outdoor landscapes for the raft-ferry and Melkovodsk, begun by Nil'sen, and filmed the Volga-Moscow canal and Moscow Sea scenes, as well as the Olimpiada finale.[96] A second crew with Pereslavtsev filmed the restaurant and ship's stern episodes.[97]

*****

When the press announced that Orlova was preparing to play a woman mail carrier in *Volga-Volga*, she began receiving letters from mail carriers offering information about their work and invitations to observe their daily rounds. The actress claims that she even delivered mail for several days:

> I saw how this sort of work influences a person's character, the kind of sociability it requires. I understood the interest and excitement with which people in a small town await the mail, newspapers, magazines, letters, and what an event the arrival of the mail carrier is for most people. [...] The newspaper *Sel'skaia sviaz'* supplied me with a great deal of material on the life of provincial mail carriers. I was given an entire album of photographs of provincial communications workers. [...] (In the beginning, my mail carrier role was much more extensive, but later, during work on the film, many traits pertaining to Dunia's profession receded into the background and, in the interests of the general concept, a new image of the girl evolved—the organizer of an amateur group.) I borrowed Dunia's external appearance from a photo I found in the album. After seeing a mail carrier carrying a letter across a field of rye, I thought that I could use the rye as a mustache during the *lezginka*.[98]

Orlova does not mention one other model. The petite, pale-skinned, blonde circus performer and film actress Janina Żejmo generally resembled Orlova as a physical type. In *Lenochka i vinograd* (*Lenochka and the Grapes*), a mediocre 1936 comedy about a group of children's struggle with a vineyard wrecker, Żejmo played the child-heroine Lenochka, the large-eyed, enthusiastic and impulsive ringleader of all activities—a younger Strelka type. In an attempt to scare away birds attacking the grape crop on a Crimean sovkhoz, Lenochka puts a stalk of long grass under her nose, mimicking a large moustache—the same comic device employed by Orlova during her demonstration of local talents for Byvalov (Fig. 35).

Orlova was terrified of water and had a double, Natal'ia Sedykh, for Strelka's dive from the ship. The close-ups of the "Water!" scene were shot at the Sandunovskie baths and required multiple takes because of Orlova's hydrophobia. She later recalled that Tutyshkin (Alesha) first tried holding her wrist to keep her under water to a count of twelve, but she broke free, shouting that she was drowning. Only when she realized that she needed to take a deep breath before submerging was she able to outlast him and complete the scene.[99]

Il'inskii's comments about his work in *Volga-Volga* at the time of its release are more critical than his memoirs twenty years later. While praising Aleksandrov's rapport with actors, he laments the lack of a proper rehearsal period before filming and the poor working conditions at Mosfil'm, where the actors for *all* films in production were squeezed into two dressing rooms. Il'inskii's nod to the politics of the day and its tendency to make even comedy serve serious ideological agendas is particularly chilling. After describing his comedic hero, Il'inskii predicts his non-humorous future: "Byvalov contains within himself the embryos of an enemy of the people. From these embryos and in this hospitable soil of unscrupulousness, self-enrichment, and complete emptiness, Byvalov may in future grow into a malicious, out and out enemy."[100]

Figure 35.

In his memoirs, Aleksandrov recalls that Il'inskii, in makeup for the Byvalov role, turned out to resemble Boris Shumiatskii, who was offended by the director's perceived lack of gratitude for Shumiatskii's assistance in bringing *Happy Guys* to realization.[101] In 1939, a year after the arrests of Shumiatskii and the Mosfil'm leadership, Aleksandrov complained in print about the dumbing down of Byvalov: "The character was initially written very pointedly. But the former cinema leaders forced us to throw out the most successful episodes with Byvalov. These cuts ruined the plot terribly and destroyed its contents."[102]

western comedians, such as Chaplin and Keaton, took pride in doing their own stunts. Il'inskii felt the same, albeit less eagerly, during the filming of Byvalov's dive off the ship near the Khimki port:

> It was a clear, sunny, but cold fall day in mid-October. It was a shame to refuse to do this episode. We could have hired a double, a swimmer, and dressed him in my suit for a long shot. But after running along the deck and taking off from it, I wanted to keep kicking my feet while falling, as if continuing to run in the air. Besides, Byvalov's actual decision to jump and the acting during take-off interested me, and I didn't want to entrust this "jump" to a double. Aleksandrov showed me the place on the middle deck from which I had to jump. Rather downcast, I said, "Better from the captain's bridge, that will be more effective!" Less than ten minutes later Aleksandrov had spread the rumor that I was going to jump from the upper captain's deck. [...] It was difficult to go back on my word now and I climbed to the upper deck in boots and carrying a briefcase. By the time I had climbed to the place that had seemed so impressive from below, I was less ecstatic about it and was about to refuse, when I suddenly remembered the incident during filming the previous day with Orlova's double, who was supposed to jump into the water at the count of one, two, three. Aleksandrov counted "three, four, seven, and nine," but she never did jump. He had to get another double who specialized in diving. People laughed maliciously at her indecisiveness. How they'll laugh at me, I thought, if I refuse, when the camera is already in position and everything is ready. One, two, three...I had no choice but to jump. Everything went well. I didn't have to jump from there again. But there was more filming in the cold water.[103]

A script dating from August-September 1937 shows Nil'sen's name heavily crossed out on the title page.[104] This version has yet another, provisional ending that incorporates Byvalov and his secretary into the action of the latter part of the film, as required by the studio: by mistake, Byvalov takes his secretary instead of Strelka to present her as the composer of the song. On the hydroplane, as Byvalov pounds on the gates of the lock, the secretary climbs into a nearby boat, attaching herself to yet another career bureaucrat, and berating Byvalov: "You booby! I can't even get into Moscow with you. Bureaucrat!" Meanwhile, Strelka reaches the Olimpiada ship and sings her song. While her group is performing, she and Alesha steal away to kiss in a corner, and Aleksandrov adds a conventional Hollywood ending:

> The camera aperture half closes—
>
> S: We'll get married and we'll definitely have a little girl.
>
> A: Who?
>
> S: A little girl.
>
> A: You take the cake, I didn't expect that from you! It will be a boy...
>
> S: No, a girl!
>
> Fade

A note in an unknown hand is appended at the end of the ms: "The ending has not yet been done and is subject to revision."

The next script submitted to GUK dates from late fall 1937 and lists Aleksandrov as sole author.[105] Most of the songs are now in place, along with notations regarding still incomplete episodes, such as the phonogram and filming of the singing quartet in the restaurant (14 frames), and Byvalov's pursuit by the townspeople, who sing snatches of different folk songs (50 frames). The town has now been renamed Melkovodsk (probably an earlier Erdman witticism, deriving from the lock theme in the original storyline), and army prodigy Fed'ka has become an innocuous worker: "Stepka the potter—since he's returned from the vacation home, spews out all of *The Demon* by heart." Byvalov's secretary criticizes Strelka's unfashionable jacket in a scene that was later cut. During the forest trek, Strelka asks directions, eliciting a witticism that could only be Erdman's: "S: 'Grannie, do you know how to walk from Asia into Europe here?' G: 'Go along this little path and when you jump across the ditch, you'll land right in Europe.'" The image of the ditch, not particularly flattering to the Russian East, was also ultimately cut from the film.

The bear and gypsy episodes, which had justified a number of comic situations, have also been cut in this script and replaced by Strelka talking to the radio in Alesha's cabin. Without saying so directly, Aleksandrov hints that the deletion was a consequence of the period's typical paranoia: "Everything had been going well, but once I was called to see Comrade Koroptsov, Mosfil'm's former deputy director. He said, "Comrade Aleksandrov, you have a bear in your film. It says about him that he's an arts person and doesn't know how to do anything. Doesn't this point to the director Medvedkin who is shooting a film on a kolkhoz topic?" I gave a start, but didn't lose my head and replied, "The more hints you see in the film, the more satisfied I'll be with my work." The next day shooting was halted and the reworking of the script began."[106]

Byvalov now confesses to Strelka that he was wrong about the lack of talents in the town: "I can see the immediate future clearly. They'll fire me again." The captain of the ship from which Strelka jumped lends her his uniform and they later go to the tower to change clothes, followed by a jealous Alesha. Here Aleksandrov introduces yet another—this time metatextual—ending, again modeled on American comedy:

> S: How nice that we're alone. (She intends to kiss him.)
>
> A Voice: Of course, it's nice...
>
> The cameraman turns the pan head from the window to Strelka and finishes his sentence:
>
> A Voice: ...You were shielded all the time.

Strelka and Alesha run upstairs and are surprised by a photographer on the next floor. They run to the roof of the tower and kiss, without noticing that the platform of the tower is rising: "The platform rises higher, revealing a panorama of the Khimki port, in which a huge crowd of people on the staircases, docks, ships, launches, yachts, and boats play and sing the song 'Volga-Volga.'" Strelka and Alesha quarrel again and are about to leave when they suddenly realize that they are seventy meters up in the air and grab each other in a panic. The entire world below—people, ships, an orchestra, even the propellers of hydroplanes—pick up the Volga-Volga melody.

> Al: How beautiful!
>
> S: You and I were born under a lucky star, Aleshka!
>
> They kiss. A pan to the star [on the mast of the tower]. Iris shot in the form of a five-pointed star. The end.

Here the dialogue alludes to V. Govorkov's popular 1936 poster of a laughing baby under a red star and the slogan "Schastlivye rodiatsia pod sovetskoi zvezdoi!" ("Happy [children] are born under the Soviet star!").

If Aleksandrov and Orlova had indeed been protected by a lucky (red) star, their Mosfil'm superiors were less fortunate. Babitskii, the studio head from late 1934 to May 1937, had left Mosfil'm for lesser positions in the theatre and circus administrations, only to be arrested in December. Sokolovskaia, who had replaced Babitskii as director of Mosfil'm in June, was herself arrested October 12, 1937; Darevskii had been arrested on December 23.[107] A new acting Mosfil'm director, A. Khachatur'ian, was appointed in December.[108] A parallel process was occurring at GUK, where administrators such as V. A. Usievich were arrested before Shumiatskii himself was brought in on January 18, 1938.[109] In the press of the purges, with the disappearance of the Mosfil'm leadership that had initially vetted the *Volga-Volga* project, it is not surprising that Aleksandrov's still unfinished film was yet again subjected to examination. In his December 2, 1937 report, Reznik, the new head of the script section of Mosfil'm, writes that the idea of the film is correct: "to show the most extensive, large-scale growth of amateur talents, coming from a working class environment...the stimulus to the discovery of talents is our wonderful, modern Soviet life that creates an opportunity for the thorough and full development of human personality, revealing the previously crushed, hidden, and lost talents in people."[110] Whereas Sokolovskaia and company had ordered Aleksandrov to *expand* Byvalov's satirical role in the film, this characterization is now seen as exaggerated, a magnified critique of Soviet reality which Reznik intuits as parodic: Byvalov's bureaucratic hindrances "acquire the character of hyperbolic improbability. At times it seems that the caricatured town of Melkovodsk is located outside the borders of Soviet reality.... Byvalov turns out to be the arbiter of all human destinies and, apart from Byvalov, we see no other force that has elevated, educated, and guided people.... At times, Melkovodsk begins to resemble Shchedrin's town of Glupov." Similarly, Reznik views the "tippling water carrier and strange caretaker" as unacceptable representatives of the Soviet people.

Reznik further sees a major flaw in the opposition of Strelka and Alesha's groups "according to the principle of the originality and complexity of the repertoire they perform. It turns out that Strelka's group performs folk songs that are qualitatively on a higher level and, in addition, her group is more democratic in its composition. Andrei's [Alesha's] group, which is made up of office workers, plays the complicated works of outstanding composers. It seems to me that the issue has been turned on its head. It is precisely our amateur performers who can be proud of mastering the most serious works, which, together with all the riches of folk creativity, have been mastered by folk talents." Here Reznik fails to recognize a basic paradigm of musical comedy, the conflict between classical and popular music, which typically resolves itself in a reconciliation of the two styles, as in the *Volga-Volga* script. Instead, in the wake of the 1936 shift in cultural policy, he underscores both folk and 19th century classical music as accessible to folk amateur performance, which stands opposed to complex and opaque modernist music.[111]

Zel'dovich's brief Dec. 7 review agrees with Reznik regarding Byvalov, critiquing the beginning and end of the script as "too drawn out," and directing the central song to be rendered in a male, as well as female, voice. Most importantly, he suggests that the finale should be constructed of "witty comic situations (Byvalov's unmasking, Alesha's meeting with Strelka)," and instructs that Aleksandrov should come to the studio meeting with proposals for reworking the finale.[112]

The director submitted a new version of the concluding episodes on December 21, 1937.[113] Strelka and the Lotsman again change clothes in the tower, and Strelka and Alesha are pursued up the tower staircase by a photographer. Meanwhile, the water carrier leads the chorus, which Byvalov joins just before he loses his voice. After Byvalov coughs, the water carrier turns Byvalov's earlier reproach to Strelka back on him in an Erdmanesque metatextual remark on professional performers vs. peasant amateurs: "It won't work, Comrade Byvalov. To sing like that you have to study for 20 years!" On the tower, Strelka and Alesha kiss, again failing to notice the rising platform, and fall off. They pull each other back up: "Strelka: 'Hold on tighter!' A male voice (the lumberjack) finishes the song: 'It's good to work and live under a lucky star!' They kiss."

This typescript bears the anonymous notation: "Presented 21/XII and rejected the same day." The next day, Shcherbatykh of GUK wrote Mosfil'm director Khachatur'ian that Aleksandrov must rewrite the ending so that *Volga-Volga* does not conclude with Orlova's "vocal performance. We forbid filming the finale in the old version."[114] As early as June 1937, in his notes to Aleksandrov prior to the beginning of filming, Dunaevskii had envisioned a grand finale with Orlova at center stage: "Strelka begins alone. Gradually the symphonic orchestra joins in, the force increases, the choir joins in, the winds, the jazz, and a shared coda (Puccini). Strelka sings the last couplet."[115] In response to Shcherbatykh, on December 25, Aleksandrov submitted yet another version of the ending, adding the "young composer" who directs the orchestra, telling Strelka, "Your theme, my interpretation!" and the comic scenes with Strelka, the Lotsman, and Alesha bumping about under the presidium table. The water carrier now tells Byvalov that he can't stand beer (another change forced by officials who saw the onscreen depiction of a drunk as harmful)[116] and a slapstick episode is added with Byvalov's boomeranging horseshoe. After appearing from under the table, Strelka is recognized by the chairman and sings one couplet of her song. This finale, which again concluded with Orlova, was also rejected.

The soundtrack of the film was completed January 19, 1938, followed by final editing. Aleksandrov submitted the film to the studio and GUK on February 7.[117] In January, former Chekist S. S. Dukel'skii replaced Shumiatskii as head of GUK.[118] The new chief reviewed the *Volga-Volga* footage and, of course, demanded further changes. In his February 15, 1938 response regarding necessary revisions, Aleksandrov notes that approximately 200 frames had been cut from the film, especially scenes of the transfer of Strelka and Alesha's groups to the ship and the appearance "of the young composer Tolia in the lounge of the steamboat... Now, with the absence of these scenes, the viewer will get mixed up and not understand what's going on."[119] Thus, the intrusion of new "authors" produced the unexpected appearance of the "young composer" in the concluding scenes of the film. Aleksandrov attaches an eleven-page list of additional scenes to be filmed to bridge the cuts required by Dukel'skii. Also attached is the new conclusion, accompanied by an epilogue in which the actors leave us with the verse "moral" of the film. The double-entendres of the new concluding scenes suggest the presence of a continuing Erdman substratum: when the adult Dunia emerges from under the table, little Dunia nudges the young composer, "Smotri, avtora poimali!" ("Look, they've caught the author!"). After the Olimpiada, the chairman runs up to give Strelka her prize ("We've found her at last!"), Strelka exclaims, "What, is it already the end?" The evidence for a subversive reading of Strelka's experience with her song as a metaphor for Erdman's own peripeties of authorship, especially the fable that earned him arrest and exile, is even more apparent in the final script where, after an extended search for the author of the Volga song, Byvalov interrogates the Melkovodsk maidens through his teeth, "Comrade Dunias, confess immediately. Which one of you wrote this song?" and the Lotsman seconds him reassuringly, "Confess, girls. Nothing will happen to you because of it."

Stepping out of their roles in the epilogue, the actors (minus Il'inskii) go on to moralize about the Byvalovs of the arts who create hindrances for talented people:

Alesha: Biurokratov takikh, kak Byvalov
Mozhet byt' i nemnogo naidesh'...

Strelka: No liuboi iz proidokh i nakhalov
Na Byvalova ochen' pokhozh.

Alesha: Chasto melkie mysli i chuvstva
Plesen' starykh, bezradostnykh let

Lesorub: Nam meshaiut v trude

Strelka: I v iskusstve,
Zamedliaia talantov rastsvet.

Vse: No v respublike svobodnoi
Nam ne strashen staryi khlam
I genii narodnyi
Kak solntse svetit nam![120]

Although, as we have seen, in the course of the production process cinema officials repeatedly voiced concerns about the idiocy of Melkovodsk-Glupov, this ambiguous figuration of provincial life "passed" for several reasons. As confirmed by the final quatrain of the original verse epilogue above, the coda was meant to leave the audience with the right perspective, reemphasizing Byvalov as the parodic target of the film, while elevating the genius of the Folk. Furthermore, Lebedev-Kumach's texts for diegetic songs, such as "Song of the Volga" and "Molodezhnaia" ("Song of the Young") created an ideologically correct protective semantic shield for the film. Toward the end of the film the idiocy of Melkovodsk dissolves in a mythical Soviet modernity of yachts, ships, and the new port, as the characters draw nearer to Moscow. Finally, the didactic epilogue spoken by the actors—the typical moralizing ending of Perrault's fairy tales—compromises the illusion of reality created by the diegesis, leading the audience to more readily accept the diegesis as fiction or "story," thereby mitigating the parody of any previously established filmic reality.

But Dukel'skii was still not satisfied with the film. On March 21, 1938, Aleksandrov sent the studio another memo outlining further cuts to the film, which were then implemented.[121] The opening kissing scene was abbreviated. At the 1941 closed film conference, in a complaint to Zhdanov, Aleksandrov used the cut as an example of bureaucratic over-cautiousness, born of the fear of possible repercussions. As one might expect, his account also betrays his own fears at the height of the purges:

> At the eighteenth congress, Comrade Stalin talked about people, narrow-minded functionaries with no prospects, who blindly carry out instructions from above. At the screening of *Volga-Volga*, Comrade Stalin said that the first kiss should be cut. Comrade Dukel'skii then decided that a kiss is a harmful thing. [Laughter in the room.] When a kiss appeared, it shouldn't be shown and must be cut. [...] Dukel'skii's deputy, Comrade Bur'ianov, told me that it was better to cut out the kiss, it would be better that way. I asked him whose opinion that was. "It's probably Comrade Stalin's opinion and Comrade Zhdanov's," and I cut it out. But I'm sure that it wasn't your opinion, but his [Bur'ianov's] opinion. But to make things easier, so that he wouldn't have to try to persuade me, he carried out this kind of psychological attack on me.[122]

Byvalov's conversation with the fisherwomen, whom he categorized as "Pishcheprom" and therefore ineligible to board the *Sevriuga*, was also deleted, as was Alesha's acquaintance with the young composer in the lounge of the ship. Also abbreviated were the comic scene in which soot is blown on the policeman out of a trombone, 10 meters of panorama (of 45) during the departure of the ship from Bol'shaia Volga pier, and the Strelka-Alesha argument under the table. Ultimately, some of the gaps had to be bridged with informational intertitles.

Political exile Erdman's name had not appeared on the final version of the script and, according to the memoirs of V. Smekhov, Aleksandrov traveled to Kalinin, where Erdman was living after Siberian exile, to explain to him why his name would not appear in the credits: "When the film was ready and it was shown to Stalin, still without titles, Grisha went to see me, to Kalinin, where I was in exile. And he says: 'Understand, Kolia, our film is becoming the leader's favorite comedy. You yourself understand that it will be much better for you if your name isn't in it. Do you understand?' And I said that I understood."[123]

Finally, after months of criticism, confusion, editing, cutting, and additional filming in a world of arrests, silences, and accusatory meetings, the director of Mosfil'm was notified on April 20, 1938 that *Volga-Volga* had been authorized for release[124] and the film premiered April 23 at the Udarnik Theatre during a spring ball and concert with the film's actors.[125] *Volga-Volga* was praised at the April 18 official discussion at Dom kino and by the major newspapers (*Pravda*, *Izvestiia*, and *Kino*), with criticism limited to weak plot development in the latter part of the film.[126] The film was so popular with audiences that it was still playing in theatres at the outbreak of the war, while *The Radiant Path*, which had premiered in the fall of 1940, was being taken out of circulation.[127] The same was true of Dunaevskii's songs for the film: his 1939 contract with Muzgiz specified a print run of 300,000 copies for "Molodezhnaia" and "Song of the Volga."[128] In 1939, Goskinoizdat published individual monographs about Aleksandrov and Orlova.[129] Meanwhile, Orlova's career was not without its troubles. In June 1938, the influential *Sovetskoe iskusstvo* published an unsigned article entitled "Unworthy Behavior," criticizing the star, who needed money for a suburban dacha, for greedily demanding 3,000 rubles per concert in Odessa instead of the established official maximum of 750 rubles.[130] But Orlova was Stalin's favorite female movie star and there was no further bad publicity.

On May 1, 1938, Aleksandrov headed a group that filmed the documentary *Fizkul'turnyi parad* using P. Mershin's new three-color hydrotype method. The film was released in November, but it was soon withdrawn from circulation because of the poor quality of the color.[131] Future plans were unclear: in May 1937, Dunaevskii had mentioned that he and Aleksandrov were planning a new color musical based on *The Marriage of Figaro* and in 1938, a literary script was submitted.[132] In August 1938, Aleksandrov wrote Dunaevskii asking for help with the music for *Fizkul'turnyi parad* and mentioning that he was also thinking about a theatrical show "Veselye zheleznodorozhniki" ("The Happy Railway Workers").[133] In the press, he talked about his next project, *Schastlivaia rodina* (*Happy Motherland*), a color film about the folk music and poetry of the eleven Soviet republics, to be co-scripted with Lebedev-Kumach, but nothing came of his plans.[134] According to Kushnirov, the proposed storyline foreshadowed the fairy tale genre of *The Radiant Path*: a boy and girl pioneer hide under a sofa at the Leningrad House of Pioneers in order to test the rumor that its frescoes come to life at night. Orlova appears as a good fairy who gives the children a magic carpet and a "shapka-nevidimka" (invisibility cap). The trio travels throughout the country admiring the deeds of Soviet people, ending their trip in Moscow, where they enter the Kremlin unnoticed to meet Stalin.[135]

In the meantime, Orlova was busy with the first negative role of her film career, in Aleksandr Macheret's *Engineer Kochin's Mistake* (1939). She played Kochin's neighbor and girlfriend, Kseniia Lebedeva, who helps a foreign spy gain access to Kochin's room in order to photograph top secret blueprints that he brought home without permission from his aviation factory. Macheret consciously exploited the Marion Dixon persona created by Orlova in *Circus* for the purposes of his spy thriller. Lebedeva has lived abroad in the past, hence the exotic looks for which Orlova/Dixon was renowned, and, like Dixon, she is a woman with a secret. For an unspecified reason—having lived abroad would be sufficient proof of corruption—Lebedeva is being blackmailed by the agent of a foreign government who now forces her to betray her native land. Both women long to find fulfillment in the land of the soviets. After losing Martynov, Marion Dixon confesses to Raika, "I wanted to be happy in the USSR, but it's impossible." After confessing her treason to Kochin and forfeiting his love, Lebedeva exclaims, "I could have been so happy!" But what is possible for an innocent foreigner is impossible for a treacherous Russian, and Lebedeva is killed by the foreign agent. Fans reacted badly to the casting of Orlova as traitor, and in Aleksandrov's next musical film, *The Radiant Path*, she returned to her accustomed positive *emploi*.

II. THE TOWN OF GLUPOV

In her two articles on *Volga-Volga*, Maia Turovskaia initiated the recovery of the film from standard Soviet-era interpretations based on Socialist Realist stereotypes and the vagaries of Stalin's taste, interpretations that elided issues of genre paradigms outside Socialist Realism.[136] Although *Volga-Volga* marked a return to the comedic style of *Happy Guys*, its show musical syntax also incorporates elements of the folk musical's setting and mode of characterization. *Volga-Volga* turns on the creation and performance of a show—in this case, a song— by the inhabitants of a small river town, with the progress of the endeavor paralleling the making of a couple. The American folk musical, like *Volga-Volga*, is a hybrid genre that often makes use of the embedded show, together with a specific syntax related to the importance of nature or country life and the formation of community.[137] The highly influential *Show Boat*, whose first two versions (1929, 1936) predated *Volga-Volga*, introduced the old-time paddle-wheel boat mise-en-scène and river journey narrative into the semantic repertoire of the folk musical. Another source for the ramshackle *Sevriuga* with its attendant comic complications is *Steamboat Bill Jr.* (1928), in which Buster Keaton, like the *Volga-Volga* characters, suspiciously tests both the floor and pillars of his father's decrepit vessel. The obstacles set up by Byvalov (the grumpy, anti-entertainment senex), the peripeties of the river journey with its striking nature scenes, the final acceptance of the song by both groups of the Melkovodsk delegation and its victory at the Moscow Olimpiada parallel the comic progress of the Strelka-Alesha Trubyshkin relationship. When Strelka and Alesha reconcile on the ship as it nears Moscow, they are framed within the locks of the Moscow-Volga canal, a major Stalinist initiative, and the Melkovodsk Olimpiada performance takes place against a background of flags and the national coat of arms. Both episodes thus affirm the larger community of individuals with the State.

Although the original secondary comic couple of Alesha Trubyshkin and Byvalov's secretary was cut early in the making of the film, we will see that Byvalov and his secretary, most of whose scenes were also deleted, still fulfill a rudimentary complementarity at the beginning of the film. As in *Circus*, the female heroine is more central to the narrative and the male hero does not sing, so that there are no duets or parallel solo performances. The action of "making the song" falls into two parts—overcoming the initial obstacle (Byvalov's refusal to recognize the town's talents), which culminates in the townfolks' carnivalistic street performance, and the picaresque journey to Moscow, climaxing in the victory of the song at the competition and the formation of community.

In the folk musical, living means singing (and dancing), which arise out of everyday existence: Okhapkin's sweeping the yard turns into a lively dance; the policeman's whistle imitates the song of a nightingale; the Melkovodskites play not only folk instruments, but also the everyday artifacts that surround them (logs, jugs, saws, kitchen utensils), and their work (driving a wagon, pulling up a sail, steering a ship) passes naturally into song and dance. Singing or other artistic performance also denotes living rightly—that is, in harmony with the natural order[138]—and all the townspeople are gifted in music or dance except for Byvalov. He cannot dance (his attempt at a *lezginka* in his office, after escaping the town's talent show, is unrhythmical and wooden); he cannot sing and at the Olimpiada performance he lets out a falsetto squawk. He knows nothing about classical music and claims personal acquaintance with a "Comrade Shul'bert," nor does he care about folk music, as evidenced by his rejection of Strelka's group and the poor quality of the balalaikas produced by his factory.

As a folk musical, *Volga-Volga* also incorporates aspects of the *balagan* or carnival street show, first adopted by Meierkhol'd and elaborated by Eisenstein in their theatrical productions, and therefore perfectly familiar to Aleksandrov, Erdman, Il'inskii, and others of Meierkhol'd's circle. Alesha lays bare the subtext by referring to Strelka's group as "your *balagan*." The film's prologue and epilogue (the verse introductions of major characters and moralizing conclusion) are double-coded as typical of folk performance, while remaining within the genre conventions of 1930s western comedy films which employ introductory cameos and direct audience address in the coda of comedian comedy.[139] In both instances, the direct address frame underscores the fictional aspect of the performance.

Advertising material published for the première of *Volga-Volga* plainly points to the one-dimensionality of the film's characters by depicting them all as comedic masks.(Fig. 36).[140] Strelka's vigor and high spirits do not devolve from our understanding of her character, but simply function as her external tag. In the same way, Alesha represents reflexive choler, Byvalov self-importance and careerism, and the Lotsman boastful dissimulation. Byvalov, the most blatantly parodic figure of the film, displays a farcical resemblance to a pig: short, stiff neck, stocky torso, short legs and mincing gait, snub nose, and the dull glance of small, swollen eyes. Lest we miss the point, in the telegram-shouting scene, he is framed with pigs in the background and finally steps on one, precipitating swine chaos in the river.

Volga-Volga is replete with folksy characters displaying the stereotypical body language of pre-revolutionary vaudeville and operettas: scratching the back of the head, pulling at one's beard, walking with a rolling gait, loudly blowing one's nose. As the collective embodiment of the Folk, Strelka serves up a set of stock peasant gestures—from wiping her nose on her sleeve to fiddling with the buttons on her jacket to hammering with her fist in rhythm to her speech to make a point.[141] Throughout the film, Strelka's femininity is subsumed to a unisex model as she mostly wears a quasi-military mail carrier's uniform (rough sailcloth jacket and trousers tucked into boots or a straight skirt with boots, headscarf tied at the back). Nevertheless, in certain episodes of *Volga-Volga* that reveal her true creative identity as author of the song, Strelka sheds her crude mail carrier's garb and dons a dress: when boarding the *Sevriuga* in order to reach the Moscow Olimpiada, where she hopes her song will be recognized; when confessing her authorship of the song in Alesha's empty cabin; when teaching her song to Alesha's orchestra. For the culminating revelation, when Strelka declares herself as author of the song to Alesha aboard the steamship, she wears an even more ornate organza dress. As in the other musicals, this true creative—and at the same time feminine—identity resembles that of Orlova herself in real life. When Strelka's authorship is finally validated at the Olimpiada, she wears an outsize male naval uniform which, by contrast to her petite form, comically underscores her femininity, and the large bow of her organza dress peeps out over her uniform collar. She soon switches clothes with the Lotsman, and in the concluding scenes, the under-the-table argument with Alesha, and the didactic epilogue, she appears in the organza dress as her feminine-creative self.

In the cinematic tradition, the transgressive female heroine has typically found a home in melodrama and romantic comedy. As an alternative to the suffering femininity affirmed by melodrama, female resistance to masculine authority has been located in romantic comedy.[142] In her relationship to Alesha and Byvalov, Strelka is clearly a transgressive heroine. Her constant bickering with Trubyshkin falls just short of the balagan's conventional battle of the sexes. Her metonymical demonstration of the town's talents to a skeptical Byvalov introduces a show that builds from individual performers (the singing waiter and cooks, the policeman, Okhapkin) to groups (the balalaika players, Alesha's orchestra, the fisherwomen, the schoolchildren) to an apotheosis of circus performance, replete with stilt-walkers, acrobats, and cavorting townsfolk (Fig. 37). In Bakhtinian terms, Byvalov, the king of Melkovodsk, is uncrowned—aggressively pursued and mocked by the townsfolk—during the carnival chaos unfolding in the public space of the town's main streets. First, the waiter Filip Ivanych forces the thirsty Byvalov to listen to an extended vocal performance of the menu and the cooks' song. Byvalov then escapes outside, but he is promptly accosted by the dancing Okhapkin, a

НОВАЯ ЗВУКОВАЯ МУЗЫКАЛЬНАЯ КИНО-КОМЕДИЯ
Б.А.Зеленский 38г.
Волга Волга

Figure 36.

balalaika orchestra, and singing fisherwomen, who ensnare the king in their nets. Next, Byvalov is pursued down the street by fire engines and then encircled by singing and dancing schoolchildren. After escaping from them, he is pursued by Alesha and his orchestra and runs up against the town's acrobats, stiltwalkers, and dancers. Byvalov climbs over a fence and sinks down on a bench by a cottage window, out of which a woman puts him in an armhold, forcing him to listen to her rendition of "Volga, Volga mat' rodnaia." He runs away and stops by a watch repair kiosk, where the watchmaker

Figure 37.

destroys Byvalov's watch by hammering it to the tune of "Ei, ukhnem!" The king of Melkovodsk is then pursued down the street by acrobats and dancers and is forced to retreat before Alesha and Strelka's aggressively advancing orchestras. Exhausted and reduced to an animal state, Byvalov crawls up on all fours to drink from a water barrel as a chorus sings "Zhil-byl u babushki seren'kii kozlik" ("Once upon a time grandmother had a little grey goat"). The carnivalistic uncrowning of Byvalov and laughter of the townsfolk force him to renew himself, i.e., to be reborn as something of a dancer, but more importantly, to acknowledge the talents of the Melkovodskites and agree to take them to Moscow, admittedly for selfish reasons.[143] Through this svistopliaska, as the scriptwriters and composer called the episode, the avant-garde's project of taking art into the streets is also paradoxically realized in *Volga-Volga*.

As comedic masks, the characters of *Volga-Volga* lack psychological development and are better situated within the paradigms of Russian fairy tales. Throughout the film, as the transgressive heroine, Strelka performs the male hero of the fairy tale, which is often populated with super-talented figures, much like the inhabitants of Melkovodsk. Like *Ivanushka-durachok*, Strelka the clever peasant is able to outwit Byvalov, the bad master, who "knows how to judge and make order" ("umeiu i sudit' i riadit'").[144] From beginning to end, the plotline of *Volga-Volga* may be seen as an elaboration of the fairy tale paradigm, according to Propp's functions of dramatis personae.[145] In an inverted interdiction, the townspeople are invited to Moscow, but this is violated by the villain Byvalov, who denies the town's talents. The villain causes harm when he prevents Strelka from taking her song to Moscow, and Strelka decides to leave home. She then encounters the lumberjack, a donor who interrogates her regarding the failed passage on the *Sevriuga* and provides magical agents (the raft and sailboat) that enable the heroine to make the trip. The donor tests her by specifying an arduous trek across mountains and forests (included in the early script, but later dropped from the narrative) in order to reach the raft. The heroine and villain join in direct combat, carried out here as the sub-category of competition, during the river journey. The heroine then arrives unrecognized in another country, the magic kingdom of Moscow, and proceeds to the royal palace of the Olimpiada. The villain appears as a false hero who makes unfounded claims (Byvalov as author of the song) and a difficult test of identity is proposed to the heroine, as Strelka sings "Song of the Volga," thereby proving her authorship. The villain is exposed when Byvalov shows himself unable to sing and is punished by being expelled from the winning collective. The tale concludes with proleptic marriage—Strelka and Alesha's final reconciliation at the conclusion of the film.

The semiotic code that unites all aspects of the film, from characterization to the battle of different "musics" is stasis versus movement. As the primary romantic couple, Alesha and Strelka embody opposing cultural values, such as psychological rigidity vs. flexibility, tradition vs. innovation and acquired knowledge vs. inborn talent. The profession of accountant had long been fair game for Soviet satirists. The pedantic Alesha, who keeps track of his orchestra's mistakes on an abacus, is a lesser version of the full-blown bureaucrat Byvalov, whose surname is associated with the past, something usual or not new, as in "eto delo byvaloe" ("it has happened before"). In the case of Byvalov, the second meaning of "byvalyi," someone with life experience, acquires the negative connotation of someone who has "been around."[146] Strelka's very name, meaning "little arrow," implies purposeful movement. She succeeds in getting her group to Moscow thanks to her flexibility and ingenuity: when the *Sevriuga*, the official avenue of travel is closed off, she takes the Melkovodskites over the mountains and on a log raft. Alesha is a literate musician who nevertheless does not dare to compose, while Strelka—a mail carrier and therefore uneducated, as he points out—cannot read music, but has the inborn talent to compose a song. The traditionalist Trubyshkin favors 19th century classical music, while Strelka the innovator performs Dunaevskii's modern (and original) mass songs. Finally, Alesha and his Neapolitan orchestra have a taste for foreign music (Mozart, Beethoven, Schubert, Wagner) played on conventional foreign instruments, while Strelka's group prefers the native arts, both folk and classical: Tat'iana's aria from *Eugene Onegin*, Lermontov's *Demon*, the *lezginka* and *gopak*, folk songs, chastushki-like couplets, the use of folk instruments and surrounding everyday realia (another sign of spontaneity and imagination).

Alesha's special preference for Wagner and his parodic performance of "The Death of Isolde" on the tuba were late additions to the *Volga-Volga* script, inserted after April 1937, that directly reference the 1936 cultural directive against difficult modernist music and in favor of transparent, harmonious classical, folk, and popular music.[147] Through the chromaticism of *Tristan und Isolde* (1857–59), Wagner had taken tonality to its limits and opened the way for Schoenberg's musical revolution. However, it is important to remember that Erdman's point is only a subtext within the larger category—the conventional opposition of classical to popular music in the musical, which validates and affirms itself by advocating popular musical forms. Alesha's tuba playing is slow, unmelodious and boring—a species of musical rigidity and stasis—while Strelka's group embraces harmonious melodies and lively dancing. The further contraposition of native music of all styles to foreign—and particularly German—works not only underscores Russia's fear of the rising fascist threat, but also elaborates the newly reconfigured cultural geography of high Stalinism that has discarded the internationalism of the twenties and defines Russia as a nationalist union of center and periphery whose signifying perimeters are now its outlying boundaries with other nations. Of Strelka's contingent, only the singing waiter uses a mix of familiar Russian and foreign music to praise kvas and Volga beer with motifs from Lenskii's aria in *Eugene Onegin* and the Duke's song in *Rigoletto*.

Byvalov's psychological rigidity is immediately manifested through physical appearance in the opening title vignette. His expression is haughty and wooden, his posture stiff. Byvalov's neck is short and rigid; when turning, he rotates the entire body. He runs from the townspeople in an upright, rigid posture. In his office, he dances in a mechanical way in the rhythm of military marching. Later in the film, he dives off a ship, again in an upright position, clutching his briefcase. In contrast, the Melkovodskites dance the *gopak* and *lezginka*, walk on stilts, run, jump, and climb through windows. Byvalov's thinking is similarly rigid and limited. There can be no talents in Melkovodsk, only in Moscow. His telephoning for a horse shows him to be unable to adapt to local conditions. In response to Strelka's declaiming verse from *The Demon*, the ignorant Byvalov barks, "I won't allow self-criticism on the street." He is a tyrant who acknowledges only people of "his own system." Byvalov's rigid mindset also emerges in his administrative egotism, which hinders the progress of the *Sevriuga* and impedes collectivity and the formation of community. The paddleboat makes its long journey relying on the dubious and sporadic services of an incompetent channel pilot and without a captain. The tugboat captain who pulls the *Sevriuga* off the shoal does address Byvalov as "captain," but Byvalov's decisions are all erroneous. The *Sevriuga has* no real captain, and therefore, its passengers' project is doomed to failure. Unlike Byvalov, Strelka is a successful administrator, the organizer of her group's river journey, and, in accord with the syntax of the folk musical, imbues the larger community with her own energy.

The folk musical is never solely about the young couple in love; they are always representative of differing segments of the community.[148] Alesha himself is an accountant and his musicians seem to be technical professionals who dress in shirts and ties. Strelka is a mail carrier and her group—a caretaker, water carrier, policeman, waiter, and fisherwomen—represent the working classes. The syntax of the musical will require the fusion of these temporarily warring social strata. In her demonstration of the townspeople's talents to a dubious Byvalov, Strelka literally embodies the collective talent of the Folk. Byvalov's condescending "To sing like that you have to study for twenty years," which, like the horseshoe he throws, boomerangs on him in his own attempt to sing at the conclusion of the film, is ironically validated in the decidedly un-amateur artistry of trained singer, dancer, and operetta star Orlova's performance. The individual members of the Folk, among them "Uncle Kuzia" and "Aunt Pasha," also represent Strelka's extended family, a stock feature of thirties American folk musicals.[149] Because the focus of the film is on the larger community, both she and Alesha lack a nuclear family.

Beyond the union of the primary couple, the folk musical always works toward the formation of a community, once obstacles in the form of natural hazards (the disastrous storm that seemingly destroys the score of the song) and human villains are overcome. In *Volga-Volga*, Byvalov, who denies the gifts of the Folk, functions locally much like a producer or backer who puts obstacles in the way of talented performers. In the national context, he acts as an impediment to the formation of the greater Soviet community, the union of the geographic margins with the center, the cultural geography of Russia newly reconfigured in *Circus*'s "Song of the Motherland." Even *after* the two Melkovodsk factions unite behind Strelka's song and the lovers are reconciled, Byvalov continues to interfere, functioning as interloper between the people of the periphery and the center. Once

Strelka's song receives public recognition, he attempts to take charge first of finding the author (the comic succession of village Dunias), and then to participate prominently in the performance of the song, pushing his way to the front row of Melkovodsk singers.

As in the folk musical, the oppositions in *Volga-Volga* are thus not based solely on the male-female dichotomy, which extends to the larger population, but also on the opposition of Byvalov to the Melkovodskites within the context of movement toward community. The dual focus of the plot therefore highlights both antipodal pairs. Alesha's desire to fulfill Strelka's wishes parallels Byvalov's secretary's role in furthering her boss's wish to move to Moscow. Alesha's orchestra corresponds to Strelka's circle ("kruzhok"). The extended townspeople's talent show contrasts to Byvalov's brief demonstration of his own talents in his office. The river journey of the two Melkovodsk factions maintains a strong dual focus narrative: Trubyshkin's orchestra on the *Sevriuga* competes with Strelka's group on a raft and the *Lesorub*, and Schubert's sedate "Musical Moment" is opposed to Dunaevskii's rousing "Molodezhnaia." On the *Sevriuga*, the orchestra's rehearsal parallels Byvalov's rehearsal of his speech. The *Sevriuga* runs aground and so must the *Lesorub*. Alesha and Strelka travel to each other's boats, and both listen to Arenskii's romance on the radio. Alesha and Strelka's enforced sojourn with each other's musicians leads to mutual understanding, as Alesha's musicians come to like Strelka's song while Alesha approves the song in the young pianist's classicized rendition and proposes a joint performance by the two Melkovodsk groups. Strelka's song is rendered classically, in jazz style, and as a march by different constituencies who pick up the floating notes. The quarrel between classical and popular genres is resolved as all unite in performance of the same musical text.[150]

In its drive toward unity, the folk musical favors the passed-around song, which *Volga-Volga* develops in extended instrumental passages. The storm blows the score to recreational sail boaters, a diver, an aquaplane, a ship, and loggers. Next, the Melkovodskites hear familiar musical phrases from a torpedo boat, a tugboat, a navy band, a steamship, a small tour boat, sailboats, the decorative metal ships on the canal, and even a dirigible. But the fact that the passed-around song is disseminated as a written text is crucial in the Soviet context. In the Stalin era the pathos of early revolutionary rhetoric was transformed into a sacral written text, whose author and interpreter is the Leader.[151] Katerina Clark has pointed out the importance of text and authorship in *Volga-Volga*.[152] The discourse of authority in the Stalinist state was based on the importance of legitimizing texts, of authorship (e.g., Stalin as the author of the 1936 constitution), and on hierarchical control over written texts: who did and did not have access to information in documents. Byvalov's jealously guarded administrative access to texts is parodied at the beginning of the film through his forced public transmission of a "top secret" telegram to Moscow. Strelka knows that her song will not be recognized as legitimate until it is transmuted into text and therefore eagerly accepts the orchestra members' offer to render it in musical notation. When the score, which was recorded on official stationery (Byvalov's notepaper), is swept away by a storm, she is devastated and exclaims, "The song is lost!" ("Propala pesnia!"), even though nothing has really been destroyed because she obviously remembers the melody and lyrics.

During the purge years, authorship was both potentially prestigious and risky, a dialectic embedded in the final personal and public episodes of the film. Under cover of musical comedy narrative, the final episodes also engage Soviet society's anxieties about class and political identity, which played out during the 1930s in a public rhetoric of masking, unmasking, and self-criticism. Strelka changes into her best dress before revealing herself to Alesha as the composer of the song, but she also uses the rhetoric of vigilance against potential enemies of the people as she tells him to "look more closely" ("smotri vnimatel'nei") to see the true author. She has dropped her mask, her conventional identity (and garb) of mail carrier, to reveal her true identity as composer. Authoring an incorrect text may merit serious punishment—a plausible explanation for Alesha's refusal, motivated by his just-declared love for Strelka, to allow her to acknowledge her authorship publicly at the Olimpiada. Nevertheless, on the Olimpiada stage, she proceeds to make a clean breast of it, using the conventional period rhetoric of confession and self-criticism: "Do with me what you will, it was *I* who wrote the song!" Of course, in this instance, she has authored a legitimizing text and we have a happy ending.

*****

The comedic devices of *Volga-Volga* are more varied and better integrated into the plot than in *Happy Guys*. At both the beginning and end of the film, Aleksandrov brackets the main plot with screwball comedy devices in which a couple's sexual attraction is displaced into antagonism. Strelka and Alesha kiss, but then immediately quarrel over musical styles. Even though they reconcile before reaching Moscow, the truce falls apart at the Olimpiada as they quarrel under the table over a typical screwball topic—whose love is greater:

> Strelka: So it's peace?
>
> Alesha: Peace.
>
> Strelka: Forever?
>
> Alesha: Forever.
>
> Strelka: Oh, I love you so much, Alyoshka! Although you won't understand it.
>
> Alesha: Me?

Strelka: Yes...

Alesha: I won't understand?

Strelka: Yes, yes.

Alesha: Well, with a disposition like yours...

Strelka and Alesha's kissing at the beginning of the film replicates the establishing shot for the secondary, comic couple of *Circus*, Raechka and Skameikin, who also proceed to quarrel throughout the film.

The humor of the first part of *Volga-Volga* is closely connected to the plot—the Melkovodskites' attempts to prove their talents to the resistant Byvalov. For the river journey in the second half of the film, more tenuous gags are employed to delay the resolution: the *Sevriuga* zigzags crazily as the Lotsman sings boastfully about his expertise; the Lotsman runs both ships aground; a log comes up on cue through the floor of the *Sevriuga*; characters repeatedly fall or jump off all ships. The search for Dunia Petrova—doubled as the little girl Dunia, the marathon swimmer Dunia, and the Melkovodsk Dunias—in the concluding scenes of the film represents an extended interpenetration of action device in which the audience understands a situation which both diegetic sides, the serial Dunias and the searchers, do not.

Incongruity, the basic building block of comedy, is exploited in its linguistic, aural, narrative, and gender code aspects. Byvalov speaks in bureaucratic clichés that are always inappropriate to the situation: "We have mass production and I do not have the opportunity to concern myself with each balalaika individually"; "I'm taking only people of my system." Byvalov can only respond to Strelka's recital of Lermontov's *The Demon* in ideological clichés: "Vy menia ne agitiruite...Ia na ulitse zanimat'sia samokritikoi ne pozvoliu" ("Don't you propagandize me...I won't allow self-criticism on the street"). He talks about his musical instrument factory in similar terms: "I must tell you that, in appropriate hands, this is a fascinating undertaking. I'm not going to boast, but having mastered musical culture and being personally acquainted with Schul'bert." The waiter provokes our laughter by mixing high and low culture, singing the restaurant's menu to motifs from *Rigoletto* and *Eugene Onegin*, and classical music accompanies various pursuit scenes: Strelka's group plays Mozart's *Turkish March* as it advances on Byvalov; the firemen pursue him down the street to the sounds of Rossini's *William Tell Overture* and Alesha's orchestra plays the march from Verdi's *Aida* as the *Sevriuga* passes the becalmed *Lesorub*. Strelka's brilliant demonstration of the town's talents (singing an aria, declaiming poetry, dancing the *lezginka*) builds to a narrative climax that culminates in ironic reversal. Byvalov objects: "Anybody can lie about other people. So what can *you* do?" Strelka: "Maybe I myself can't do anything. That's not important."

Like *Happy Guys*, *Volga-Volga* abounds in slapstick humor, particularly during the river journey. With the image of Cossack bandits floating down the Volga fixed in national memory, Soviet audiences were receptive to the chaos of the Melkovodskites' river journey. The antiquated *Sevriuga*, with its collapsing decks and smokestacks, is a natural source of physical comedy. The ship turns chaotically as the Lotsman sings; passengers fall into the water (one episode is shown twice); Byvalov dives off the steamship in full administrative attire and continues to run in the air; Alesha and Strelka's argument causes the presidium table at the Olimpiada to bump and jump, thereby undermining the dignity of the occasion.

However, a striking difference between *Volga-Volga* and other Soviet comedy films of the time, such as *Three Comrades* (1935), *Once in Summer* (1936), and *Lenochka and the Grapes* (1936), is its narrative tempo. The action of *Volga-Volga* moves quickly, almost frantically, and Aleksandrov accelerates it even further in gag scenes as a natural way of magnifying the comic effect. In later years, Il'inskii recalled the director's preoccupation with timing in these episodes, such as Byvalov's taking off and putting on his jacket in one continuous movement while exhorting the musicians to help the stokers when the *Lesorub* passes the *Sevriuga*, avoiding work himself (Fig. 38). "Grigorii Vasil'evich rehearsed this scene several times and I had to spend half a day learning how better to take off and put on a jacket quickly. And only after the director got a precise execution of his idea, did filming begin."[153]

The verbal slapstick of the film operates via malapropism ("Tovarishch Schul'bert"), the repetition of comic sayings ("you just want to tear and throw", ["prosto khochetsia rvat' i metat'"]) and outright insults, often relating to the animal world. Alesha and Strelka mock each other's groups in barnyard terms:

Alesha: The artistic ensemble "Enough to make a cat laugh" ("Kuram na smekh").

Strelka: "Enough to make a cat laugh"? Well, to speak frankly, an orchestra like yours should only play in the dairy, and in summer at that.

Alesha: And why is that?

Strelka: There won't be any flies—they'll all die off.

Alesha: No flies? There won't be any flies because of your choir, and no dairy either.

Strelka: Why is that?

Alesha: Because voices like that will make the milk go sour.

Figure 38.

In *Volga-Volga,* Aleksandrov again borrowed gags and comic devices from early American comedy, as adapted in Disney cartoons.[154] Here again, a common transformation gag changes everyday objects into musical instruments. Disney had pioneered the gag for animation in *Steamboat Willie*, and in *The Whoopee Party* (1932), where Mickey and friends play bottles, pots, pipes, wooden tubs, and other household objects. In the Melkovodsk restaurant, the three cooks perform a jazz song on kitchen utensils and during the river journey on the *Lesorub*, Strelka's group plays logs, bottles, and a saw (Fig. 39-40). Also typical of Disney was the use of classical music in chase scenes, notably the *William Tell Overture*, which similarly accompanies Byvalov's escape from music-making firemen. The kiss with iris shot that begins *Volga-Volga* is borrowed from the endings of such Disney shorts as *Building a Building* and *Ye Olden Days*, both from 1932. In *Volga-Volga*, although Strelka's group is covered with soot from the passing *Sevriuga*, she continues her animated song and dance performance of "Molodezhnaia" with even greater gusto in blackface. Jolson's blackface performance of "Mammy" was notoriously parodied in early Disney cartoons. In *Mickey Steps Out* (1931), Pluto chases a cat into a stove which shakes, covering everyone with soot, and Pluto exclaims "Mammy!" In *The Whoopee Party* (1932), several matchsticks strike their heads together, igniting a flame that turns them into blackface heads who also shout "Mammy!" In American minstrel comedy, the blackface mask worn by white performers served not only as form of ridicule, "but as means of gaining access to supposedly 'black' qualities, such as spontaneity, carefree charm, and natural vitality."[155] Strelka's blackface performance of "Molodezhnaia" thus integrates this American appropriation of black energy with the dynamism, vitality, and enthusiasm emblematic of early Stalinist culture.

Several types of verbal humor employed by Erdman in *Volga-Volga* are also typical of the Marx Brothers. A seemingly positive statement is belied by its concrete realization. Byvalov's secretary flatters him shamelessly, "For you life is work. Just think, a person of such elemental ability for work..." But then, as various townspeople appear with complaints about the quality of the factory's instruments, it becomes obvious that Byvalov is completely indifferent to his work. In a proximate scene, Alesha tells Strelka, "Do you know what I would like most of all right now [...], to fulfill all your wishes, so that you asked me for something and I complied, you asked and I complied. Go ahead and ask what you want..." Strelka: "You know what, come to our rehearsal today from four to five." Alesha: "I can't from four to five." Strelka: "Why not?" Alesha: "I have a rehearsal myself." Finally, the humor of Byvalov's telegram to Moscow lies in its confidentiality, which is immediately violated as Byvalov asks bystanders to shout its contents to Strelka on the ferry:

> —Comrades, comrades, help me send a telegram, a very important telegram, top secret. All together now!
>
> —To-op se-cret.
>
> —Louder, louder.
>
> —S-e-e-cret.

Figure 39.

Both concretization and polysemy pervade the comic fabric of *Volga-Volga*: the Lotsman boasts that he knows all the shoals on the Volga and almost immediately runs aground: "—You old devil, you were bragging that you know all the shoals!—Of course I do. This is the first one." The script plays on the dual meaning of "provalit'sia" ("to flop" and "to fall through") when Alesha and Strelka argue about their respective groups' performances and Strelka falls through the deck of the *Sevriuga*:

Alesha: You'll disgrace our whole district with this nonsense, and you'll be a complete flop ("...s treskom provalites').

Strelka: See that you don't flop yourself ("Kak by vy sami ne provalilis'").

Alesha: We'll see about that yet, which one of us flops ("...kto iz nas provalitsia").

Strelka: It's clear that you'll flop! ("...vy provalites'!").

Alesha: We won't flop! ("Ne provalimsia!").

Strelka: Yes, you will flop! ("Net, provalites'!").

Alesha: No, we won't flop! ("Ne provalimsia!").

Strelka: You will flop! ("Provalites'!") A-a!

(Strelka falls through [provalivaetsia]).[156]

Figure 40.

When Byvalov refuses to board Strelka's group on the *Sevriuga*, she tells the logger:

—We ourselves didn't want to go with them.

—I see. Why?

—Our artistic direction is different. ("U nas khudozhestvennoe napravlenie raznoe." "Napravlenie" = both physical direction and orientation)

—You're not going the same way then.

The script also comments on the dangers of creativity via the polysemy of "sochiniat'" ("to compose," but also "to fabricate"). When the chairman of the Olimpiada presidium asks Byvalov to play his song, he refuses:

—I don't play.

—Then how do you compose? ("A kak zhe vy sochiniaete?")

—Comrades, I don't make anything up, I tell the truth. ("Ia, tovarishchi, nichego ne sochiniaiu, ia pravdu govoriu.")

This exchange is part of a longer dialogue based on the humor of context reversal, a misunderstanding arising from differing initial premises. When the presidium chairman asks Byvalov to talk about his work, meaning song composition, Byvalov begins to expound on the manufacture of balalaikas: "So, comrades, we make balalaikas. Of course, many people think this is a trivial occupation." When the chair invites Byvalov to sit down at the piano, he refuses: "Comrades, a mistake has occurred. My system doesn't make pianos."

Given the directive from above ordering Aleksandrov to return to the situation comedy and slapstick of *Happy Guys*, together with the mounting ideological pressures of 1936–38, satire—always politically problematic—is the weakest comedic line of *Volga-Volga* and instead the film returns to the gaiety and high spirits of *Happy Guys*. Writing in 1939, Aleksandrov distinguishes between "funny" (in the sense of ridiculous) and "merry" comedy, meaning the characterization of Byvalov vs. that of Strelka. In the first type, a character falls into situations worse than the viewer's, who must feel smarter than the character, and the character's defects are ridiculed. The funny is rarely buoyant (*zhizneradostnyi*). "Happy laughter is a sign of confidence, strength, and optimism. A funny person elicits laughter by his behavior; a happy person infects us with his laughter, we're carried away by his liveliness (*bodrost'*) and high spirits (*vesel'e*)."[157]

Apart from Byvalov, the traditional bureaucrat-target, it is the secondary characters who carry the weak satirical charge of the film in different ways. The three cooks who perform in Marx Brothers fashion for Byvalov sing in the military imagery of the five-year plans: "On the food front we'll manage to win thousands of sweet victories." The chef who recites Mayakovsky's poetry is ridiculed as a stereotypically gay man with a tenor voice, the polar opposite of his literary idol, and consequently Byvalov has him "thrown off the ship of modernity":

> Byvalov: …And who are you?
>
> Cook: I'm a reader-reciter.
>
> Byvalov: From what institution do you recite?
>
> Cook: I don't recite from an institution. I recite Mayakovsky.
>
> Byvalov: I'm asking where do you work?
>
> Cook: Oh...in the kitchen. I'm a chef.
>
> Byvalov: Who?
>
> Cook: I'm a cook.
>
> Byvalov: A food guy? Clear the deck!

Like the Lotsman, who is satirized as a stock braggart character, Uncle Kuzia, the water carrier, first appears to be the typical comedic drunk, who has trained his horse to make an automatic stop at the local tavern. But contrary to expectations, the water carrier who sings couplets about the necessity of his profession ("bez vody i ni tudy i ni siudy"), also proves himself to be the crucial moral barometer of the film by producing a sober assessment of Byvalov's moral-ethical qualities. In the telegram scene by the river, the water carrier unmasks Byvalov by playing on the polysemy of "otvechat'" ("to answer" and "to answer or be responsible for"):

> Byvalov: Shout "otvechaiu" (I'm answering/I'm responsible) with me.
>
> ……………………………………………………………………..
> Water carrier: So you've been up to all this funny business here, and I'm going to answer/answer for it/ with you...
> Byvalov: You idiot, you just shout, and I'll be responsible.
> Water carrier: So I'm going to shout, and you'll be responsible. Agreed.
> Water carrier sings: It used to be, in happy days…
> Byvalov: What are you shouting?
> Water carrier: Why shouldn't I shout, if you're going to answer for it?

The water carrier then reappears at the end of the film to turn Byvalov's own words against him as he tries to sing and to sweep him offstage:

> Byvalov: Kuz'ma Ivanych, it [my voice] caught again.
>
> Water carrier: It won't work, Comrade Byvalov, to sing like that you need to study for twenty years.
>
> Byvalov: What did you say?
>
> Water carrier: I said…clear the deck.

Aleksandrov's speech at the May 1941 conference on film outlines his original satirical strategy for the character, which was derailed by overly cautious functionaries:

> Take the film *Volga-Volga* where there's a water carrier who liked to have a drink and was always tipsy. Apart from that, at the end, when Byvalov wanted to suck up to the water carrier, he bought two mugs of beer and treated him, but the water carrier didn't drink at all, he refused the beer. They decided that a drunk water carrier is harmful and began to sober him up. He was cut. And I have to say that, because of this, the plot of the second half of the picture changed, because he didn't need to be sobered up. He had been sober from the very beginning. I have to say that, thanks to this, he had no motion forward. There's nothing terrible about some water carrier appearing on screen tipsy. I have to say that with us, these things are looked at separately from the impression. Because they're afraid of something, both the script section and the Committee heads play it safe. This happens because they forget about the slyness that greatly facilitates artistic success.... If the hero comes out at the very beginning and says that I'm going to make you laugh with this and this, it won't elicit any laughter from the viewer. The viewer isn't going to laugh, because you need slyness, and for that you sometimes need to pretend to be stupid and turn out not to be by the end.[158]

*****

In *Volga-Volga*, Dunaevskii's music became even more central than it was in *Circus* because the very plot revolved around a musical text, the fate of the song composed by Dunia Petrova (Strelka). To his friends, Dunaevskii was always known as "Dunia." According to Dunaevskii family tradition, just as Aleksandrov was conferring with his co-authors about characters' names, Liubov' Petrovna asked whether Dunia had called from Leningrad (as he often did in the course of work on the film), inspiring Aleksandrov to name the heroine Dunia Petrova.[159] The plot has several points of contact with Dunaevskii's career as well: at one point, Strelka doubts the quality of her song; she is later suspected of plagiarism by the Melkovodskites, but triumphs in the end when "Song of the Volga" gains national recognition. Like all artists, Dunaevskii had occasion to doubt himself and the value of his music. Initially, his jazz-influenced work had not been accepted by RAPM critics and he had been accused of plagiarizing the march from *Happy Guys*, but he nevertheless achieved national prominence with *Happy Guys* and then *Circus*. Orlova's "Dunia—moia podruga" (Dunia is my friend) and Alesha's contemptuous "Dunia kompozitor" ("Dunia the composer") thus inscribed into the narrative a private joke about the peripeties of authorship.

Dunaevskii worked on the score for the film between May 1937 and February 1938 and, for the first time during his collaboration with Aleksandrov, almost all the music was recorded before filming began in June 1937.[160] "Dorogoi shirokoi" ("Along a broad path") was the only song composed toward the end of work on *Volga-Volga* and is first mentioned in Aleksandrov's February 1938 response to Mosfil'm. Because of its centrality, Dunaevskii agonized over the quality of "Song of the Volga" and its potential mass appeal:

> The content of not only Strelka's image but also, to a significant degree, the persuasiveness of the entire plot of the film, depended on this song: if the song had turned out to be unsuccessful, the viewer would not have believed in Strelka's talent. In addition, the song was supposed to become popular, to be well received by listeners. Overall, it wasn't an easy task. That's why work on Strelka's song continued until various kinds of doubts stopped tormenting me.[161]

Dunaevskii explained that his compositional method with "Song of the Volga" reversed the musical chronology of the film. He himself began with a more complex orchestration, the symphonic version of the song conducted at the Olimpiada by young Tolia Shalaev, and then worked backwards to the simple song, the "primitive form" Dunia had found "in nature, in the forests, mountains, in the water."[162]

In composing for *Volga-Volga*, Dunaevskii followed the formula he had discovered with *Circus*: for songs to be assimilated and sung by Russian audiences, they must be consistent with the native melos. *Volga-Volga*'s plot allowed Dunaevskii to use many more folk and urban song melodies than *Circus*, thereby contributing to the film's success. As the Melkovodskites pursue Byvalov while demonstrating their talents, Dunaevskii's accompanying divertissement includes Okhapkin's "Kamarinskaia," the fisherwomen's waltz based on "Samara," the woman in the window's phrase from "Iz-za ostrova na strezhen'," the watchmaker's "Ei, ukhnem," and the children's songs

"Shire krug" and "Zhil-byl u babushki seren'kii kozlik." Dunaevskii creates typical balalaika melodies for Melkovodsk performers. "Molodezhnaia" is based on the folk song "Po Donu guliaet kazak molodoi." The water carrier and Lotsman's songs resemble folk chastushki, and "Dorogoi shirokoi" is composed in the lyric style of a classic romance.[163]

In a 1937 talk to fellow composers, Dunaevskii once again reiterated his three strategies for composing in the cinema: extensive use of illustrative music to convey the plot peripeties to the viewer, very close association of music to content, and creation of a central song that determines the musical design of the film.[164] In following these principles, Dunaevskii created an intricate cinematic score. In a true musical film, instrumental music and songs not only reiterate and reinforce the plotline but also extend meaning by providing independent information. For example, in *Volga-Volga*, the Lotsman's ditty "Amerika Rossii podarila parokhod" ("America gave Russia a steamship") references a naval rivalry between the two countries that is implicit in the film (and was made explicit in Shumiatskii's communications with Aleksandrov). According to Dunaevskii, the "Moon Waltz," Marion Dixon's leitmotif in *Circus*, had been intended to reveal her true life situation more explicitly than the script. In *Volga-Volga*, "Dorogoi shirokoi" serves the same purpose for Strelka. The melody plays at the beginning of the film when Alesha says he would like to fulfill all of Strelka's desires and when she asks him whether he has ever composed a song. She sings the first stanza of "Dorogoi shirokoi" as she goes to the *Sevriuga* to make peace with Alesha. The melody sounds again as the two make peace while framed by the Volga-Moscow canal locks, as Strelka dives off the ship followed by Alesha, and after the lovers make peace again in the "Water!" scene and the camera pans across an expanse of shimmering water. The lyricism of the "Dorogoi shirokoi" melody with its words of happy love ("Dorogoi shirokoi, rekoiu glubokoi / Khorosho nam plyt' vdvoem s toboi," ["Along a broad path, on a deep river, / We feel fine sailing, the two of us together"]) thus illustrates the romantic line of the film and tells us repeatedly that the two are meant for each other despite their musical rivalry, screwball antics, and verbal jousting throughout the film.

The first part of *Volga-Volga* is concerned with the Melkovodskites' attempts to disprove Byvalov's denial of their amateur talents. The ad hoc talent show builds from individual performances to the crescendo of the "Svistopliaska" with its speeded-up action, and then subsides through individual performances, ending in Byvalov's display of his *lack* of talent. Musically, the plotline culminates in the crazily eclectic "Svistopliaska," which illustrates the townspeople's gifts in both the classical and folk genres. Although the rival musical groups compete for Byvalov's attention as they pursue him through the town, in "Svistopliaska," which skillfully blends classical, folk, and popular music, Dunaevskii makes his own musical statement, demonstrating that, for him, there is no conflict among the differing styles, that popular, contemporary music is simply a natural continuation of the earlier forms.

As Strelka and Alesha bump up against each other while conducting their respective groups, Dunaevskii introduces the "Molodezhnaia" melody played by Strelka's musicians, which competes with Alesha's classical repertoire in the episode. Dunaevskii's contemporary song "Molodezhnaia" thus becomes associated with Strelka's folk performers and characterizes them in ways that both complement and go beyond the script. Strelka's group projects youthful energy and dynamism as it performs "Molodezhnaia," a rousing song and dance melody, on the raft and the *Lesorub*. The melody also provides a musical bridge as the group transfers from the raft to the *Lesorub*, and from the *Lesorub* to the steamship, again underscoring the dynamism of travel. In contrast, Alesha's Neapolitan orchestra makes the river journey practicing Schubert's sedate "Musical Moment" and the pompous Verdi march from *Aida*.[165] The lyrics of "Molodezhnaia," the only *Volga-Volga* song whose text is included in toto in the film, serve to further extend meaning by associating Strelka and company with a broader cultural notion of youthfulness defined as natural joy ("Oi ty radost' molodaia" ["Oh, you youthful joy"] and "Slovno kolos, nasha radost' nalivaetsia" ["Our joy ripens, like an ear of wheat"]), fairy tale into reality ("Chto mechtalos' i khotelos', to sbyvaetsia" ["What we dreamed of and wished for, is coming to pass"]), and spontaneous merriment ("V pliaske nogi khodiat sami, sami prosiatsia" ["Our legs move on their own in a dance / They ask for it themselves"]). Much like "Song of the Motherland," the song defines youth in terms of almost orgiastic maximalism (largeness, unlimited expanses, extreme motion) and unity ("Vsekh razbudim…Vse dobudem" ["We'll wake everyone up...We'll get everything"]):

> *Beisia* dymka zolotaia, pridorozhnaia,
> Oi ty radost', molodaia, *nevozmozhnaia.*
> *Tochno nebo, vysoka ty,*
> *Tochno more, shiroka ty,*
> *Neob"iatnaia* doroga molodezhnaia.
>
> Chto mechtalos' i khotelos', to sbyvaetsia—
> *Priamo k solntsu nasha smelost' probivaetsia.*
> *Vsekh razbudim, budim, budim,*
> *Vse dobudem, budem, budem,*
> Slovno kolos, nasha radost' nalivaetsia.[166]

Dunaevskii was careful to link music to content by using only those sections of Lebedev-Kumach's lyrics for songs which corresponded to the on-screen action. As they pull on the rigging to raise their sails, Strelka and friends sing: "Ei, grianem sil'nee, / Podtianem druzhnee" ("Hey, let's sing it out louder, / We'll pull it up/join in the song/ together"). As Strelka and the logger dance on the *Lesorub*, they sing: "Ei, podruga, vykhodi-ka / i na druga pogliadi-ka, / Chtoby shutkoiu veseloi perebrosit'sia" ("Hey, friend, come on out and take a look at your pal / So that we can trade a happy joke,") (Fig. 41). Apart from the two initial lines of "Dorogoi shirokoi," the only lyrics of the song used in the film accompany nature scenes: "Vysokie gory, / Rodnye polia, / Stepnye prostory— / Liubimaia zemlia! / I plyt'—legko, / I pet'—legko!" ("High mountains, / Our native fields. / Expanses of steppe / Beloved land! / And it's easy to sail, / And easy to sing!"). The lyrics of the Lotsman, cooks', and water carrier's songs are similarly abbreviated so as to parallel the action.[167]

"Song of the Volga," the central melody of *Volga-Volga*, is almost absent in the early parts of the film, which are concerned with Byvalov's non-recognition of Melkovodsk's talents. Dunaevskii gives us two lines of the song instrumentally in the raft scene, as Strelka and Alesha kiss and the camera pulls back to reveal the town, and Strelka introduces her song to Alesha (and to us) by singing the first quatrain of the fourth stanza ("Mnogo pesen pro Volgu propeto, / No eshche ne slozhili takoi, / Chtoby, solntsem sovetskim sogreta, / Zazvenela nad Volgoi-rekoi," ["Many songs have been sung about the Volga, / But they haven't yet made up one, / Warmed by the Soviet sun, / That would ring out over the Volga river"]) and the refrain. "Song of the Volga" then reappears only in the latter half of the film where it becomes dominant, repeating in the series of ingenious stylistic variations that infuse an otherwise rather sketchy plot with enormous energy.

In line with Dunaevskii's coordination of lyrics with events, Strelka's first performance on the raft is indeed the first time the song sounds on a tributary of the Volga system. Her initial rendition of the song, as she accompanies herself on the accordion, is a simple, unadorned, straightforward, even unemotional performance. When the song reappears much later in the film, she sings a few lines on deck at night, but with a *lyrical* intonation. After Strelka and Alesha are stranded aboard each other's boats, we hear Tolia Shalaev playing a waltz version of the song with flourishes, and the lumberjack sings an appropriate stanza as the travelers near Moscow: "My sdvigaem i gory i reki, / Vremia skazok prishlo naiavu, / I po Volge svobodnoi naveki, / Korabli priplyvaiut v Moskvu" ("We move both mountains and rivers, / The time of fairy tales has come to our waking hours, / And along the forever free Volga, / Ships come into Moscow").[168] Next, Strelka sings to Alesha's musicians, also in a waltz rhythm, which goes "straight to the heart": "Grianem pesniu i zvonko, i smelo, / Chtoby v nei nasha sila zhila, / Chtob do samogo solntsa letela, / Chtob do samogo serdtsa doshla!" (We'll sing the song resonantly and boldly, / So that our strength lives in it, / So that it flies up to the very sun, / So that it reaches the very heart!"). The storm scene demonstrates the musical's axiomatic preference for non-diegetic sound over image as we hear dramatic instrumental phrases of "Song of the Volga" on the soundtrack—and not the sounds of wind, rain, and thunder. As sail boaters, divers and others pick up the notes, we hear an energetic instrumental rendition of the song. Alesha's orchestra then performs it as a march, but he comments, "We're not singing it right. Strelka sang it really well!" (Strelka never performs "Song of

Figure 41.

the Volga" as a march.) Another extended variation follows as a band aboard a patrol boat plays the song in march rhythm. This is followed by a chorus, and then a jazz version as we see a tugboat, and yet another march version played by a military band, culminating in a series of consecutive phrases performed by each of the preceding groups, finally fading away into the air to the vibrating sounds of a metalophone and Hawaiian guitar as sailboats and a dirigible appear on screen. In her cabin, Strelka hears the song as a slow romance over the radio. A jazz rendition follows as the first Dunia is dragged to the Olimpiada hall, and Strelka runs up the stairs in her oversize sailor suit to a march version. She herself performs the song solemnly and majestically, almost as an anthem or hymn, and this is followed by an orchestral version conducted by the young composer. As Strelka disappears under the table, we hear a jazz rendition of "Song of the Volga," which moves seamlessly into "Dorogoi shirokoi," when she quarrels with Alesha. In Strelka's absence, the Melkovodskites then perform the song as a march, which is cut off by Byvalov's squawk, and the jazz version resumes as Strelka and Alesha make peace under the table. In the course of the film, Dunaevskii takes us through all possible styles of performance, but he seems to prefer both Strelka's serious rendition of "Song of the Volga" as anthem—marked because unique for the film—and the multiple jazz variations rather than the more conventional marches. Dunaevskii's stylistic variations again blur the divide between classical and popular music. Nevertheless, in the moralizing epilogue, the actors conclude with the "Krasavitsa narodnaia" refrain again performed in march rhythm.

The first stanza's lyrics of "Song of the Volga" establish the river's historical importance as a main national waterway, personified as freedom fighter and staging ground for the folk rebels Sten'ka Razin and Pugachev: "Ne sdavalas' tsepiam i obmanam / Golubaia doroga strany, / —Ne zadarom Stepan s Emel'ianom / Vniz po Volge vodili chelny" ("The blue road of the land would not yield to chains and deceptions, / It was not in vain that Stepan and Emel'ian guided their boats down the Volga"). The song turns on a series of semantic oppositions located within the larger category of past/present: wrong melody vs. right melody (the folk songs of the *Volzhskaia vol'nitsa* vs. Soviet songs); clouds vs. sun and spring; melancholy vs. joy; fairy tales vs. reality.

Mnogo pesen nad Volgoi zvenelo,
Da napev byl u pesen ne tot.
Prezhde pesni toska nasha pela,
A teper' nasha radost' poet.
....
Razorvali my serye tuchi,
Nad stranoiu vesna rastsvela
....
My sdvigaem i gory i reki,
Vremia skazok prishlo naiavu
....
Mnogo pesen pro Volgu propeto,
No eshche ne slozhili takoi,
Chtoby, solntsem sovetskim sogreta,
Zazvenela nad Volgoi-rekoi.[169]

In its definition of cultural geography, the song is analogous to "Song of the Motherland," with the difference that the Volga river is made metonymical for the entire homeland—"Krasavitsa narodnaia" ("National Beauty"). As in "Song of the Motherland," the broad expanses of the river ("neob"iatnaia nasha reka" ["our boundless river"], as congruent to the vast national space of the earlier song), give rise to freedom, strength, and national unity. The broad geographical expanses are also congruent to the all-encompassing song: "Grianem pesniu i zvonko, i smelo, ...Chtob do samogo solntsa letela, / Chtob do samogo serdtsa doshla!" and the free-flowing river denotes social freedom and strength: "I kak Volga, rekoiu moguchei / Nasha vol'naia zhizn' potekla" ("And, like the Volga, our free life began to flow like a mighty river"). The Volga both facilitates contact between the periphery and center and unifies the geographical extremes of the nation:

I po Volge svobodnoi naveki,
Korabli priplyvaiut v Moskvu.
Ot Moskvy do vorot stalingradskikh,
Kak bol'shaia zhivaia ruka,
Vse narody privetstvuet bratski
Vsenarodnaia Volga-reka.[170]

The national unity of geographical expanses, freedom, and strength are all recapitulated in the refrain of "Song of the Volga":

Krasavitsa narodnaia.
Kak more—polnovodnaia,
Kak rodina—svobodnaia,
Shiroka,
Gluboka,
Sil'na![171]

Finally, because center and periphery have been unified, the national boundary is now set at the country's border with external enemies:

Pust' vragi, kak golodnye volki,
U granits ostavliaiut sledy—
Ne vidat' im krasavitsy Volgi
I ne pit' im iz Volgi vody![172]

Chapter 3 Endnotes

1. G. V. Aleksandrov, "Uspekh metoda," *Kino* (May 28, 1936): 3. In 1935, Aleksandrov had made a proposal to the studio for "Zolotoi poezd" ("The Gold Train"), a scenario based on the story, "Zolotoi zapas" ("The Gold Deposit"), but nothing came of the idea. (GFF, f. 154.) Parts of this chapter were published in Rimgaila Salis, "U istokov "Volgi-Volgi," *Kinovedcheskie zapiski*, 76 (2005): 314–343.

2. G. Aleksandrov, "Nasha tema—rastsvet tvorchestva," 18.

3. Stenogramma, doklad Dunaevskogo v Muzykal'nom nauchno-issledovatel'skom institute (May 7, 1937).

4. G. V. Aleksandrov, *Vecherniaia Moskva*, Apr. 5, 1938.

5. See Jan Plamper's introduction, *Personality Cults in Stalinism*, eds. Klaus Heller and Jan Plamper (Göttingen: V & R Unipress, 2004) 19.

6. G. Aleksandrov, "Nasha tema—rastvet tvorchestva," 18. In Lydia Chukovskaia's *Sof'ia Petrovna*, the elevator operator in the publishing house engages in the same rhetoric of big little people as she criticizes the purged director's secretary: "You think the elevator woman's just a little person, Comrade Timofeyev, that she don't understand? Well, you're wrong! It's not the old days now! Under Soviet rule there aren't no little people, everyone's big." (Lydia Chukovskaya, *Sofia Petrovna* (Evanston, IL: Northwestern University Press, 1994) 66.

7. *Kul'turnaia zhizn' v SSSR 1928–1941*, Vol. 1, 173, 189, 215.

8. See L. Maksimenkov, *Sumbur vmesto muzyki. Stalinskaia kul'turnaia revoliutsiia 1936–1938* (Moskva: Iuridicheskaia Kniga, 1997) 213 and Petrone, 154.

9. "Sumbur vmesto muzyki," *Pravda* (Jan. 28, 1936): 3; "Baletnaia fal'sh'," *Pravda* (Feb. 6, 1936): 3. In a January 29 conversation with Stalin, Shumiatskii declared himself on the side of music "based on folklore, on the sources of folk music and the best classical music" (B. Shumiatskii, "Moia kratkaia zapis' besedy s Ios. Vissar, 29/I-1936 g. (10 chas. vechera)", No. 31, www.idf.ru/15/31.shtml. Accessed Nov. 11, 2006).

10. A. Bek-Nazarov, "Talanty iz naroda," *Kino*, Mar. 26, 1936: 3. Other folk and *samodeiatel'nost'* activities contemporaneous with the making of *Volga-Volga* include: Jan. 10– Feb. 5, 1936, I Moskovskaia oblastnaia vystavka samodeiatel'nogo iskusstva; Feb. 17, 1936, Tsentral'nyi dom khudozhestvennoi samodeiatel'nosti moskovskikh profsoiuzov established; Mar. 5–20, Vystavka samodeiatel'nogo iskusstva Krasnoi Armii i NKVD; July 9, 1936, Bol'shoi Theatre brigade travels to the Volga in search of talented singers among collective farm workers and working youth; Mar. 2, 1937, Tret'iakov Gallery opens an exhibition of folk art; April 14, 1937, a new production of Glinka's *Ruslan i Liudmila* opens at the Bol'shoi Theatre; August 1937, opening of Vsesoiuznaia vystavka samodeiatel'nogo iskusstva in honor of the 20th anniversary of the revolution; Oct. 17, 1937, first performance of I. Moiseev's Gosudarstvennyi ansambl' narodnogo tantsa SSSR.

11. Aleksandrov, "Uspekh metoda," 3.

12. Erdman, *P'esy. Intermedii. Pis'ma. Dokumenty. Vospominaniia sovremennikov*, 260.

13. G. Aleksandrov, V. Nil'sen, "Khudozhestvennaia samodeiatel'nost'," *Pravda* (Nov. 17, 1936): 3. The lumberjack's comic performance of Ol'ga's aria from *Evgenii Onegin* survived obliquely as Strelka's performance of Tat'iana's aria for Byvalov.

14. Poor administration and leadership of *samodeiatel'nost'*, together with a lack of books, musical instruments, and sheet music, are a continuing refrain in articles about the movement. See, for example, "Khudozhestvennaia samodeiatel'nost," *Sovetskoe iskusstvo* (Jun. 6, 1938): 1.

    In his memoirs, Aleksandrov also mentions, as an inspiration for the film, a talented woman tractor driver who is prevented from performing in Moscow by her boss: "We arrived in Ramenskoe. They organized something like an agricultural amateur show for us. A kolkhoz ensemble performed, and this girl sang and danced. Her abilities really were outstanding and I decided to invite her to Moskinokombinat for a screen test. But the MTS director didn't let the girl go to Moscow, explaining his motive in approximately the following way: 'There's no point in her caterwauling there, let her work on the tractor properly. Some artist!'" (Aleksandrov, *Epokha i kino*, 205).

15. G. Aleksandrov, "Nasha tema—rastsvet tvorchestva," 8.

16. K. V. S., "Volga-Volga," *Za bol'shevitskii fil'm*, No. 32 (1936): 3; G. V. Aleksandrov, "Kak my rabotaem nad iubileinymi temami," *Kino*, Sept. 28, 1936: 1.

17. Anon., "Volga-Volga," *Komsomol'skaia pravda*, Sept. 27, 1936: 4.

18. Van Geldern, "The Centre and the Periphery," 62–9. If the Volga waters metaphorically represent the blood of the motherland's body, then Moscow, to which the Melkovodskites travel, is its heart (Giunter, "Arkhetipy sovetskoi kul'tury," 771–72).

19. Gr. Aleksandrov, "Prezhde pesni toska nasha pela, a teper' nasha radost' poet," *Za bol'shevitskii fil'm*, No. 19 (1938): 2.

20. L. V., "Volga-Volga," *Izvestiia* (Apr. 5, 1938): 4.

21. To reinforce the paradigmatic composition, Aleksandrov included a very fleeting shot of Merkurov's Stalin statue on the opposite bank in the pre-Khrushchev era version of the film. The Stalin statue was dynamited in February 1961 (A. V. Beliaev i A. A. Rastorguev, "Istoriia Dubny," http://www.dubna.ru/rastor/History/Channel.htm. Accessed Jul. 8, 2007).

22. Modern Soviet seafaring vessels are, of course, contrasted to the antiquated paddleboat given to Russia by the US. Stalin ordered the steamship with his name taken out of the film. *Volga-Volga* is now shown with the original footage (Iurii Saakov, "Oborvan 'na schast'e,'" *Pravda* [23–30 Jan. 1998]: 6).

23. Anon., "'Volga...Volga' Beseda s rezhisserom-ordenonostsem t. Aleksandrovym," *Komsomol'skaia pravda* (Oct. 27, 1936): 4. In this same interview, Aleksandrov named Orlova, Volodin, and Kurikhin as actors in the film—and Nikolai Cherkasov, presumably to be cast as accountant Alesha.

24. G. V. Aleksandrov, V. S. Nil'sen, "Skhema siuzheta," RGALI, f. 2450/2/321.

25. Aleksandrov and Nil'sen, Sept. 30, 1936 note to Z. Iu. Darevskii, RGALI, f. 2450/2/321.

26. RGALI, f. 2753/1/6 and f. 2753/1/7.

27. Anon., "'Volga...Volga' Beseda s rezhisserom-ordenonostsem," 4.

28. See M. Grishin, "Bol'shaia Volga," *Pravda* (May 10, 1937): 2.

29. Aleksandrov borrowed the motif from the Marx Brothers' *Monkey Business* (1931), in which the film credits appear on a revolving barrel.

30. In 1895, Karl Teodor Kazimir Meierkhol'd changed his name to Vsevolod (in honor of Garshin, his favorite writer) and his religion from Lutheranism to Orthodoxy.

31. A 1933 entry in the diary of Aleksandr Afinogenov, never one of Meierkhol'd's fans, attests to the director's larger than life persona: "Oh you old wolf, you hardened beast. You retreat, without admitting it even to yourself. You shiver with cold, exposing a thatch of hair to the stormy wind of a harsh winter. You've lost a sense of the road. Master, you are perishing, covered with snow—majestic, unbending Meierkhol'd." (Aleksandr Afinogenov, *Izbrannoe*, vol. 2 [Moscow: Iskusstvo, 1977], 213).

32. All quotations relating to the first version are from literary scripts, RGALI, f. 2450/2/321, 2753/1/6, 2753/1/7.

33. Acrobatics were used in *Mystery-Bouffe* and *The Magnanimous Cuckhold*. In his landmark 1926 production of *The Inspector General*, Meierkhol'd had the floor built on a slant in some scenes. ("Revizor. Eksplikatsiia spektaklia," V. E. Meierkhol'd, *Stat'i, pis'ma, rechi, besedy. 1917–1939*, Part 2 [Moskva: Iskusstvo, 1968] 111).

34. Anon., "Sumbur vmesto muzyki," *Pravda* (Jan. 28, 1936): 3.

35. Anon., "Baletnaia fal'sh," *Pravda* (Feb. 3, 1936): 3. Maksimenkov identifies Platon Kerzhentsev as the most likely author of both *Pravda* articles (Maksimenkov, 88–112). Informers reported Meierkhol'd's politically correct comments on the ballet: "Amateur art should be put on the stage, instead of showing a woman collective farmer in a tutu and little wings." ("Spravka sekretno-politicheskogo otdela GUGB NKVD SSSR ob otklikakh literatorov i rabotnikov iskusstva na stat'i v gazete "Pravde" o kompozitore D. D. Shostakoviche," *Vlast' i khudozhestvennaia intelligentsia*, eds. A. Artizov and O. Naumov [Moskva: Demokratiia, 2002] 294).

36. P. Kerzhentsev, "Chuzhoi teatr," *Pravda* (Dec. 17, 1937): 4. Meierkhol'd was arrested June 20, 1939.

37. V. Meierkhol'd, "Meierkhol'd protiv meierkhol'dovshchiny. Iz doklada 14 marta 1936 g," Meierkhol'd, *Stat'i, pis'ma, rechi, besedy*, 330–47.

38. V. Meierkhol'd, "Vystuplenie na sobranii teatral'nykh rabotnikov Moskvy, 26 marta 1936 goda," Meierkhol'd, *Stat'i, pis'ma, rechi, besedy*, 353–54.

39. P. M. Kerzhentsev, "Problemy sovetskogo teatra," *Sovetskoe iskusstvo* (Apr. 5, 1936): 2.

40. Osoaviakhim (Union of Societies for Assistance to Defense and Aviation-Chemical Construction) was a militarized youth organization with its own airports, parachute jumping towers, and firing ranges.

41. Nil'sen worked closely with Shumiatskii on the project, a plan to build new studios and centralize Soviet filmmaking in the Crimea, whose sunny and warm climate was favorable for year round production. In January 1936, Nil'sen published an article strongly advocating the project ("Amerikanskii i sovetskii Gollivud," *Kino* [Jan. 11, 1936]: 3), and in August, Shumiatskii notified him that it would soon be presented to the government: "In a day or two we're submitting the plan target for the *kinogorod*. Things are going pretty well." (B. Shumiatskii, Aug. 3, 1936 letter to V. Nil'sen, RGALI, f. 2753/1/39). The plan failed, apparently opposed by Beria.

42. Dem'ian Bednyi, "Kanonizatsiia" ili "chto trebovalos' dokazat'," *Izvestiia* (Apr. 6, 1930).

43. George O. Liber, *Alexander Dovzhenko. A Life in Soviet Film* (London: British Film Institute, 2002) 133–36.

44. Nil'sen solved some technical problems with the soundtrack and was rewarded with an M-1 car for his efforts. (Interview with E. S. Al'pers, 2002).

45. See "Spravka Tomskogo gorotdela NKVD ob otbytii ssylki" and "V komissiiu po chastnym amnistiiam pri verkhovnom sovete soiuza SSR dramaturga Erdmana Nikolaia Robertovicha zaiavlenie," in Erdman, *P'esy. Intermedii. Pis'ma. Dokumenty. Vospominaniia sovremennikov*, 293, 295. Erdman was present at a Mosfil'm meeting on the script, Feb. 5, 1937.

46. N. Erdman, "Volga-Volga," *Sovetskii ekran*, 17 (1967): 18.

47. RGALI, f. 2450/2/321. The *Volga-Volga* file specifically identifies Erdman as co-author of this version.

48. "Literaturnyi stsenarii, Volga-Volga," RGALI, f. 2450/2/317.

49. G. Aleksandrov in "Nad chem my budem rabotat' v iubileinom godu," *Iskusstvo kino* (November 1936): 54; G. V. Aleksandrov in "Nad chem my budem rabotat' v 1937 godu," *Kino* (Dec. 31, 1936): 3. The draft of Lebedev-Kumach's "Zastol'naia pesnia" lyrics for the film survive in his archive (RGALI, f. 2450/2/321).

50. "Soveshchanie u Zam. dir. kino-studii tov. Sokolovskoi ot 5-go fevr. 1937 g.," RGALI, f. 2450/2/321.

51. G. Aleksandrov, V. Nil'sen, "Volga-Volga (muzyk. kino-komediia), 3 marta 1937, Moskva," RGALI, f. 2450/2/317. Erdman's name was not included as co-author.

52. Quoted in Sheila Fitzpatrick, *Tear off the Masks! Identity and Imposture in Twentieth-Century Russia* (Princeton: Princeton University Press, 2005) 165.

53. Aleksandrov and Nil'sen, "Volga-Volga (muzyk. Kino-komediia), 3 marta 1937. Toptygin is the name of the three bear heroes of Saltykov-Shchedrin's tale, "Medved' na voevodstve" (1884).

54. "Zakliuchenie direktsii Mosfil'ma na stsenarii *Volga-Volga* ot 8.III.37," RGALI, f. 2450/2/321; "Protokol soveshchaniia po rezhisserskomu stsenariiu *Volga-Volga* 9 marta 1937 g.," RGALI, f. 2753/1/53.

55. This is the conventional reconciliation of opposites in musical comedy.

56. "Zakliuchenie direktsii Mosfil'ma na stsenarii *Volga-Volga*."

57. "Protokol soveshchaniia po rezhisserskomu stsenariiu *Volga-Volga*."

58. "Protokol soveshchaniia po rezhisserskomu stsenariiu *Volga-Volga*." There is no evidence that Erdman came to Moscow at this time.

59. "Protokol soveshchaniia po rezhisserskomu stsenariiu *Volga-Volga*." Aleksandrov's ideas about a fluid comedy script are, of course, naive in the face of the growing administrative initiative to censor by forbidding any deviation from approved scripts.

60. "Postanovlenie GUKa o khode podgotovki k proizvodstvu," RGALI, f. 2450/2/321. See also memo to GUK from Babitskii and Bliumenfel'd of Mosfil'm, mid-March 1937, about stopping funding for the film because of the delay in GUK approval. Preliminary expenses were listed as 72,200 rubles, of which 32,700 were used for Aleksandrov's earlier trip on the Volga.

61. Anon. note, *Proletarskaia Pravda* (Kalinin) (Mar. 30, 1937).

62. "Literaturnyi stsenarii, *Volga-Volga*," RGALI, f. 2753/1/9.

63. G. Aleksandrov, V. Nil'sen, "*Volga-Volga* (muzykal'naia kino-komediia), 3 Marta 1937 g., Moskva ["Marta" crossed out and replaced by "Aprelia",]," RGALI, f. 2450/2/319.

    I'm leaving you for a long time,
    I'm going to other lands.
    Good-bye my Volga beauty,
    Good-bye my friend.

64. Aleksandrov finally settled on "Trubyshkin," by analogy to "Tutyshkin," the surname of the actor playing the role and "truba" (trumpet).

65. "Postanovlenie direktsii Mosfil'ma po 2-mu variantu rezhisserskogo stsenariia Volgi-Volgi, 15 Aprelia 1937," RGALI, f. 2450/2/321. In April, Mosfil'm approved a pre-production budget of 581, 831 rubles. (RGALI, f. 2450/2/321).

66. "Zakliuchenie GUK po rezhiss/montazhnomu stsenariiu "Volga-Volga" (2-oi variant), 3 Maia 1937," RGALI, f. 2450/2/321. Approximately a month later, GUK approved the slate of actors we see in the film ("Zakliuchenie GUKa, 25 Maia 1937," RGALI, f. 2450/2/321).

67. RGALI, f. 2450/2/321.

68. Volodin's contract was signed April 17, 1937. He was paid 3,000 rubles for 9 days filming per month and 400 r. per day for overages. Nil'sen's friend, S. M. Gofman, recalled that the cinematographer objected to Aleksandrov that Orlova was too old for the Strelka role, but to no avail (Bernshtein, "Gollivud bez Kheppi-enda," 234).

69. "Usievich, Itkina, Danil'ian Babitskomu, 28 Aprelia 1937," RGALI, f. 2450/2/321.

70. "Pis'mo Orelovicha Usievichu i Babitskomu, 14 Apr. 1937," RGALI, f. 2450/2/321.

71. Kh. Khersonskii, "Il'inskii protiv Il'inskogo," *Kino* (Aug. 11, 1936): 3.

72. Byvalov duplicates Pobedonosikov's vanity, ignorance, and bureaucratic clichés, and Pobedonosikov is also protected from petitioners by an aggressive (male) secretary.

73. "Akterskaia kharakteristika vtorostepennykh i epizodicheskikh rolei po kartine *Volga-Volga*," RGALI, f. 2753/1/53. Mironova stated that her role in the film had originally been much larger but was cut during editing. She was offended and did not attend the première. (Maia Turovskaia, "*Volga-Volga* i ee vremia," *Kinovedcheskie zapiski*, 45 [2000]: 136.) According to Orlova, the character was considered a blot on Soviet contemporaneity by film industry officials who insisted upon its deletion. (Skorokhodov, *V poiskakh utrachennogo*, 407–08.)

74. "Zakliuchenie GUKa, 25 Maia 1937," RGALI, f. 2450/2/321.

75. Anon., "Nachalis' s"emki fil'ma *Volga-Volga*," *Kino* (Jun. 4, 1937): 3.

76. Tikhon, "Pod vympelom *Volgi-Volgi*," *Kino* (Jul. 4, 1937): 4.

77. Ark. Litvin, "*Volga-Volga*. Na s"emkakh fil'ma," *Vecherniaia Moskva*, No. 148 (1937): 3.

78. E. V-kh, "*Volga-Volga*," *Za bol'shevitskii fil'm* (Jul. 13, 1937): 4.

79. Starikov review (undated clipping), RGALI, f. 154.

80. E. V-kh, "*Volga-Volga*," 4.

81. R. M., "S"emki na Volge," *Kino* (Aug. 22, 1937): n. p. a.; Igor' Il'inskii, *Sam o sebe* (Moscow: VTO, 1961) 315.

82. I. Ivanov, "Na reke Chusovoi," *Kino* (Sept. 4, 1937): 3; Il'inskii, *Sam o sebe*, 315.

83. R. M., "S"emki na Volge."

84. E. P. Nesterov, "Moia rabota v kartine *Volga-Volga*," *Za bol'shevitskii fil'm*, No. 21 (1938): 4.

85. R. M., "S"emki na Volge."

86. Underlined twice.

87. "Pis'mo B. Shumiatskogo, 16 Iiulia 1937," RGALI, f. 2450/2/321.

88. "Zamechaniia po prosmotru naturnykh kuskov k fil'mu *Volga-Volga*, 11 Avgusta 1937, RGALI, f. 2450/2/321.

89. The possible context here is also the initial phases of the dismantling of the GUK administration, beginning with its lower ranks: Al'bert Moiseevich Slivkin, an assistant to Shumiatskii, had been arrested Aug. 3.

90. "Zapiska Darevskogo, 9 Avgusta 1937," RGALI, f. 2450/2/321.

91. V. Valina, "*Volga-Volga*. Na s"emke fil'ma." *Rabochaia Moskva* (Sept. 30, 1937).

92. Anon., "Bystree likvidirovat' posledstviia vreditel'stva," *Kino* (Oct. 28, 1937): 4.

93. Nil'sen was executed in January 1938. See *Vernite mne svobodu!*, 69–76; Arkadii Bernshtein, "Vozvrashchenie iz nebytiia," 6. For an overview of purges in the film industry, see Jamie Miller, "The Purges of Soviet Cinema, 1929–38," *Studies in Russian and Soviet Cinema*, 1.1 (2007): 5–26.

94. "Operatory ob operatorskoi rabote v fil'me *Volga-Volga*," *Za bol'shevitskii fil'm*, No. 20 (1938): 4.

95. S"emochnaia gruppa kartiny *Volga-Volga*, "*Volga-Volga*," *Za bol'shevitskii fil'm*, No. 29 (1937): 2.

96. S. Galadzh, "B. Petrov and V. Pereslavtsev," *Za bol'shevitskii fil'm*, No. 19 (1938): 2.

97. E. V-kh, "*Volga-Volga*," 3.

98. L. Orlova, "Zritel' i akter sovetskogo kino," *30 let sovetskoi kinematografii*, 376. Same in G. Zel'dovich, *Liubov' Orlova*, 24.

99. Vit. Zaseev, "Vody! Vody!" *Vecherniaia Moskva* (Jan. 17, 1970).

100. I. Il'inskii, "Rabotali khorosho i druzhno," *Za bol'shevitskii fil'm*, No. 19 (1938): 2.

101. Aleksandrov, *Epokha i kino*, 206.

102. G. Aleksandrov, "O sovetskoi kinokomedii," *Sovetskoe iskusstvo*, Feb. 4, 1939.

103. Il'inskii, *Sam o sebe*, 315–16. In later years, both Aleksandrov and Il'inskii exaggerated the number of dives to seven and eight.

104. "*Volga-Volga*, rezhisserskii stsenarii," RGALI, f. 2450/2/320.

105. G. Aleksandrov, "*Volga-Volga*, stsenarii muzykal'noi kino-komedii," RGALI, f. 2450/2/318.

106. "Iz doklada tov. G. Aleksandrova," *Kino* (Jun. 11, 1939): 2; see also Aleksandrov, *Epokha i kino*, 207.

107. *Letopis' rossiiskogo kino 1930–1945*, 488, 509, 519–20. Sokolovskaia was particularly vulnerable as the wife of People's Commissar for Agriculture Iakov Arkad'evich Iakovlev-Epshtein (1896–1938), who had supervised collectivization and had been executed as a participant in a military conspiracy. On Babitskii, see *Kremlevskii kinoteatr 1928–1953*, 1056–57, 465 (on his relationship with Shumiatskii, according to G. V. Zel'dovich).

108. K. A. Polonskii, head of the recording studio at Mosfil'm, was appointed as director in April 1938.

109. For information on these arrests, see www.memo.ru/memory/ and stalin.memo.ru. On Shumiatskii, see www.jewish.ru/8680.asp. Accessed Sept. 18, 2006.

110. "*Zamechaniia po fil'mu Volga-Volga*, Reznik," RGALI, f. 2450/2/321.

111. Reznik also criticizes what he considers hackneyed jokes used in the script (the horse that stops three times at the tavern, Byvalov on the phone to his driver) and crude lines, such as "Sama takaia", "Tvoi Vagner—durak."

112. "K obsuzhdeniiu prosmotra kuskov fil'ma Volga-Volga, Zel'dovich, 7 Dek. 1937," RGALI, f. 2450/2/321.

113. "Novaia razrabotka finala, Dekabr' 1937," RGALI, f. 2450/2/321.

114. "Shcherbatykh, Vrio Nach. KhPU GUK, Khachatur'ianu, dir. Mosfil'ma, 22 Dek. 1937," RGALI, f. 2450/2/321.

115. I. Dunaevskii, "Zametki, 8 June 1937," RGALI, f. 2062/1/137.

116. "Stenogramma soveshchaniia v TsK VKP(b) pod predsedatel'stvom A. A. Zhdanova po voprosam khudozhestvennogo kinematografa, 14 Maia, 1941," RTsKhIDNI (Russian Center for the Storage and Study of Modern History Documents), f. 77/1/919.

117. Notices in Jan. 20 and Feb. 10 1938 issues of *Za bol'shevitskii fil'm.*

118. Maksimenkov, 284.

119. "Pis'mo Khachatur'iana KhPO GUK-a, 15 Fevr. 1938," RGALI, f. 2450/2/321. Kushnirov has an account of Dukel'skii's first meeting with Aleksandrov at the studio and Stalin's identification of Byvalov with Dukel'skii (173–74).

120. Alesha: Maybe you won't find
Many bureaucrats like Byvalov,

Strelka: But any of the sneaks and insolent fellows
are a lot like Byvalov.

Alesha: Often petty thoughts and feelings,
The mold of old, joyless years,

Lumberjack: Interfere with our work

Strelka: And in art,
Holding up the flowering of talents.

All: But in a free republic
Old trash doesn't scare us,

And the folk genius
Shines for us like the sun!

Text by Lebedev-Kumach. In the film, the last quatrain above was replaced by the lines, "Staryi khlam ubrat' nedolgo, lish' metlu voz'met drugoi," ("It doesn't take long to get rid of the old junk, once another takes up the broom") and a properly grand rendition of the refrain from the theme song ("Krasavitsa narodnaia"). One thinks of Shumiatskii being swept away in the cinema administration purges.

121. G. Aleksandrov, "Predlozheniia k popravkam i sokrashcheniiam fil'ma Volga-Volga, 21.III.38," RGALI, f. 2450/2/321.

122. "Stenogramma soveshchaniia v TsK VKP(b) pod predsedatel'stvom A.A. Zhdanova po voprosam khudozhestvennogo kinematografa."

123. V. Smekhov, "Erdman na Taganke," Erdman, *P'esy, intermedii, pis'ma, dokumenty, vospominaniia sovremennikov*, 435.

124. "Linov, nachal'nik GUPKhF direktoru Mosfil'ma, 20 Apr. 1938," RGALI, f. 2450/2/321. The permission form was signed April 11.

125. *Letopis' rossiiskogo kino 1930–1945*, 555.

126. "Stenogramma diskussii po fil'mu "Volga-Volga" v Dome Kino, 18.IV—1938 goda," RGALI, f. 2450/2/321; Brat'ia Tur, "Volga-Volga," *Izvestiia* (Apr. 14, 1938): 4; D. Zaslavskii, "Khoroshii smekh," *Pravda* (Apr. 16, 1938): 6; A. Korchagin, "Volga-Volga," *Kino* (Apr. 17, 1938): 2.

127. Kushnirov, 181. Citing Averell Harriman as his source, Aleksandrov recounts the story of Stalin's gift of the film to Roosevelt in his memoirs (*Epokha i kino*, 208–09). For doubts about the factual basis of the story, see Valerii Golovskoi, "Legenda o 'Volge-Volge,'" *Kinovedcheskie zapiski*, 69 (2004): 333–38.

128. RGALI, f. 2062/1/565.

129. G. Zel'dovich, *Liubov' Orlova* and R. Iurenev, *Grigorii Aleksandrov* (Moscow: Goskinoizdat, 1939).

130. Anon., "Nedostoinoe povedenie," *Sovetskoe iskusstvo* (Jun. 10 1938): 4. In 1937–38, there was also talk of Orlova's drinking problem, which she was able to overcome.

131. *Letopis' rossiiskogo kino 1930–1945*, 580.

132. RGALI, f. 2062/1/332; GFF, f. 154.

133. "G. Aleksandrov 13 Aug. 1938 letter to I. Dunaevskii," RGALI, f. 2062/1/433.

134. H. Kolin, "Film-reviu," *Iskusstvo kino*, 4–5 (1938): 42; G. Aleksandrov, "Volga-Volga," *Moskovskii ekran*, No. 6 (1938): 10.

135. Kushnirov (182–83) points out the preoccupation of Soviet writers with modern-day fairy tales and the Stalin-children theme, which Aleksandrov apparently also considered.

136. See M. Turovskaia, "'Volga-Volga' i ee vremia," *Iskusstvo kino* (March 1998): 59–67; Maia Turovskaia, "'Volga-Volga' i ee vremia," *Kinovedcheskie zapiski*, 45(2000): 120–36.

137. *Show Boat* (1929, 1936, 1951), *Every Sunday* (1936), and *Summer Stock* (1950) are examples.

138. Altman, 306.
139. Karnick, 32.
140. RGALI, f. 1104/1/295.
141. Bulgakova, *Fabrika zhestov*, 256–57.
142. Karnick, 41.
143. Mikhail Bakhtin, *Problems of Dostoevsky's Poetics*. Trans. by R.W. Rotsel (Ann Arbor: Ardis, 1973) 100–07.
144. "Ivanushka-durachok," A. N. Afanas'ev, *Narodnye russkie skazki* (Moskva: OLMA-PRESS, 2004) 421.
145. V. Propp, *Morphology of the Folktale* (Austin: University of Texas Press, 1998) 25–65.
146. Hence Gaidai's criminal hero "Byvalyi."
147. See Katerina Clark, "Grigorii Aleksandrov's *Volga-Volga*," *Language and Revolution*, 219. Reprinted as "'Chtoby tak pet', dvadtsat' let uchit'sia nuzhno...': sluchai *Volgi-Volgi*," in *Sovetskoe bogatstvo. Stat'i o kul'ture, literature i kino*, 371–90.
148. Altman, 315.
149. Altman, 274.
150. Similarly, the Sevriuga, a rickety gift from America, competes against a more traditionally Russian raft and sailing vessel, the Lesorub. The quarrel between the two groups is resolved aboard the modern steamship, the *Iosif Stalin*, as if symbolically mediated by the Leader himself.
151. V. Podoroga, "'Golos vlasti' i 'pis'mo vlasti', in *Totalitarizm kak istoricheskii fenomen*, eds. A.A. Kara-Murza et al. (Moskva: Filosofskoe obshchestvo SSSR, 1989)108-11.
152. Clark, "Grigorii Aleksandrov's *Volga-Volga*," 227–32.
153. G. Sveshnikov, "Pesnia o rodine," *Sovetskii ekran*, No. 17 (1980): 15. Aleksandrov's student, Frolov, also notes that the director worked with Il'inskii to speed up his tempo in scenes such as Byvalov's jump into the cutter on the way to the Olimpiada (Frolov, *Grigorii Aleksandrov*, 96).
154. Aleksandrov may have seen more cartoons at the first Moscow international film festival, Feb. 27—Mar. 2, 1935, where Disney received third prize.
155. Susan Smith, 6.
156. See Robin La Pasha, "Snimaia komediiu. Muzykal'nye fil'my Aleksandrova i brat'ia Marks." *Kinovedcheskie zapiski*, 41 (1999): 232–36.
157. G. Aleksandrov, "Muzykal'nyi fil'm," *Kino* (Oct. 17, 1939).
158. "Stenogramma soveshchaniia v TsK VKP(b) pod predsedatel'stvom A. A. Zhdanova po voprosam khudozhestvennogo kinematografa."
159. Minchenok, 343.
160. RGALI, f. 2062/1/138, f. 2062/1/334.
161. I. Dunaevskii, "Kak sozdaetsia pesnia," *Pionerskaia pravda* (Sept. 9, 1955), reprinted in Isaak Dunaevskii, *Pesni*, introd. G. Golub (Moscow: Izdatel'stvo "Muzyka," 1983) 11.

162. Stenogramma, doklad Dunaevskogo v Muzykal'nom nauchno-issledovatel'skom institute (May 7, 1937).

163. N. Shafer, *Dunaevskii segodnia*, 40. Shafer also points out that Dunaevskii was able to work in various styles simultaneously: while writing for Utesov's jazz orchestra in the early thirties, he arranged "Ei, ukhnem" for the opera singer, B. Freidkov (38).

164. Stenogramma, doklad Dunaevskogo v Muzykal'nom nauchno-issledovatel'skom institute (May 7, 1937).

165. Dunaevskii, Mass, and Erdman had already exploited the comic potential of the Schubert piece in their 1932 production of *The Music Store* at the Leningrad music-hall. Under attack by RAPM, acknowledging the error of his (jazz) ways, Utesov sings satirical stanzas to the Schubert music.

166. Throb, golden smoke by the road,
Oh, you impossible youthful joy.
High as if the sky,
Wide as if an ocean,
Boundless path of youth.

What we dreamed of and wished for is coming true.
Our daring forces its way right up to the sun.
We'll wake up, wake up, wake up everyone,
We'll get everything, get it, get it.
Our joy is ripening like an ear of wheat.

167. I have used the early editions of the songs as published in *Moskovskii ekran*, No. 6 (1938): 2–3, 10–12. Lebedev-Kumach later added stanzas to many of the original lyrics. An April 21, 1938 contract gives Muzgiz exclusive publication rights to "Molodezhnaia," "Song of the Volga," and "Liricheskaia" ("Dorogoi shirokoi"), along with two songs from Pyr'ev's *The Rich Bride* with a print run of 50,000. Lebedev-Kumach was paid 4,000 rubles. (RGALI, f. 1104/1/7).

168. Cf. the first line of German and Khait's "Vse Vyshe": "My rozhdeny chtob skazku sdelat' byl'iu."

169. Many songs have sounded above the Volga,
But the melody of the songs was not right.
Before the song it was our melancholy that sang,
But now it is our joy that sings.
....
We've ripped open the grey clouds,
Spring has blossomed over our land.
....
We move both mountains and rivers,
The time of fairy tales has come to our waking hours.
....
Many songs have been sung about the Volga,
But they haven't yet made up one,
Warmed by the Soviet sun,
That would ring out over the Volga river.

170. And along the forever free Volga,
Ships sail into Moscow.
From Moscow to the gates of Stalingrad,
Like a great living hand,
The national Volga river
Salutes all nations as brothers.

An earlier variant is even more specific about the Volga's uniting function: "I ot radosti svetitsia Volga / Podruzhiv Stalingrad i Moskvu" ("The Volga shines with joy, / Having made Stalingrad friends with Moscow") (RGALI, f. 1104/2/7).

171. National Beauty,
Full-flowing like the sea,
Free like the motherland,
Broad,
Deep,
Strong!

In popular usage, the coda became a tongue-in-cheek allusion to female sexual physiology.

172. Let enemies, like hungry wolves,
Leave tracks at our borders.
They will not see the Volga beauty,
And they will not drink water from the Volga!

Orlova performed "Song of the Volga" at the front during the winter of 1943 at Stalingrad and gestured toward a line of passing German POWs as she sang the last stanza (Kushnirov, 179). Lebedev-Kumach's lyrics for "Boevye druz'ia" ("Combat Friends"), a military song intended for *Volga-Volga*, survive in the archives (RGALI, f. 2450/2/321).

Chapter 4

Svetlyi Put’

The Radiant Path

"Technology directed by people who have mastered technology, can and must work wonders."

– Joseph Stalin, May 4, 1935

"The pathos of the film is contained in the proverbial words of the song: 'We were born to make fairy tales come true.'"

– Grigorii Aleksandrov, *Epokha i kino*, 218

"In days of long ago, when there was almost none of the technology that surrounds us today, the Russian people composed fairy tales. Now, when we glance through these dreams, we often find that the people dream of flying on a magic carpet, dream of creating a magic spindle, a magic mirror, in which they could see everything that interests them, everything they want. In reality, we ourselves create this magic mirror. We turn this fairy tale idea into practical life; every evening we light this magic light in a modern mirror and the people see the facts, passing on the screen."

– Grigorii Aleksandrov, Nov. 16, 1939[1]

I. THE PERILS OF HEROIC COMEDY

Although each of the heroines of Aleksandrov's musical films—whether Aniuta, Marion Dixon, or Strelka—is in some respect a Cinderella type who escapes obscurity, poverty, or degradation to achieve fame, deserved recognition of her talent, personal happiness, and—beginning with *Circus*—political consciousness, this persistent paradigm emerges in its most literal form in Aleksandrov's last musical comedy, *The Radiant Path*. Tania Morozova, an uneducated country girl working as a servant and nanny in a provincial town, is fired by her bourgeois mistress for disparaging her employer to a handsome new arrival, engineer Lebedev. Party organizer Pronina takes Tania in hand (Fig. 42), sends her to literacy classes, and places her in a textile factory, where Tania gradually rises through the ranks to become a skilled weaver. After reading about Stakhanov's record, Tania devises a plan to operate a greater number of weaving machines, overcomes the factory director's opposition, and eventually sets a Stakhanovite record herself. She is awarded the Order of Lenin in a Kremlin ceremony and afterward, looking into a magic mirror, imagines her future as a people's deputy and Lebedev's partner.

Figure 42.

The Radiant Path takes place during 1930–35, from the end of collectivization to the beginning of the Stakhanovite movement, which evolved and flourished in a specific economic context. "In the years 1934–36, [Soviet] industry expanded very rapidly, drawing on the immense investments carried out during the first five-year plan. However, as early as 1934, it became clear that investment had not achieved the amounts provided for in the five-year plan, and that major projects would have to be delayed or canceled altogether, even in key branches of heavy industry."[2] In the second half of 1935, the investment plan for 1936 was increased, on Stalin's initiative and over the objections of Molotov and Gosplan, by as much as 50%. The planned increases assumed that labor and capital productivity would also increase.[3] It was in the context of this need for greater labor productivity that Ordzhonikidze, the commissar for heavy industry, having noticed the brief report of Stakhanov's record-breaking output of coal, printed on the last page of the September 1 issue of *Pravda*, ordered an enthusiastic publicity campaign about Stakhanov's achievement in the national newspapers. (This was apparently not Stalin's initiative.) A flood of records in other industries followed during September and October, among them the efforts of Evdokiia and Mariia Vinogradov at the Nogin textile mill in Vychuga. In different shifts, each worker had operated 94 and, a few days later, 100 automatic weaving machines.[4] The highly publicized First All-Union Conference of Stakhanovites was held November 14–17 and was attended by all members of the Politbiuro and 3,000 managers and Stakhanovites. "The reports of the proceedings became one of the main propaganda documents of the second half of the 1930s. Stalin, in his address to the conference, which was his first known reference to Stakhanovism, described the Stakhanov movement as 'fundamentally, profoundly revolutionary.'"[5]

However, even during the "Stakhanovite year" of 1936, the economic significance of the movement began to decline. Record-breaking workers complained in the press about supply and repair problems. After visiting her mill in November 1936, Evdokiia Vinogradova, by then a Promakademiia (Industrial Academy) student, learned that 20% of its weavers were not fulfilling their norms. High achievers were undermined by poor equipment maintenance, while the mill administration had begun listing workers achieving only 85–90% of planned production as Stakhanovites. Her former 216-machine complex had fallen into disrepair, with puddles on the floor and dirty machines.[6] Although publicity in the press continued, the effects of the Stakhanovite movement were negated by the 1937–38 purges in the industrial sector, overwhelming all economic planning. In subsequent years, Stakhanovism was deemphasized, but it remained one element in the effort to improve the operation of the economy."[7]

In his memoirs, Aleksandrov wrote that Tania Morozova's life trajectory was based on the achievements of Stakhanovite weavers Evdokiia and Mariia Vinogradov, and the script picks up many features associated with Stakhanovism.[8] In the language of the media, Stakhanovites as "new people" (*novye liudi*) went to the extreme, "breaking" established production norms: "It is these new people who broke (*slomali*), overturned a multitude of norms and coefficients, sanctified by the name of "science" in almost all branches of production."[9] In the film Aleksandrov concretizes the breaking metaphor. Looking straight at the audience, the factory director and his colleague ask, "So, will you order walls to be broken on account of her fantasy?" Responding, also in direct address, Pronina quotes Ordzhonikidze, "We'll break everything! We'll turn everything upside down and throw it out to the devil! We're going to break everything obsolete!" In the next frame, Lebedev and friends break through a factory wall to provide room for Tania's growing number of machines.

Vinogradova's innovation in achieving her records was the establishment of a strict walking pattern that eliminated return trips to troublesome machines: "Many people wonder...how one person works on 100 machines.... We have worked out an *exact route of movement.* One hundred machines have been set up four in a row. We walk in a coil pattern...going first to the front area of machines, then to the back.... We've calculated that we do 14 kilometers. We walk calmly, we don't hurry or fuss, we keep track of the machines. *If you don't keep to the route, you'll get confused.*"[10] Tania makes the same discovery one night: after reading the newspaper headlines about Stakhanovite records, with a shuttlecock she plots out a route among the machines, using boxes and a perfume bottle laid out on her bed. With the wind of inspiration in her hair, she runs to call Pronina to confirm that she is able to work on a greater number of machines, and then writes to the Sovnarkom about the possibility of moving from the standard eight machines to sixteen.

From the beginning, a strongly competitive spirit drove Stakhanovite achievements. At the 1935 conference of Stakhanovites, Mariia Vinogradova asserted: "If workers turn up who take 144 machines, then we will definitely go to 150. If anyone announces that she is going to 150, then we'll take 200. We won't give away our record to anyone!"[11] But the personal jealousies that accompanied record competition were soon nixed by officials. Individual ego satisfaction did not serve to raise overall production norms: "The person who gets angry because of the success of another comrade is not a Stakhanovite." Genuine socialist competition operates not on the basis of competitiveness but by help to other workers.[12] Tania is angry and resentful when it turns out that her new record has already been surpassed by another textile worker. It is the Party, in the guise of her mentor Pronina, who scolds her and ultimately motivates Tania to add her name to Pronina's congratulatory telegram.

Although the extent to which Stakhanovism was resisted by workers, engineers, managers, and factory directors has not been established, an official campaign against saboteurs and wreckers was launched almost simultaneously with news of Stakhanovite records in the autumn of 1935.[13] In early December, Chief Prosecutor Vyshinskii issued a circular defining terrorist acts against Stakhanovites, among which were: forcible acts in connection to the work of Stakhanovites, resulting in their death, and preparation for such actions; damage to machinery and tools in order to disrupt the work of Stakhanovites;

deliberate hindrance of the activity of Stakhanovites by official persons. Threats against and beating of Stakhanovites should also carry severe penalties.[14] In September 1935, Ordzhonikidze spoke out against administrative personnel, arguing that the significance of Stakhanovism was to demonstrate "how far behind life lag those pseudo-leaders who seek objective reasons to justify their bad work, their bad leadership."[15]

Given the conventions of musical comedy film, Tania's enemies in *The Radiant Path* are not particularly dangerous. Samokhin, the worker villain, who steals from the factory warehouse and then sets fire to it, turns out to be a former kulak, a criminal type who threatens the entire factory rather than Tania as Stakhanovite. Instead, her resistance to him demonstrates rather her new social consciousness as proletarian owner of the enterprise. The foreman Kurnakov, who is allied with the factory director in opposition to the new movement, gives apprentice Tania a defective machine which she is unable to operate, and later makes sure to give her the newspaper report of a Stakhanovite weaver who has bettered Tania's new record. As a Stakhanovite, Tania meets real resistance only from Dorokhov, the factory director, who calls her records absurd, thinks the enthusiasts will work for a short time and then abandon the pace, while he and Pronina will have to answer for not fulfilling the production plan. Dorokhov sets up a factory committee "trial" of Tania, but she is saved by an approving telegram from the Sovnarkom.

At the 1935 Conference of Stakhanovites, Evdokiia Vinogradova bragged about her pay: "If earlier I earned 180, 200, 270 rubles a month, now while working on 144 machines, my pay reaches 600 rubles. See how I've raised my earnings!"[16] Stakhanovites were rewarded for their achievements via two avenues. Factory administrations provided them with modern apartments and awarded prizes, such as motorcycles, bicycles, cars (rarely), phonographs, and other household goods. Their own high earnings also enabled Stakhanovites to purchase clothing and other consumer goods.[17] Aleksandrov conveys Tania's rewards in a visual metaphor: after her record feat, she is tossed in the air by fellow workers. In one toss, she flies up into the air, just under a portrait of Stalin on the factory wall, thereby metonymically linking him to her achievement. Various household goods are also propelled skyward, then fall to earth, as if showering Tania with gifts. In the following inserted musical number, Tania is shown moving to a new apartment. Her cart is loaded with clothing, an umbrella, a mirror, rugs, furniture, and a rubber plant as a sign of middle-class affluence.

Unlike the wives of Stakhanovites, who gloried in domestic life as an incentive to their husbands' productivity, female Stakhanovites rarely mentioned family. They were often single or, if married, childless, preferring to focus on career advancement.[18] In recognition of her achievements, Evdokiia Vinogradova received the Order of Lenin in January 1936. She studied at the Moscow Promakademiia during 1936–41. Vinogradova later served as a people's deputy and worked as director and deputy director of several factories.[19] Tania Morozova has no family ties: she is an orphan and will marry only after achieving her career ambitions; in fact, the latter is a pre-requisite for the former, since she believes marital partners must be equals. Tania too receives her Order of Lenin and will also serve as a deputy. But she outdoes most real-life Stakhanovites, who remained at a lower technical level, by becoming an engineer. As part of their research for the film, Aleksandrov, script author Ardov, and Orlova traveled to Vychuga to interview Evdokiia Vinogradova, who made a strong impression on them by her simplicity, good will toward others, and joyful consciousness of her own success. Aleksandrov recalled, "We met a genuinely happy person."[20]

In a 1971 interview, Orlova made a comment on Tania Morozova as her favorite film role that also casts Aleksandrov's making of *The Radiant Path* in a new light:

> In the figure of Tania, I wanted to express that confidence of the Soviet person in himself and in the future that defined the moral atmosphere of the first five-year plans. All of us were elated at a scale of national construction never before seen in the world. We all delighted in the thrilling destinies of such wonderful workers like the miner Aleksei Stakhanov, the steelworker Makar Mazai, the tractor driver Pasha Angelina, the pilot Valentina Grizodubova.[21]

Aleksandrov began working on *The Radiant Path* during the fall of 1938 in a changed country that had been battered by the purges and a cinema community whose creative freedom was eroding under stricter state supervision. By this time, the Stakhanovite movement had lost its momentum and had been largely marginalized. The government had lost confidence in Stakhanovite methods and, beginning in 1939, the progressive piece-rate system, which had brought Stakhanovites high pay, was curtailed.[22] For Aleksandrov, Tania's story may well have represented a nostalgic return to the simpler world of unalloyed optimism in which he had thrived during the mid-thirties. Stakhanovism was initially a spontaneous, grass-roots movement, motivated by enthusiasm for the goals of the early five-year plans. In fact, Evdokiia Vinogradova's first records were achieved four months before the September 1935 announcement of Stakhanov's feat, but had been kept secret by the factory administration. However, Kushnirov points out that the fall of 1939, when Aleksandrov began filming, still seemed a golden era for the country, even to sophisticated observers like Eisenstein who was buoyed by Zhukov's victory in Mongolia, the non-aggression pact with Germany, the incorporation of western Ukraine and western Belorussia into the USSR, the Fergana Valley project, and the opening of the VSKhV (The All-Union Agricultural Exhibition).[23] The paradoxes of the time were embodied in the delayed opening of the exhibition—the material apotheosis of national achievement—in August 1939, postponed from 1937 because of the arrests of its planners for wrecking activities.[24] Released in 1940, *The Radiant Path* may thus be seen as Aleksandrov's nostalgic tribute to the best, most idealistic aspects of the now more equivocal and uncertain world of "fairy tale come true."

*****

Sometime during 1938, the satirist Viktor Efimovich Ardov took Aleksandrov to see his new play *Zolushka* (*Cinderella*) at the Satire Theatre.[25] In spite of its title, Ardov's three-act comedy presented a more realistic, down-to-earth narrative than what Aleksandrov was to envision for his eponymous film. Nevertheless, Ardov's play provided Aleksandrov with the basic plot, characters, and a first title for his film: Nastia Kozhina, an orphaned peasant girl, works as nanny and servant for Anna Konstantinovna, the indolent wife of a technical expert sent to the provincial town of Kostrov. Nastia mispronounces words and irritates the guests at the modern hotel by her loud chastushka singing. She is pursued by the hotel manager Taldykin but pines for engineer Lebedev, who is interested in Agniia, an elegant Moscow actress. Party official Pronina takes Nastia in after she is fired by Anna Konstantinovna and gets her a job at the Nogin textile factory. From their dormitory window, Nastia and her co-workers see the factory warehouse burning. Pronina and Lebedev quarrel with factory director Dorokhov. In the park, Lebedev tries to kiss Nastia but is rebuffed, and Samokhin attacks Nastia, who is about to report him as an arsonist. Taldykin fights him, thinking that the former kulak is kissing Nastia, and has his cheek slashed, but Lebedev saves the day by subduing Samokhin. When a fellow worker falls ill, Nastia takes over her machines, in addition to her own, and writes a letter to the Kremlin about increasing productivity. An encouraging telegram arrives from the Sovnarkom, just as Dorokhov prepares to fire Nastia. Taldykin tries to stir up sympathy with his wound and continues to propose marriage to Nastia. Lebedev and the foreman quarrel over taking responsibility for Nastia's record-breaking work. The engineer has forgotten about his actress and is now openly interested in Nastia, though she seems out of reach. As a Stakhanovite, Nastia is invited to Moscow to receive a medal. At her luxurious hotel, she learns, from a friend's letter, that a worker at her factory has beaten her record and reacts angrily, for which she is scolded by Pronina, who has become factory director. Nastia receives a who's who questionnaire from a British firm, asking about her titles, servants, diamond jewelry, and villa, to which she gives comically proper socialist answers. Lebedev arrives and declares his love, despite interruptions from a photographer and others who phone Nastia at the hotel. The couple want to be alone and order dinner in Nastia's room. Instead of the waiter, a girl dishwasher, obviously fresh from the country, appears to take their order. Nastia takes down her name in order to place her in school, thereby beginning the story of another Cinderella.

Aleksandrov was so eager to film *Zolushka* that he submitted the actual text of Ardov's play as the script proposal in late summer 1938. His haste provoked a negative reaction from the studio reviewer, who criticized Ardov's lack of political consciousness in the depiction of a Stakhanovite worker, but also panned the structure, characterizations, and language of the play: "For a film script, Ardov's play lacks events. What might, with a stretch, be called a convention in a play, must be shown in a script, but it's hard to judge how the author intends to do this. Ardov's comedy is mediocre and vulgar. The idea of representing a girl-Stakhanovite in the guise of Cinderella is a snobbish scheme ('zateia barskaia')." He argues that Tania's transformation from a peasant hick to a cultured Stakhanovite in the course of the play is improbable and that Tania has no political consciousness. Furthermore, "the honorable engineer, the wrecker, the apathetic director, the partkom secretary—you don't even have to give these characters names, we're so accustomed to the clichés. The character of Taldykin, the failure and toady, is done much better than these clichés. Although he isn't a typical figure (nowadays toadies are more subtle), he's done in a fresh and interesting way.... In terms of plot, the play is constructed terribly schematically and abstractly. The conflicts are completely far-fetched. The author knows little about village life, very little about manufacturing and especially about political education work at factories. In terms of language, the comedy is mediocre and not funny.... In my opinion, we can sign a contract for a closed competition with Ardov only after a literary script has been submitted."[26]

Between fall 1938 and spring 1939, Ardov, working with Aleksandrov, produced three versions of the *Zolushka* script. Ardov acknowledged the help of two Mosfil'm consultants: "Trauberg and Gromov helped me very much and, as a matter of fact, they are co-authors, for which I express my thanks."[27] The first manuscript preserves the basic plot of the play while adding scenes with visual possibilities as well as performance opportunities for Orlova. The Moscow cigarette box, which will later dissolve to a real view, and various photographs with potential for motion to freeze frames, make their appearance. A photographer who now shares a hotel room with Lebedev drops the cigarette box that Tania retrieves because of its Moscow panorama. The same photographer snaps Tania at three different stages of her life to highlight her peasant, worker, and Stakhanovite personas. Taldykin uses an artfully folded photo of himself (as mess cook with oversized ladle) to present himself instead as warrior with bayonet. The factory club is introduced in this script, mostly for visual effect at this point. Seemingly ignored by Lebedev, Tania sees the club dancers as unattractive people dancing to bad music. After Lebedev stops to chat with her, she perceives a different club: "The hall has become much higher than it was, the out-of-tune wind orchestra has turned into a powerful symphonic orchestra that plays extremely well. And all the dancers are well-dressed and elegant."[28]

Tania's character is fleshed out by inserted scenes that provide Orlova additional performance opportunities. Tania now peels potatoes with comic efficiency and carries the samovar outside, blackening her face in the process. Petrov (later Kurnakov) trains Tania in a detailed work scene, but she fails after he assigns her a defective machine. She later dreams about setting a record by magical dream motions. In Moscow, Tania is impatient with a hairdresser accustomed to an elite clientele. The Kremlin episode has now been added, with Kalinin himself awarding Tania the medal. Lebedev's role has been expanded in the literary script: he and Tania carry goods from the burning warehouse, and he catches her in his arms as she drops from exhaustion.

The second version of the script enlarges upon the themes of the preceding text, particularly responding to the studio consultant's earlier criticisms of the play. Ardov's descriptions of the textile factory are much more concrete, and the second script contains a new comic scene in which Tania, when first hired, follows the mechanic around, wiping off the moving parts he has just oiled, thereby causing all the factory weaving machines to grind to a halt. Ardov's note in the text makes it clear that he visited a textile factory before writing the first script and wants to go again with Aleksandrov in order to fill out the details of this episode.[29] Taldykin's ongoing pursuit of Tania is expanded by another episode, most likely coming from Aleksandrov's bag of American tricks: Taldykin hands Tania a love letter and, while she reads, sets her trunk at the top of an icy slope. The trunk slides down; Taldykin tries to get it back, falls and smashes his nose against its side, while Tania watches with amusement. Lebedev's role in the fire scenes is reduced: Tania now carries boxes with Pronina. Tania's visit to Moscow is expanded: she is shown traveling by train to the capital, and two clothes-buying scenes (also satirizing frivolous ladies) have been added to the hairdresser episode. Documentary footage of the 1935 Stakhanovite conference is to be included, along with a telling addendum to the Kremlin award scene from Ardov: "Here the kinokhronika shots showing artist L. P. Orlova receiving her decoration should be used."[30] The finale now acquires additional scenes that duplicate the quintessential Aleksandrov ending in which the characters' world opens out into the larger Soviet world. After taking down the name of the illiterate dishwasher she intends to help, "Tania goes out onto the balcony, where Lebedev is already standing. Tania puts her arm around Lebedev. The music begins. They look at the city from the tenth floor balcony. Several shots of Moscow, as seen from the tenth floor of the hotel Moskva: the Kremlin, Historical Museum, US Embassy, Lenin Museum..."[31]

The third and final script is close to the plot of the film's final version, although Aleksandrov still has not worked out the process photography scenes and has not resolved the conclusion. In Pronina's room, Tania listens to the radio through earphones and hears singing from Moscow and abroad, "One motif drowns out another. Many voices sound. Someone is making a speech. Someone is reading sad poetry. Someone jokes and laughs. And all of it in different languages...the sounds of machines, steamship sirens, the buzzing of propellers, the cheep of the radio-telegraph all intertwine in an unusual symphony. It seems that the entire planet with its noises has flooded into Tania's consciousness." Inspired by the radio, she sees pale images of cities, seas, clouds, streets, animals, and people in the night sky.[32] In this script, Kurnakov's hostility toward Tania in the film is motivated by his making passes at her in the factory and at the club, always meeting with a firm rebuff. As yet, there is no New Year's celebration at the club. In the Kremlin, Tania asks her mirror reflection, "You were a country girl and where have you climbed to now?" The reflection makes a gesture denoting height. Tania responds, "Go on, we'll crawl even higher! I know you!" The mirror fogs over, then clears, revealing a country road on which Tania sets out, as it changes, first to cobblestones and then to a modern highway. Tania finally arrives at the Kremlin gates for the Stakhanovite conference. In a series of dissolves, she climbs staircases at the Pushkin Museum, Moscow University, and other major city sites. A series of signs records her progress from Promakademiia student to deputy of the Supreme Soviet. She then drives to the agricultural exhibition, gives a speech at the textile pavilion, and chats in French with foreign journalists and diplomats. Instead of Taldykin's burning hair gag in the film, Tania muzzles him by using her nimble weaver's fingers to tie his whiskers to his pointed beard. Tania and Lebedev then go outside to wander among the fountains, with a cut to an express train along the Moscow Sea, dissolving to a car driving to the small Grand-Hotel in Kostrov. Now married, they help a new Cinderella. The camera tracks back and tilts up to show a new factory building and hotel. The film ends with a bird's eye view of the Moscow-Volga canal and its locks, a highway, orchards, a column of tractors, and the white letters "The End" that dissolve into birds.

Aleksandrov's frequent comment during the period of his work with Ardov on the script was: "Davaite uvodit' v skazku." ("Let's take it into fairy tale.")[33] Judging by the early scripts, it becomes clear that the director's contribution was indeed the literal representation and extension of the fairy tale motifs implicit in Ardov's play, specifically the addition of dream and fantasy sequences: Tania's dream of reaching castle-Moscow with fairy godmother Pronina's help; the magic mirror conversation and flying car; the explicit fairy tale references of the lyrics. The fantasy world of the *skazka* meshes naturally with two of Aleksandrov's invariant stylistic traits—the Grand Style of the Stalin era, which he helped create, and the integration of western cinema's entertainment and glamour into Socialist Realism. The monumentalism and pomp of the Agricultural Exhibition scenes (large external reliefs, the imaginary textile pavilion with its rendering of the Palace of Soviets in the background, images of Mukhina's iconic *Factory Worker and Collective Farm Laborer*) embody the Grand Style, particularly in its strong architectural-sculptural emphasis. The New Year's carnival with its illuminated building, fireworks, costumed guests, and professional skaters borrows from the Hollywood ice extravaganzas made popular by Sonja Henie.[34]

In late April 1939, Ardov told *Vecherniaia Moskva* that *Zolushka* had been approved for production, adding yet another fairy tale referent: "For the umpteenth time we have a repetition of the great and enchanting Andersen fairy tale about the duckling that grows up and becomes a beautiful swan."[35] Three weeks later, Aleksandrov told the same newspaper that Igor' Il'inskii had been invited for a major role, along with Volodin, Mikhail Zharov, and Mariia Mironova (Byvalov's secretary in *Volga-Volga*). Filming was scheduled to begin at the end of June at Mosfil'm.[36] Dunaevskii and Lebedev-Kumach were again tapped to provide music and lyrics for the film.[37] The obligatory reading and discussion of the script with textile Stakhanovites and industry leaders took place on June 9.[38] The available documents and newspaper reports show that the script met with objections from various parties during the summer, and the beginning of filming was repeatedly postponed. Two issues, one relating to the ideological implications of the genre and the other to plot development, were preventing approval of the script by the Cinema Committee.

The years 1938–39 had been chaotic for the film industry. Boris Shumiatskii, arrested in January 1938, was replaced by NKVD official Semen Dukel'skii, who proved to be even more autocratic than his predecessor. In March, the film industry was placed under the control of the newly established Committee for Cinematography. Under Dukel'skii, administrative control of the creative process was tightened through both personal fiat and additional layers of bureaucracy in the script approval process. It became all but impossible to satisfy the different consultants and script section committee members, first at the studio and then at the Cinematography Committee levels. In addition, Dukel'skii himself could and did halt production, edit, and forbid the release of films.[39] I. G. Bol'shakov replaced Dukel'skii in the summer of 1939. In the thematic plan for 1939–40, he particularly noted the absence of comedy scripts and proposed a prize competition as a way to promote submissions.[40] With encouragement from a new administrator, the cinema establishment spoke up via articles and conferences. *Kino* noted that only two comedy films (*The Rich Bride* and *Volga-Volga*) had been released in 1938 and two so far in 1939 (*Devushka s kharakterom* [*A Strong-willed Girl*] and *Traktoristy* [*Tractor Drivers*]). In June 1939, the newspaper hosted a symposium on film comedy, publishing excerpts from speeches by Aleksandrov, Trauberg, Ardov, and others.[41]

In "Snaiperskoe iskusstvo," an article published a few weeks before the symposium, Aleksandrov had called for a conference on film comedy, which Bol'shakov did, in fact, organize in November 1939. Speaking at the conference, Aleksandrov defined the problem succinctly: "Many leaders—and this was during the time of the previous leadership of the Committee—are afraid 'that something [bad] might happen' because of a comedy, and so nothing does happen."[42] Like everyone else, Aleksandrov laid the blame on censorship at various intermediate administrative levels, without alluding to the role of the country's Chief Censor.

Comedy is potentially both the most popular and most subversive cinematic genre within any social system. Given the demand for comedies (and consequently, their profitability), the thirties saw a continuing debate over the goals and failures of Soviet comedy. The two issues were ideological content and satire. The 1939 comedy script competition defined the paradoxes of the first in its guidelines: Comedies must combine "comedic form with a high ideological-political standard. They should be cheerful and funny, and at the same time have serious content."[43] During the NEP years, the reliable satirical target had been *meshchanstvo* (a petty-bourgeois mentality). Satire became problematic in the heroic era of five-year plans: the number of permissible targets progressively decreased as the country approached socialism, and administrative *perestrakhovka* (playing it safe) had increased after the purges. If fairy tales had become reality, who or what was left to criticize? At the May 1941 filmmakers' meeting with Zhdanov, Aleksandrov complained about his experience with *The Radiant Path*:

> When we make up lists now of people, employees at whom you can and can't laugh in a comedy, few such people are left.... Not long ago, while making up such a list, I was asked about this. I declared that it was about followers of Pavlov. Then they tell me that I need to choose another figure. I say that it will be about a hypocrite. 'Of what profession?' [they asked.] I say, 'A [factory] director.' They reply that making a fool of a director is not permitted here, let's take someone else. Here's where the nitpicking begins. We were permitted a house manager in our comedy, but it turns out that I can't include him in the list of such personages either, since we have been raising and strengthening the authority of house managers recently, and you can't touch them now. Our comedies will be funny when people don't rummage around in the lists when characters are being selected.[44]... And besides, each of our pictures is regarded as bureaucratic instructions. If a picture is being made and a long sea voyage is shown, the film is shown to Comrade Dukel'skii. He says, 'How can you show my fleet that way and make fun of it—no.' And the film *Doctor Kaliuzhnyi*. Narkomzdrav wanted to forbid it because there was something there with the doctor.... I often want to show a chase in a film. For example, the chases are done wonderfully in American pictures: a car is speeding through town, it's being chased. But with us ORUD won't let me do it for love or money, and we'll never have chases in our films because ORUD considers this a traffic violation.[45]

After his experience with *The Radiant Path*, Aleksandrov complained, at the closed meeting with Zhdanov, about the consequences of fewer released films: "Every film is perceived as a performance by the entire cinema industry. When a film goes into production, they begin to load it up with all the tasks, all the questions that comedy should address in general. With us, each film is examined separately, rather than as one color or note in the overall composition of comedy as a whole."[46] Once again, directors were caught between a rock and a hard place: when serious satire is disallowed, writers fall back on silly behavior and light plots to make audiences laugh. Nevertheless, in a September 1940 speech, Zhdanov, following Stalin's increasingly conservative view of cinema, accused filmmakers of depicting the Soviet people as fools in such films as *Serdtsa chetyrekh* (*Hearts of Four*) and *Shumi-gorodok* (*Bustle-Town*), while simultaneously implying that serious satire was possible:

> After releasing a series of good film comedies (*Volga-Volga*, *Tractor Drivers*, *The Rich Bride*, *Circus*), film workers have not made a single significant comedy lately.... The incorrect view of comedy as a means of entertainment has become widespread among some filmmakers. Undemanding, clichéd gags take the place of profound content. Instead of ridiculing people's real defects and faults, the authors of comedies deliberately turn Soviet people into fools, put them in absurd situations, transforming film comedy into a light amusement, and the viewer's laughter—into an end in itself. Based as a rule on untruthful situations that are distant from life, comedies have no educational significance and consequently do not achieve their goal.[47]

In "Snaiperskoe iskusstvo," Aleksandrov had argued that western comedy based on social conflict was impossible in Russia because the Soviet hero was no longer at odds with his environment. Comedy now has a twofold purpose: to satirize the remnants of bourgeois morality afflicting Soviet society (e.g., envy, greed, flattery, hypocrisy) and, at the same time, to educate audiences by depicting new Soviet people—"brave, proud (in the good sense of the word), performing heroic deeds, possessing a sense of friendship... loving their homeland and devoted to the cause of Communism." A new form of comedy that combines elements of the parodic-eccentric and heroic is needed.[48]

The Radiant Path was clearly an attempt at such a hybrid form: the retrograde Taldykin is parodied and subjected to slapstick accidents; peasant Tania operates a comically mechanized kitchen; Stakhanovite Tania heroically achieves her record and eventually becomes a deputy of the Supreme Soviet. Yet the two lines could not blend in the way Aleksandrov suggested. The authorities considered the deeds of Stakhanovites and the dignity of deputies to the Supreme Soviet to be completely serious topics, too sacred to be profaned by eccentric comedy.

During the scriptwriting process, Ardov consistently characterized *Zolushka* as comedy. In contrast, Aleksandrov, ever attuned to the prevailing political winds, moved away from the genre designation in his public pronouncements, even to the point of paradox, given the fairy tale accent of the film: "In attempting to show the new Soviet person, naturally I cannot use the genre of eccentric comedy. *Zolushka* is a realistic genre film.... I can't call the film a comedy; it's more a melodramatic cinema tale. But this doesn't mean that the film should not be happy."[49] After the completion of *The Radiant Path*, in order to justify his blend of fairy tale and life, Aleksandrov wrote about searching for new forms, just as at the 1939 comedy conference: "In our work on the new film, we did not abandon our principles for constructing a jolly, cheerful film, filled with music and humor, but we tried to find new forms for the depiction of our reality."[50] Nowhere in this official *Izvestiia* statement did the director mention comedy. Finally, at the 1941 filmmaker's meeting with Zhdanov, Aleksandrov acknowledged that he had not been permitted to make a comedy: "Sometimes I think that this is my own fault, that I mechanically carry out instructions. For example, I announced that *Zolushka* would not be a comedy because it was impossible to do within the limits that were given to me.... I should not have given up on the comedy, until I got the terms I needed for making a comedy."[51]

After both the literary and director's scripts had been approved by the Cinematography Committee, and on the same day that Bol'shakov submitted the 1939–40 thematic plan to Molotov, the same Committee, in the person of A. U. Kur'ianov, one of Dukel'skii's NKVD protégés, demanded that Aleksandrov and Ardov drop the kulak villain Kurnosov-Samokhin from the script.[52] The Committee considered the arsonist-wrecker character politically undesirable, i.e., an anachronism in 1939, and judged the entire warehouse fire episode as superfluous to the narrative. Ardov defended himself tooth and nail: "In the script, Samokhin is not presented as a conscious class enemy or wrecker. This is a man who stands on the road to crime. It would be absurd to maintain that we have now rid ourselves of that sort of person. And besides, it happened in 1934. (The fire episode relates to precisely this time.)" Ardov regarded the warehouse fire as a necessary dramatic conflict that allowed the heroine to develop a strong character by overcoming serious obstacles. "The comedy genre forces us to deviate from life in this point." Here the mixed genre issue resurfaces. Ardov is arguing that comedy is not the most suitable vehicle for demonstrating heroic character development. The fire episode artfully allows Tania to overcome her peasant fear of the déclassé kulak and selflessly defend factory property: "I can't imagine it being possible to make and release the film if Tania loses her motive for speaking the monologue on the theme that she feels herself to be the mistress of the factory at which she works ("khoziaika fabriki"), the socialist mistress of all factory property. This is very essential. Without this episode we don't have a Stakhanovite, but rather a lucky worker who could also exist in the West, in capitalist conditions."[53]

Aleksandrov made similar arguments about character formation in his letter to Bol'shakov, while also insisting on the reality of enemies in the life histories of women Stakhanovites:

> Our group has worked a great deal on examining the factual materials related to the biographies of our famous women Stakhanovites. We have had conversations with Dusia [Evdokiia] Vinogradova, Tasia Odintsova, Podsobliaeva, Orlova, Shulandina, Ganabobleva, Klavdiia Sakharova, and others. All of these conversations, conducted in Ivanovo, Vychuga, and Moscow were recorded in shorthand, and in each biography of the above-mentioned women Stakhanovites, there occur figures resembling Samokhin.[54]

With their backs against the wall, Ardov and Aleksandrov politely threatened the Committee with delays that they knew would disrupt the annual production plan. If forced to make changes to the script, Ardov wrote that he required one and a half month's time, while Aleksandrov argued that any delay beyond August 15 would make filming impossible because of bad weather beginning in the fall, and production should then be postponed to the following year. Bol'shakov gave in and filming began on August 26, 1939. Orlova wrote that she had driven a car past the pavilions at the recently opened Agricultural Exhibition that day: "I myself was at the wheel. No casualties."[55]

During the next two weeks, Aleksandrov filmed at the exhibition: the Stalin monument, the fountains on Kolkhoz and Kolos squares, the Moscow pavilion, and the Georgian pavilion for the crowd scene of Tania's meeting with cotton pickers.[56] The outdoor scenes of Tania and Lebedev walking at the exhibition were shot September 7. Aleksandrov had scaffolding erected along the lower part of the Moscow pavilion in order to place the couple on a level with the life-size agricultural high-reliefs of the building, thereby foregrounding the equivalence between the living and sculptural figures. By mid-September, Aleksandrov had filmed Tania's arrival at the Kremlin. Many of these scenes were later cut from the film.[57]

Aleksandrov chose Zagorsk for his cinematic textile factory town because he initially intended to show not only its architectural monuments, but the neighboring narrow, dirty streets and lopsided houses, which are transformed into modern buildings in the course of the film[58] (Fig. 43). In late August, cameraman Boris Petrov filmed the aerial shots of the town for the opening titles of *Zolushka* from a dirigible.[59] During the fall, filming seems to have been halted, possibly because the general plan, including the sequence of episodes and set construction schedule, was not finalized until the following spring.

In December or January, Aleksandrov filmed an episode using a fellow director:

> Zolushka is setting a world record. While working, she runs out of bobbins. The factory warehouse must be opened. The storekeeper is sleeping among the bales of cotton. Zolushka's friends, the weavers, try to explain to him the meaning of what is occurring. But in vain. The lazy and inert storekeeper just can't reach an understanding with them. Afterwards, he took off the large moustache and shaggy eye-brows, and we recognized the well-known director, Vsevolod Illarionovich Pudovkin.[60]

According to Aleksandrov, this episode, in which the girls end up taking the bobbins without permission, was inspired by his own "breaking and entering" a Leningrad electrical store to get safety fuses needed for the filming of crowd scenes in the storming of the Winter Palace in Eisenstein's *October*. The studio administrators laughed at *The Radiant Path* episode with Pudovkin, but nevertheless insisted it be cut as modeling inappropriately high-handed behavior.[61]

Figure 43.

During the winter, the set for the girls' dormitory was constructed in the center of Mosfil'm's Studio One. Next to it was the interior of the workers' club and the Hotel Moskva (later cut). In February, Aleksandrov filmed Taldykin serenading Tania on a ladder and Tania tying knots on her roommates' possessions (and told Orlova to knot faster, since she would be observed by real weavers).[62] Commenting on these scenes, a journalist reflected on the serious side of making comedies:

> Volodin doesn't fall to the ground from a ladder near Tania's window, but onto a mattress. Nothing difficult, but one should add that, after performing the lover's serenade with a guitar on a ladder, Volodin fell onto the mattress fifteen times from a height of three meters. He must make us laugh, but it's not at all funny to him.... During the fight in the snow, his whiskers (glued on, of course) are torn off, but this was happening in 25 degrees of frost and repeated twenty times or so, and the whiskers were glued on pretty firmly...[63]

From late February through mid-March, Aleksandrov worked on the outside ice carnival episodes. A set from *Lenin in October* and *Minin and Pozharskii* was recycled for the workers' club, located in a former monastery. When a sudden thaw melted the snow on the set, the entire film crew pitched in to scatter New Year's tree spangles over roofs.[64] Aleksandrov used professional figure skaters (Granatkina, Nekrasova, Iakovlev, Tolmachev, and others) for the night skating scenes, which were lit by more than 100 projectors.[65]

Sometime during early 1940, Aleksandrov changed Tania's surname from the neutral "Kozhina" to "Morozova." Orlova later explained that the intention was to contrast the peasant Morozova to the pre-revolutionary merchant millionaire Morozovs, the long-time owners of textile mills in the Ivanovo region.[66]

True to her training with Stanislavsky, Orlova initially looked inward to her own experiences in conceptualizing the Tania Morozova character: "I also recalled many events preserved in my memory, but this was not enough, and I began collecting additional material. I visited several textile factories, went with the director and film crew to Ivanovo, the center of the textile industry, where I visited factory workshops, apartments, cafeterias, clubs—the locations where the life and work of our textile workers takes place."[67] For two hours daily, from December through February, Orlova studied at the Moscow Institute of Textile Industry with Stakhanovite Varvara Petrovna Orlova, learning technique and the specifics of different weaving machines.[68] The actress recalled the difficulties of learning to thread the shuttle ("potseluinyi chelnok") and to tie a weaver's knot with the required speed. While studying with Orlova, she once inhaled a length of thread so enthusiastically that it was only pulled out of her throat with difficulty.[69] Liubov' Orlova acquired finger dexterity by constantly practicing weaver's knots: "In my purse I always carried a skein of thread like other women carry knitting. I tied weaver's knots always and everywhere. At home I tied knots in the fringes of tablecloths, towels, and curtains."[70] After her course of instruction, Orlova passed the technical minimum exam and qualified as a weaver.[71] And again, the actress follows Stanislavsky in preparing her role: "I took notice of all my inner sensations and feelings. I noted how the first sensation of fear before the machine gradually, as I mastered it, turned into a keen feeling of interest, excitement, pride, and I collected all these fleeting, momentary sensations into a chain, link by link, in order to show them in the character of Tania Morozova."[72]

During the second half of March, the film crew traveled to the textile factories at Glukhovo, where Tania's record was filmed in part and Aleksandrov was able to use local workers in factory floor scenes.[73] In April, Aleksandrov was shooting the opening scenes of *Zolushka* at Mosfil'm—Tania's awakening and morning work routine. True to his instinct for entertainment, the director integrated a physical comedy routine (Tania's potato peeling) into her initial peasant persona, since this was incompatible with her later Stakhanovite image.

In February 1940, Aleksandrov complained publicly about administrative micromanagement: "The following question was under consideration for a long time: in the course of the action, how many changes of blouse should one of the characters in the film, party worker Pronina, make during ten years of her life? The director decided—ten blouses. The studio planners—three. After many months of discussion, the Committee approved—six."[74] The rooster in the opening scene of the film also proved to be a bureaucratic problem: "The property department said it was not a prop; it belongs to the actors' section. The actors' section was offended and said the rooster was not any of its business." It took Aleksandrov four days to convince the prop department to acknowledge the rooster as one of its own. A large bird was bought in a gastronom for 20 rubles.[75] On the appointed day, the rooster was brought to the studio by its trainer and caged together with a small but aggressive gamecock that, by its crowing, prompted the rooster-actor to cockadoodle on cue. The kitten to which Tania calls in the morning scene was pitched onto the set (repeatedly) by the head of the lighting crew, A. Dudarev. Because of difficulties with a smoke-producing device and the complexities of coordinating physical motion with the phonogram, Orlova was forced to rehearse Tania's lighting of the morning samovar some twenty times.[76]

Another journalist, recruited to Aleksandrov's American-style publicity campaign for the film, has left us a comic description of working with the baby in Tania's morning scenes: "...the youngest artist of the collective got bored with 'working.' He grabbed the edge of the carriage with his little hands and rose to his feet. He was on the verge of falling out. The director: 'Stop! Tie down the artist!' The eight-month-old actor was tied to the carriage with a bandage. Just as the crew was ready to film, the baby began to cry. People danced in front of him and brought toys—to no avail. Aleksandrov leaned over the carriage. 'The artist is damp," he said. 'Change his diaper.'"[77]

In technical terms, *The Radiant Path* was the most advanced film of its day, using cartoon graphics (the cranes at the beginning and end of the film) superimposed on landscape footage, rear projection and double exposures (Tania's dream), and double rear projection (the street panorama and Taldykin in the mirror) in Tania's moving scene. The flying automobile scenes used rear projection and, for the first time in Soviet cinema, the traveling matte method invented by Boris Gorbachev. The Molotov auto factory supplied an experimental model of the six-cylinder GAZ 11-40.[78] The car was mounted on a specially constructed half-sphere in order to provide a rocking motion against the background of the rear-projection screen and lifted in the air by ropes and cranes for the traveling matte shots. Tania's mirror duet scene was accomplished via rear projection with Orlova recorded singing along with her first recording of the song while hearing it over a telephone receiver. Tania's walk to receive her award in the Kremlin was filmed by placing Orlova on a specially constructed moving track.[79]

According to the studio, *Zolushka* was due to be completed July 28, 1940. Because the film had been approved without an initial general plan, Aleksandrov and his cameraman, Boris Petrov, while busy filming were unable to map out subsequent scenes with the composer and artist, and the Mosfil'm administration halted production from March 23 through April 3. In the Stakhanovite spirit of *Zolushka*, the film crew then promised to move up the completion deadline to July 1, while also making up 45 lost work days. The crew began parallel filming—outdoor scenes in good weather, with an indoor set held in reserve for inclement weather. Another headache was Soiuzmul'tfil'm's inability to supply 100 meters of animated footage before early July.[80] *Zolushka*'s rough footage was vetted by party and studio officials at a May 11 preliminary screening. The film was generally well-received, but some criticism interestingly pointed out Tania's somewhat hysterical personality.[81] The concluding textile pavilion episode was shot at the end of May against a huge panneau of Soviet peoples at the Agricultural Exhibition.[82] In June, Tania's record-setting scenes were completed at Mosfil'm.[83]

Aleksandrov had initially planned to film the award ceremony on location in the Kremlin's Georgievskii Hall, but after permission was refused, the episode was shot at Mosfil'm. Grigorii Belov, made up as Kalinin, presented Tania with the Order of Lenin medal. The scene merges Orlova with Morozova: in February 1939, Orlova had received the award from Kalinin, a biographical detail that helps explain Orlova's preference for the film. The *Zolushka* script describes the ceremony in detail: "M. I. Kalinin is walking, holding the medal in his right hand and the little box with documents in his left. Tania enters the frame. With his right hand, Kalinin places the medal in Tania's left hand, and then shakes her right hand, after which he gives her the box."[84] Sometime between August and September, Aleksandrov was told to remove the award scene, presumably because of the implicit ban on depicting the leadership in a frivolous, i.e., comedic genre. Aleksandrov reshot the episode (Tania now wears a light colored dress, instead of the earlier print).[85] The awarding of the medal is implicit in the movement of her shoulder and arm, and the exaggerated reflections of the gold medal on her face, but the leader is invisible.

Aleksandrov missed his Stakhanovite deadline, completing the flying car scenes, editing, and soundtrack only by July 19. The studio's artistic council met to discuss *Zolushka* on September 11, 1940 and readily passed the film, criticizing only Aleksandrov's focus on Tania, rather than showing the development of the Stakhanovite movement as a whole.[86] Aleksandrov responded that he had cut a failed episode called "Ulei" ("The Beehive") in which the girls, who are lying in trucks full of cotton, begin to sing, after which a buzzing is heard from the factory and town as many Stakhanovites begin to work. The

Cinema Committee's objections had also weakened Aleksandrov's intended treatment of the mirror symbolism in the film. After learning that her new record had already been surpassed, angry Tania breaks the mirror in her room with a flower pot. The Committee wanted the entire scene cut as inappropriate Stakhanovite behavior, but after prolonged negotiations with the director, agreed to have the damage take place off-screen.

Aleksandrov himself was surprisingly critical of the film: "Now when I compare my dreams with what ended up on the screen, I feel nauseous. It's true that when I forget about this, I feel happy about what did turn out right."[87] He himself was disgusted with the flying automobile episode, which had been ruined by the Cinema Committee's objections to his original plan: "The car simply dangles in the air, like, if you'll excuse me..." Tania was supposed to return from the Agricultural Exhibition in the car, with the cartoon birds from the beginning of the film following behind in formation. The cranes were then to turn into gliders piloted by women, who would perform the title song, "Vysoko, pod samoi tuchei" ("High up, right under a cloud"), thereby completing the envisioned metaphor of the title graphics, in which the young bird on its first flight struggles to keep up but in time becomes the leader and guide of a new generation of young. "Then this would have had a completely different political meaning.... They [the Cinematography Committee] considered this impracticable, strange, incomprehensible."[88] It is indicative of the times that neither Aleksandrov nor the artistic council, which included directors Romm, Raizman, and Dzigan, viewed the flying car phenomenon as strange or excessive in any way.

Stalin saw the film later in September, noted that it lacked the satirical charge of *Volga-Volga*, and, according to Aleksandrov, zeroed in on the title:

> ...a good film and...without a portrait of Comrade Stalin," he smiled with his eyes. "But I consider its title inappropriate. The old Perrault fairy tale (he knows that too, I thought) "Cinderella" was part of the past life, but here it's a question of the new man..." "But, Comrade Stalin," I allowed myself to interrupt, "the advertising for the film has already been prepared, not only the art, but the material too—matches, candy, perfume..." Stalin heard me out and, without changing his posture and intonation, as if my words hadn't been spoken, as if nothing had happened, continued: "The film needs a new title. I'll think about it today and tomorrow morning you'll get my suggestions." In the morning, a note in Stalin's hand with twelve titles for the film was delivered to the studio. I settled on "The Radiant Path."[89]

Stalin may have included "The Radiant Path" in his list because of its strong association, even before 1917, with revolutionary rhetoric—the radiant path to socialism. In 1915, the poet and revolutionary Semen Astrov published *Svetlyi put'. Liricheskie otryvki*, and in 1919, proletarian poet Nikolai Rybatskii published his first collection of verse *Na svetlyi put'*.[90] Stalin was not fully enthusiastic about the film. At a Kremlin reception, he told Aleksandrov, "We value you for your boldness, but you wanted to please us with this film. You wanted to please the authorities."[91] Aleksandrov's account of Stalin's "a good film and...without a portrait of Comrade Stalin" is probably fictional, since the original version of *The Radiant Path* showed Tania, after landing at the Agricultural Exhibition, driving her car under the arch of the Pavilion of Mechanization and then past Merkurov's gigantic statue of Stalin, before entering the fictional textile pavilion, in which stands yet another Stalin statue.[92]

The Radiant Path was approved by the Cinematography Committee on October 3.[93] The film premiered at the Pervyi Theatre on October 7 with the usual fanfare: before the screening, Dunaevskii conducted the Cinematography Committee orchestra in the waltz from the film; after the screening, the cast performed songs from *The Radiant Path* and participated in an open discussion with the audience.[94] *The Radiant Path* opened a few days later at the Khudozhestvennyi Theatre, where Aleksandrov and the film crew talked about their work on the film, and at the Udarnik, both of which also staged textile exhibitions on their premises. In Moscow, more than 500,000 people saw the film during

Figure 44.

the first nine days after release.[95] Although newspaper reviews were generally enthusiastic, *The Radiant Path* does not seem to have been as popular with audiences as Aleksandrov's previous films.[96] The official Central Committee Propaganda Division report once again reflects the suppression of satire, prompting directors' escape into light plots, as discussed earlier in this chapter: recent films display a "simplified representation of Soviet reality. Some film workers depict the life path of the Soviet person as an easy stroll; they foster a frivolous attitude toward life among Soviet viewers."[97] An appended review of *The Radiant Path* highlights the irresolvable tension between the genre practices of the musical and the demands of Socialist Realism for contemporary particularity: "The film lacks a depiction of the real labor life of workers at a Soviet enterprise. The film about Stakhanovite labor gives a superficial depiction of their work, the real and difficult struggle of the new against the old, the grandeur of the victory of the new.... Tania Morozova's path in life is presented as relatively easy. She achieves her records in a surprisingly simple way."[98] On March 15, 1941, Aleksandrov and Orlova received Stalin prizes, first degree, awarded for *Circus* and *Volga-Volga* but not for *The Radiant Path*.[99]

*****

Dunaevskii began working on the music for *The Radiant Path* in 1939 and "Zolushka's Song" ("V staroi skazke govoritsia" ["An old fairy tale tells"]) was completed September 24 of the same year.[100] He also began composing what he called the "Stakhanovite March" (later "Marsh Entuziastov ["The Enthusiasts' March"]) at the same time, but the work proceeded with uncharacteristic difficulty, leading Aleksandrov to complain to cinema administrators that the composer was sabotaging the film with his delays. In April 1940, Dunaevskii wrote Lidiia Smirnova that he just couldn't get the march right and was on the tenth version.[101] Elsewhere he complained: "I've been working on it for ten months. I have a superb refrain and a first theme that doesn't satisfy me. The bastards should be glad that I'm searching for something better, that I strive to produce high quality music. No, it's: 'Help! A disruption!' The bastards. All the same, I won't give it to them until I myself feel happy with my music."[102] Years later, Dunaevskii explained that the march was the first Soviet "hymn to labor," hence his struggle with the complexity of the task.[103] Lebedev-Kumach, who was initially ill and then participated as an officer and war correspondent in the 1939 western Ukraine-Belorussian campaign and the 1940 war with Finland, was unavailable to work on *The Radiant Path*. Mikhail Vol'pin composed the lyrics for "Vysoko pod samoi tuchei;" "The Enthusiasts' March" lyrics and the chastushki couplets were written by D'Aktil'.[104]

In 1939, the Council of People's Commissars had set the maximum pay to authors of film music at 15,000 rubles—what Dunaevskii had earned for *Circus* three years earlier. On November 13, 1939, the composer, who was at the height of his popularity and serving as a deputy to the Supreme Soviet, wrote to A. Kur'ianov, the head of GUPKhF, asking for more money and citing his reputation and extensive work on the film. Kur'ianov replied in a conciliatory fashion: compensation would be decided after the conclusion of the composer's work on the film.[105] On March 22, 1940, Mosfil'm formally contracted with Dunaevskii for payment to be decided after completion of *The Radiant Path* and approving reimbursement for hotel and piano rental expenses during his stays in Moscow. For his part, Dunaevskii was expected to deliver music on schedule.[106]

While *Circus* began with a visual-musical reference to *Happy Guys*, pointedly overlaid by the poster and music of the later film, the opening scenes of *The Radiant Path*, Tania's morning exercise guided by the radio announcer, conclude with the same march from *Happy Guys*, as if now reconnecting to the comedic tradition of the first Aleksandrov-Dunaevskii film. In keeping with Dunaevskii's views on the function of both repetition and variation in musicals, as well as the effect of the folk tradition on audiences, his music for *The Radiant Path* falls into two clusters: the lyric-comic Cinderella narrative with its fairy tale-folk accent, and the heroic theme of work and will arising from ideological paradigms. Dunaevskii stressed that the treatment was different from his preceding musicals in that he had not written Cinderella's song as the usual heroine's piece, but as a song *about* Cinderella. And "The Enthusiasts' March" denoted "the authors' attitude toward the events, the behind-the-screen expression of the happiness of our labor, will, and strength, that knows no limits."[107] Dunaevskii's statement thus goes some way toward explaining the completely over-the-top apotheosis of labor and Soviet achievement in the film.

For the Cinderella theme, Dunaevskii uses the same melody, but with differing iterations, in "Vysoko, pod samoi tuchei," "V staroi skazke govoritsia," and the chastushki in the girls' dormitory. The title song, "Vysoko, pod samoi tuchei," performed by Bol'shoi Theatre diva Elizaveta Antonova in operatic style, elevates the beginning and end of the film to the grandeur characteristic of High Stalinism. "V staroi skazke govoritsia" is sung in the slow, deliberate tempo of fairy tale narration, while the chastushki melody is slightly faster, with the strong, even beats of folk performance. The latter are sung with an accordion, balalaika, and guitar accompaniment that begins visually with two men Tania sees through the window, strumming and singing on the street. Aleksandrov's private joke was to include Dunaevskii himself (the shorter man) in this scene.

The lyrics of "Vysoko, pod samoi tuchei" and "V staroi skazke govoritsia" operate via metaphors from the folk universe—the natural world of crane migration and the Cinderella fairy tale. In "Vysoko, pod samoi tuchei," the young bird making her first flight is afraid: "Oi boius', boius' otstanu. Oi boius', ne dolechu!" ("Oh, I'm afraid, afraid I'll fall behind. Oh, I'm afraid I won't make it flying!"). The fear motif, which humanizes Tania, recurs throughout the film as she makes the different transitions to textile worker ("Oi boius', ne douchu!" ["Oh, I'm afraid I won't learn it all!"]), to Stakhanovite ("Oi boius', ne dokruchu!" ["Oh, I'm afraid I won't tie it all!"]), and the summarizing mirror duet episode that returns to the crane metaphor ("Oi boius, ustanu! Oi boius', ne dolechu!" ["Oh, I'm afraid I'll get tired! Oh, I'm afraid I won't make it flying!"]). The Cinderella song is a transformation tale in which Tania moves from servant to Stakhanovite and from hopelessness to success, while the narrative remakes the old fairy tale into Soviet reality: "Skazka-byl' u nas tvoritsia / I stanovitsia blednei / Starykh skazok nebylitsa / Pered byl'iu nashikh dnei." ("A fairy tale-true story is happening here, and the fantasy of old fairy tales pales before a true story of our time"). Aleksandrov had originally envisioned the title song, "Vysoko, pod samoi tuchei," as a parallel transformation tale in nature: "In the finale of the film, ten years later, a new generation of birds flies over a changed landscape, over socialist cities. Among them again are young birds making their first long-distance flight. The bird that was so anxious at the beginning of the film has become the leader of the flock. She has reached her intended goal and continues on her way. Now she, in turn, leads the growing young ones."[108] Dunaevskii introduces "V staroi skazke govoritsia" instrumentally as Lebedev tells Tania the Cinderella story at their first meeting, and then ties their romance implicitly to the fairy tale by accompanying Tania's flirtatious questioning of Lebedev about his name and profession with the same instrumental music.

Early in the film, Tania sings a version of the song comparing herself to Cinderella ("Ia kak Zolushka toskuiu" ["I'm sad like Cinderella"]) and doubting that her fairy godmother will ever arrive. At the high point of her success, after the Kremlin ceremony, she performs the full version of the song, the verbal charm of which survives in its humorous treatment of the paradigm of the Socialist Realist hero:

Ne volshebnitsa sedaia
Podavala ei sovet
I ne feia molodaia
A tovarishch srednikh let.

Podderzhala, podskazala,
Kak sud'bu svoiu naiti.
Zamarashka zashagala
Po shirokomu puti.[109]

I rabotala otlichno,
Kak Stakhanov nauchil.
I Kalinin samolichno
Orden Zolushke vruchil![110]

According to Dunaevskii, two categories of chastushki were originally planned for the film: "The Languor of Love" (for the girls' dorm scenes in the film) and "Tania's Growth," intended to show her professional progress toward Stakhanovite status.[111] The lyrics of the latter, originally with seven singers, largely expressed consumer envy of Stakhanovite rewards and were dropped: "Nu-uzh, plat'e sh'et Morozova! Sh'et puntsovo...Vasil'kovo…

Rozovo...Da na shee brosh'! Da na iubke klesh! Da eshche galosh troe!" ("You should see the dress Morozova is having made! A crimson one…a cornflower blue one…a pink one. And she has a brooch on her neck! And she has a flare to her skirt! And three pairs of galoshes!")[112] Only the chastushka for Tania's move to the new apartment was preserved (this group had a different, livelier melody) as a showcase number for Orlova that summarizes Tania's evolution: "Ekh, mamka by zhila moia! Mama, vstan'-ka! Eto Tan'ka! Eto-zh ia! Nezabitaia, Delovitaia, Znamenitaia. Von kak!" ("Gee, I wish my Mom was alive! Mama, get up! It's Tan'ka! It's me! Unintimidated, businesslike, famous. That's how it is!"

The dorm chastushki give each girl a kernel of personality, to be developed subsequently in the film. The gullible Marusia, who will be betrayed by the kulak-arsonist, sings: "Ne khodi ko mne, Nikita. / Ne volnui devich'iu krov'. Tvoe serdtse vrode sita, / V nem ne derzhitsia liubov'" ("Don't visit me, Nikita. Don't stir a girl's blood. Your heart is like a sieve, it doesn't hold love"). The plain Varia is often alone: "Ne davaite interesnym / Vashi ruki pozhimat'. / Interesnye ne mogut / Nashi muki ponimat'" ("Don't let attractive men press your hands. The attractive ones can't understand our torments"). Frivolous, flirtatious Klasha sings: "Mazhu guby ochen' gusto / I vyshchipyvaiu brov'. / Okh, i khlopotnoe chuvstvo / Eta samaia liubov'!" ("I put on a lot of lipstick and pluck my eyebrows. Oh, what a troublesome feeling—this love is!"). Tania shows the determination that will define her in future: "Nichego, chto on smeetsia / Pravo slovo nichego! Serdtse b'etsia, b'etsia, b'etsia / I dob'etsia svoego!" ("It doesn't matter that he laughs. Really, a word is okay! The heart beats, and beats and beats / And will get what it wants!").[113] In *The Radiant Path*, romance is always contingent upon successful production: as Tania sings the last two lines, she holds her textile worker's manual up to her face, and she will later repeat the same lines when she is inspired to work on sixteen machines. Taldykin's serenade-chastushki introduce his role as Lebedev's comic rival in the romantic triangle of the film: "Ia ne p'iushchii i ne b'iushchii / Sushchii angel vo ploti. / Eto promakh vopiiushchii / Za takogo ne poiti" (I'm not a drinker or a beater, I'm a regular angel in the flesh. It's a flagrant blunder not to marry someone like that").

The second, heroic thematic cluster of *The Radiant Path* music develops in two closely related lines—the themes of Tania's will and the pathos of labor.[114] A two-note rising horn motif characterizes Tania's will to achieve, sounding each time she faces a challenge: at the beginning of her dream with the silhouette of Moscow; when she first enters the factory with Pronina; as Samokhin runs past her on his way to set fire to the warehouse (she will fearlessly capture him); as she reads the newspaper headlines about the Stakhanovite movement and is inspired to take on 16 machines; as she is about to begin her record-setting shift; and finally, just before she climbs to the dais to give a speech at the Agricultural Exhibition. The labor theme is elaborated in "The Enthusiasts' March," the second central song of the film, which Dunaevskii weaves into the narrative, gradually increasing its presence, while avoiding monotony by introducing new lyrics appropriate to the action, culminating in Tania's recitation and song at the textile pavilion. "The Enthusiasts' March" first plays instrumentally in Tania's dream as Pronina leads her toward Moscow, and the related, contiguous motif of will is then gradually submerged in the rhythm of weaving machines as Tania enters the factory. Once Tania becomes a qualified worker—and one with the machines—the direction reverses: in the record-setting scene, the machines' steady mechanical rhythm precedes Tania's vocal performance in march tempo:

> Nam li stoiat' na meste?
> V svoikh derzaniiakh vsegda my pravy.
> Trud nash est' delo chesti,
> Est' podvig doblesti i podvig slavy.
>
> K stanku li ty skloniaesh'sia,
> V skalu li ty vrubaeshsia—
> Mechta prekrasnaia, eshche ne iasnaia,
> Uzhe zovet tebia vpered.[115]

The song builds momentum as a choir picks up the refrain: "Nam net pregrad, ni v more, ni na sushe, / Nam ne strashny ni l'dy, ni oblaka. / Plamia dushi svoei, znamia strany svoei / My pronesem cherez miry i veka" ("For us there are no barriers, either on sea or land, / Neither ice nor clouds terrify us. / Through worlds and ages we'll bear / The flame of our souls, the banner of our country"). Tania's success is marked by a grand instrumental ending accented by kettledrums as she stands by the factory window at dawn, after completing her record, wiping her brow and inhaling the fresh morning air. In Tania's tour of the country during the flying car episode, she sings an earlier version of the lyrics: "Zdravstvui, strana geroev, / Strana mechtatelei, strana uchenykh! Pesen veselym roem / Ty perepolnila serdtsa millionov."[116] Dunaevskii expresses Tania's ecstasy after the Kremlin experience by altering the melody of the last line and adopting operatic style at this point, in contrast to the more subdued tone of the stanza ending elsewhere. As Tania steers the car toward the Agricultural Exhibition and drives past the Mukhina sculpture, she sings lyrics that exist only in the film but are more appropriate to the cinematic narrative than what became the canonical printed text:

> Vse to, chto bylo pesnei,
> O chem my grezili i chto liubili,
> Stalo eshche chudesnei,
> Zhivoi segodniashnei sovetskoi byl'iu.

I net strany krasivee,
I net strany schastlivee,
Tsveti, liubimaia, neobozrimaia,
Nesokrushimaia moia![117]

Once again the chorus performs the refrain. Finally, at the textile pavilion, Tania, instead of making a speech, first declaims the last stanza of the march:

Sozdan nash mir na slavu,
Za gody sdelany dela stoletii.
...I zvezdy nashi alye
Sverkaiut nebyvalye
Nad vsemi stranami, nad okeanami
Osushchestvlennoiu mechtoi.[118]

Tania then breaks into song, performing the refrain, with the chorus echoing her every line, and culminating in a grand orchestral finale. Unlike *Volga-Volga* and the earlier musicals, Dunaevskii moves away from purely diegetic singing in *The Radiant Path*, introducing an unseen large chorus in order to magnify the sense of grandeur and spectacle.

Given the production theme of *The Radiant Path*, the lyrics of "The Enthusiasts' March" have a narrower thematic focus as in the "Nam li stoiat' na meste?" stanza. However, like "Song of the Motherland" and "Song of the Volga," the lyrics of the march operate via a dialectic of largeness with unity, whether referencing geographic space or cultural markers. "Largeness" may be present in boundless physical expanses or hyperbolic maximalism: "I *net strany krasivee*, / I *net strany schastlivee*, / Tsveti, liubimaia, *neobozrimaia*"; "*Za gody sdelany dela stoletii*...I zvezdy...sverkaiut *nebyvalye* / Nad *vsemi* stranami, nad okeanami." Physical and emotional opposites are unified, as well as space and time: "*Vse* to, chto *bylo* pesnei, / O chem my *grezili*...Stalo eshche *chudesnei*, / *Zhivoi segodniashnei* sovetskoi *byl'iu*"; "Nam net pregrad *ni more ni na sushe*, / Nam ne strashny, *ni l'dy ni oblaka*. *Plamia dushi svoei, znamia strany svoei* / My pronesem *cherez miry i veka*." The defense of national boundaries, as in *Circus* and *Volga-Volga* ("No surovo my brovi nasupim / Esli vrag zakhochet nas slomat'"; "Ne vidat' im krasavitsy Volgi / I ne pit' im iz Volgi vody"), is not even an issue in this apotheosis of national might, for the country is now portrayed as invincible: "Tsveti... *nesokrushimaia* moia!" The pathos and pomp of "The Enthusiasts' March" reaches a ridiculous extreme at its culmination in Tania's speech at the textile pavilion. Perhaps for this reason, even though both *Circus* and *Volga-Volga* concluded with their central ideological songs, Dunaevskii chose to end *The Radiant Path* with the lyrical and more restrained "Vysoko, pod samoi tuchei."[119]

The third melody in *The Radiant Path* is a waltz, which first plays during the New Year's celebration (the arrival of club revelers, the ice skaters' performance, Lebedev's pursuit of Tania, including their awkward dancing), and drives the festive, joyful tone of these scenes. The waltz then recurs twice, making a point about Tania's life experiences through the musical dramaturgy. After the Kremlin ceremony, Tania dances exultantly around the room to the same melody. (At the New Year's celebration she did not yet know how to dance.)[120] In the later flying car episode, her good fairy double sings, "Tania, Tania, pogliadite. / Vse dorogi, vse prostory vam otkryty" ("Tania, Tania, take a look. All roads, all expanses are open to you") to the opening phrase of the same waltz melody. In this way, the composer unites Tania's public and private tasks musically—the making of a Stakhanovite and the making of the couple—and locates both in a higher fairy tale reality.

The New Year's celebration was filmed during March 1940, so it is possible that Dunaevskii's dancing waltz was influenced by the music of Julien Duvivier's *The Great Waltz* (1938), which had reached Russia by late 1939 or early 1940.[121] The fictionalized version of Johann Strauss the younger's life had a useful radical political tinge: the composer is portrayed as an adherent of the 1848 revolution, writing a march for demonstrators demanding a constitution, free speech, and free press, and participating in a clash with the emperor's guard. The film, which sparkles with Dimitri Tiomkin's arrangements of Strauss waltzes, lyrics by Oscar Hammerstein and performances by émigré opera singer Miliza Korjus, soon became Stalin's favorite foreign work, which he ordered released to the general public in June 1940. Aleksandrov recalled that in 1939, planned awards to directors in honor of the twentieth anniversary of Soviet cinema the following year were vetoed by Stalin, who made invidious comparisons to *The Great Waltz*: "The thoroughly discussed lists of awardees had already been printed up. All that remained was to get Stalin's signature. And it was here…that something unexpected occurred: taking his famous pipe out of his mouth, Stalin took up a pencil and with a sweeping gesture, pressing down with the pencil, crossed out the entire list with two heavy lines. It was not customary to ask the Leader about anything, but here he himself answered the unasked question: 'When they learn how to make films like *The Great Waltz*, then we'll give them awards. For now, it's early.'"[122]

In a July 1940 article, Dunaevskii, in response to Stalin's wish for a Russian version of *The Great Waltz*, addressed the immense popularity of the American film and proposed an alternative: Why has *The Great Waltz* turned all our heads? Not because of Strauss's life story, but because of his music. "Strauss's waltzes live to the present, striking us by their inexhaustible optimism, their life-affirming qualities.... What can we in Soviet cinema counterpose to *The Great Waltz* in the area of musical genres? What do we have at our disposal, what riches do we have that the people love, with which they live, work, conquer, go to their death in battle?... The riches that we have and of which we can rightly be proud—are the song, our resplendent folk song, our golden Soviet song fund.

A song may become the basis for the creation of a great Soviet film, and this film will be a hymn to the song."[123] Dunaevskii never pursued the project, but the Russian alternative to *The Great Waltz* that he proposed was consistent with his musical strategy since the time of *Happy Guys*: to be remembered and sung outside the movie theatre, film music must be based on the Russian folk tradition.

II. PEASANT'S PROGRESS

The storyline of *The Radiant Path* plays out in three different stylistic registers. In the first of these, Tania's peasant persona and interactions early in the film are conveyed via genre comedy of the American type. Pronina jokingly dubs Tania "kurnosaia" (snub-nosed), which initially links her to fellow villager Samokhin, whose real name is Kurnosov, and both speak with a provincial "khe-khe" to express knowing awareness. Tania inadvertently blackens herself with soot, thereby suggesting the "darkness" of country people. Her encounter with Lebedev at the New Year's ball is comic rather than romantic. The second segment, the Stakhanovite plot, which begins with Tania's reading the newspaper and sketching out her own idea for increasing productivity and culminates in the Kremlin award ceremony, is largely serious, focusing on the drama and pathos of industrial production. The final section, which outlines Tania's future, moves into a fairy tale-mythic register, accompanied by the grand style initiated with the Kremlin scenes. The vision of Tania's future corresponds to the dream sequence of 1940s American musicals which became an alternative to the conventional final production number.[124] In characteristic fashion, Aleksandrov refuses to eliminate comedy altogether from the last two serious sections, instead retaining Taldykin and his farcical pursuit of Tania, which throughout the film is beset by physical mishaps—falling into a manhole, a surprise shampoo and styling by a street cleaning machine, hair set ablaze by a photographer's flash.

As a folk musical, *The Radiant Path* is concerned with doing the country's work, which is paralleled by the making of a couple. Tania's life path as a Stakhanovite benefits the Soviet community as she contributes to economic progress. Her achievements, first as a Stakhanovite, then as an engineer and people's deputy, make her increasingly attractive to engineer Lebedev until, in the final scenes of the film, her triumphant appearance at the textile pavilion is followed by the union with Lebedev. While the American folk musical is often characterized by nostalgia for an ideal time in the 19th century past, as in *Meet Me in St. Louis* or *Oklahoma!*, *The Radiant Path* focuses on a more recent—but also idealized—past: the early years of the first five-year plan.

In spite of its genre mix of comedy, drama, and fairy tale, *The Radiant Path* maintains the musical's traditional hierarchy of image-sound reversal at climactic moments. Peasant Tania sings into a mirror as she contemplates her future. She sings as she sets her production record and as she moves to a new apartment. She sings into the mirror after the Kremlin award ceremony and breaks into song in the middle of her speech at the textile pavilion. Aleksandrov's attention to the musical's conventional dual focus narrative (giving equal time to male and female heroes), began to erode with Orlova's growing stardom after *Happy Guys* and is all but absent from *The Radiant Path*. Although initially, the male and female heroes have radically divergent values (peasant vs. urban professional), they must be reconciled in the end, and they are, but only because Tania, not Lebedev, undergoes a change. Lebedev, the male lead, is hardly prominent and shows little development over five years. In his review of *The Radiant Path*, director Grigorii Roshal' likened Evgenii Samoilov's role to that of the male ballet dancer whose only task is to adroitly hold his female partner aloft at the proper moment.[125] The film does, however, maintain a traditional romantic triangle of serious and comic male lovers playing opposite the female heroine and, just as Kostia and Aniuta's kiss is interrupted by a comic character in *Happy Guys*, Taldykin conveniently interrupts Tania and Lebedev at the crucial moment—conveniently because this old comic device supports the era's ban on kissing after *Volga-Volga*. Aleksandrov also recycles previous character types: Tania shares the cleverness, energy, and peasant ways of Aniuta in *Happy Guys*; Tania's first employer, Anna Konstantinovna, the indolent wife of a technical specialist, resembles the "Nepmansha" of the same film; the factory director with his sycophantic secretary are diluted versions of Byvalov and his secretary from *Volga-Volga*.

In its comedic devices, *The Radiant Path* returns to the style of *Happy Guys*, but it lacks the earlier film's preoccupation with verbal humor. Peasant Tania and Taldykin are developed via comedic incongruity and physical humor. Tania works in the Small Grand Hotel and her morning exercises, so familiar to Soviet listeners from Radio Moscow, turn out to be rhythmically performed chores. Using the *Happy Guys* march as broadcast over the radio in part of the episode, Aleksandrov and Dunaevskii foreground their own national popularity. Physical humor abounds: Tania grimaces at the smell of a rotten potato, then throws it so that the observing baby and kitten must duck; Lebedev laughs at Tania's soot-smeared face; Taldykin makes a pass at Tania, which develops into farcical reciprocal hand-slapping in the style of the Marx Brothers. In screwball comedy, sexual attraction is displaced into violence. At the New Year's celebration, Tania reacts blissfully to Lebedev's sudden kiss, but then shoves him into a snowdrift. Just before this scene we are shown skaters gliding and pirouetting gracefully on the ice, but at this point in the narrative, Tania and Lebedev have not yet learned how to "skate together." In the dormitory, Tania and Taldykin follow the flight of a giant bumblebee, which she swats, knocking Taldykin down a ladder—an episode borrowed from American cartoons. Trailing Tania to her new apartment, Taldykin falls into a manhole, above which a passing street cleaning machine brushes his hair straight up, followed by a shampoo from a water truck. At the textile pavilion, Taldykin steps in front of a photographer's magnesium flash and has his hair set ablaze. An extended gag demonstrates Tania's native talents as she prepares potatoes, shoving peels to the left with a knife, while simultaneously raising the pot lid on a string with her foot and pushing the potatoes to the right, straight into the pot, all without looking (Fig. 45). Her mechanical kitchen gag is borrowed from early silent comedians, such as Harold Lloyd, who prepares meals by pulling levers that manipulate the food in *The Chef* (1919), and Buster Keaton in *The Scarecrow* (1920), who has an automated kitchen with plates nailed to the table for easy spray washing and lifting to the wall, a condiment trolley that runs the length of his table, and a napkin on a retracting string.

Aleksandrov uses interpenetration of action humor (the audience is aware of the real state of affairs, while characters misinterpret it) when Taldykin attacks Tania and Samokhin, who is choking her, thinking that they are embracing. Lebedev has the repetitive—and therefore comic—verbal tag "Khm?" expressing puzzlement (in response to the conversation with Tania about Christmas gifts for children and as a reaction to her refusal to hug him, as she does other co-workers, after achieving her record), which is reversed at the end of the film, when Tania reacts with a "Khm?" after Lebedev is unable to explain his late arrival at the textile pavilion.

A new device used several times in *The Radiant Path* is physical-verbal contradiction: Tania is happy but crying because Lebedev has kissed her at the New Year's ball; after receiving the Sovnarkom telegram approving her Stakhanovite project, Tania cries while affirming, "Ia smeius'" (I'm laughing). At the conclusion of the film, Taldykin gives up his pursuit of Tania after seeing her with Lebedev:

> —So now you won't marry? ["me" is implicit here, but elided]
>
> —I will, I'm so happy. (Tania kisses Taldykin on the cheeks.)
>
> —It's all clear now, she doesn't love me!

As one would expect, the cinematography of *The Radiant Path* differs in each of its three narrative segments. In part one (Tania as peasant), camera work is frontal with only one close-up (Tania's imagining herself studying). Process shots are limited to Tania's dream of Moscow and her arrival at the factory. In the second section (Tania as Stakhanovite), there are two extended close-ups of her at triumphal moments (the arrival of the Sovnarkom telegram and news of the Order of Lenin). Lighting is generally stronger, especially in the record setting episode and the close-ups, and the tempo is faster, in accord with and highlighting Tania's achievements. The third section, beginning with Tania's Kremlin award, employs fairy tale motifs and the Grand Style, which use a large number of process shots and a slower, statelier tempo in the concluding scenes.

As a student of Eisenstein, Aleksandrov devoted special attention to editing.[126] While *Volga-Volga* is characterized by conventional classical cutting, *The Radiant Path* returns to the foregrounded match cuts of *Circus*. Like the earlier film, *The Radiant Path* has

Figure 45.

several sound bridges. In Tania's school, a dinosaur model's roar is ironically connected to Anna Konstantinovna's wailing baby at the hotel. In a more effective word-sound bridge, Pronina's Stakhanovite "We will break everything" speech and fist banging down on the photographs of Tania and other workers is followed by the sight and sounds of a breaking wall as Lebedev and co-workers create space for Tania's multiplying machines. A match on movement connects Tania's record to the Stakhanovite reward—her move to a new apartment in the next scene: co-workers first toss Tania in the air, then gifts of household goods are thrown upward and fall into a moving wagon, in which she sits, thereby providing the transition to the next scene. Most frequent, however, is editing for image matches as bridges to location changes. A candle in Tania's dorm room morphs into a burning torch at the warehouse fire. As Tania chases pigeons away from her factory window, they reappear on her dormitory window in the following scene. The dial of the factory director's home telephone becomes the face of the factory clock as the camera switches location. In the moving episode, Tania's umbrella with a tractor pattern establishes the bridge to the same fabric in the director's office. Tania's profile in a factory poster becomes her profile in a mirror. The Kremlin postcard pasted into Tania's trunk dissolves into the actual scene as Tania travels to Moscow. A Kremlin tower clock is matched in the face of Tania's wristwatch as the scene moves indoors. Finally, a series of related images marks the passage of Tania's time at the factory in an extended sequence: the cotton fluff she sweeps up on the factory floor gradually changes into snowflakes, which turn into rain, and then into shower water for the girls at the end of their shifts. In true Hollywood style, Aleksandrov provides a voyeuristic moment by making the girls appear to be nude behind the shower enclosure. But, upon closer inspection, it is obvious that they have been made to shower in their underwear![127]

Of all the Aleksandrov musical comedy films, *The Radiant Path* displays the fullest encoding of socialist values. Tania's life story both follows the evolution of the Socialist Realist heroine from spontaneity to consciousness and also metonymically models State policy—the transformation of the peasantry after collectivization into an urban working class. The film illustrates paradigmatically the central socio-cultural values inherent to High Stalinism: a reorientation from the horizontal and fraternal social relations of the 1920s–early 30s to a vertical hierarchy and the concomitant philosophical shift from egalitarian positivism to a more elitist form of mystical idealism.[128] The film's single-minded exploitation of folklore and fairy tale motifs comes out of a second aspect of High Stalinism, the drive toward transcendence, expressed in a hyperbolic register and via convergence between the fictional and the real. "We were born to make fairy tales come true," the opening line of German and Khait's "Aviamarsh" (1920), became the byword of the 1930s, when the fairy tale metaphor was widely applied to Soviet life in the press: in the early thirties the Volga improvement project is described in a newspaper headline as "Not a Fairy Tale, but Life."[129] Fictional and real converge as Aleksandrov claims that the life of a Stakhanovite has overtaken fairy tale: "In the film *Zolushka*, we want to show the Soviet viewer how real life surpasses fairy tale fantasies. Life turns out to be more powerful and more interesting than a fairy tale."[130] The description of the extraordinary New (Wo)man demanded extraordinary forms—the supernatural, fantastic, and archetypal images of folklore and fairy tale. At the same time, the incorporation of folklore into the practice of Socialist Realism furthered the legitimization of Soviet power as from and by the people through continuity with established popular tradition.[131]

In *The Radiant Path*, Aleksandrov draws upon literary fairy tales such as *Cinderella* and the central folkloric archetype of weaving, as well as various fairy tale motifs, such as the magic mirror, flying carpet, and magic kingdom, to encode the dominant Socialist

Realist narrative. The very familiarity of the folkloric and fairy tale motifs in *The Radiant Path* provided a recognizable, comfortable vehicle for conveying the ideological message to both peasant and urban proletarian and professional audiences (vydvizhentsy), who were often only one generation removed from the countryside. The imagination of the new urban population with peasant origins thus remained folkloric.[132] An advertising brochure for the film highlighted this message as the fulfillment of popular hopes, historically embodied in fairy tales: "If we compare the facts of our reality with the fairy tale dreaming of the past, it turns out that our present is, in fact, the realization of the people's aspirations and strivings."[133] The fairy tale form also allowed Aleksandrov to elide psychological motivation and character development, always a problematic area for Socialist Realism. The same holds true of dramatic motivation: the film dwells more on Tania's rise to success than any real obstacles on her path. Finally, the fantasy aspect of the fairy tale allowed the director to indulge his love of spectacle by inserting Hollywood-type glamour and magnificence into the narrative.

In the introductory cartoon graphics of *The Radiant Path,* the flock of cranes diagonally intersects the frame, followed by the bird that struggles to keep up with the group. The same bird reappears during the flying car episode, and the final credits show the entire flock traveling in perfect formation. By using cartoon graphics, Aleksandrov marked the cranes as fictional, possibly even imitating Disney's fairy tale cartoons and the full length *Snow White and the Seven Dwarfs* (1937), while envisioning the following specifics: "Migratory birds fly high over the earth. Among them is a young bird, making its first distance flight. It worries and flaps its wings more than necessary. It's afraid of the unknown, but nevertheless flies toward it.... The [other] birds comfort it, advise it to stay close to the flock and follow the wise lead bird." Years later, the same novice crane is in charge of a new generation. "It had reached its intended goal and continues on its path. Now it, in turn, leads the growing younger generation."[134] In Russian folkloric tradition, the crane is a familiar and beloved totemic bird, associated with the coming of spring and with hope and renewal. Consequently, Aleksandrov's metaphorical representation of Tania as a young crane and her life path from novice to leader as part of the natural order of things would have resonated well with Russian audiences.[135]

The fairy tale model for *The Radiant Path* is, of course, Perrault's *Cendrillon.*[136] Tania, whom Lebedev labels "Zolushka" at their first meeting, is the servant of her two lazy "sisters," Anna Konstantinovna and the director's secretary, both of whom show interest in "Prince" Lebedev as they spy on him from an upstairs window.[137] Tania is aided by fairy godmother Pronina, who leads her to the factory, which Pronina calls "our palace." In the course of the film, Tania will enter four palaces (the factory, the workers' club, the Kremlin, the Agricultural Exhibition), each foregrounded by her crossing thresholds and opening doors or gates into a new territory. Her entrance through gates to the club is accompanied by conventionally magical harp music. Like Cinderella, who must leave the ball, Tania must leave the factory-palace when she fails to operate a machine properly.

She then goes to the New Year's ball at the factory club but sits marginalized outside. Prince Lebedev dances with Tania, crowns her with a costume tiara (also echoing the Snow Maiden), and kisses her in the elaborate latticework mise-en-scène Aleksandrov uses here and in the textile factory gates to enhance the aura of fairy tale spectacle. But because she is not yet a true princess (i.e., Lebedev's professional equal), Tania must escape the ball after the midnight kiss. At the Kremlin palace, she is transformed by the award and, after passing through yet another door-threshold, dances ecstatically in a palace ballroom. As material evidence of a supernatural location, crystal occurs frequently in the palaces and mountains of fairy tales.[138] After Tania receives the approving Sovnarkom telegram, she drinks water to calm herself, and the glittering bottom crystal pattern of the glass fills the frame. The Kremlin award scenes are accompanied by oversize crystal chandeliers. As Tania enters the looking glass world of the future, she is led not by fairy godmother Pronina, but by her own hypostasis as would-be princess-lover, dressed in tiara and sheepskin coat, as she appeared at the New Year's ball. In the course of the flight, the two Tanias (lover and Stakhanovite) merge into one, intimating Tania's self-actualization as engineer-people's deputy and spouse of Lebedev. Tania's arrival at the Agricultural Exhibition is marked by an implied passage through its arched entrance. In the final episodes of the film, Tania and Lebedev, now social equals, pass through elaborate tall doors that open magically into the palatial garden space of the Agricultural Exhibition, where Tania is united with her prince.

The Radiant Path also elaborates Propp's fairy tale morphology in a general, non-sequential way.[139] An act of villainy (Tania's firing by Anna Konstantinovna) initiates the action, but with donor Pronina's help, Tania is provided with another job that allows her to progress. At the factory, she must overcome the villainies of foreman Kurnakov and kulak Samokhin, and she completes a difficult folkloric task, the Stakhanovite record for weaving. With herself as helper, Tania is transported by magical agent (the late model convertible) to another kingdom (the Agricultural Exhibition), where Lebedev and Taldykin initially fail to recognize her. Nevertheless, by the conclusion, the lovers are united with the expectation of future marriage.

Mirrors are scattered throughout *The Radiant Path*, as their function progresses and builds from the mundane to the supernatural. Traditionally, the mirror reflects reality and true character: the pursuing Taldykin is visible in Tania's mirror during her move; when beaten by another Stakhanovite, Tania berates herself in the mirror. As a reflection of the self, the mirror also mediates hopes for the future. Peasant Tania's assessment of her situation and dreams at the beginning of the film ("V staroi skazke govoritsia…) is sung into the mirror. In the wake of Tania's record, the factory director regards himself smugly in the mirror, while alluding to "our record." The Kremlin looking glass episode, which introduces the final section of the film, exploits three features of folkloric mirror symbolism—liminality, divination and *dvoedushie* (dual souledness). In Slavic folk belief, the mirror represents a portal or point of access into the other world and is the site of

Figure 46.

magic rituals, as is characteristic of all boundaries. "Zerkalitsa," the mirror spirit, inhabits the looking glass world and therefore knows the future, hence the Slavic divination rituals in which girls use a mirror to see or dream of future husbands. Mirroring, the production of a second, reflected image, may also cause bifurcation between the world of people and that of unclean forces, which transforms a human female into a sorceress.[140] Finally, magic mirrors have also been used to show the past, present, and future.[141] In the Kremlin award ceremony, Tania undergoes a transformation that gives her access to higher knowledge. Afterward, with the help of the mirror, she reviews her past (exaggeratedly crude peasant) and present (no nonsense Stakhanovite). Divining the future requires the power of a relatively innocuous *dvoedushie*: Tania's split into good fairy, in her costume of Snow Maiden, who literally steps out from behind her in the mirror episode, and her present Stakhanovite self (Fig. 46). The fairy self opens the frame of the mirror, the portal to the world "there," which Tania enters. The fairy double is, of course, able to fly and takes Tania on a tour of the Soviet land. The film screen has often been equated to a magic mirror. In a self-reflexive gesture, Aleksandrov projects

Tania's future in the Kremlin magic mirror-movie screen, the epitome of illusion, loaded with the greatest concentration of special effects in the entire film.

Weaving, which is the fundamental female ritual activity in Slavic folklore, is also at the center of *The Radiant Path* (Fig. 47). Spinning-weaving-knotting symbolism is associated with the Great Mother goddess, and female figures spinning the thread of fate occur in most Indo-European traditions. In Slavic folklore, the complex is also connected to the transition from girlhood to marriage, the girl's meeting with her intended one.[142] The three brides in "The Frog Princess" must weave shirts to please the king and the heroine

Figure 47.

Elena the Beautiful later turns into a spindle which Prince Ivan must break to return her to human form.[143] Vasilisa the Beautiful (also initially a Cinderella figure) spins flax and weaves fine cloth that brings about her meeting and marriage with the king.[144] It is Tania's Stakhanovite weaving skill that makes her most attractive to Lebedev: after her record-setting feat, he looks longingly at her image on a factory poster.

Weaving is also one of the cosmogonic archetypes in the Slavic world. The folkloric semantics of weaving are based on the likening of the creation of cloth to the creation of the world and of human life. The spinner creates thread out of the chaos of raw material. The weaver symbolically creates order (cloth) out of chaos (threads), thereby organizing space. The length of fabric traditionally represents the road or path of life.[145] Because a woman appropriates the function of demiurge in weaving-creation, the activity may also be regarded negatively as unclean or ungodly work.[146] As an impossible or extraordinary task, weaving may be performed, facilitated, or hindered by supernatural agents. When Kroshechka-Khavroshechka's stepmother assigns her the impossible task of producing cloth from raw flax in one day, the magic cow has the girl crawl through one bovine ear and out the other, after which the fabric is ready.[147] During the night, Vasilisa the Beautiful's doll builds her a loom on which the girl weaves marvelous cloth.[148] The Slavic goddess Mokosh' was depicted as a night spinner who could ruin bundles of raw flax left out overnight.[149]

Ardov's play and an early script of *The Radiant Path* explicitly highlight Tania's magical powers. When Taldykin asks her about her success at the factory, how she knows the needs of her machines, Tania replies jokingly: "The machine itself tells me everything. I'm a sorceress ("koldun'ia")."[150] In the earliest *Zolushka* script, Tania dreams of magic control over the machines. When a thread breaks, she shakes her finger at it, adding "I'll get you!" and the thread, wiggling furtively, reconnects itself.[151] Taldykin himself is conscious of Tania's powers, which are harmful to him—or at least as harmful as they can be in a comedy film. He does not recognize her initially at the textile pavilion, but after his hair is set ablaze by the photographer's flash, he *knows*: "It's her. If there's damage, that means it's her!"

In his review of *The Radiant Path*, Grigorii Roshal' calls the textile factory "the source of fairy tale power."[152] This is demonstrated when, coming to the shop floor for the first time, Tania is overwhelmed by its larger than life bobbins. She demonstrates her own folk power ("sila") through the ritual act of weaving. Her Stakhanovite record is performed overnight on the late shift—an act of sorcery. Tania herself is depicted as both saint and sorceress, two image complexes familiar to the Folk and put to good use by Socialist Realism. Her dormitory is located in a former monastery decorated with reliefs of the saints. Just after Tania devises her Stakhanovite plan of work, out of nowhere (because she is sitting on her bed indoors), her hair begins to blow with the wind of inspiration common in depictions of saints, and later in Socialist Realist art, as she exclaims: "Serdtse b'etsia, b'etsia, b'etsia i dob'etsia svoego" ("My heart beats and

Figure 48.

beats and beats, and will get what it wants"). From a wall telephone held by a saint, Tania calls Pronina to announce that she is able to work on sixteen machines (Fig. 49). For most of the scene, she is framed together with the saint. When Tania receives the approving Sovnarkom telegram, Pronina suddenly arrives with a shawl-veil over her head, visually metamorphosing into the Virgin Mary, with Tania as Baby Jesus, as she

Figure 49.

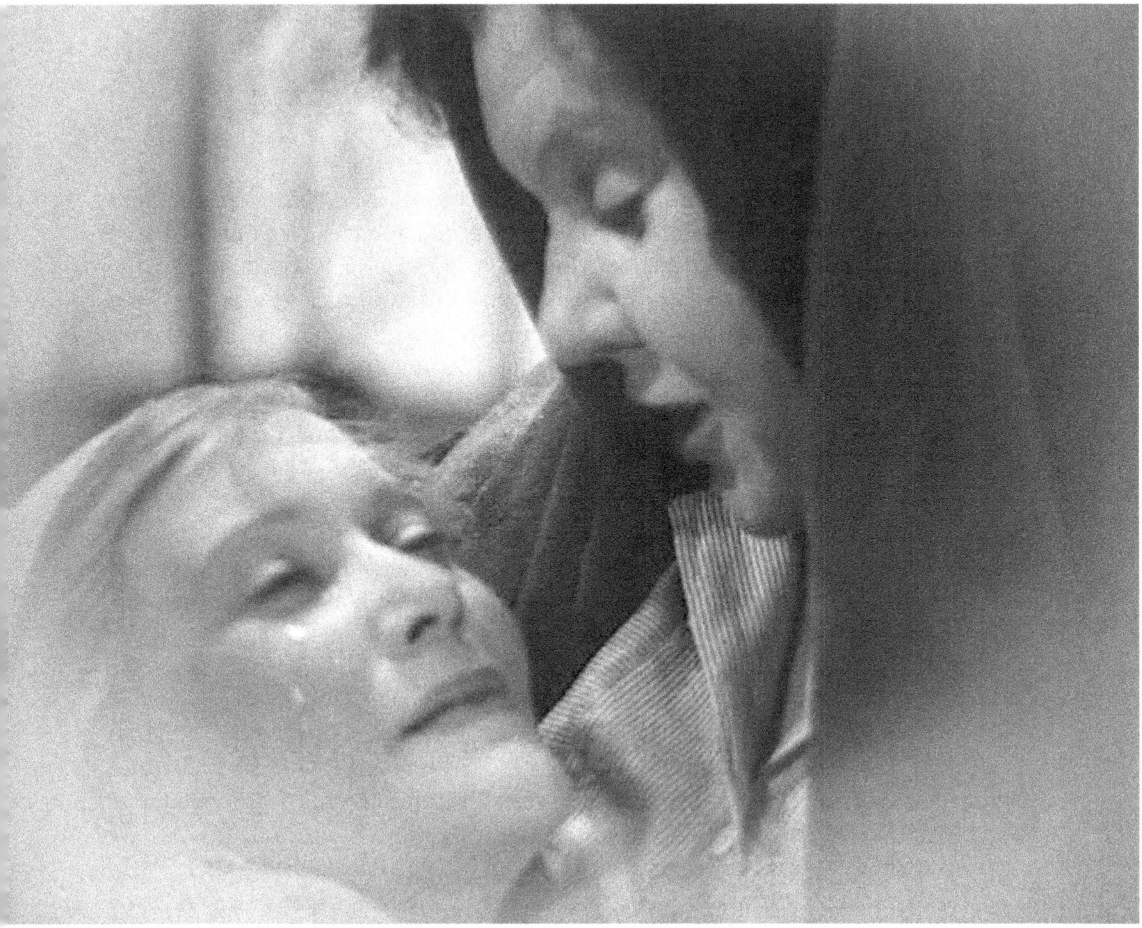

Figure 50.

comforts the semi-hysterical Tania lying in her lap (Fig. 50). Aleksandrov apparently intended the scene as a metaphor for Tania's rebirth as a Stakhanovite. A publicity photo of Pronina and Tania in the Mary-Jesus pose, enclosed in a masked shot of a five-pointed star, survives in the archives.

Extensive screen time in *The Radiant Path* is devoted to Tania's learning to tie the weaver's knot. She practices obsessively on objects in the dorm room, but always on the property of others. Like most ritual activities that carry binary signification, a knot may function both as a protective amulet against evil forces and as a means of causing harm. Multiple knots were worn under peasant clothing to protect against evil spirits, who could not do harm, it was thought, before undoing all the knots. Knots were also used harmfully to prevent the fertility of the earth and of women, especially when tied into a bride's clothing.[153] Tania ties knots only in the shoelaces and on the shawl belonging to frivolous roommate Klasha, who cares more about men than her work. Consequently, Tania's knotting, which is a work-related skill, functions simultaneously here as a punishment. In an early script, Tania ties the ends of Taldykin's moustache together into a weaver's knot in order to forestall yet another proposal of marriage.[154]

Tania's speech in the textile pavilion is highly stylized and therefore implicitly symbolic. The mise-en-scène carries a mythical charge: She is surrounded by representatives of various Soviet nationalities; in the background stands a large building resembling the Palace of Soviets, and Tania's monumental posture generally mimics that of the Stalin statue, situated higher, at the far right of the frame (Fig. 51). Tania first declaims the third stanza of the film's central song "The Enthusiasts' March": "Our world was created for glory, / In years we have accomplished the deeds of centuries, / And our prodigious stars blaze / Over all countries, over oceans as a realized dream." With the last words, she raises her right arm in a classic orator's gesture. Music is then foregrounded over speech, as she breaks into song: "Nam net pregrad ni v more ni na sushe" ("We have no barriers, neither on sea nor on land"), the refrain of "The Enthusiasts' March."[155] In this apotheotic scene, she stands beside a weaving machine that disgorges an endlessly flowing length of patterned fabric. Here, with the staging of the culminating weaving archetype, Tania emerges triumphantly as demiurge, as symbolic creator of the world, directing the path of life and human destiny.

Tania's progress from uneducated peasant to Stakhanovite textile worker to engineer and public figure is conveyed via the acquisition of the speech, body language, and clothing of the 1930s cinematic urban heroine.[156] Orlova plays the young Tania as the stylized country bumpkin of comedy and operetta. Her speech is substandard ("Ish' ty!," "dadeno," strong dialectal *okan'e*); her body language connotes the stereotypical peasant: slumping posture, touching one's body (rubbing the nose, hiding the face with an arm), fidgeting with clothing, squinting, soot on the face. Once in school, Tania switches from a garish flowered blouse and skirt to a more restrained print dress with a stylish zigzag overlay. As a factory worker, she still chews with her mouth open, uses dialect language, and bawls loudly and expressively over her failed New Year's encounter with Lebedev. Nevertheless, she has acquired new speech etiquette, responding to Lebedev's "Kak zhivete?" with a polite "A Vy?" She argues and jokes with Lebedev, prompting him to observe, "They've issued you a different personality at the factory too!" While still a cleaner, Tania discards the peasant scarf tied under the chin for the tied back scarf of the proletarian worker. Outside the factory, she now wears a fashionable beret.

Figure 51.

As Tania morphs into a Stakhanovite, her physical appearance and body language change accordingly. When inspired to work on sixteen machines, Tania already has a short haircut á la Mariia Vinogradova. In the record-setting episode, she adds a hair ribbon, enhances her overalls with a polka dot blouse, and marches between the rows of machines in an erect posture. Now she no longer waves her arms about but holds them close to the body as she pulls levers and carries a cleaning rag. At the Kremlin ceremony, Tania sports an urban hairstyle, stylish dress, and a watch (a marker of culture and affluence), but still uses some dialect speech (*okan'e*). Once in the looking glass world of the future, Tania acquires the perfected bearing of a Stalinist heroine (Fig. 52). She speaks standard Russian (and even French), moves in a measured, deliberate, and dignified way, subduing all body language, and uses the gestures of a professional orator in her speech at the textile pavilion. Oksana Bulgakova has demonstrated that

Figure 52.

in the cinema of high Stalinism, the public (rhetorical) gestures of speeches and official meetings migrate into the private sphere of family, love, and friendship.[157] As Tania and Lebedev stroll through the Agricultural Exhibition during their romantic interlude, Tania clasps her hands behind her back, as if discussing a thorny production problem, and puts her hands into the pockets of her coat—both gestures displaced from the public sphere denoting authority and confidence.

Gender relations in *The Radiant Path* are elaborated in the farce tradition of comic violence, but with an ideological twist. At different times, Tania is accosted by Taldykin, Kurnosov, and finally Lebedev, but she resists all of them. She reacts to Taldykin's groping in the peasant manner, by slapping him and scratching his face. She resists Kurnosov verbally, but has no need to go further because Taldykin's hidden presence scares off the cowardly kulak. At the New Year's celebration, Lebedev becomes uncharacteristically insistent, attempting to kiss her three times in spite of her protestations of "ne nado." In spite of her affection for him, Tania resists, pushing him away into a snowdrift. The outcome is her comic wailing ("he ki-i-i-ssed me!"), distress motivated by her understanding of the intellectual distance between them and his implicit lack of respect for her as an uneducated country girl. As a Socialist Realist heroine, Tania mostly appears in public space (the factory, the Agricultural Exhibition, the New Year's ball), and when we do see her in private space, on her bed, she is ruminating over a public task. Tania's sexual energy is displaced into service to the State: she appears as a sexual being only at the moment of industrial inspiration. When she discovers a way of working on sixteen machines, Tania rumples her hair in excitement and runs to call Pronina, dressed only in a nightgown slipping off one shoulder. Production zeal is thus conveyed via the devices of sexual ecstasy. It is also Pronina who assumes the erotic gaze denied Lebedev, flirting with Tania at their first meeting by flicking her nose and tucking flowers into her bodice.[158] In her relations with the various men, Tania fulfills the traditional ideal of the girl who "keeps herself" for her intended, in line with conservative Stalin era views on marriage. At the same time, her reserve is an elaboration of official policy on equality between the sexes in all areas: not until they are professional equals will she become romantically involved with Lebedev.

Of all the Aleksandrov musical films, *The Radiant Path* most clearly fulfills Socialist Realist narrative paradigms in which the heroine typically has a dual goal: to fulfill a task in the public sphere and to resolve the tension between spontaneity and consciousness.[159] Like other Socialist Realist heroines, Tania begins with marked native talent, which will be developed in a Soviet environment. Initially, she is a clever house servant who invents labor-saving devices to enable her simultaneously to prepare breakfast and look after Baby Misha. Tania's task in the public sphere is the achievement of a Stakhanovite record which, as she affirms to Pronina, is for the benefit of the State. Tania is angry and petulant, breaking glasses and sulking in bed, after she reads that Zvantseva (the surname is etymologically related to "vyzvat'" [to challenge]) has surpassed her record. Pronina, her Party mentor, decries this outburst of "spontaneity," points out Tania's egotism, and brings her to rational "consciousness": "Get up this minute, comb your hair and get yourself and the room in order. For whom do you produce, for yourself personally or the State?... You should be *glad* that another girl also produces a lot during her shift." Tania stops sulking and, with Pronina's approval, pledges to take on 240 machines. Although the Stalinist hierarchy is strongly vertical, Socialist Realism preserves the motif of personal communication between the bottom of the social pyramid and the apex. Consequently, Tania writes a letter directly to the Sovnarkom about her plan to work on sixteen machines and duly receives a personal reply in the form of an approving telegram.

Tania's strangely ecstatic behavior in three episodes of the film is comprehensible only in terms of the mysticism and belief in an inexpressible higher knowledge, characteristic of High Stalinism. When the Sovnarkom telegram arrives, Tania bursts into tears and is comforted like a child by Pronina. After the news of Tania's Order of Lenin is announced, she drinks the water from a glass vase full of lilacs and then pours the remaining water—flowers and all—over her head, exclaiming, "No, it can't be!" At the Kremlin ceremony, both before and after the receipt of the award, she lifts her arm to her forehead, exclaiming "Akh," as if about to faint from an excess of emotion. Within the context of the panegyric rhetoric of High Stalinism, it is also possible to see Tania's behavior as a compensatory-defensive reaction to the psychological pressures of the purge years. Her response to positive communications from authority visually demonstrates her loyalty to the regime. Extreme emotion is meant to signify extreme devotion.

Tania's ritual initiation into a higher world (she wears a white dress and the set is flooded with light) will both transform her into a leader who will now mentor others (the public context) and will allow her to love (the private sphere). Tania's flight to the mountains, coming as it does after the award ceremony, functions as the physical expression of transcendence, the upward vector signified by the paradigmatic "ever higher." Her travels take her from the Kremlin out over the city to distant snow-capped mountains, thereby uniting periphery and center before she returns to Moscow, the sacred omphalos, for the finale of the film. As Tania's song addressed to the country ends ("Hello, land of heroes, land of dreamers, land of scholars"), her white Kremlin dress is replaced by a dark power suit and she takes the wheel of the car, thereby actualizing her transformation from worker into leader and public figure. In the textile pavilion, Tania's suit is replaced by a less severe, but still business-like, pale dress covered by a dark duster, more appropriate to the love scenes that will conclude the film.

Tania's movement toward the center is adumbrated from the very beginning of the film. At her first meeting with Lebedev, he throws down an empty cigarette box embellished with a classic view of Moscow, exactly the perspective on the Stone Bridge and the Kremlin familiar to cinematic audiences since the silent era. Curious Tania picks up the box, and the symbolic movement toward the center is established as she pastes the image into the lid of her hope chest. In the Likbez classroom episode, Tania spits out the answer to a question about Moscow with which her co-worker, Agrafena

Lukinichna, struggles: "It's the capital of the RSFSR!" (Fig. 53). Tania's dream, which marks the beginning of her career path, includes a collage of Moscow buildings, such as the Kremlin and Bol'shoi Theatre, that culminates in "our palace," as Pronina calls the textile factory entrance in which audiences recognized the elaborate metalwork gates of one of the Moscow metro stations.[160] When the announcement of Tania's Kremlin award comes, she opens up her hope chest once again to look at the Moscow panorama, which then dissolves into the living city.

Figure 53.

After her automobile flight, Tania returns to Moscow, to the Agricultural Exhibition, another symbolic space metonymic to the "fairy tale come true" of the entire land. The actual agrarian countryside is represented by the exhibition grounds as a well-manicured park. Although Tania's transformation is initially located in the future (underscored by the gilded mirror frame visible around the edges of the flying automobile scenes), as she descends to the Agricultural Exhibition, steering her car toward Mukhina's gigantic *Factory Worker and Collective Farm Woman*, the looking glass frame disappears, leading the audience to perceive the subsequent Agricultural Exhibition scenes as present reality. The mise-en-scène—actual exhibition grounds and fictional textile pavilion—together with Tania's metamorphosis into engineer and deputy to the Supreme Soviet, has collapsed time, staging the future in the present. The finale of *The Radiant Path* elevates the narrative to the symbolic register of Socialist Realist representation.

Lebedev arrives after Tania's speech at the textile pavilion and asks, "Which one is Tania?" to which Pronina responds jokingly, "Oh, you Onegin. It's that one over there." She has introduced Pushkin's pairing of older, sophisticated male with young, naïve female as a template for *The Radiant Path* couple, but posits a happy ending in post-imperial Soviet society. Having fulfilled her public task, now initiated into higher knowledge at the Kremlin, Tania is at last able to love. The final episodes of the film gradually move the couple from the organic to the monumental and from the personal to the universal. In Marxist terms, social harmony once existed—and will again exist—when man is not alienated from the means of production. The Agricultural Exhibition grounds denote such a utopia, which for an agrarian nation is logically pastoral and fertile. As Tania and Lebedev leave the textile pavilion, its elaborate, monumental doors signal an entrance into just such a Garden of Eden, complete with a view of the "Kolos" (ear of wheat or corn) fountain.

Outside, on the exhibition grounds, the camera first lingers over columnar fountains that fill the entire frame. In the next scene, the couple are united with the natural world as black silhouettes moving in this watery landscape. The use of wipes rather than cuts for transitions through differing levels of signification contributes to the stately and deliberate tempo of these culminating scenes. A wipe takes the couple to the agricultural reliefs decorating the Moscow pavilion (Fig. 54). Tania and Lebedev stroll against a background of monumental carved gardeners, shepherds, tractor drivers, luxuriant fruits, vegetables, and farm animals, among which a large pig with piglets and decorative bulls' heads, implying the couple's future fertility, are most prominent. Here and in the final scenes with Mukhina's *Factory Worker and Collective Farm Laborer*, Aleksandrov makes effective use of the special mise-en-abîme effect popular in both Socialist Realist poster graphics and painting: the ordinary human subject is depicted against a background of larger sculptural figures, often idealized leaders, with whom the smaller subject is associated both by physical and intellectual proximity (shared ideological goals), so that the larger image is symbolically doubled in a smaller human version.[161] Tania and

Figure 54.

Lebedev are assimilated to the ideal of pastoral fertility and plenitude as they walk in front of the stone reliefs, which by their size and substance move the couple from the organic towards the monumental, from motion, however subdued their gait and gestural language, toward the stasis of the Mukhina sculpture.

Another wipe brings us to the climactic love scene, in which the lovers' kiss is thwarted by the appearance of the comic rival, Taldykin. Instead, their affection is channeled into a monumental register. As an operatic voice performs the film's theme song, imparting a majestic tone, Tania and Lebedev appear in front of the towering figures of Mukhina's *Factory Worker and Collective Farm Laborer*, which they even resemble physically (Fig. 55). The camera then cranes upward in mise-en-abîme: Mukhina's sculpture is doubled in the couple—a smaller version of itself. Lebedev holds his arm around Tania protectively, while she puts a hand on his chest, acknowledging his protection. But the camera assimilates their private relationship to the public and ideological symbolism of the sculpture. This progression is then repeated: the couple turn their backs on us, heads together (a stock ending of American romantic comedy), as the camera again cranes up and fixes on the sculpture. With this monumental apotheosis, but with less spectacle than in *Happy Guys* or *Circus*, Aleksandrov again moves the narrative from the localized story of a single couple into the greater world of Soviet peoples.

Figure 55.

Chapter 4 Endnotes

1. "Stenogramma tvorcheskogo soveshchaniia, sozyvaemogo komitetom po delam kinematografii v Dome kino po voprosu o razvitii sovetskoi kinokomedii," RGALI, f. 2456/1/443.
2. R. W. Davies and Oleg Khlevniuk, "Stakhanovism and the Soviet Economy," *Europe-Asia Studies,* 54.6 (2002) 897.
3. Davies and Oleg Khlevniuk, 897.
4. Lewis H. Siegelbaum, *Stakhanovism and the Politics of Productivity in the USSR, 1935–1941* (Cambridge: CUP, 1988) 76.
5. Davies and Khlevniuk, 880.
6. O. A. Ermanskii, *Stakhanovskoe dvizhenie i stakhanovskie metody* (Moscow: Gosudarstvennoe sotsial'no-ekonomicheskoe izdatel'stvo, 1940) 317–18.
7. Davies and Khlevniuk, 889; Siegelbaum, 100.
8. Aleksandrov, *Epokha i kino*, 221.
9. Ermanskii, 282.
10. Ermanskii, 163.
11. M. I. Vinogradova speech, *Pervoe vsesoiuznoe soveshchanie rabochikh i rabotnits-stakhanovtsev, 14-17 noiabria 1935. Stenograficheskii otchet* (Moscow: Partizdat TsK VKP(b), 1935) 48.
12. Ermanskii, 9.
13. Davies and Khlevniuk, 882–83.
14. Davies and Khlevniuk, 883.
15. Siegelbaum, 74.
16. E. V. Vinogradova speech, *Pervoe vsesoiuznoe soveshchanie rabochikh i rabotnits-stakhanovtsev*, 27.
17. Siegelbaum, 227–30.
18. Siegelbaum, 237–38.
19. http://ortoys.ru/wiki. Accessed Jul. 28, 2007.
20. Aleksandrov, *Epokha i kino*, 217.
21. "Svetlyi put' dlia millionov," Interview with L. Orlova and G. Aleksandrov, *Leninskoe znamia* (Dec. 21, 1971): 3.
22. Siegelbaum, 292.
23. Kushnirov, 194.
24. Papernyi (1996), 196.
25. Kushnirov, 183. V. E. Ardov (Zil'berman, 1900–76) wrote for the journals *Krasnyi perets* and *Krokodil* and variety shows during the 1920s, helped organize the Moscow Satire Theatre in 1925, and published more than forty collections of stories and sketches during his lifetime. He and his wife were close friends of Anna Akhmatova.
26. "Zolushka," 4/IX/38 g., GFF, f. 154.
27. "Stenogramma tvorcheskogo soveshchaniia," Nov. 19, 1939, RGALI, f. 2456/1/460.

28. V. Ardov, *Zolushka. Literaturnyi stsenarii (pervyj variant)*, GFF, 69.
29. V. Ardov, *Zolushka. Stsenarii polnometrazhnoi zvukovoi komedii*, GFF, 41.
30. V. Ardov, *Zolushka*, GFF, 105.
31. V. Ardov, *Zolushka*, GFF, 114.
32. V. E. Ardov, *Zolushka. Literaturnyi stsenarii polnometrazhnoi zvukovoi komedii. Moskva 1938–39*, g., RGALI, f. 1822/1/28.
33. Kushnirov, 183.
34. For example, *One in a Million* (1936) and *Thin Ice* (1937).
35. Anon., "Zolushka," *Vecherniaia Moskva* (Apr. 21, 1939).
36. Anon., "Zolushku stavit G. Aleksandrov," *Vecherniaia Moskva* (May 15, 1939); for a summary of the director's script, see Iurii Saakov, "'Poterpet' polnyi kriak...', ili chego ne uvidel zritel' v kinoteatre 'Khudozhestvennyi' 8 oktiabria 1940 goda," *Kinovedcheskie zapiski*, 57 (2002): 226–236.
37. Anon., "G. Aleksandrov," *Kino* (Jul. 5, 1939).
38. R. B., "Zolushka. Khudozhestvennyi fil'm o tekstil'shchikakh," *Legkaia industriia* (May 27, 1939).
39. For an enumeration of common grievances against Dukel'skii, see "Document 191, "Stat'ia A. Dubrovskogo i A. Volozhenina 'Pochemu malo kinokartin' ob oshibkakh v rabote S. S. Dukel'skogo," in *Kremlevskii kinoteatr 1928–1953. Dokumenty*, 523–28.
40. "Document 206, "Dokladanaia zapiska I. G. Bol'shakova V. M. Molotovu o tematicheskom plane proizvodstva kinokartin na 1939–1940 gg," *Kremlevskii kinoteatr*, 550.
41. See Jun. 11, 1939 issue, 1–2. Medvedkin's *New Moscow* had been banned in January 1939.
42. "Tvorcheskoe soveshchanie, sozvannoe Komitetom po delam kinematografii v Dome kino po voprosu o razvitii sovetskoi kinokomedii 16-17 noiabria 1939 goda," *Zhivye golosa kino*, 152.
43. *Kremlevskii kinoteatr*, 561.
44. The references are to the factory director, Dorokhov, and Petr Ustinovich, the hotel manager in *The Radiant Path*.
45. "Stenogramma soveshchaniia v TsK VKP(b) pod predsedatel'stvom A. A. Zhdanova po voprosam khudozhestvennoi kinematografii." At the same May 1941 conference, Pyr'ev added that a script sent to the Committee lies there for 6–7 months or, on average, 3–4. "It is held up because it is being checked in various departments, in narkomaty. They send the script to Narkomzdrav: and what will Narkomzdrav say to us? After that they send the script to another organization. And when they collect a pile of reports about the script, then they express their own point of view. And after that they're surprised why Narkomzdrav or another narkomat isn't minding its own business."

    Established in 1931, ORUD (Otriad regulirovaniia ulichnogo dvizheniia) regulated traffic.

    During the summer of 1940, six directors, including Aleksandrov, had written a collective letter to Stalin about the catastrophic state of the film industry: low morale under the pressures of self-criticism; the cinema leadership's distrust and over-supervision of directors; poor quality scripts; and outdated equipment. Stalin declined to meet with the directors, and instead established a government commission for the review and release of films, and ordered some new equipment. ("Pis'mo kinematografistov I. V. Stalinu," in *Vlast' i khudozhestvennaia intelligentsia*, 446–48).
46. "Stenogramma soveshchaniia v TsK VKP (b) pod predsedatel'stvom A. A. Zhdanova."

47. A. Zhdanov, "O zadachakh khudozhestvennoi kinematografii, proekt," Sept. 1940, RGASPI, f. 77/1/908. See also Stalin's Dec. 28, 1940 letter to A. Korneichuk about his comic play in Evgenii Gromov, *Stalin: Iskusstvo i vlast'* (Moscow: Eksmo, 2003) 223.
48. G. Aleksandrov, "Snaiperskoe iskusstvo," *Kino*, No. 24 (1939): 3.
49. G. Aleksandrov, "Tvorcheskie zamysly," *Kino* (Jul. 5, 1939): 3.
50. Gr. Aleksandrov, "Fil'm 'Svetlyi put'"," *Izvestiia* (Oct. 1, 1940): 4.
51. "Stenogramma soveshchaniia v TsK VKP (b) pod predsedatel'stvom A. A. Zhdanova."
52. Orlova's account of how Aleksandrov was forced to insert the character by the Cinematography Committee is contradicted by Ardov's earliest scenario, which already includes Kurnosov as arsonist. (See Skorokhodov, *V poiskakh utrachennogo*, 408).
53. V. E. Ardov letter to Bol'shakov, undated, GFF.

    At the November 1939 comedy conference, Ardov, now at odds with Trauberg, who served on the advisory board to the Cinematography Committee, reacted emotionally to Trauberg's criticism of his inability to use repetition for comedic purposes in the film: "Comrades, they threw everything out of my script, and then they say that I didn't know how to do it." (*Zhivye golosa kino*, 177).
54. G. Aleksandrov letter to Bol'shakov, undated, GFF.
55. Saakov, *Liubov' Orlova. 100 bylei i nebylits*, 58.
56. B. Vladimirov, "Zolushka," *Kino* (Sept. 17, 1939). In the film, Tania is welcomed to the pavilion by Vysokovskaia, the real-life director of Glavtekstil' (Kushnirov, 193).
57. B. Vladimirov; Vl. Rudnyi, "Na s"emkakh 'Zolushki'," *Vecherniaia Moskva* (Apr. 5, 1940).
58. B. Vladimirov.
59. Vl. Rudnyi.
60. Vl. Rudnyi.
61. Iu. Saakov, " 'Poterpet' polnyi kriak...'," 232–233.
62. E. Grinberg, "Dve s"emki," *Moskovskii komsomolets* (Feb. 15, 1940); photo of filming Taldykin serenade in *Izvestiia* (Feb. 15, 1940).
63. Vl. Rudnyi.
64. Vl. Rudnyi; anonymous notice in *Kino* that Aleksandrov has completed the ice carnival scenes (Mar. 17, 1940).
65. Anon., "'Novogodnii bal' na Potylikhe," *Moskovskii bol'shevik* (Mar. 12, 1940).
66. "Svetlyi put' dlia millionov," 3.
67. L. Orlova, "Zritel' i akter sovetskogo kino," 377.
68. Kushnirov, 185.
69. Saakov, *Liubov' Orlova. 100 bylei i nebylits*, 56–57.
70. Aleksandrov, *Epokha i kino*, 222. A photo of Orlova being coached by a Stakhanovite weaver is reproduced in the same volume, 192–93.
71. Accelerated and specialized technical minimum courses, lasting 6–10 months rather than the 1–3 yrs of conventional education, were introduced in June 1932 as part of the drive to raise productivity. (Siegelbaum, 22).

72. L. Orlova, "Zritel' i akter sovetskogo kino," 378.
73. L. Orlova, "Zritel' i akter sovetskogo kino," 378.
74. G. Aleksandrov, "Zametki o kinokomedii," *Pravda* (Feb. 2, 1940): 6.
75. Stenogramma soveshchaniia v TsK VKP(b) pod predsedatel'stvom A. A. Zhdanova.
76. Vl. Rudnyi.
77. H. Kholmin, "Den' v kinostudii," *Trud* (Mar. 23, 1940).
78. Anon., "Zolushka," *Kino*, Jul. 14, 1940.
79. S. Bronshtein, "Tekhnika fil'ma," *Kino*, No. 47 (1940): 2.
80. B. Chizov, "Na 22 dnia ran'she sroka," *Kino*, No. 23 (1940): 1.
81. Anon., "Predvaritel'nyi prosmotr," *Za bol'shevistskii fil'm*, No. 23 (May 16, 1940): 2.
82. Anon., "Zakliuchitel'nyi epizod," *Kino*, (May 29, 1940).
83. Anon., "Na s"emkakh fil'ma 'Zolushka'," *Pionerskaia Pravda*, (Jun. 8, 1940).
84. Saakov, *Liubov' Orlova. 100 bylei i nebylits*, 269.
85. See illustration in Saakov, *Liubov' Orlova. 100 bylei i nebylits*, 269.
86. RGALI, f. 2453/2/64.
87. RGALI, f. 2453/2/64.
88. RGALI, f. 2453/2/64.
89. Saraeva-Bondar', *Siluety vremeni*, 199. In *Epokha i kino*, Aleksandrov gives a shorter account of the meeting (220). The director's official explanation of the title change, after consulting with "avtoritetnye tovarishchi," can be found in Gr. Aleksandrov, "Fil'm 'Svetlyi put''," *Izvestiia* (Oct. 1, 1950): 4.

    Aleksandrov's admiration and fear of Stalin emerge in his comments to Saraeva-Bondar': "His judgments and demands were never groundless, his decisions were logical and uncompromising. The sense of artistic and civic responsibility in meeting with him grew to such self-torturing and soul-terrifying heights that in one of these discussions, to my own and everyone's surprise, I fell into the most banal ladies' faint" (200).
90. In a 1912 May Day proclamation, Stalin wrote: "[Rabochie] gordo shestvuiut k obetovannoi zemle, po puti k svetlomu sotsializmu." ("Da zdravstvuet pervoe maia!" in Iosif Vissarionovich Stalin, *Sochineniia*, http://www.petrograd.biz/stalin/2-7.php. Accessed Sept. 10, 2006).

    After the release of the film, the title became a communist cliché, e.g., Vladimir Zhukov, *Svetlyi put'. Stikhi* (1952); Ivan Kuchin, *Svetlyi put'. Povest' v stikhakh* (1952); *Svetlyi put'. Ocherk o zhizni i rabotakh geroia sotsialisticheskogo truda V. P. Filatova* (1955); *Svetlyi put': Kommunisticheskaia partiia Sovetskogo Soiuza—borets za svobodu, ravnopravie i schast'e zhenshchiny* (1967); *Svetlyi put': o laureate gosudarstvennoi premii SSSR T. M. Sokolenko* (1981); Kim Chong-il, *Svetlyi put': stat'i i vystupleniia* (1996).
91. Because the film mentioned Molotov, Ordzhonikidze, and Kalinin, Aleksandrov speculated that Stalin was displeased that he had been omitted (Kushnirov, 195).
92. These scenes were cut during the Khrushchev era. See the deleted footage at www.landscape-design.ru in the "Moskva v kinofil'makh" section (accessed 8/12/07). The DVD version of the film released in 2006 restores the footage.

93. *Letopis' rossiiskogo kino 1930–1945*, 680, 682.

94. Anon., "Prem'era fil'ma 'Svetlyi put',"' *Vecherniaia Moskva*, Oct. 5, 1940. Saraeva-Bondar', based on information from Aleksandrov, gives October 8 and the Khudozhestvennyi for the première. According to the director, viewers were so enthusiastic about the film that they asked for the last part of the film to be shown again (Saraeva-Bondar', *Dunaevskii v Leningrade*, 180).

95. Anon., "Na ekranakh Moskvy," *Kino*, Oct. 14, 1940; Anon., "Uspekh fil'ma 'Svetlyi put'," *Za bol'shevistskii fil'm*, No. 46 (Oct. 16, 1940): 3.

96. More substantive reviews are: P. Bliakhin, "Realisticheskaia komediia. Stsenarii 'Zolushka'," *Iskusstvo kino*, 9 (1939): 34–36; G. Roshal', "Melodiia i dissonansy," *Kino*, No. 44 (1940): 2; B. Faians, "Vymysel i zhizn'," *Iskusstvo kino*, 10 (1940): 15–17.

97. G. Aleksandrov and D. Polikarpov, "O polozhenii del s vypuskom kinofil'mov," Jan. 18, 1941, RGASPI, 17/125/71.

98. "Retsenziia sotrudnika Upravleniia propagandy i agitatsii TsK VKP(b) na fil'm 'Svetlyi put','" *Istochnik*, No. 3 (1995): 77–8.

99. *Letopis' rossiiskogo kino 1930–1945*, 701.

100. RGALI, f. 2062/1/139.

101. L. Smirnova, *Moia liubov'* (Moskva: Vagrius, 1998) 85.

102. Minchenok, 402–03.

103. Dunaevskii letter to R. Ivanycheva (Oct. 24, 1954), I. Dunaevskii, *Izbrannye pis'ma*, 220.

104. Saraeva-Bondar', *Dunaevskii v Leningrade*, 176. Satirist and scriptwriter Mikhail Davydovich Vol'pin (1902–1988) had been arrested with frequent co-author Erdman in 1933 and sent into exile. Satirist and translator D'Aktil' (pseudonym of Anatolii Adol'fovich Frenkel', 1890–1942) wrote material for the music hall, authored the libretto for Dunaevskii's operetta *Dorogi k schast'iu* (1941) and the lyrics for his music in the film *Moia liubov'*.

105. Kur'ianov letter to Dunaevskii (Nov. 29, 1939), RGALI, f. 2062/1/577.

106. Chizhov memo to N. M. Kiva, deputy director of Mosfil'm (Mar. 22, 1940), RGALI, f. 2062/1/565.

107. I. Dunaevskii, "Podlinno muzykal'nyi fil'm," *Za bol'shevistskii fil'm*, No. 34 (Jul. 19, 1940): 2.

108. G. Aleksandrov, "Muzykal'nyi fil'm, *Kino*, No. 48 (1939): 3.

109. The song originally contained another stanza here: "Ne suprugoi-shchegolikhoi / Korolevskogo synka, / Stala Zolushka tkachikhoi / U fabrichnogo stanka" ("Not the fashion-plate spouse of a king's son did she become, Cinderella became a weaver at a factory machine). (RGALI, f. 1822/1/595.)

110. "It was not a grey haired sorceress who gave her advice, and not a young fairy, but a middle-aged comrade. She supported her, made suggestions on how to find her fate. Little soot-face set out on the broad way. And she worked excellently, as Stakhanov had taught, and Kalinin in person presented her with the Order (of Lenin)."

111. Typescript of interview with I. Dunaevskii, c. 1939, RGALI, f. 2062/1/346.

112. RGALI, f. 2062/1/139.

113. RGALI, f. 2062/1/139.

114. Typescript of interview with I. Dunaevskii, c. 1939, RGALI, f. 2062/1/346.

115. Is it for us to stand in place?
We are always right in our daring attempts.
Our labor is a matter of honor,
It is a feat of courage and of glory.

Whether you bend down to a machine
Or cut into rock—
A beautiful dream, not yet clear,
Already beckons you forward.

Part of the first stanza above is a close paraphrase of Stalin's "Trud v SSSR –est' delo chesti, delo slavy, delo doblesti i geroistva." Naum Shafer notes that the line "Mechta prekrasnaia, eshche ne iasnaia" was cut from the film at one point, although it was always preserved in songbooks. (N. Shafer, "Dunaevskii i kino," *Dunaevskii segodnia*, 88–89.) Rather than being a sign of weakness, Tania's doubts about the future serves to nuance an otherwise sorely one-dimensional character. Parts of the following analysis borrow from Shafer's "Dunaevskii i kino," 87–92.

116. The last two lines are: "You have filled the hearts of millions to overflowing with a merry swarm of songs."

117. Everything that was a song,
What we dreamed about and what we loved,
Has become even more marvelous,
As today's living Soviet reality.

And there is no land more beautiful,
And there is no land more happy,
May you flourish, my beloved, vast
My invincible one!

118. Our world was created for glory,
The work of centuries has been done in years,
...And our prodigious crimson stars
Flash above all lands, above the oceans,
Like a dream come true.

Two lines reminiscent of the *Happy Guys* march were omitted from the film performance: "Schast'e berem po pravu, / I zharko liubim i poem, kak deti" ("We take our happiness by right, and love and sing, like children").

119. In 1940, Muzgiz published 50,000 copies of sheet music for "The Enthusiasts' March" and "Vysoko, pod samoi tuchei," paying Dunaevskii 2,000 rubles (RGALI, f. 2062/1/565).

120. In the music for *The Radiant Path*, Dunaevskii had subtitled the waltz "Tanets s ordenom" ("Dance with the Decoration") and inscribed it to G. V. Aleksandrov, who was a previous Kremlin award winner (RGALI, f. 2062/1/139).

121. Most commentators state that the film was purchased by the Soviet government; Saraeva-Bondar' claims that it was received as part of war reparations from Poland (Saraeva-Bondar', *Siluety*, 253).

122. Saraeva-Bondar', *Siluety*, 254–55.

123. I. Dunaevskii, "O sozdanii muzykal'nogo fil'ma. Moia tvorcheskaia zaiavka," in "Dunaevskii—kinematografist," *Iskusstvo kino*, 10 (1961): 101–02. (Shorter version first publ. in *Kino* [Jul. 5, 1940].) Dunaevskii, who was in the middle of an affair with Lydia Smirnova during the first half of 1940, saw himself and Smirnova as Strauss and Karla Donner, even signing himself with Strauss's nickname "Shani" in letters to the actress (Minchenok, 413).

124. Altman, 61.

125. G. Roshal', "Melodiia i dissonansy," 2.

126. Aleksandrov borrowed the extreme close-up of Marusia's terrified eyes when she is discovered telling Tania about the arson from a similar close-up of a woman in the Odessa steps episode of *Potemkin*.

127. See Saakov, *Liubov' Orlova i Grigorii Aleksandrov*, 156–57, for a story about Stalin's supposed reaction to the episode. Orlova does show her legs up to her garters as she gets up from bed, where she has been sulking over Zvantseva's record.

128. Clark, *The Soviet Novel*, 136.

129. S. F., "Ne skazka, a zhizn'," *Komsomol'skaia pravda* (Nov. 22, 1933): 4.

130. G. Aleksandrov, "Zolushka," *Za bol'shevistskii fil'm* (May 16, 1940): 2.

131. Clark, *The Soviet Novel*, 147, 150–51.

132. Ryklin makes this point about the appropriateness of the "rejoicing" motif, as linked to earth and fertility, in the Moscow metro (Mikhail K. Ryklin, "Bodies of Terror: Theses toward a Logic of Violence," *New Literary History*, 24.1 (Winter 1993) 59.

133. "Undated brochure in Russian and Latvian," RGALI, f. 2434/1/64.

134. G. Aleksandrov, "Muzykal'nyi fil'm," *Kino* (Oct. 17, 1939).

135. In world folklore, the crane is often linked to human/avian transformations: in a Japanese fairy tale, a wounded crane turns into a beautiful girl who is a skilled weaver. (M. Oesting, "Cranes in Folklore," *The ICF Bugle*, 10.1 (1984): 2–3.

     At the beginning of *Cranes are Flying* (1957), Kalatozov uses the same symbolism, along with Veronika and Boris's games in the paradisiacal garden by the Kremlin, to establish their utopian pre-war existence in mainstream Soviet society. Boris points out to Veronika the cranes flying overhead in V-formation as a harbinger of hope and happiness. However, their ironic reward for bird-watching is a drenching from a passing water truck. The Stalinist values of *The Radiant Path*—cranes flying in perfect, collective formation, along with the historical optimism implied by the image—will be deconstructed by Thaw era film.

136. It is worth noting that the Perrault Cinderella is largely passive and silent as she carries out the fairy godmother's benevolent plan, while Tania is always outspoken, even sassy, and actively pursues her goals.

137. His surname, derived from "lebed'" (swan) also has fairy tale connotations, as in "The Ugly Duckling" or "Gusi-Lebedi."

138. For example, "Khrustal'naia gora," in *Narodnye russkie skazki*, comp. A. Afanas'ev, Vol. 1 (Moscow: GIKhL, 1957) 393–94.

     After 1937, Grandfather Frost (Ded Moroz), accompanied by the Snow Maiden (Snegurochka), became the symbol of the New Year's holiday that replaced Christmas. It is possible that the motif of Snegurochka's virginal coldness and conflicted inability to love, as developed in Ostrovskii's play (1873) and Rimsky-Korsakov's opera (1882), in intertextually present in Tania-Snegurochka's similarly conflicted resistance to Lebedev's forced advances during the New Year's celebration.

For *The Radiant Path* and New Year's films, see Alyssa DeBlasio, "The New-Year Film as Genre of Post-war Russian Cinema," *Studies in Russian and Soviet Cinema*, Vol. 2, No. 1 (2008): 43-61.

139. V. Propp, *Morphology of the Folktale*, 25–65.
140. *Slavianskaia mifologiia*, eds. V. Ia. Petrukhina et al. (Moscow: Ellis Lak, 1995) 195.
141. According to Polish legends, the magician Tvardovskii called up the spirit of Barbara Radziwill, King Sigismund Augustus's deceased wife (Peter Greif, "Zerkalo," http://www.simbolarium.ru. Accessed Jul. 18, 2006). In Andersen's "The Snow Queen," the evil stepmother learns the whereabouts of the princess through a magic mirror.
142. S. B. Adon'eva, "Ikonografiia blagoveshcheniia: Atribut—siuzet—mif," *Imia-siuzhet-mif*, ed. N. M. Gerasimova (St. Petersburg: Izd-vo S.-Peterburgskogo universiteta, 1996) 30.
143. "Tsarevna liagushka," *Narodnye russkie skazki*, vol. 2, 329–331.
144. "Vasilisa prekrasnaia," *Narodnye russkie skazki*, vol. 1, 164.
145. "Tkachestvo," *Slovar' slavianskoi mifologii*, www.pagan.ru. Accessed Jul. 17, 2006.
146. N. S. Koshubarova, "Tkan' kak veshch' i znak v russkoi traditsionnoi kul'ture" (http://ethnography.omskreg.ru/page.php?id=694. Accessed Jul. 29 2006).
147. "Kroshechka-Khavroshechka," *Narodnye russkie skazki*, vol. 1, 150.
148. "Vasilisa prekrasnaia," 164.
149. "Mokosh'," *Mify narodov mira*, ed. S. A. Tokarev et al., Vol. 2 (Moscow: Sovetskaia entsiklopediia, 1988) 169.
150. Ardov, *Zolushka* (Moscow: Iskusstvo, 1940) 76.
151. "Zolushka," GFF, 92–93.
152. G. Roshal', "Melodiia i dissonansy," 2.
153. "Uzel," *Slovar' slavianskoi mifologii*, www.pagan.ru. Accessed Aug. 5, 2006.
154. "Zolushka" (1938–39 literary script), RGALI, f. 1822/1/28.
155. Several restored video/DVD versions of *The Radiant Path* cut off the performance of the refrain in mid-stanza, jumping to the applause of the diegetic audience. The Gosfil'mofond print has a full performance of the refrain, followed by a symphonic finale.
156. Oksana Bulgakova, *Fabrika zhestov*, 221. I expand upon Bulgakova's observations on body language.
157. Bulgakova, *Fabrika zhestov*, 264.
158. See Ann Eakin Moss, "Stalin's Harem: The Spectator's Dilemma in Late 1930s Soviet Film," *Studies in Russian and Soviet Cinema*, Vol. 3, No. 2 (2009): 168-69
159. Clark, *The Russian Novel*, 162.
160. The early metro stations were described as underground palaces, precursors of the future city above ground. (Mikhail Ryklin, "The Best in the World," *The Landscape of Stalinism*, 271).
161. See for example, the 1951 poster "Izuchaite velikii put' partii Lenina-Stalina!"

Appendix A

A Day of Filming with Director G. Aleksandrov's *Circus* Crew

18:00 The driver turned off the motor and headlights. Up above in Room 213, a door slammed and the director's assistants began running about with pages of the working script. A brief report to the director about the progress of preparations for filming.

18:20 Drawings showing the position of the actor in the frame are glued onto pages of the working script. Director G. V. Aleksandrov looks over the frames, puts them in the order in which they will be filmed, and hands them over to his assistant.

18:30 The director goes to the studio. The circus set is already filled with spectators. The overwhelming majority of them are dolls, made by the artist Grivtsov, and between them here and there sit actors. Today, long shots of the revue are going to be filmed. The shooting will be dangerous. Thirty-one jugglers will get up on the rotating pandus in the center of the arena, and each one will juggle three burning torches. The studio director has already positioned firemen at the ready, having ordered them to douse every spark.

18:40 The director calls the jugglers together. He demands absolute precision, emphasizing that each of their faces will be visible on screen. The director talks to three members of the film crew simultaneously: he explains the assignment to the actor, suggests that his assistant check the phonogram, and that the cameraman set up the lighting.

19:15 The director clambers up to the flies, along dark passageways piled high with construction refuse, along creaking staircases long in need of repair, and chooses the spot from which the next shot will be filmed. From below, an assistant asks the director through a megaphone, "Grigorii Vasil'evich, from where should I start the phonogram?" "Look at the music, see which numbers are circled in black." Downstairs, the director is immediately surrounded on all sides: the assistant, holding the music, checks the spot to start the phonogram; the actor again checks his assignment with the director. But the director, who is upset that the lighting hasn't been set up, goes up the huge staircase, studded with two thousand electric lights, to the very top, where the camera stands under the propellers of a stage airplane. The head lighting technician is banging the microphone with his fist, swearing through his teeth. Today radio contact with the lighting technicians is working badly, and consequently rays of light feel their way timidly and uncertainly around the set. Setting up the lighting delays filming.

19:40 The director stands at his microphone. He gives the order: "Start the phonogram! Order in the hall!" And he begins the rehearsal of the burning torches scene with the actor. The director consults with the cameraman about the lighting. The rehearsal is repeated in front of the camera. The lighting has finally been set up, but the director tells the cameraman that the pandus is too bright; the torches won't be visible on it.

19:55 The positioning of the jugglers and ballerinas begins. "Pandus to the left," commands the director. The pandus is motionless for a long time, then turns rapidly in the opposite direction, then suddenly stops, and begins to rotate just as rapidly, when people shout, "Stop!" The thing is that the pandus is turned by people under the floor. They don't hear the command well, and no one had the sense to connect them to the director's microphone. At last the pandus is tamed. The rehearsal with the girls and jugglers begins.

20:15 Preparations for filming.

20:17 ...The torches are doused and the pandus is stopped...

20:25 There are fumes in the air and flecks of soot fly about. The director again shows the actor how he should use the torches. The cameraman is busy with the camera. The motor has broken down and he'll have to turn the crank manually during filming of the next shot.

20:35 The actors have again soaked their torches. The lighting has been set up again. The standard command rings out: "Start the pandus! Camera! Action! Jugglers begin!"

20:37 One shot has been completed. The camera is carried downstairs into the circus loge, breaking dozens of light bulbs on the staircase en route. The electricians are busy with the lighting; radio communication isn't working.

21:00 The artist Stoliarov stands at the middle of the staircase and rehearses his work with the torches. The assistant checks that the staircase works. Finally, everything is ready. Stoliarov rehearses for the last time, and again the command sounds from the megaphone, "Good."

21:15 Another take is filmed, and after this the cameraman's assistant drags the equipment up to the flies. For some reason, the staircases leading up aren't lit in the evening and carrying the camera up rickety steps in the dark takes a long time, and is difficult and fairly dangerous. While the cameraman's assistant is climbing to the top, the director's assistant arranges the jugglers on the pandus, according to Aleksandrov's directions. Two doubles are involved in this shot. The acrobat Gusarova stands at the top of the pandus in place of the actress Orlova; the acrobat Litvinenko stands in for Stoliarov. Both must juggle burning torches. The doubles are standing in place; everything is ready, but again there is trouble with the lighting. "Number 13," the head lighting technician hisses into the microphone, "where are you shining the lights? I'm telling you to aim at her feet, and you're shining them in her face." The director looks over the rushes of the first shots.

21:55 The lights have been set up. The pandus turns slowly; the smoky flames of the torches glimmer; firemen rush about below, catching the burning tow and falling torches. The camera is running.

21:57 One more shot has been finished, but the director isn't satisfied.

22:00 The torches were not sufficiently soaked with kerosene. The shot has to be redone. Within two minutes the shot is repeated but, through the fault of the lighting technicians, it must be repeated yet again.

22:15 Reshooting begins. The jugglers begin to throw the torches, but half of them, hastily soaked with kerosene, won't burn.

22:20 The lights are turned off again and the jugglers quickly run to the kerosene bucket.

22:25 The lights are on, the torches fly, the camera chatters.... After a few seconds, the director, who is now satisfied, announces:

22:30 "Thirty minute break."

23:00 The camera is set up downstairs, almost by the circus ring. The director looks over the set from the new angle and checks all the details. He looks at the propellers of the stage airplane and tells the assistant to the director, "Check the plane so that it doesn't turn out that the propellers don't work, just at the moment we begin shooting." Aleksandrov's intuition is correct. Two of the five propellers don't work. While the propellers are being repaired, the director gives his assistant directions on how to position the ballerinas on the edge of the ring. Radio communication with the lighting technicians finally begins working and the delighted director tells them over the microphone, "Lighting technicians, put on your earphones." Now setting up the lighting goes better, and very soon the rays of light on the figure of the woman juggler at the top of the pandus crisscross in precisely the way the director wanted them to. "Stop the 'boulevard' in front of the camera," a strict voice from the megaphone is heard.

23:25 "Jugglers, start rehearsing. Remember that, when we begin shooting, the torches must be hidden behind your back. During shooting I count to three, and on the count of three, you turn around."

23:30 When it's time to turn on the lights, it turns out that radio communication isn't working again, and the technicians are sitting with their earphones on, hearing nothing. While the lights are being set up, the director gives orders to prepare the "cradle" for the next shot.

23:45 "Get ready for shooting. We remind the jugglers that they turn around on the count of three. Light the torches, turn on the plane. Attention! Camera! Stop!"

23:48 It's slightly dark at the center of the pandus and needs more lighting. Besides that, some of the jugglers have dropped their torches. The scene has to be reshot. Jostling one another, the actors pour sand over the burning torches, and again soak them with kerosene.

23:55 They take their places quickly and filming begins again.

23:58 But several torches fall again and the director prepares one more take.

24:00 The tired ballerinas stand close up to the camera, waving their burning torches. They get slightly burned, but bear it, and even find the strength to smile.

24:05 The shot is finally completed, and a wooden platform, swaying on steel cables, comes down from the ceiling. The camera is placed on the platform and the director and cameraman climb onto it. The cradle swings back and forth for a long time, and lists strongly first to one side, then the other. During these manipulations with the cradle, the director manages to give orders to the actors and instructions to the assistants.

24:30 The firemen stand motionless below. Now the actress, who is Orlova's double, is going to throw burning torches from the top of the pandus to the actor replacing Stoliarov on the platform of the staircase. The director gives the actress final directions.

24:37 The actors change the torches. Shooting continues. The woman acrobat at the top of the pandus blows on her scorched fingers.

24:45 The cradle must be lifted higher for the next shot. Long and boring negotiations with the technical people begin again. The creaking cables pull up the platform, lifting it up by one end. The director and cameraman hang by their hands.

0:10 Finally, filming is completed. But the director and crew don't leave the studio.

0:30 A quick meeting is going on in the director's room. The past work day is being discussed, and plans are made for the next day. Tomorrow we're shooting, beginning at twelve midnight. We've fallen behind by one day. Tomorrow we have to do ten shots. After discussing tomorrow's plan with the assistant director and assistants to the director, and recording it in a notebook, the director stands up.

0:50 The day is over.

"S"emochnyi den' gruppy rezhissera G. Aleksandrova. 'Tsirk,'" *Iskusstvo kino* (January 1936): 42–44.

Index

www.ingramcontent.com/pod-product-compliance
Lightning Source LLC
LaVergne TN
LVHW060728310826
846742LV00016B/48
9781841502823